PROPAGANDA
IN WAR
AND CRISIS

PROPAGANDA
IN WAR AND CRISIS

materials for American Policy

edited

with an introduction

by Daniel Lerner

George W. Stewart, Publisher, Inc., New York

a Policy Sciences Book

JF
15.25
.P8
L4
1951

31792

MANUFACTURED IN THE UNITED STATES OF AMERICA
BY THE CORNWALL PRESS, INC., CORNWALL, N. Y.

To

ALBERT A. WEINSTEIN

for whom
the arts of persuasion
served
the purposes of justice

THE CONTRIBUTORS

WALLACE CARROLL, an officer of the Overseas Branch of OWI, has written an account of his propaganda experience in World War II entitled *Persuade or Perish*.

RICHARD H. S. CROSSMAN, Labor M.P. from East Coventry and an editor of *New Statesman and Nation*, was Deputy Chief of Psychological Warfare Division (SHAEF).

ELMER DAVIS, newsman and radio commentator, was Chief of OWI during World War II.

HENRY V. DICKS, medical psychiatrist associated with the Tavistock Clinic in London, was a senior intelligence officer in the British Directorate of Army Psychiatry.

LEONARD DOOB, Professor of Psychology at Yale University and author of *Public Opinion and Propaganda*, held several important posts in OWI.

LEWIS F. GITTLER, field intelligence officer (OWI-PWD) in World War II, collaborated on the book *German Psychological Warfare*.

MURRAY I. GURFEIN, formerly public prosecutor and now practising attorney in New York City, was Chief of Intelligence in PWD.

MARTIN F. HERZ, Chief Leaflet Writer at PWD, is now a Foreign Service Officer with the American Embassy in Paris.

CHARLES D. JACKSON, Deputy Director of PWD, has recently taken leave as Publisher of *Fortune* Magazine to direct the Committee for Free Europe.

MORRIS JANOWITZ, intelligence analyst at PWD, is now Assistant Professor of Social Science at the University of Chicago.

ERNST KRIS, Visiting Professor of Psychology in the New School for Social Research, was co-author of *German Radio Propaganda*.

HAROLD D. LASSWELL, Professor of Law at Yale University, opened a new field of research with *Propaganda Technique in the World War;* during World War II he directed the Experimental Division for the Study of Wartime Communications at the Library of Congress.

NATHAN LEITES, formerly with OWI and now with The RAND Corporation in Washington, has published *Some Psychological Hypotheses on Nazi Germany* (with Paul Kecskemeti) and *The Operational Code of the Politburo.*

DANIEL LERNER, Visiting Professor of Sociology at Columbia University (on leave from Stanford University), has described PWD operations in *Sykewar: Psychological Warfare Against Germany.*

PAUL M. A. LINEBARGER, Professor of Asiatic Politics at the School of Advanced International Studies, has published a synoptic account of World War II propaganda in *Psychological Warfare.*

ROBERT BRUCE LOCKHART, Director-General of Britain's Political Warfare Executive in World War II, has reviewed this experience in *Comes The Reckoning.*

MARGARET OTIS was, for several years, Press Analyst at the American Embassy in Paris.

SAUL K. PADOVER, Dean of the School of Politics at the New School for Social Research, has recounted his experiences as field intelligence officer (OSS-PWD) in *Experiment in Germany.*

JAMES RESTON has been a "number one voice" in *The New York Times* for many years.

EDWARD A. SHILS, Professor of Sociology at the University of Chicago, was a senior intelligence officer in the formative period of PWD.

HANS SPEIER, Director of Social Science in The RAND Corporation, held several important government posts connected with international propaganda during World War II and is co-author of *German Radio Propaganda.*

PAUL R. SWEET, Professor of History at Colby College, was a field intelligence officer (OSS-PWD) and is now on a State Department mission concerned with documentation of the Nazi period.

JAMES P. WARBURG, an officer in the Overseas Branch of OWI, has published *Germany, Bridge or Battleground* and *Unwritten Treaty.*

ELLIS M. ZACHARIAS, Retired Admiral of the U. S. Navy, has evaluated his World War II propaganda operations to Japan in *Secret Missions.*

TABLE OF CONTENTS

PART IV. THE EVALUATION OF PROPAGANDA EFFECTS

INTRODUCTION

Some Problems of Policy and Propaganda

By

DANIEL LERNER

THE VOICES here mingled are soloists. They perform on a variety of themes, and their individual tones have been only lightly orchestrated for this performance. Their effect, nevertheless, is choral. The careful listener will detect that they are rendering different passages in the same score. Some program notes on the score and its present performance may help to delineate the pattern.

1. The Book

We have in hand the first collection of writings on the use of propaganda in war and crisis, recently rebaptized psychological warfare. They have been selected and arranged with the aim of clarifying some key problems that confront American policy in the present time of high tension. A variety of hands were needed for this purpose, as the subject has many dimensions and no one man has yet covered them all.

The contributors are men with wide and varied experience in the matter. Represented here are social scientists who have contributed to a theoretical framework for systematic inquiry into the propaganda process. Represented, too, are those social scientists who have codified their own experience in particular propaganda operations to illuminate general aspects of the process.

Important witnesses are those men who were responsible for the conduct of various psychological warfare activities in World War II. Elmer Davis was Chief of OWI; Wallace Carroll and James P. Warburg were responsible officers of its Overseas Branch. C. D. Jackson and Murray Gurfein were top officers under General Robert A. McClure in the Anglo-American Psychological Warfare Division of General Eisenhower's headquarters staff (SHAEF). Richard Crossman was the senior British officer in this Division, and Bruce Lockhart was Director General of the British PWE. Their influence upon American operations, as that of Dr. H. V. Dicks, was so large as to justify their inclusion in this otherwise All-American collection.

Some of our valuable insights come from those rare operating propagandists who can both exercise symbol skills and talk about them descriptively. Martin Herz was our Chief Leaflet Writer in Europe, and Ellis M. Zacharias broadcast a top-level series of talks to Japan, during World War II. James Reston knows how to sociologize political behavior as well as journalize it.

We have, then, an abundant spectrum of skills focussed in this volume upon the problems of psychological warfare. It is a rare subject which brings together such a variety of expert consultants from the academy and the world of affairs. Well represented are the communication industries—publishing (Jackson), films (Gittler), and the "working press" (Carroll, Davis, Reston). The professions represented include the legal (Gurfein), medical (Dicks), economic (Warburg). Spokesmen from the government community include an elected legislator (Crossman), an executive official (Lockhart), intelligence specialists (Herz, Otis), and a military officer (Zacharias). The academic delegation includes historians and political scientists (Lasswell, Leites, Linebarger, Padover, Sweet), psychologists (Doob, Kris), and sociologists (Janowitz, Lerner, Shils, Speier). Too often talk within such groups is strictly intramural. Here they confront each other in public.

The papers here assembled reflect the range and habitat of their authors. Several items were prepared especially for this volume; others are declassified war documents here printed for the first time. A substantial number are reprinted from the learned journals and from specialized volumes designed to reach only small professional groups. We have made no fetish of using only inaccessible materials, however; several items were taken from current publications because they were most relevant to the problem at hand.

We have, in short, made our selections with a resolute eye on the book's purpose: to assemble and arrange "materials for American policy." The problems of policy we consider as threefold: to clarify goals; to organize the best available means of reaching those goals; to evaluate, continuously and rigorously, the degree to which past and present activities are contributing to these goals. We turn next to summarize briefly the bearing of these policy problems on propaganda operations in war and crisis.

2. *The Problems*

Psychological Warfare is the phrase current in American usage for propaganda designed to achieve national policy goals in the world political arena. The term may be misleading: decisions about propaganda are no more (and no less) "psychological" than decisions about boycotts or bombings; and international propaganda is by no means confined to "warfare." We may get the sort of effects on morale sought by "psychological warfare" when, in peacetime, Gromyko walks out on the Security Council; or when a gift of American hydro-electric equipment brings power to Italian farmers for the first time. Yet, these are political and economic activities. The distinctive propaganda function is to emphasize, by talk, the effects on audience morale which such activities are designed to produce. What we are talking about, then, when we speak of "psychological warfare," is the use of symbols to promote policies, i.e., *politics*.

The British, with greater candor, designate these activities as "political warfare." Why the Americans have sought refuge from this term is an interesting question, on which Professor Lasswell offers enlightenment in the present volume (chapter 12). This is perhaps another illustration of that pervasive American antipathy to theory and generality which often misleads us into preferences for whatever can be made to seem technical and "empirical." We are not here directly concerned with American culture traits, however. Our interest in such traits is to see how they, among other factors, affect our ability to use propaganda in effective support of our policies. One consequence is expressed wittily by Colonel Gurfein (chapter 9), who calls the term "an unhappy one in that it brings to mind the picture of unsoldierly civilians, most of them needing haircuts, engaged in hypnotizing the enemy."

The point to be emphasized is that concentration on technique often obscures the fact that propaganda, in war or peace, is first and always an instrument of policy. Propaganda is politics conducted by the symbolization of events. It differs from other instruments of policy which act directly upon the material environment (e.g., battles, boycotts, blockades). Propaganda manipulates only the *language* in which such activities are talked about.

However, manipulation of the symbolic environment can itself produce major *events* in the political life of the world. Hitler drew world attention to his pronouncements, and so at various times did Wilson, Roosevelt, Churchill, Stalin, and Truman. James Reston's discussion of "The Number One Voice" (chapter 18) indicates that such claims upon the world focus of attention are a function of power and purpose. Public utterances are widely attended events when they are felt to be auguries of the future.

This is a central lesson of the volume at hand. Policy is the continuous effort to shape the future by decisions in the present. What is meant by "confused policy" is the failure to *clarify* in present actions the future toward which one is moving. A "faulty policy" is one that fails by present actions to *achieve* desired events in the future. "Sound policy" integrates all available means in making decisions which increase the likelihood that the future will conform to postulated goals.

One requirement of sound policy is the *clarification* of goals; a second is their *instrumentation*. The two interact incessantly in the course of political life. Goals without instruments constitute utopianism; instruments without goals is nihilism. The art of democratic politics consists in discovering those alternatives which make the most of "what is possible" with the least compromise of "what is desirable." Hence, the "soundness" of any policy decision is to be judged by its effectiveness in modifying given conditions toward desired goals, as Dr. Hans Speier demonstrates in his analysis of "War Aims in Political Warfare" (chapter 5).

The step from clarification of goals to their instrumentation requires, in the first instance, adequate intelligence of the conditions which are "given." This crucial service rendered to policymaking by the intelligence function is perhaps the most serious area of ignorance in our present understanding of the political process. Clarification of this function is a central purpose of Policy Science and should be among the problems which concern all social scientists. We call particular attention to Part

II of this volume—on "Policy, Intelligence, and Propaganda Strategy"—as a modest contribution in this direction.

The instruments of policy activate policy decisions by continuously modifying present conditions toward future goals. Policy specifies the desired ends; intelligence appraises the available means. Each of the policy instruments—propaganda, diplomacy, economics, war—has its distinctive techniques, but all are to be appraised by the criterion of effectiveness. A treaty is "good" if it effectively furthers a determinate policy; it is "bad," however admirable the contracting diplomats, if it does not. Similarly a propaganda Strategy of News is good if it activates current policy decisions more effectively than available alternatives; if it does not, it should be replaced immediately, despite the discomforts virtuous propagandists may suffer from the use of ideas instead of "facts." Part III therefore treats the problems of organizing the purposes and persons concerned with propaganda operations so that policy is served most effectively.

The evaluation of propaganda effectiveness involves some of the knottiest problems confronting social scientists and policy-makers. Nothing less than a comprehensive conception of the future is needed to give perspective to questions about effectiveness. Whether effects are to be long-range or short-range, whether they are to result in action, whether submission or revolt or apathy are the effects desired—all these are policy questions regarding the future. Such questions must be answered before it is possible to evaluate the extent to which the effects desired have been achieved. Systematic analysis of this sort lies in the future. The distinctive contribution of Professors Shils and Janowitz (chapter 23) toward this end is to demonstrate what can be done by bringing relevant data to bear systematically upon one short-range propaganda goal, formulated *a posteriori*. The USSBS report (chapter 22), apart from the technical interest of its procedures for gathering and processing data, is a useful reminder that morale is a continuing process involving multi-dimensional situations. Since systematic analysis must isolate variables, we welcome a study whose design emphasizes that variables are interactive in "real life." The appraisals concluding the volume specify some of the many dimensions on which alert political analysts wish to have information. The study of Aachen by Professor Padover and his associates (chapter 25), for example, brings to focus on a concrete situation the very factors which are isolated in his subtle and sensitive portraits of individual German personalities (chapter 8). These chapters are clues, therefore, to problems with which systematic students of effectiveness will be concerned in the future.

3. Acknowledgments

I wish to thank here the contributors and their publishers, named elsewhere, for generous permission to borrow their past writings for the present volume. Whether our common purpose has been served will be determined by the future activities of those for whom the book is intended.

Professors H. H. Fisher and C. E. Rothwell, officers of the Hoover Institute and Library, showed their usual uncommon generosity with materials in that treasure-house of modern history. Stanford University granted me a leave which substantially advanced the completion of the book. Professors P. F. Lazarsfeld and R. K. Merton, my present colleagues, made suggestions which were used. So, vigorously, did Dr. Leo Rosten.

I wish to thank especially the editors of the Library of Policy Sciences. From Saul K. Padover I have learned to clarify values and goals which reach beyond the limits of this volume. Joseph M. Goldsen helped to specify the function of this book and exerted himself to increase its utility. It is a pleasure to acknowledge the extraordinary fact that my intellectual debt to Harold D. Lasswell continues to grow with the years.

As always my wife, Jean Lerner, stood by.

DANIEL LERNER

Columbia University
March, 1951

Part I

THE 20TH CENTURY BACKGROUND

THE PROPAGANDA one nation directs toward another is limited by many factors beyond the immediate control of propagandists. These limiting factors are the "given conditions" which propagandists may seek to modify as their goal, but which they must take into their initial calculations as to means. Chief among these limiting conditions are: the current and impending world political situation, the characteristics of the propagandizing society, and those of the audience society. To illustrate, we may specify a few relevant factors.

In the world political situation, a controlling factor is the current balance of power and impending changes (or expectations thereof) in the balance. It makes an enormous difference to propagandists whether they speak for the most powerful nation (or coalition) in the balance, or for the chief contender for this role, or for the powers receding toward the periphery of the balancing process. Top power position is not invariably the most desirable spot for the propagandist: e.g., for two centuries the aspiring United States spoke to the world confidently as the embodiment of a revolutionary new ideology on earth; for the past two decades the world-powerful United States has felt itself forced into a defensive ideological posture viz-a-viz world opinion.

With respect to the social structure of either party to the propaganda process—whether sending or receiving—the following factors will constitute limiting conditions: the prevailing system of values and goals which compose the social myth; the structure and stability of political institutions; the pattern of educational practices; the condition of technology, and particularly of communications industries.

The opening chapter by Speier elaborates and analyzes the conditions of modern life which define the scope and limits of propaganda, particularly in wartime. Lasswell's analysis of Soviet propaganda strategy sets its past development in a context

which clarifies its observable· present and probable future alternatives. Kris and Leites present a basic proposition regarding
the 20th Century background for current propaganda in the
West: "Our general hypothesis is that responses to political
propaganda in the Western world have considerably changed
during the last decades; and that these changes are related to
trends in the sociopsychological conditions of life in the twentieth century."

Each of these chapters looks at the present as a movement in
time from the past to the future. It is such "developmental"
consideration of the present which contributes to policy thinking in a way that neither antiquarianism nor prophecy can do.
Since we live in a world which always has both a past and a
future, it is useful to keep our attention focussed on the *process*
of change through time. The man who must decide what to do
now in order to get certain results he wants later—i.e., the policymaker—is a man concerned with both *trends* and *conditions*.
The study of trends will tell him what has been happening; the
analysis of conditions will clarify the probable direction and
rate of changes that will result from alternate decisions. For
decision making that is not capricious, such evaluations and estimates are indispensable. The development of surer ways and
means for making more relevant and reliable evaluations and
estimates is a goal of the "policy sciences."

Chapter 1

MORALE AND PROPAGANDA *

By

HANS SPEIER

I

In the last year of the World War the French succeeded in producing a special shell to be fired from regular infantry rifles. It contained paper instead of steel, and when it exploded in the air 150 pamphlets or 5 to 10 newspapers dropped upon the enemy lines. The shell had a range of about 200 meters. Bigger shells, with a considerably wider range of 4 to 5 kilometers and a correspondingly larger load, were fired from guns. According to a French propaganda expert the French once shot between one and two million pamphlets to the Germans in a quarter of an hour. Thus the demand for the use of "moral ammunition," made by the London *Times* as early as 1915, was at last complied with, and literally, by an invention which deserves to be recognized as an instance of warfare waged by means of verbal symbols.

The total number of pamphlets distributed by the Allies in the World War has been estimated at 66 million. In September 1918, at the peak of their propaganda, the French and English alone distributed 17.7 million pamphlets over the German lines by balloon, airplane and shell. Plans existed for an unprecedented propaganda campaign by balloon that was to flood large parts of the interior of Germany in 1919. Apart from following these measures of offense all belligerents strained their organizational, financial and intellectual resources in order to keep up the morale of their own populations at home. In view of these stupendous efforts it is not surprising to find that many

* Reprinted from *War in Our Time,* edited by Alfred Kähler and Hans Speier, published by W. W. Norton (1939).

writers have declared that propaganda, with the threefold objective of strengthening the martial spirit at home, influencing public opinion in neutral countries and demoralizing the enemy, constitutes an innovation in modern, totalitarian war.

It appears that the magnitude and technical perfection of modern war propaganda have somewhat obscured the historical perspective. There was such propaganda in earlier centuries, and there were even elaborate discussions as to how to conduct it properly. In its moral implications propaganda has not changed. The differences between war propaganda today and in earlier epochs result from differences in technological and social circumstances. Therefore in order to understand what is new in modern war propaganda it is necessary to focus attention on its organization, its scope, the persons it is intended to reach and the character of modern social life.

The distinctly new feature of modern war propaganda is its extension to non-combatants. Propaganda at home to bolster up the martial spirit or at least the will to resistance among the millions of workers and farmers, men and women and children, is a phenomenon unknown to earlier centuries of modern history. It was in its infancy even as late as the nineteenth century and was entirely unknown in the eighteenth century. One may properly speak of diplomatic propaganda during the *ancien régime,* intended to influence the decisions of foreign courts, but there was nothing of modern propaganda devised to arouse war enthusiasm in civilians. Frederick the Great curtly expressed his desire that his subjects should not concern themselves with the wars he was waging; and in France when a battle had been lost the conscience of the nation, the intellectual elite that frequented the salons, found consolation by making jokes about the generals. The situation in this century, which later military writers have so often accused of inefficient and formalized warfare, hesitation in strategy and constraint in tactics, offers the most striking contrast to the conditions which underlie symbol conflicts in modern war.

The new situation arose with the participation of nationalistic masses in war—during the French Revolution, the Napoleonic wars and the popular resistance in Spain, Austria and Prussia to the Napoleonic rule. Europe entered the "century of words," as Metternich, then Austrian Ambassador to France, neatly remarked; he advised his government in 1808 that public opinion required "peculiar cultivation" since "it penetrates like religion the most hidden recesses where administrative measures have no influence."

Democracy and nationalism unleashed political passions which no sovereign in the *ancien régime* had been able to draw on. The absolute ruler had to rely on his soldiers, his funds and his administration. But when each citizen became identified with the cause of his country at war the limited warfare of the eighteenth century was transformed into a national undertaking. War gained a new momentum; it became instinct with the energy and unrestricted vigor of conscripted masses urged by enthusiasm for *la patrie,* "liberty," "revenge."

The situation conducive to modern war propaganda was brought about not only by new forms of military organization, such as universal conscription, and by the nationalistic spirit that pervaded both the social and the military system, but also by the development of war technique. The influence of technology on modern war operates, generally speaking, in two directions. With the development of long-range guns and motorized vehicles, and particularly with the production of fast bombing planes, the fact of distance from the theater of war has lost much of the protective value it formerly had. Russia and the United States are the only major countries today whose urban areas are not within the easy flying range of their neighbors. In a large-scale war the civilian population would be as exposed to aggressive action of the enemy as were non-combatants in a besieged fortress in earlier times. War between nations with highly industrialized war equipment has come to resemble campaigns in which whole countries besiege one another. The military front has become merely the skirmishing line of the entire nation.

Less obvious, but hardly less important, is the influence of modern war technique on the interdependence of soldier and civilian, army and nation, as established by the mere production of war material. The interdependence of the industrial production, transportation system and food supply of the nation on the one hand, and the military effort of the armies on the other, has become closer as the technological quotient in war has been increased. Today the strength of the armed forces depends to a much greater extent than in less industrialized societies on the productive resources and the organizational skill of the nation.

No modern army can wage a war without the persistent support of the whole country. Political conflicts at home, sabotage in the factories and offices or mere malaise among the citizens may incapacitate the best armies. With more truth than ever the ancient metaphor of the fighters as the arm of the state can be applied to modern war. When the body, the economic and social system, is sick, the arm cannot strike.

Thus under the conditions created by these three factors—the development of technology, mass participation in war, and nationalism—the morale of the nation itself becomes of decisive *military* importance. A major war assumes the character of siege warfare on a huge scale, with economic and symbol war supplementing the strictly military effort.

II

There is a strong temptation to ignore the fact that the modern forms of symbol warfare are consequences of the organization of modern society as a whole and not the sinister inventions of governments or military castes. In a liberal democracy the benefits of governmental policy are easily attributed to the virtue and intelligence of the average citizen, but when the body politic suffers from weaknesses and mistakes, failures and evils, the government itself will often be held exclusively responsible. The logic of political representation rules supreme as long as the state of the nation meets the voter's approval. If it does not he substitutes for the logic of representation what may be called, with some exaggeration, the shibboleths of tyranny: he accuses those in power and no longer thinks of them as representatives chosen by himself.

This distribution of responsibilities is comforting rather than fair or correct. It is understandable, however; in the atmosphere of disillusionment which has spread in the last twenty years a great deal of what was accepted during the last war as fact and sincere expression of feeling has been revealed as lies and deplorable madness. It is difficult for anyone to call himself a liar, but his self-respect is even more threatened when he has to debunk his emotions. War's psychological aftermath of resentment and cynicism accounts perhaps for the widespread forgetfulness concerning the agents of war propaganda. Much of the propaganda in war is inevitably conducted by those who later prefer to consider themselves as having been its victims.

The following facts and quotations are from the "Complete Report of the Chairman of the Committee on Public Information," which during the World War was the central propaganda agency in the United States. They illustrate how greatly the official effort toward nation-wide mental control depended upon social organizations that already existed in times of peace. It is hardly an exaggeration to say that in the World War no special machinery had to be built up for promotional activities. The major task in symbol warfare was not one of construction but was one of co-ordination and guidance. It was voluntary co-operation which made the amazing accomplishments possible.

The Pamphlet Division of the Committee "commanded the services of any writer that it chose to call, and at its back were over 3000 of the leading historians of the country." The Committee "gathered together the leading novelists, essayists and publicists of the land, and these men and women, without payment, worked faithfully in the production of brilliant comprehensive articles that went to the press as syndicate features." The objective of the Division of Syndicate Features was "to sell the war" to the people, and to present in acceptable newspaper style not only the story of the war but also "the spirit that was back of the whole adventure." The stories reached a circulation of about 12 million a month. Of the 75 million pamphlets that were distributed three quarters were sent out on request. Similarly, American painters, sculptors, designers, poster men, illustrators and cartoonists were "mobilized . . . on a volunteer basis, and another volunteer staff of several hundred translators helped the committee to keep in touch with the foreign language press."

Germany had bought up all the moving-picture houses in some neutral countries. "The heads of the American exporting companies met with the Committee's officers and agreed that no American film should be exported unless a certain amount of American propaganda film was included in the order." In a short time the strong bargaining position of the American companies led to a signal victory in symbol conflicts: "Charlie Chaplin and Mary Pickford led 'Pershing's Crusaders' and 'America's Answer' into the enemy's territory and smashed another Hindenburg line."

Through teachers' institutes, summer sessions and educational organizations the school was reached. Twice a month a sixteen-page paper was issued to every one of the 520,000 teachers in the United States. "It gave to the schools the needs and messages of Government in concise and usable form and to the Government a direct medium of reaching the 20,000,000 homes represented in the schools." Children were used in other ways as well: 5 million copies of the President's Flag Day address were distributed by boy scouts.

Most ingenious was the creation of the four-minute man. No less than 75,000 speakers volunteered as four-minute men operating in 5200 communities of the United States. They spoke chiefly in moving-picture houses, but later also in Sunday schools, churches, lumber camps, colleges, lodges and women's clubs. Within a period of eighteen months they made about a million speeches and reached a total of about 400 million people. The official expenditures for salaries, traveling, slides and the printing of bulletins were surprisingly low, a little more than $100,000 for the entire eighteen-month period. The additional costs, met by non-official contributions, were estimated by the Committee as follows: $2 monthly for each speaker's traveling and incidental expenses; $10 monthly for the expenses of each local chairman's office; the value of the speeches themselves, computed on the basis of $1 a minute, which the Committee considered a conservative estimate; for rent of theaters and other places where the speeches were delivered a lump sum amounting to half the total value of speeches; the publicity freely contributed by the press, regarded as worth $750,000. The grand total of costs met by voluntary contributions was 9.5 million dollars, or ninety-five times the official appropriations.

Nor was this all. The big organizations representing advertising agencies, advertising clubs and business papers were requested to name a board of control that would "mobilize the advertising forces of the country." The magazines, farm papers, house organs, newspapers, college papers and other periodic publications which gave space to the Division of Advertising had a total circulation of about 549 million. This advertising space was purchased by advertisers of merchandise and turned over to the state, or was contributed by the publishers without charge. The value of donated space totaled about $2,250,000 in

1918. This amount, of which the "sudden cessation of activities" caused only about 70 per cent to be used, does not include the services which the advertising agents offered free of charge, nor does it include the value of outdoor advertising, in the form of posters and billboards, or of window displays. By the cooperation of the International Association of Display Men the entire "display resources" in 600 cities were turned over to the Committee, so that 60,000 patriotic window displays, "timed to the minute," could supplement the campaigns in periodicals.

To complete the record of the Committee's activities, which were indeed the activities of the nation, or to review the corresponding measures in other countries would be tedious and on the whole repetitious. The degree of centralization varied from country to country, with the United States heading the list. Details differ, but the main lesson is the same: modern war propaganda is the upshot of modern society. It is not confined to any particular country, nor can it be attributed to any specific form of government. It is a concomitant, or rather an integral element, of modern war as such, which originates in the structure of modern society in times of peace. For that reason we should not be surprised to find that in all major countries today there are elaborate plans for repeating the mobilization of "opinion," possibly on a large scale, in the event of another war.

During the World War propaganda was most efficiently organized in the highly industrialized nations which had a liberal rather than a militaristic or autocratic tradition. It developed very slowly in czarist Russia, an almost wholly rural and illiterate country, and only after the collapse of the old government do we find the beginnings of symbol warfare on the Russian side; Belgian and French socialists arrived and tried to revive the will to resistance among the soldiers and thus to transform a meaningless conflict into a "war of opinion." Correspondingly propaganda was organized with greatest efficiency and comprehensiveness in that liberal country which offered not only its sons and its money to the cause of the Allies but also the slogan "Make the world safe for democracy."

With some exaggeration it might be said that the amount of war propaganda varies from epoch to epoch and from country to country in proportion to the development of advertising in times of peace. The propagandist is anything but a military type; he is a specialist in selling attitudes and opinions. The

successful propagandists in the World War were not soldiers
but newspapermen and intellectuals accustomed to contriving
for success. The military profession was reluctant to realize the
potentialities of propaganda, and not rarely resented a form of
warfare which conflicted with its traditional notions of proper
military conduct. Even in August 1914 the General Secretary of
the National Liberal Party in Germany suggested to the military authorities the distribution of pamphlets by airplane in
the enemy countries, but in 1915 high military authorities were
still declaring malicious propaganda against foreign governments inadmissible. One of the first English pamphlets protested in November 1914 against the Germans distributing
proclamations among the Indian soldiers; officers who lent their
hand to the distribution of such writings were called "unmindful of honor." In the present war between Japan and China
this professional military aversion to propaganda has reached
an amusing climax in the argument of a Japanese writer that
"lip-fight" is incompatible with Bushido, the true spirit of
Japanese knighthood, an argument which under the prevailing
conditions of comprehensive Japanese propaganda is but a
particularly mendacious weapon in symbol warfare.

III

The enormous efforts that have been made to perfect the
technique of war propaganda and to widen its range should not
blind us to the fact that its power is limited. Its function is to
influence the morale of civilians and soldiers, but only when
morale is already shaken may hostile propaganda succeed in
dealing a decisive blow; only when the conditions for a strong
morale are already present may the mood be intensified. Not
only propaganda affects morale.

A victorious nation cannot be defeated by slogans; an army
whose food supply functions satisfactorily will not be demoral-
ized by the however often repeated statement that it is starving;
civilians who suffer from air attacks cannot very long be fooled
by pronunciamentos that there is no reason to fear them; the
propagandistic denunciation of a general whose authority is
unshaken may prove a boomerang turning against the propagandist himself. Morale is a function of a situation in which
human impressibility and propagandistic attempts to make use

of it are only two elements among many. The effectiveness of propaganda is by no means determined merely by the skill with which it is conducted but depends also on the responsiveness of the public, which in turn depends on various elements, including objective facts.

Thus the resistance to hostile propaganda comes not merely from counter-propaganda but to a large extent from the concrete situations of the persons exposed to the hostile propaganda. In part these situations can be manipulated, in part they are the incidence of chance. The morale of a nation at war may be improved by adequate protection against air raids, by a tax system which curbs profiteering, by success of the armies and by other measures or events that are in themselves not propaganda but conspicuously influence the responsiveness to it.

Especially resistant to propagandistic manipulation are those elements of concrete situations which may be called the simple and immediate facts. Every hostile propagandist encounters them as certainties in the attitudes of his public. They are so stubborn that it would be futile for him to deny what they affirm. These facts reveal their meaning for us in immediate experience, while for the understanding of remote or complicated facts there is required more imagination, special information or a greater intellectual effort. Many simple social facts are experienced in face-to-face relations, although it is not this origin in primary relations which makes them simple but our immediate access to them. To put it in a different way, facts and events, and propositions referring to them, are simple if no aid from experts is needed in order to perceive or verify them. The superior strength of the enemy's artillery is a simple and immediate fact to the soldier at the front but a remote fact to the civilian at home. The shifts in the distribution of income, as they occur in every society at war, are remote and complicated facts which become comprehensible only when they are presented and interpreted properly; a slight change of a neighbor's economic status in relation to one's own income, however, may easily be perceived and thus has the character of a simple and immediate fact.

The social world we live in is of the greatest functional importance to us but we are often baffled in trying to comprehend its strikingly remote and complicated character. In various ways we tend to obliterate this intellectual shortcoming: we overestimate the relevance of the simple facts for the total situation, since it is through them that we participate in that remote totality of social life; or we put our confidence in experts who interpret to us the meaning of remote facts of which we experience only immediate repercussions; or, finally, we attach to simple and immediate facts of our experience a symbolic meaning with reference to which we form our judgments concerning that remote totality. Thus the sluggishness of an individual officer may be responsible for his men's attitude toward leadership in general.

Experience seems to prove, and skillful propagandists certainly act on, the psychological presupposition that simple and immediate facts have a more important bearing on morale than remote and complicated facts. Propagandists cannot change the simple meaning of immediate facts but they can try to manipulate the interpretation of remote facts, and this they do chiefly by manipulating the symbolic relevance of concrete experiences.

In passing it should be noted that the distinction between remote and immediate facts is helpful in understanding an otherwise baffling paradox in human behavior. Disillusionment about the aims of war may be widespread and the ideological justifications for its outbreak or even for its mere continuation may be rejected with disgust—and yet, the fighters may keep their morale. During the World War German soldiers, years before their "morale" was definitely shaken, referred to the war as the "swindle"; the factors which influenced their morale resided chiefly within the range of their everyday experience. War, taken as a whole, is a remote fact.

In September 1918 an inquiry was conducted, on the basis of 54,000 letters sent home from the front, into the extent and the causes of malaise and diffidence among the soldiers of the 6th German army in France. The following reasons for low morale were ascertained: [1] first, superiority of enemy artillery and aircraft; second, lack of dugouts in the first line; third, insufficient care for the material welfare of the soldiers (this item constituted by three specific complaints—the losing of food on the way from kitchen to line, no potatoes and too little meat, and, finally, not enough water); fourth, soldiers being kept too long in positions they considered untenable; fifth, too strenuous service behind the lines and at the same time reduced food portions; sixth, privileges for officers regarding leave and food (in the few cases in which officers ate the same food as their men, there were no complaints about food in the letters, and the behavior of the officers was praised); seventh, occasional defeatism of officers; eighth, general knowledge of the immense war profits; ninth, propaganda of the enemy. Most interesting is the frankness of the report regarding the patriotism of the soldiers: "there seems to prevail almost a certain sense of shame even to express a patriotic idea" (p. 269).

The list illustrates the significance which facts lying within the range of immediate experience have for the morale of the soldiers, and thus the limited importance of propaganda.

An inference suggests itself. The importance of propaganda in war is likely to increase when there is little change in the constellation of facts, that is, under conditions of stalemate such as prevailed during the larger part of the World War. The chance for successful symbol warfare is likely to increase when the odds in military and economic warfare proper are about equal. When there obtains a military stalemate propaganda is so to speak the only changing element in a situation in which all other variables remain deadly constant. It provides the factor of surprise which has disappeared from a military warfare that has become immobile. Conversely, the greater the mobility in warfare, the less important will be the effect and possibly the amount of propaganda, since the changing conditions will tell their own story. The extent and effectiveness of propaganda in a future war will thus depend not only on the technology of communication but also on the influence of modern weapons on the character of military operations.

IV

Propaganda in war operates in three main directions: it may be used to focus attention on facts which favorably or unfavorably affect morale; it may be conducted in such a way as to suggest a desired meaning for remote facts, this largely by manipulating the symbolic meaning of immediate facts, through dramatization or otherwise; finally, it may be used for directing loyalties.

Much of the morale of a group living in danger, be it the army or the nation as a whole, can be understood in terms of the psychology of fear and anxiety: morale can be strong in the face of danger, particularly when it rests on the notion that one is prepared to meet it; undefined danger, which causes anxiety, destroys morale. Fundamental safeguards against demoralization in war are superior strength, in modern war above all superiority of matériel, and adequate protection, especially of the defenseless civilians who cannot conquer their fear through action. As regards these factors the task of propaganda is chiefly an informative one, of the character of advertising. It may indulge in exaggeration or minimization, as the case may be, but it must mind its limits, which lie where remote facts become immediate, that is, where stories can be checked. A poster used by the Allies in the World War showed nothing but a soldier with the American flag and the curt legend "The First Million." Its effectiveness may be inferred from an observation of a competent American, Edward L. Munson: "There was a noticeable improvement in the morale of the French troops whose homes were in the districts where the Americans landed, before the effect was apparent elsewhere."

Naturally the importance of informative propaganda within the ranks of the enemy is greater when an inconvenient truth has been withheld by his censors or distorted by his deceitful propaganda, or when he has tried to divert attention from it or when its realization requires comparisons of immediate with remote facts. It was an American idea to distribute the same newspaper in the trenches of both the American and the German soldiers. Its demoralizing effect was believed to lie simply in its true information.

Success in war makes for high morale. Victory and defeat, however, are rather remote facts, save for the soldiers immediately experiencing them. Thus the agencies which control the news will be inclined to exaggerate victory and to cover up or deny defeat. It is not so much a habitual indifference to truth which makes the reports of high military and civil authorities in times of war an almost continuous narration of successes. Rather, the inability of the average citizen to penetrate into the darkness of remote facts induces the propagandists to maintain as long as possible their stolid optimism; in attempting to spread this attitude they have justification in the fact that confidence is a prerequisite of sustained effort and future success.

The chances of the propagandist are more limited regarding such simple facts as the food supply. As long as there is no severe shortage he may strengthen morale at home by denouncing luxury and declaring that it is patriotic to endure hardships, but against the odds of hunger he is impotent. Thus, because of its immediacy, one of the most important facts influencing the morale of a nation at war is largely exempt from verbal manipulation.

The effect of undefined danger, that is, danger whose magnitude is not known, is frequently out of proportion to its actual import. Undefined danger is infinite danger. It cannot be faced. It overwhelms the imagination. It crushes all hope. It terrifies. The story of surprise in war, particularly of the moral effect of new weapons, has often been told. Their psychological power is that they suggest unknown danger and create panics. The soldier's terror of poison gases and tanks has probably decreased with their technical perfection, because in the meantime he has experienced them, knows their potentialities and limits and can, to a large extent, act against them; they have thus been defined. In the civil war in Spain even civilians have grown accustomed to the horror of devastating air raids because they know exactly what to expect. The moving-picture houses remain open though death may strike at virtually any hour.

Particularly illuminating in this context is the psychology of panic. In a recent series of German studies it has been found that panics never had an "adequate" cause in the World War and that nobody under their spell seemed to know why he was struck. In panic, since the danger is not defined, demoralization can hardly be cured by the advice, be it persuasive or threatening, to face the danger. Very often in the World War the panic disappeared as abruptly as it had arisen if there was incidentally introduced into the situation some element which had no relation whatever to danger or to the panic or to the soldiers' duty to overcome fear but added a normalizing factor of familiarity. For example, it vanished when someone began singing a song or simply asked in surprise what everybody was doing.

If we pass from the psychology of morale to its moral foundations, which modern analysts tend to belittle, it is clear that nothing is more important than justice. Morale is strengthened by confidence in the justice of the cause one is fighting for and lowered by distrust of one's right. At the beginning of war it is always the aim of the professional interpreters of political events to drive home the argument that "they" are wrong and that "we" have been forced to defend our rights. In the later stages of the war sincere or feigned peace offers may serve the same purpose: the enemy's rejection of them, for whatever reason, gives renewed proof of his viciousness. Similarly, critical and discriminating opinions which differ from the official version as to the guilt and aims of war are relentlessly suppressed at home and, like all dissenting opinions that come from the other side, noisily disseminated by the enemy. More than anything else they lend to his own story the air of truth and thus buttress his monopolization of justice.

Only to a superficial observer will it appear paradoxical that the "just war" is universally felt to be the war that is ultimately waged for peace. Many pacifists, of course, participate in a "last war" or a "war against war," but in our time even the dictators have so far paid homage to the goddess of peace, regardless of the fact that their overt life-philosophies and their actual policies are irreconcilable with their popular enunciations of how much they cherish the pacification of international relations. There has not yet been a modern war, not even the violent ventures of English imperialism or Mussolini's conquest of Ethiopia or the invasions of China by the Japanese or the war of fascism against democracy in Spain, that has been justified as an evil which one is entitled to commit. Peace is good, the breach of peace is evil. Thus wars are justified as means toward peace.

In modern war, in which mass opinions count, the enemy has to be wholly identified—if need be at the cost of all intellectual sincerity—with the principle of evil, so that one can mobilize the power of right for one's own cause. Individual fighting is simple and can therefore be fair, even chivalrous. Mass war is a remote fact. In order to attract the attention of masses and to secure their moral participation war must be propagandistically simplified by creating symbols of danger and evil. Since its public interpretation cannot be discriminating it must be unfair. The "huns," the "tartars," the "reds" and all the other targets of hatred serve the purpose of focusing diffuse emotions and uniting diversified opinions. Thus an atmosphere of exaltation is created, of pride in one's own righteousness, of blind determination to save the group even at the sacrifice of one's life. It is that moment in the history of a nation which later promoters of jingoism delight in recording and which gives them a chance to disparage the boredom of peace.

As the war continues and its origins lose news value the emphasis tends to shift from denunciation of the enemy's breach of peace to his atrocious and cruel conduct. This gradual reorientation of propaganda has been noticed by students of the World War as well as of the present Japanese-Chinese conflict. The charge of villainy is thus perpetuated and reinforced, but this must be done in terms that are simple enough to be understood regardless of religion, age, party or race. Causal chains of events are difficult to understand; fairness may have its repercussions by correcting the desired allotment of right and wrong in the conflict; a decent silence might promote fatigue; besides, modern wars have to be noisy—the propagandists have it that everybody is thrilled by cruelty. In a recent investigation of propaganda during the English Civil War it has been found that the Puritans indignantly accused their enemies of precisely the same atrocities which they boasted of having committed themselves against their adversaries. Such distortions of moral judgment are indigenous to the war climate of opinion. The poisonous air that propagandists breathe is the same that nourishes their germs of hate.

There is another side to the story, however. Either a founded conviction or a manipulated belief that the war is waged in order to fight injustice strengthens the will to resistance, not only because the nation is in danger but also because in struggling for interests and rights the whole people imagines itself to be defending something general and sublime, the law itself, the moral order of life. The actions of everyone thus rise to a status of extraordinary moral significance. For this participation in a common cause which is greater than the self the French found a word of adequate solemnity. They spoke of *union sacré*, sacred union. Compared with it *Burgfriede,* the corresponding term used by the Germans, is feeble, being only an archaic word for truce.

This collective exaltation that may prevail at the beginning of war does not stand the test of time. It has to be embodied in the regularities of life, and under institutionalization it fades into a verbal trimming, a mere justification of hardship and sacrifice. The ideal merely conceals a form of existence which cannot fail to be imperfect and ugly. With this institutionalization, which in itself tends to wear off high morale as it offers routine for a substitute, discontent about the unjust distribution of hardships is bound to crop up. Actual or imagined injustice on the part of the in-group is definitely destructive of morale.

A favored object of this discontent is profiteering, in the narrow or wider sense of the term. Profiteering represents an overt and cynical denial of the value of sacrifice, the public praise of which helps everybody to bear the burdens of war. It is ubiquitous, since even the wisest laws against profiteering on a large scale leave loopholes for profiteering in a smaller measure. Moreover, in a situation of extreme stress, such as comes to prevail in war, any difference in the conditions of life may give occasions for disappointment and indignation. Even the exemption of munitions workers from military service may constitute profiteering in a psychological sense, when their lot is compared with that of their comrades at the front. Finally, profiteering strikes a particularly tender nerve, because though everybody is constantly urged *not* to profit, there are perhaps many who would like to if they had a chance and were sure of not being caught.

An alert government, however, will do whatever it can to curb profiteering. The importance of such measures on the preservation of morale is obvious. But those who assume that proper legislation can eliminate all profiteering should remember that even the best law removes only some conspicuous facts in terms of which discontent would otherwise be defined, but leaves other facts that will be seized upon for that purpose. Legislation cannot really eliminate all occasions for this discontent; in modern society it is, so to speak, part of the mores, and it is one of the reasons why the "sacred union" is euphoric and transitory.

Discontent destroys morale and may destroy order. Propagandists will therefore make every effort to arouse it among the enemies. They will dramatize conspicuous cases of profiteering and try to intensify their reprehensible character, in order to evoke resentments. But in practicing the odious vocation of handling human attitudes, which in war gains respectability, propagandists who destroy loyalties do not get very far if they offer nothing to take their place. Out of the stuff of loyalty much of our self-respect is formed, and much of our emotional security. For this reason a propaganda confined to criticism and debunking would arouse violent reactions against the propagandists. Their objective must be conversion rather than subversion, manipulation rather than destruction of the personal loyalty structure. They use the method of replacement, suggesting substitute loyalties. In this process the citing of apposite facts is of merely instrumental importance.

The choice of substitute loyalties is limited. As a rule what propagandists actually do is to invoke loyalties which are submerged. This will be more concretely understood after a short digression.

Everyone takes part in the life of many social groupings, from his family or his local community to his nation, and from affiliations into which he was born, such as race or age group, to relationships which, like clubs or parties, he enters at will. All these groups, which overlap to a certain extent, prescribe actions and demand loyalties. The subjective loyalty structure, that is, the inner relationship of a person's loyalties and their relative weight, depends partly on his preferences, partly on the particular activity in which he happens to be engaged at the moment, partly on natural or social events beyond his control.

A society too can be viewed as a field with a specific, objective structure of loyalties, differing as to goal and intensity. This structure reflects both the heterogeneity and the cohesion of society. It expresses not only traditions and institutionally entrenched differences, but also the extent to which, on the institutional level of life, willing co-operation supplements mere routine, public approval or indignation, and violent coercion as means of social control. The loyalty structure also comprises dissenting valuations which lack institutional incorporation, and thus, on the opinion level, it reflects the extent to which the existing institutions satisfy wishes. It is more or less focused around central values and, in this sense, more or less integrated. The degree of integration depends, among other things, on the actual relation of the society to other societies.

As a rule, there is much diffuseness and diversification of loyalties in a society, but under modern conditions the transition from peace to war effects a marked integration. This is in accordance with the organizational co-ordination of activities in times of war, which has been mentioned before. The government demands an inclusive consensus and an unqualified loyalty to "the nation." All other loyalties, whether they pertain to church or family, class or party or region, become subsidiary and indeed subservient to the foremost virtue of nationalistic patriotism. This spectacular intensification of one subjective loyalty has not only its grandeur but also its reckless crudity. It demands and entails a simplification of life, which the unbalanced mind tends to confuse with its enrichment.

The less the enemy is capable, for technical or other reasons, of paralyzing the organizational and material strength of his adversary, the more will his success depend on his skill in impairing morale by fomenting internal conflicts. Naturally the enemy propaganda will attempt to revive the subsidiary loyalties since, under the prevailing conditions, the adversary's power of resistance depends upon their insignificance.

The values with reference to which the skillful enemy propagandist operates are chiefly those that are relevant *within* the field he tries to influence. During the World War one hardly attempted to impair the morale of soldiers by strengthening their loyalties toward Christianity or humanity. Propaganda was concentrated on breaking up the objective loyalty structure from within, according to the principle of schism, rather than on prostrating it according to the principle of inclusion, by stressing wider obligations. Wider obligations remain vague and remote, unless they can be felt and practiced within the range of immediate experience, for example in an occasional fraternization. In general the wider obligations are stifled in war by the assumption that they are private feelings, not shared by others, especially not by the soldiers in the opposite trenches. As a rule a man does not remember his standards as a humanitarian when he stands behind a machine gun, or his standards as a Christian when he has to drop bombs from the air. The propagandist will work upon those submerged loyalties which can easily be related to war experience and which were intense and widespread before the outbreak of hostilities. Loyalties which were never intense cannot seriously endanger the spirit of resistance. Loyalties which were not widely diffused are difficult to arouse, since hostile propagandists cannot make use of individualized methods.

In the World War the Allies tried to arouse, among non-Prussian German soldiers, separatist feelings against Prussia, and corresponding aims were pursued in Austria-Hungary and

Poland; the Germans, less effectively, tried similarly to stir up Irish-English animosities. It seems, however, that the emphasis on national divisions was not so successful as that propaganda which stressed class and party oppositions. Whether the dramatization of national divisions will lead farther than that of class or party divisions cannot be decided on principle. It depends on the extent to which those divisions are easily associated in the nation with a tradition of internal conflicts. For example, the propaganda among the German soldiers which identified the war as one of special classes, parties and leaders was called for by the political setup in Germany before and during the war. It will suffice to mention two incidents in the internal situation which illustrate the situation. While the nation was waging a national war the Conservatives elaborated plans for perpetuating a system of suffrage in Prussia giving plural votes to members of the upper classes, thus attempting to entrench their political power. When measures for counteracting enemy propaganda were being considered high military authorities objected to introducing political education among the soldiers for the reason that such education would undermine discipline and foster the spirit of the Soviet Russian workers' and soldiers' councils. This "educational" service was finally established, but the soldiers were not permitted to discuss freely the question of war aims, the main issue of interest to them. At the same time chauvinistic organizations at home had a free hand in conducting their provocative speculations as to which European territories would have to be annexed at the end of the war.

Apart from the substitution of collective loyalties there is only one other device at the disposal of propagandists who manipulate valuations. Its objective is what might be called "privatization." This device, which involves the "decollectivization" of the individual, may assume the power of religious admonition and have the air of ultimate truth which in previous ages was ascribed to revelation. In it are combined the plain appeal to the fear of meaningless death and the attempt to give voice to one of the profoundest emotions man is capable of: happiness in being alive. A quotation from a pamphlet distributed by the English in the last year of the World War may serve as an illustration:

To the Soldier Who Marches West

You are still alive. It is wonderful. Everything that lives is wonderful, even the green grass and the birds.

The dead and the rocks and the soil and the dung—they are nothing, for they have no life.

We who have life have everything; we possess fabulous wealth.

The rocks, the dead and the soil have nothing, are nothing.

Where will your road lead you, soldier? Are you going West? Are you going to Paris?

Do you know what is in the West, soldier? I shall tell you, soldier; listen.

In front of you are the English, you know that. The French and the Americans are behind them. You also know how they fire into the lines of your comrades. Perhaps they will retreat and new regiments will march ahead. Then they will fire again. Then the Allies retreat again.

But the firing never ceases. . . .

There is something else in the West. I shall tell you what this "something" is. Nobody can tell you exactly where it is, but it surely is in the West.

Your grave lies in the West.

If you march West, you can't help finding it. Possibly it is far ahead of you, behind the mountains. But possibly it is very near you, perhaps you can see it. Today or tomorrow—nobody knows. But surely, the grave lies there, as surely as does the sunset.

Do you march West, soldier? Then, we say good-by to you. All of us who live say good-by.

There are only two things on earth, the living and the dead. The difference between these two things is greater than that between friend and foe, greater than that between man and animal. It is the greatest difference in this world. With the dead one you cannot marry, to the dead one you cannot be a friend, you can't talk with him, you don't touch him. If you march West, soldier, we say good-by, we who are alive.

Men and women, dogs and birds and insects—they shall not be with you any more. . . .

Soldier, farewell.

Today, you are one of us; you are one with men and women

and everything that lives. You are master of the rocks and the woods and all inanimate things.

Tomorrow you march West.
Soldier, farewell.
Do you hear our voice?
Farewell.

Naturally this pamphlet was reserved for distribution among the enemies. The more deeply one is moved by the simplicity and beauty of its content, the more difficult will it be to find a specimen of more vicious propaganda, anywhere, at any time.

V

It is idle to indulge in predictions concerning the spiritual strength of democracies and dictatorships in a future war. As has been mentioned before, there is little likelihood that democracies will shrink from using all available means of propaganda. Also one should clearly realize that there is no dictatorial type of warfare as opposed to a democratic type, either with respect to the technological aspect of military strategy and tactics or with respect to economic and propagandistic measures: the character of a major war under modern social, economic and technological conditions approaches the totalitarian type regardless of the political organization of society. Democracies are not free to choose a "limited war" if their adversaries wage a "total war."

Democracies in modern wars will have to adopt dictatorial devices of political organization, at least for a time, while dictatorships will have to show more respect for democratic principles than they have so far done. This seems paradoxical, but it is only a necessary consequence of the interdependent structure of modern international society and of the fundamental democratization in each country. The tendency of democracies to approach the dictatorial pattern of political organization in national emergencies could be observed in the World War and can be seen in various measures and mobilization plans for the war of the future. Dictatorships, however, will have to take more cognizance of international mores than they have so far done, not on account of any moral or legal considerations but for reasons of expediency. In the event of war they will have to offer explanations of their policy both at home and abroad. The causes and the aims of their wars will demand interpretations in terms which are not easily reconciled with the political philosophies dictators have hitherto acclaimed. They will have to speak about right and justice, while their past record is largely one of persecution and violence. Their history, moreover, will provide the enemies with a stock of invaluable propaganda material. The bill which the suppressed minorities and majorities could not present in times of peace, under the constant threat of violent sanctions, will be presented by the enemies in the next war. In this respect modern dictatorships will have to enter a major war under spiritual conditions which do not favor their success. It should be noted that this handicap arises not from the injustice inherent in their existence but from the mass demand for legitimations and interpretations of their policy and from the enemy's technical opportunities to satisfy this demand possibly better than the dictators are able to do.

True as it is that dictatorships may have an initial advantage at the beginning of a war on account of their comprehensive preparations, it is probable that this efficiency will have reduced the spiritual "war potential." In dictatorial regimes the violent suppression of political tensions will have to be increased when war comes. There exist elaborate plans in Germany as to how to organize the war on the home front, that is, how to suppress opposition at a time when dissatisfaction is bound to spread, when the thirst for revenge may grow stronger and when, in any case, a nation intoxicated by anticipated glory may have to look into the face of defeats.

The maximum war strength of dictatorially governed nations can be reached only when the organizational accomplishments are cemented by an inclusive consensus; this consensus, however, would make dictatorship technically superfluous. So far nothing resembling this exists. There is more likelihood of a devilish than of a sacred union in a future war. It is significant that the critics of fascism and many of its military experts meet on common ground when they consider the question of fascist morale in a future war: this ground is skepticism.

A short war, to be sure, would favor dictatorships, because their strength is hectic. They have to fear the sustained national effort by which democracies would probably gain. But the next major war is by no means likely to be short. That it will be long, and so much the more disastrous, is one of the reasons which render the dictatorial policy of intimidation in times of peace so effective. Dictators are masters of bluff and stunt, in domestic policy as well as in international relations. Only the patience, not the morale, of their nations has so far been put to a severe test.

Chapter 1. Notes

1. Hans Thimme, *Weltkrieg ohne Waffen* (Stuttgart 1932), pp. 264 ff.

Chapter 2

THE STRATEGY OF SOVIET PROPAGANDA *

By

HAROLD D. LASSWELL

IT IS NO NEWS to anyone that Soviet propaganda is full of inconsistencies whether you look at it through time or at the same time. At first there was fervent stress upon the themes of world revolution and the inevitable triumph of communism over capitalism. Suddenly at the Genoa Conference, Chicherin told us of "peaceful coöperation of two social systems during a given historical epoch." And the see-saw between coöperation and war to the death has been going on ever since. For years the Socialist and Liberal parties of the world were vilified by the Russian leaders as "Social Fascists," until suddenly a terrific threat appeared in Nazi Germany. And then the "united front against war and fascism" took top billing. But not for long. Came the Pact, and Stalin drank the health of the Führer. Came the German offensive, and slogans uncongenial to the West sank into the shadow, while Stalin made news by mentioning God in a favorable tone of voice. Came the end of hostilities, and the beginning of a new epoch of separatism and hatred. The United States now rises to the dignity of chief devil, taking the place occupied by the Nazis and the "Anglo-French plutocracies" in earlier times.

If there are differences, there are also consistencies in Russian propaganda. Many of the key symbols and slogans of the Marxist inheritance linger on.

Is there an interpretation capable of accounting for the zigzags of Russian propaganda? I suggest that there is unity of strategic aim: *to maximize the power at home and abroad of the*

* Reprinted from *Proceedings* of The Academy of Political Science, Columbia University (1951).

ruling individuals and groups of Russia. Propaganda is an instrument of total policy, together with diplomacy, economic arrangements and armed forces. Political propaganda is the management of mass communications for power purposes. In the long run the aim is to *economize the material cost of power.* Even more specifically: *the aim is* to *economize the material cost of world dominance.*

What will happen if this strategic goal is perfectly attained? There will be no general war. Indeed, it is doubtful that there will be local aggressions of the Korean type. Nation after nation will fall into the Russian orbit through complacency, division and intimidation. The United States will adopt policies that weaken its economic, political and social fabric; the United States will decline peacefully into a secondary place in world affairs. Perfect success by Russian propagandists will cut down the material costs that would be entailed by general war, or by a series of local aggressions, or by colossal preparations for war.

A fraction of the success just described can contribute mightily to the reduction of the material cost of Russian domination. Whatever shortens war, without compromising success, saves Russian resources.

Perhaps it is superfluous to point out that the use of propaganda as an instrument of power is no idiosyncrasy of the Russian ruling class. All ruling classes in large-scale communities resort to propaganda. There are, however, factors in the Russian case that set it somewhat apart. The contrast is particularly great when we think of the United States. The leaders of Russia are operating in a tight, supercentralized garrison-police state, while the leaders of the United States are still dispersed through government, business, education, and other relatively independent institutions. The elite of Russia is oriented toward power, and possesses a tradition of calculating power at home and abroad. In the United States the ruling elements are much less conscious of power as a predominating value, since they are more preoccupied with wealth, respect and other values.

The top rulers of Russia possess a doctrine and a tradition in which the use of propaganda plays a conspicuous part in the execution of total policy. No one is unmindful of the fact that the power seizure of 1917 was prepared by years of activity in

which every member of the revolutionary party was supposed
to devote most of his energies to propaganda.

It would be a mistake, however, to assume that the Russian
elite emphasizes propaganda out of deference to the human
mind, or to the rôle of ideas in history.[1] It is much closer to
the mark to say that the tradition of the Russian ruling class
is to discount both ideas and the human mind; for the strategy
of Russian propaganda acts upon pessimistic assumptions about
the capabilities of mankind for enlightenment by peaceful
persuasion.

Consider for a moment the doctrinal framework in which
propaganda operations are conceived. Distrust of the "ideological" can readily be derived from the stress put upon the
primacy of "material" factors in history. This inheritance from
Marxism was given a special twist in the lives of the chief
conspirative leaders of Russian socialism. Lenin was only too
conscious of being in a minority. His conceptions of revolutionary action reflected the helplessness that he felt in the face
of the task of winning the Russian masses by peaceful persuasion. He saw in the ideological structure of Russian peasants
and workers the imprint of the material ascendancy of the old
ruling class. The sluggishness, stubbornness and stupidity of
the Russian masses, against which Lenin railed at times, were
ideological factors in history. But these gigantic icebergs were
frozen into shape by the "material" forces at the disposal of
the older elites.

And how were these ideological residues to be broken up and
melted down? Not by persuasion, concluded Lenin. Only by
sweeping material transformations. But how was this to be
reconciled with the use of propaganda? [2]

It is not necessary to assume that Lenin solved the problem
of the interplay of material and ideological factors in a manner
free of contradiction or entirely in harmony with scientific
knowledge. But the conspirative activists of Russian hammered
out strategy and tactics that continue to influence Russian
leaders. The making of propaganda is primarily a "material"
activity in the sense that it depends upon the control of instruments of production, such as presses capable of turning out
magazines, pamphlets and books; and it depends upon hours
of labor devoted to processing and distributing the product.
It is "material" in the added sense that it is possible to con-

centrate upon audiences who occupy disadvantageous material positions, and who are therefore susceptible to programs for the betterment of their material state. The number of such "susceptibles" depends upon the intensity of the contradictions prevailing at a given time and place. If the material instruments of communication are skillfully employed, a very small concentration of material factors can reshape the ideas of an ever-expanding aggregate. Eventually those in control of the expanded material resources may seize power, and control enormously enriched means for transforming mass ideologies on a colossal scale.

Once the workers have attained the new ideological perspective, they can make sure of perpetuating it intact by utilizing the material instruments of communication which can then be accessible. This is the background for the provisions appearing in Article 125 of the Constitution of 1936 relating to freedom of communication. The Article says that the rights of the individual to free speech (and such) are secured by turning over to the workers and their organizations the printing establishments, stocks of paper, public buildings, streets, means of communication, and other material conditions essential for the realization of these rights.

The standing charge against the capitalist world is that the working masses are full of the illusions disseminated by the press, which is said to be under the control of the plutocracy. Obviously, the assumption is that whoever controls the material instruments of communication can imprint upon the passive mind of the audience images that protect the material relationships then prevailing or in prospect. Thus propaganda is viewed as an activity, low in material cost, by means of which the receptivities created by material contradictions can be made politically effective.

The disregard of persuasion on the part of the Russian elite is apparent in the dogmatic finality with which the eventual goal of policy is treated. The elite possesses a rigid, non-debatable conception of the future. In this future commonwealth man is within the realm of freedom and not of necessity (Engels). The gloss on the doctrine as applied by the Russians is that those who pursue this aim may deny freedom to others until such time as no material contradictions remain which are capable of imprinting ideas hostile to the functioning of such a free society. Not the least of the menaces that must be obliterated are the streams of communication directed toward Russian audiences from the material facilities at the disposal of foreign elites. The Russian ruling group has no hesitation in using whatever material means are at hand to seal off the Russian audience from such "subversive" exposure.

The directors of Russian propaganda do not ignore the sentiments and assumptions of their current or prospective audiences. But this is not for the sake of sharing with the masses the task of creating a consensus, through free discussion, concerning the aims, major policies and top leaders of the body politic. On the contrary, the scrutiny of the audience is a one-way affair in which the deviation of the audience from some leadership objective raises only a tactical problem: namely, what are the most economical means of overcoming such deviations? At moments Lenin was brutally frank about his contempt for the thoughts and feelings of the masses when they were other than he wanted them to be. In common with other modern tyrannies, the present leaders of the Russian garrison-police state recognize that so much candor is a source of weakness. Hence the Stalinists now congratulate themselves upon having the "most perfect democracy" on earth in which the will of the people is more fully expressed than anywhere else. Thus is revived the mystic conception of democracy which makes it possible for a tyranny to pretend to "intuit," free of representative mechanisms, the most profound sentiments of the people.

Within the framework provided by the secular revelation of the commonwealth of freedom, all questions are reduced to the level of tactical expedients. A decent regard for the opinions and sentiments of others is superfluous or worse; it is an act of pandering to the accumulated errors stamped upon the human mind by the weight of the material at the disposal of previous ruling classes. Honesty is of no value as an expression of rectitude; there is always the higher rectitude of whatever contributes to the ultimate goal.

The major task of propaganda strategy is proper timing in relation to the specific dangers and opportunities of a given set of circumstances for the power position of the Russian elite. It is possible to trace the prevailing offensive and defensive strategies of Russian propaganda. Many essential features were exhibited in the preparation by Lenin for the seizure of power in

Russia. If we go back to the years of deepest depression for the revolutionary movement (after the collapse of 1905), we find that the first task of Lenin was to form primary nuclei capable of further expansion. Lenin and his followers provided the man-hours for propaganda work. They were often able to gain recruits by direct personal propaganda, often preceded and facilitated by the output of the party presses.

When the primary nuclei became sufficiently abundant to operate as a significant part of the power process in trade unions, in political parties and in parliament, a second task took shape. The problem was to find allies without losing independence. Now allies, whether inside or outside of the socialist movement, were full of danger to the towering ambitions of a Lenin (or Leninists). Without allies there is the threat of being crushed entirely by a combination of hostile elements whose strength is potentially overwhelming. The propaganda strategy of Lenin was to keep alive an attitude of suspicion toward allies, while at the same time lulling the ally into complacency, or diverting his attention to a common enemy, or fanning disunity. Propaganda has many means of contributing to the complacency of an ally. There is the direct declaration of mutual friendship and admiration. And there is the nullifying of hostile or disturbing manifestations. The propaganda goal of diverting attention to a common enemy is comparatively obvious, but the tactic of fomenting disunity is exceedingly complicated. Plainly the ally must not be allowed to weaken below a point where his usefulness against a common enemy is lost. But internal tension can absorb attention, and thus divert attention from inconvenient features of the Leninist-led group. The strategy of division paves the way for coöperating with minorities in wrecking or taking over the control of the ally at some future date.

The third stage is the seizure of power, and this sets a somewhat different propaganda task, which is to demoralize the potential opposition, and to gain support, by creating an impression that all further opposition, or noncoöperation, is both useless and immoral.

At any given moment the Lenin-led groups might find it necessary to assume a defensive posture, which consisted for the most part in masking all hostile potentialities of policy toward an ally; and in redoubling attempts to prevent or to break up hostile combinations by spreading complacency, fear of a common enemy, and disunity.

To recapitulate the strategic rôle of propaganda as a means of reducing the material cost of expanding and defending power (as exemplified by the Leninists, and followed subsequently by the Stalinists): *Stage one.* The creation of primary nuclei in which fully indoctrinated individuals provide the solid corps of full-time labor for the cause. *Stage two.* Coöperation with allies in the arenas of power accessible to the nuclei, who are by this time sufficiently strong to act as "parties," "unions," and the like. The propaganda task is to maintain the sentiment of having a distinctive mission (inside the party or "own" group), while at the same time fostering certain attitudes among potential enemies (including allies). The attitudes include complacency toward the party; the diversion of hostile attention to a common enemy; the spreading of disunity. *Stage three.* Seizure of power. Propaganda demoralization of the opposition and of noncoöperators: spreading fear or confidence in the inevitable triumph of the party, and of the hopelessness and immorality of further opposition or noncoöperation.[3]

Consider briefly the application of these strategic principles to the seizure of power in countries adjacent to Russia (the present satellites). The first task of propaganda in Hungary or Czechoslovakia was to win enough support to begin to play a bargaining part in the ordinary processes of local and national parliamentarism and administration. This was accomplished by penetrating the trade unions, and other private associations. The second task arose when the party was strong enough to join coalitions, and to work with allies at every level of government (including special attempts to permeate the ministries concerned with public order and information). The third stage came with the seizure and consolidation of power by *coup d'état* (within a "framework of legality"). It was during the second stage that the greatest versatility was required in the handling of Russian propaganda, since it was necessary to keep in balance the often contradictory tasks of fostering a distinctive sense of mission, complacency on the part of potential enemies (including allies), diversion of attention to common enemies, and disunity. This was the period in which such illusions were useful as that Russian policy has at last "settled down" to peaceful coexistence and to the restoration of genuine coöperative effort. The third stage is less subtle and far more ruthless, since it involves the spreading of terror, often by means of close correlation and coöperation with acts of violence.[4]

Looking at the world picture as a whole, it can be said that Russian propaganda is best served at the first stage (penetrating a new community) by propaganda that possesses high doctrinal content. It is the function of propaganda during this period to provide a professional nucleus of revolutionaries to give skillful direction to ensuing activities. Suppose we ask ourselves why the propagandists of the Kremlin continue to repeat so many of the time-worn doctrines of the Marxist tradition. Clearly the answer is that most of the traditional doctrines are of demonstrated effectiveness in appealing to the disaffected of many lands, whether in the heartlands of modern industrialism, or among the peoples long subject to the economic expansionism of Western states. It is an old story that the dissolution of ancient loyalties and the break-up of old religious faiths and philosophical traditions have been signs of, and in turn contributory to, the vast transformations through which mankind is passing in our historical period. It is an old story that Marxist doctrine has provided a secular substitute for the universality of aim, of cosmic outlook, and of personal identification with destiny which were part of earlier systems. No doubt it is an old story that Marxism and liberalism were co-ideologies which were alike in attacking the institutions of a caste society, and in proclaiming the importance of renovating society for the sake of realizing human dignity in theory and fact.

Several of the doctrines carried forward from historical Marxism by the elite of Russia have a plausible ring to millions of human beings who live exposed to the material and ideological tensions of our time. (Note that I now speak only of plausibility, not of truth or falsity.)

Consider the familiar thesis that there is a tendency toward monopoly in capitalistic economies. Can the plausibility of this be denied in the United States, for instance, where monopoly trends have been the subject of lament for years?

Consider the thesis that the capitalistic system generates periodic crises of mass unemployment. In the light of "panics," "crises" and "depressions," can we sweep this entirely to one side?

Consider further the thesis that movements of protest arise among the nonowners in capitalistic societies. This is not implausible in view of the vitality displayed by protest movements in the name of "labor," "socialism" and other political symbols.

Again, think of the doctrine that in parliamentary countries the owners abandon democracy in favor of non-democracy when they feel seriously threatened by movements of protest. Is this altogether implausible in view of the aid received from big industrialists and landlords in the formative stages of Mussolini's fascism, Hitler's Nazism, or Franco's falangism?

Think also of the thesis that imperialism is a result of capitalistic rivalries for the control of raw materials and markets. Obviously this gains plausibility from the scramble for colonies which enlarged the empires of England, France, Germany and Belgium, and which put the United States in the place of Spain in the Caribbean and the Philippines.

Consider the thesis that imperialistic rivalries generate wars among imperial Powers. In this connection it is possible to point to the rivalries between England and Germany before 1914, and the German thrust for "living space" in the recent past.

Think finally of the revision which the "imperialism and war" thesis has undergone in recent years. I refer to the conception of capitalist encirclement of the "Socialist Fatherland," and the promotion of armament and war as means of preparing an attack upon Russia, particularly in the hope of diverting against an outside group the gathering rage of the unemployed masses of a collapsing capitalism. Is it not true that capitalistic countries have been stepping up their expenditures of arms?

These doctrinal lines have an important place in the strategic balance of Russian propaganda appeals. Recruits continue to be sought by means of study groups devoted to the writings of Marx, Engels, Lenin, Stalin and other acceptable figures in the canonical list. That these study groups are effective instruments of Russian power has been demonstrated more than once. May I remind you that when the Canadian government looked into the spy ring in Canada, the trail led to study groups organized privately as recruiting stations for persons of high intellect and culture. Wherever Marxism-Leninism-Stalinism is ignored in the advanced educational systems of a country, or tossed aside with conspicuous prejudice by teachers who are obviously ignorant of the subject, the basis is laid for curiosities that may be gratified in private and faintly (or overtly) clandestine study groups. In these intellectual "speak-easies" the doctrinal system is expounded in a pious atmosphere free of the critical, deflating effect of vigorous evaluation on a comparative basis. Study groups are an important example of the tactical principle that it is possible to move toward effective power in an indifferent or hostile society by limited concentrations of superiority of books and man-hours in propaganda work. (The step from private study to espionage or sabotage is not too long for many persons to make.)

It is noteworthy that the greatest successes of Russian propaganda have been scored among nonindustrial peoples. This is a good example of the choice of audience anywhere in the world wherever material or ideological factors have created tension. These activities are vital at all stages of the power-seizing process, but create special resonances at stages one and two above. The Russian elite has become progressively clearer about the potential rôle of the "ex-colonial" victims of "imperialism," especially since so many of the "ex-colonials" live on the continent of Asia within the shadow of the Russian world. The new noncommunist elites of these countries are relatively weak, while the old elites are largely discredited. The sentiment of nationalism can be turned against former "oppressors" and directly toward complacent coöperation with Russia. Further, the resentment of ex-colonials is fed by the rankling memory of the indignities imposed upon them by the "white imperialists." In the traditional literature of socialism the link between race prejudice and capitalism has long been forged. The formula is that capitalists seek to divide the workers from one another, and to drive wages down, by setting black against white, yellow against white, and so on. Seizing upon these cleavages in the respect structure of the non-Russian world, the strategy of Russian propaganda is to identify imperialism and ethnic discrimination with capitalism. For this purpose the chief target is the strongest capitalist Power, the United States; hence, the distorted image of America as a land with Negroes hanging from the lampposts, lynched by miserable gangs of sharecroppers and unemployed workers, incited by ruthless agents of the plutocracy who are commissioned to keep the workers at one another's throats.[5]

The conspirative tradition of pre-revolutionary times has left an imprint upon the channels as well as the content and the strategic-tactical correlation of propaganda with total policy. Consider from this point of view the method of dual organization. This is the use of an open channel of propaganda which is closely paralleled by a closed, secret channel. The technique can be applied in many ways, as when one is labeled "governmental" and the other "party." If the upper corridor is closed for reasons of expediency, the basement is kept in operation (as when the Comintern was publicly extinguished in 1943). The secret channel can be a faction which is entrusted with the mission of controlling the policy of organizations which are nominally independent of party control. Hence the vast network of "come-on" organizations which are used by the party to permeate every national community, seeking to reach the armed forces, the police, the foreign service, business, the professions, trade unions, coöperatives, schools, publishing houses, radio-television, films, and the like. There is a slot for housewives who hate high prices, for mothers who hate war, and for humanitarians of every hue. Through these organizational networks a great number of special environments are made available for the restamping of minds, and for expanding the material facilities within the reach of the Russian leadership. The Russian technique parallels in a curious way the means by which in a capitalist economy the control of a gigantic network of private corporations is obtained through a series of minority stock ownerships. The parallel includes the use of "fronts" who are called "dummies" in the vernacular of capitalism, and something less complimentary in the private language of Russian propaganda.

Dual control was a congenial method in the hands of conspirator Lenin, who employed a small clique of disciples to continue to do what he wanted to do regardless of the formal prohibitions of his party. One striking example is the secret organization by means of which funds were raised through robbery, counterfeiting, seduction of rich women, and the like. To this day the channels of Russian propaganda continue to use the dual structure appropriate to conspiracy. In this way it is possible to conduct activities of the utmost unscrupulousness.

We can sum up the strategy of Soviet propaganda by saying that the chief strategic aim is to economize the material cost of protecting and extending the power of the Russian elite at home and abroad. Such propaganda is a struggle for the mind of man, from the Soviet point of view, only in the sense that it is a struggle for the control of the material means by which the minds of the masses are believed to be molded. Hence the purpose of Russian propaganda is *not* peaceful persuasion of the majority of the people in a given country as a prelude to the taking of power. Rather, the task is conceived as that of a minority that must remain an ideological minority until it succeeds in accumulating the material means of obtaining consensus. In the early stage of penetrating a new community, the basic task of propaganda is to assist in establishing and shaping primary nuclei of potential leadership at the next stages. When enough strength is assembled to admit of a strategy of coalition, the task is to maintain separatism, coupled with propaganda designed to prevent or break up potentially more powerful combinations. The fostering of complacency, the diversion of attention to common enemies, and the fomenting of division among potential enemies (including momentary allies) are part of the strategic tasks to be carried through. At the stage of power seizure the strategy of propaganda is that of demoralization, which is sought in synchronization with terror as a means of impressing all with the "inevitable" triumph of Soviet power and the hopelessness, and indeed the immorality, of resistance or even noncoöperation. Possessing a world-encompassing goal that is treated as beyond the reach of discussion or inquiry, the ruling few of the Kremlin have no self-limitations of principle upon the choice of message, channel or audience. Soviet propagandists and their agents can lie and distort without inner restraint, for they are largely immunized from the claims of human dignity in any other sense than the dignity of contributing to the ultimate goal of the free man's commonwealth by contributing to the present and future power of the Kremlin elite.

Chapter 2. Notes

1. The most important study of the perspectives of the Soviet elite is by Nathan Leites (forthcoming).

2. Concerning the theory of propaganda used by Soviet leaders see Alex Inkeles, *Public Opinion in Soviet Russia* (Cambridge, 1950).

3. The seizure of power in Russia was but one step in the expansion of the Communist movement, though the most decisive. In relation to most of the world arena, the Soviet elite is at stage one or two. Stage three has been achieved piecemeal in adjacent states. On the internal transformations in Russia since 1917, see especially Barrington Moore, Jr., *Soviet Politics—The Dilemma of Power* (Cambridge, 1950).

4. Consult these authoritative and concise case studies: Ivo Duchacek, "The Strategy of Communist Infiltration: Czechoslovakia, 1944-48," *World Politics,* vol. II, No. 3 (April 1950), pp. 345-72, and "The February Coup in Czechoslovakia," *ibid.,* July 1950, pp. 511-32; Stephen D. Kertesz, "The Methods of Communist Conquest: Hungary, 1944-1947," *ibid.,* October 1950, pp. 20-54.

5. For the whole picture consult Frederick C. Barghoorn, *The Soviet Image of the United States; A Study in Distortion* (New York, 1950).

Chapter 3

TRENDS IN TWENTIETH CENTURY PROPAGANDA *

By

ERNST KRIS AND NATHAN LEITES

IN SPEAKING of propaganda, we refer to the political sphere and not to promotional activities in general. We define acts of propaganda, in agreement with H. D. Lasswell (1927, 1946) as attempts to influence attitudes of large numbers of people on controversial issues of relevance to a group. Propaganda is thus distinguished from education which deals with non-controversial issues. Moreover, not all treatments of controversial issues of relevance to a group fall under the definition; they are not propaganda if they aim at the clarification of issues rather than at the changing of attitudes.

In the following, we deal mainly with propaganda by agents of government and exclusively with propaganda using the channels of mass communication, i.e., principally print, radio and film.

However, neither the potentialities of any one medium, nor the variety of promotional devices used by all will be discussed here. We are concerned with the place of propaganda in Western civilization. Our general hypothesis is that responses to political propaganda in the Western world have considerably changed during the last decades; and that these changes are related to trends in the sociopsychological conditions of life in the twentieth century.

We shall not be able to offer conclusive proof for the points we wish to make. We do not know of the existence of data comprehensive and reliable enough to demonstrate in quantitative terms broad hypotheses about changes in responses to propa-

* Reprinted from *Psychoanalysis and the Social Sciences* (vol. I), edited by Geza Roheim, published by International Universities Press (1947).

ganda. We start out from changes in content and style of propaganda, assuming that they reflect the propagandist's expectation as to the response of his audience. The propagandist may be mistaken in his expectations, but finally he will be informed to some extent about his audience's response and adapt his output, within limit, to its predispositions.

We choose two situations in which propaganda was directed towards comparable objectives: the two World Wars.

Wartime propaganda is enacted in a situation with strictly limited goals. Under whatever conditions, the objective of propagandists in wartime is to maximize social participation among members of their own group and to minimize participation among members of the enemy group. Social participation is characterized by concern for the objectives of the group, the sharing of its activities, and the preparedness to accept deprivations on its behalf. High "participation" is therefore identical with high "morale." Its psychological dynamics are mutual identifications among group members, and identification of individual members with leaders or leading ideals of the group, strong cathexis of the goal set by the group, and decreased cathexis of the self; processes that at least in part are preconscious and unconscious. Low participation may manifest itself in two ways: first, participation may be shifted partly or totally from one group to another. In this case, one may speak of a split in participation. Second, low participation may manifest itself as a withdrawal of individuals from the political sphere; in this case, we speak of privatization (H. Speier and M. Otis).[1]

The psychological dynamics of a split in participation are obvious; one set of identifications and objectives has been replaced by another. The only dynamic change consists in the fact that, as a rule, the old group has not lost its cathexis, but has become the target of hostility.

The dynamics of privatization are more complex: withdrawal of cathexes from the group and its objectives leads to a process comparable to, but not identical with a narcissistic regression. Concern with the self becomes dominant. Since the striving for individual indulgence is maximized, the individual becomes exceedingly vulnerable to deprivation.

Modern warfare is distinguished from older types of warfare by the fact that it affects larger numbers of individuals. In total war "nations at arms" oppose each other with all their resources.

Hence participation becomes increasingly important. To the extent that preparedness for war infringes upon life in peace, the problem continues to exist in peacetime.

Participation of whole nations was more essential during World War I than during any previous war; and yet it was somewhat less essential than during World War II; the first World War, especially at its onset, was "less total" than the second. On the other hand, the media of mass communication were less developed; radio and film had hardly been tested. Three areas of difference between the propagandas of the two wars seem particularly relevant in our context:

1. Propaganda during the second World War exhibited, on the whole, a higher degree of sobriety than propaganda during World War I; the incidence of highly emotionalized terms was probably lower.
2. Propaganda during the second World War was, on the whole, less moralistic than propaganda during the first World War; the incidence of preference statements as against fact statements was probably lower.
3. Propaganda during the second World War tended to put a moderate ceiling on grosser divergences from presently or subsequently ascertainable facts, divergences that were more frequent in propaganda during the first World War. Also, propaganda during the second World War tended to give fuller information about relevant events than propaganda during World War I.

In summarizing the psychological aspects of these differences, we might say that propaganda appeals were less frequently directed to id and superego, more prominently to the ego.

In this respect, these areas of difference are representative of others. At least two qualifications to the points mentioned above are essential: first, most of the differences we stress became ever clearer the longer the second World War lasted; second, they were more accentuated in the propaganda of the Western democracies than in that of Germany and Russia.[2]

The use of emotionalized language was, at the outset of World War II, almost completely absent in British propaganda. When, in the autumn of 1939, Mr. Churchill, then First Lord of the Admiralty, referred to the Nazis as "Huns", thus using the stereotype current during World War I, he was publicly rebuked. Basically, that attitude persisted throughout the war in Britain and the United States. "We don't want to be driven into hate" was the tenor of opinion. There were modifications of this attitude: in the United States in regard to Japan, in Britain after the severe onslaught of bombing. However, hate campaigns remained largely unacceptable. In Germany, a similar attitude persisted: attempts of German propaganda to brandish the bombing of German cities by British and later by American planes as barbarism, to speak of the crews of these planes as "night pirates" and of German raids against Britain as retaliatory largely failed to arouse indignant hate.

The waning power of *moral* argumentation in propaganda is best illustrated by the fact that one of the predominant themes of propaganda during World War I played no comparable part in World War II. The theme "Our cause is right; theirs is wrong" was secondary in the propaganda of the Western powers; its part in German propaganda was limited; only in Russian propaganda was its role presumably comparable to that it had played in World War I propaganda. In the democratic countries and in Germany, the moral argumentation was replaced by one in terms of indulgence and deprivation (profit or loss): "We are winning; they are losing;" and: "These will be the blessings of victory; these the calamities of defeat." There is evidence indicating that both in the democracies and in Germany this type of appeal was eminently successful. In other words: success of propaganda was dependent on the transformation of superego appeals into appeals to the ego.[3]

The third area of difference, the increased concern for some agreement between the content of propaganda and ascertainable facts, and the increased concern for detailed information was to some considerable extent related to technological change. Thus, during the first World War, the German people were never explicitly (and implicitly only much later) informed about the German defeat in the battle of the Marne in September 1914. A similar reticence during the second World War would not have proved expedient, since in spite of coercive measures, allied radio transmissions were widely listened to by Germans. However, technological progress was not the only reason for the change. The concern with credibility had increased, independently of the technology of communication. The tendency to check statements of one's own against those of enemy governments existed both in Germany and in the democracies; while it was limited in Germany, it was widely spread in Britain and the United States.

The differences of propaganda during World Wars I and II are epitomized in the treatment of a theme related to all three areas discussed—enemy atrocities. As far as we know, only Russian propaganda on German atrocities, and German propaganda on Russian atrocities gave to this theme about the same importance in World War II that all propagandists had given it during World War I. But German reports on allied atrocities were rather timid, if compared to the inventiveness of German propaganda in other areas; and German propaganda about Soviet atrocities was largely designed to create fear and defensive combativeness rather than hate and indignation. In the democracies, however, the "playing down" of reports on enemy atrocities was a guiding principle of propaganda, at least until 1945. While during World War I, allied propagandists did not refrain from exaggerating and even inventing atrocities, uncontestable evidence of enemy atrocities was, for a long time, withheld during World War II. It is needless to say that the atrocities to which this documentation referred and which, at the end of the war and after the war became manifest to the soldiers of armies traversing Europe, were of a kind totally different in horror from anything the world of the earlier twentieth century had known. The purposeful reticence of the democratic governments becomes thereby even more significant.

No adequate understanding of these propaganda trends is possible, unless we take two closely related trends in the predispositions of the public into account. Our thesis is that the differences between the propaganda styles during both World Wars are largely due to the rising tendencies towards *distrust* and *privatization*—tendencies that we believe to have existed in the Western democracies as well as in Germany.

Distrust is directed primarily against the propagandist and the authority he represents, secondarily also against the "suggestibility" of the "propagandee." (E. Kris, 1942, 1944)

> The first mentioned manifestation of distrust can be traced back to the last war. Propaganda operated then on a new level of technological perfection; the latent possibilities of the mass communication media became suddenly manifest; in all belligerent countries, outbursts of enthusiasm for war occurred. Propagandists, like children playing with a new toy, charged their messages with many manufactured contents. After the war, they reported on their own achievements—sometimes ex-

aggerating the extent to which they had distorted events. These reports helped to create the aura of secret power that ever since has surrounded propagandists. In Britain and the United States, some of this prestige was transferred from the propagandist to the public relations counsel; some of the men who had successfully worked in government agencies became pioneers of modern advertising. Beliefs in the power of propaganda led to a phobia of political persuasion: propaganda became "a bad name", an influence against which the common man had to guard himself.

The political and economic failures of the postwar era, the futility of the idealistic appeals which had helped to conclude the first World War, reinforced this distrust. Its spread and influence on the political scene, however, was sharply different in different areas. In Germany, the distrust of propaganda was manipulated by the nationalist, and later, the national-socialist movement. Propaganda was identified with those allied propaganda efforts that had accompanied German defeat.[4] While distrust was directed against one side, nationalist and national-socialist propaganda could operate more freely under the guise of anti-propaganda. In the Western democracies, the propaganda phobia rose during the Great Depression. It became a lasting attitude both in the United States and possibly to a lesser degree, in the United Kingdom; and it took years of experience to discover a propaganda style that would at least not provoke distrust. While the disdain of propaganda had been initiated by the upper strata, it was during the second World War more intense with lower socio-economic groups.

At this point, it becomes essential to supplement our analysis of the distrust of propaganda by a discussion of contemporary privatization tendencies. Many motivations contribute to such tendencies. Some of them are not taken up here.[5]

Individuals in the mass societies of the twentieth century are to an ever increasing extent involved in public affairs; it becomes increasingly difficult to ignore them. But "ordinary" individuals have ever less the feeling that they can *understand* or *influence* the very events upon which their life and happiness is known to depend. (Mannheim, K.; Kecskemeti, P. and Leites, N.) At the same time, leaders in both totalitarian and democratic societies claim that decisions ultimately rest upon the common man's consent, and that the information supplied to him fully enables him to evaluate the situation. The contrast between these claims and the common man's experience extends to many areas. Thus in economic life ever more depends upon state interference. But, on the other hand, people increasingly regard economic policy as a province in which the professional specialist is paramount and the common man incompetent. The increasing "statification" of economic life has been accompanied by a rising mass reputation of scientific economics as a specialty. The emotional charges of simple economic formulae such as "free enterprise" or "socialization of the means of production" seem to have decreased (one might speak, at least in certain areas, of the silent breakdown of "capitalism" and "socialism" as ideologies). While the economic specialist is to fulfill the most urgent demand of the common man, that for security of employment, the distance between him and his beneficiary grows; he becomes part of a powerful elite, upon which the common man looks with a distrust rooted in dependency.

This is but one instance of the experience of disparity—of insight as well as power—between the common man and the various political organizations into which he is integrated. That disparity counteracts the feeling of power which accompanies the manipulation of increasingly effective machinery, whether of production or destruction: the common man is usually acutely aware of the fact that the "button" he is "pushing" belongs to an apparatus far out of the reach of any unorganized individual.

This feeling of disparity greatly affects the common man's attitude to foreign policy. The potential proximity of total war produces situations that not only seem inherently incomprehensible, but that he, the common man, feels cannot be made comprehensible to him by his government. "Security considerations", he infers, are the reason why the "real dope" is kept away from him. Thus the distance between the common man and the policy maker has grown to such an extent that awe and distrust support each other.

The common man feels impotent in a world where specialized skills control events that at any moment may transform his life. That feeling of impotence bestows upon political facts something of the solidity of natural events, like weather or hurricane, that come and go. Two attitudes result from this feeling: First, one does not inquire into the causation of the events thus viewed; second, one does not inquire into their morality.[6]

The feeling that politics as such is outside the reach of morals is an extreme form of this attitude. Probably moral indignation as a reaction to political events has been declining since the turn of the century. One may compare the intense reactions to injustice against individuals under comparatively stable social conditions—the Dreyfus affair, the cases of Ferrer, Nurse Cavell, Sacco and Vanzetti—with the limited reactions to Nazi terror and extermination practises as they gradually became notorious. In the case of the Nazis, public reaction went through a sequence of frank disbelief, reserved doubt, short lived shock and subsequent indifference.

The psychological dynamics operating the interplay of distrust and privatization can now be formulated more sharply. We here distinguish in the continuum of distrustful attitudes, two cases: One we call critical distrust; the other projective distrust.[7] In the child's development, the former arose not independently from the latter. Critical distrust facilitates adjustment to reality and independence; it is at the foundation of scientific thought, and is an essential incentive in the battle against what Freud called the prohibition of thinking in the individual. Critical distrust has gained a decisive importance in modern society, since technology has played havoc with many kinds of magic. Projective distrust, on the other hand, is derived ultimately from ambivalence; it is an expression of hostility, in which aggressive tendencies against others, frequently against authority, are perceived as tendencies of others, frequently as attitudes of authority.

We allude to these complex questions only in order to round off our argumentation: in the world of the twentieth century, the exercise of critical distrust by the common man meets with many obstacles; it is at the same time increasingly stimulated and increasingly frustrated. He therefore regressively turns to projective distrust: He fears, suspects and hates what he cannot understand and master.

Privatization is, amongst other things, a result of the hostility between the individual and the leadership of the group: We mentioned that it is comparable to what is known as a narcissistic regression. In order to maintain this attitude in which self-interest predominates over group interest—the self in this case may include "primary" groups such as the family—projective distrust is set into operation. Scepticism becomes the guarantor of privatization: scepticism here acts as a defense. If the individual, for instance, were to accept available evidence on atrocities, his emotional involvement in politics might rise;

he might hate or experience enthusiasm. Thus privatization could not be maintained. The propagandist's concern in war-time is therefore to reduce such scepticism.

That concern, we said, was more clearly expressed in the democracies than in Germany or Russia. In order fully to understand this difference, we turn to a more detailed discussion of the relationship between propagandist and "propagandee." Every propaganda act occurs in such a relationship; in the case of propaganda by agents of governments, it is the relationship between the individual and his government.

We discuss this relationship in regard to two types of political organization: the totalitarian state with the charismatic leader and democracy. In both cases, the propagandists speak for the leaders, who are the chief propagandists. In both cases, propaganda presupposes, and attempts to strengthen identifications of the propagandees with the propagandists. These identifications, however, have a different character under the two regimes.

In a totalitarian state these identifications concern, to a large extent, id and superego functions. These identifications facilitate the gratifying completion of impulses, as superego functions have been projected upon the propagandist, and as he is idealized in an archaic sense: omnipotence, omniscience and infallibility are attributed to him.

In democratic states, the corresponding identifications concern, to a large extent, ego functions which are delegated to the propagandist. Amongst these functions, the scrutiny of the existing situation and the anticipation of the future are of predominant importance. While the propagandee relies upon the propagandist for the fulfillment of these functions, he retains a critical attitude in relation to him.

Superego and ego identifications, of course, constantly interact. The distribution of their intensities, however, is clearly dependent upon the institutionalized relationship between propagandist and propagandee. In this sense, we may say that the one is typical of totalitarian, the other of democratic propaganda relations.

That difference is reflected in the devices of propaganda. Totalitarian propaganda tries to sway the audience into participation; its preferred setting is the visible leader talking to the masses; it is modeled after the relations between the hypnotist and his medium. Democratic propaganda gives greater weight to insight as basis for participation; it is to a greater extent modeled after the principles of guidance or education.

The nature of the two propaganda situations accounts for the fact that for each of the two kinds of propagandists different goals are difficult to reach. The totalitarian propagandist finds it arduous to stimulate initiative among his followers. When German propaganda was faced with the task of stimulating co-operative action "from below" among the citizens of bombed towns, that difficulty became apparent: the devices then adopted were plain imitations of the techniques of British propagandists in a similar situation. Democratic propagandists meet a comparable difficulty when faced with the task of manifestly denying information on reasons for government action, that is, of demanding implicit trust for a limited time. The impasse in which allied leadership found itself when faced with a public demand for the opening of a second front, especially in 1943, is an example.

The two types of propagandists react to the impact of distrust and privatization in different ways; these tendencies show a different incidence under the two political orders. In a totalitarian state, privatization grows with deprivation. Then the latent cleavage of the totalitarian state becomes manifest, the cleavage between the faithful, from whose ranks elite and sub-elite are recruited, and the indifferent, who are controlled by the faithful. Their mounting privatization renders this control more difficult. Superego identifications cease to function with ever more individuals, and finally they function only with the fanatics. When that situation crystallized in Germany with the approach of defeat, two devices were adopted: First, a gradual revision of propaganda policy. Appeals to superego identifications became less and less important and increased weight was given to the stimulation of fear: ego interests should now motivate continued allegiance. But this did not prevent further privatization. Thus the central method of all totalitarian social control was applied ever more consistently: violence. In its last phases, Nazi propaganda hardly fulfilled the purpose of gaining participation in the present; building the Nazi myth, it addressed its appeals to future generations.

Democratic propaganda is better equipped to deal with the tendency towards privatization, since it puts greater emphasis on the creation of insight. Its appeals are better in tune with a high level of distrust. In totalitarian regimes, there is a polarization between the politicized and the privatized, which is, however, difficult to perceive from the outside. In democratic states, tendencies towards privatization are clearly perceptible but their distribution within the society is less clear cut.

There are periods when this tendency decreases: in America after Pearl Harbor, in Britain after May 1940. While enthusiasm was kept at a low level, determination prevailed and sacrifice was willingly sustained.

What was the part of the propagandist in such situations? It may be illustrated by turning to one specific situation, in which democratic propaganda reached its greatest success.

We refer to Churchill's propaganda feat during the spring of 1940. The series of speeches he made in May, June and July of 1940 are remembered for the singular depth of feeling and the heroic quality of language. But these qualities were only accessories to the major political impact of these speeches. Their function was a threefold one—to warn Britain of the danger, to clarify its extent, and to indicate how everyone could help to meet it. In order to illustrate this point, we refer to one topic only: the announcement of the Battle of Britain.

The first intimation was made on May 12th, three days after Churchill's appointment, when the Battle of Flanders had not yet reached its climax. After having described the battles on all fronts, Churchill added that "many preparations had to be made at home." On May 19th, after the surrender of Holland, and during the climax of the Belgian battles, he devoted well over one-third of his speech to announcing "that after this . . . there will come the battle for our island." And after demanding full mobilization of production, he gave for the first time the "box score": he reported that the R.A.F. had been downing three to four enemy planes for each of their own. This, he inferred, was the basis of any hope. On June 4th, in his famous speech after Dunkirk, the theme was taken up anew and an elaborate account of the chances of the fighter force in a battle over the homeland was given. Churchill went into technical details; at a time when France seemed still vigorously to resist, he acquainted the British people with the chances of their survival. While the enemy had broken through the allied front with a few thousand armored vehicles, he forecast the future by saying: "May it not also be that the course of civilization itself will be defended by the skill and devotion of a few thousand airmen." And while he discussed the necessity of ever increasing production, he spoke at this time of imminent defeat of "the great British armies of the later years of war."

In the later speeches of that unforgettable spring, he elaborated on the subject. Every one could understand how his own behavior was related to the total situation, and how this situation was structured; how supplies were needed for the repair and construction of fighter planes, and how in this matter every detail, even the smallest one, could contribute to the final result. All this information was released well in advance of any German attack.

Thus Churchill had not only given the "warning signal" and mobilized "emergency reactions." His detailed analysis of the situation also contributed to the prevention of an inexpediently large and rapid increase in anxiety: unknown danger was transformed into a danger known in kind and extent. He fulfilled those functions of leadership that can be compared to those fulfilled in the life of the individual by the organization of the ego (E. Kris, 1944). At the same time, Churchill offered his own courage as a model: "If you behave as I do, you will behave right." He not only spoke of Britain's "finest hour" but was careful to add that in this hour "every man and woman had their chance."

The propagandist thus seems to fulfill a double function: first that of structuring the situation so that it can be anticipated and understood, and second, that of offering himself as a model.

It is essential to understand the difference between the democratic leader who functions as a model and the charismatic leader (F. Redl). The latter offers himself as an object that replaces superego functions in the individual. The model function of leadership implies that in identifying with the leader, the individual will best serve the ideals he shares with him. But the understanding of the situation is a precondition for such moral participation.

The general problem which we here finally approach concerns the relation between ego and superego functions. One might tentatively formulate the hypothesis that in a situation in which the ego functions smoothly, the tension between ego and superego is apt to be low. In fact, we find in the study of superego formation in the child some evidence in support of such a formulation (K. Friedlander). However, other evidence is contradictory. Frequently, successful ego performance is accompanied by intense conflicts between ego and superego. We therefore reject this formulation and substitute another: unsuccessful ego functions endanger the positive relationship between ego and superego. They tend to encourage regressive trends. Individuals who feel impotent in the face of a world they do not understand, and are distrustful of those who should act as their guides, tend to revert to patterns of behavior known from childhood, in which an increase of hostility against the adults and many neurotic or delinquent mechanisms may develop. The incidence of such maladjustments may increase in a society in which privatization tendencies have become dominant.[8]

Little can be said here about what conclusions can be drawn for the future of democratic propaganda from these considerations. They clearly point to the desirability of sharp and wide increases of insight into events in the world at large among the citizens. Briefly, the trend towards distrust and privatization among the audience of the propagandist should be turned into a trend towards increase of insight. That trend would find a parallel in changes of related techniques: psycho-therapy and education, largely under the influence of psychoanalysis, have substituted or are substituting insight for pressure. If the appropriate education, on a vast enough scale and at a rapid enough rate is not provided for, the distrust and privatization of the masses may become a fertile soil for totalitarian management.

BIBLIOGRAPHY

Deutsch, H. Zur Psychologie des Misstrauens, *Imago* 7, 1921, pp. 71-83.

Friedlander, K. Formation of the Antisocial Character, *The Psa. Study of the Child,* New York, Int. Univ. Press, I, 1945, pp. 189-204.

Kecskemeti, P. and Leites, N. *Some Psychological Hypotheses on Nazi Germany,* Washington, D. C., Library of Congress, 1945 (multigraphed).

Kris, E. The Danger of Propaganda, *Amer. Imago,* 2, 1941, pp. 1-42.

——. Some Problems of War Propaganda. A Note on Propaganda, Old and New, *Psa. Quart.* 2, 1943, pp. 381-99.

——. Danger and Morale, *Amer. J. Orthopsych.,* 14, 1944, pp. 147-155.

——. Speier, H. and Associates, *German Radio Propaganda,* New York, Oxford Univ. Press, 1944.

Lasswell, H. D. *Propaganda Techniques in the World War,* New York, Alfred A. Knopf, 1927.

Mannheim, K. *Man and Society in an Age of Transition,* K. Paul, Trench, Trubner & Co., London, 1940.

Masserman, J. H. *Principles of Dynamic Psychiatry*, Phila., Saunders, 1946.
Redl, F. Group Education and Leadership, *Psychiatry* 5, 1942, pp. 573-96.
Smith, B. L., Lasswell, H. D. and Casey, R. D. *Propaganda, Communication and Public Opinion*, Princeton Univ. Press, 1946.
Speier, H. and Otis, M. German Radio Propaganda to France, *Radio Research* 1942/43, New York, Duell, Sloan & Pearce, 1944.

Chapter 3. Notes

1. Two kinds of decreased participation in the direction of privatization can be distinguished: first, a decrease of active attitudes towards the political sphere, in favor of passive or merely adjusting attitudes; in this case, one must speak of a decrease of attitudinal participation; second, a decrease of the actual sharing in political action; in this case, one might speak of a decrease of behavioral participation.

2. In the following, we shall in the main limit ourselves to examples from American, British and German propaganda, and some data on response; information on reactions of Russian and Japanese audiences is not accessible.

3. See Jules H. Masserman, p. 219, who makes a similar point. He speaks of "resonance with personal incentives."

4. For the question of the actual contribution of propaganda to this defeat and generally for the question of the limited influence of propaganda on warfare, see E. Kris, H. Speier and Associates.

5. For instance, we do not propose to discuss how privatization is related to changes in values.

6. American soldiers during the second World War were frequently explicitly opposed to discussions of its causation: going into its pre-history was frequently regarded as futile and somewhat "out of this world."

7. We do not propose here to discuss in detail their genetic interrelation, nor their pathological manifestations, especially in obsessional neuroses and paranoid syndromes. (See H. Deutsch's classical expositions.) A fuller treatment would also have to consider the question of retaliatory and self-punitive distrust.

8. We here note that the traditional discussion of the applicability of "individual" psychological hypotheses to "social" events lacks substance, since events dealt with in the empirical analysis of human affairs, "psychological" or "sociological," occur in individuals. We deal with frequencies of incidence.

Part II

POLICY, INTELLIGENCE, AND PROPAGANDA STRATEGY

POLICY DEFINES the limits within which propaganda must work by specifying the goals to be achieved. Intelligence defines the limits within which propaganda must work by specifying the limits of what the audience will believe and what they will do. Propaganda strategy consists of making the most of the terrain that lies between the boundaries defined by policy and intelligence.

Only the impetuous amateur among propagandists ignores these boundaries. Without policy goals firmly in control of utterances, propaganda may move its audience—but in no direction or in the wrong direction. Without audience predispositions at the center of its strategy, propaganda may be brilliant —but leave its audience unmoved or more hostile than it was before. Professional propagandists learn to distrust ingenious "stunts" until their utility has been evaluated in terms of policy goals, audience predispositions, and the "tactical situation."

Part II is mainly a case-study of a difficult propaganda strategy: that which operated in World War II on the terrain between the Allied policy directive of "unconditional surrender" and German predispositions toward a Nazi hegemony over Europe. This is a particularly instructive case since many observers have attacked this policy because it supposedly hamstrung our propaganda. Yet, no less a professional than R. H. S. Crossman has asserted: "Surprisingly enough, we found more room for maneuver than might have been expected."

After a chapter by Lasswell which provides a perspective on the policy uses of intelligence, we consult two evaluations of Unconditional Surrender by men who worked with this policy in World War II. Speier, writing before VE-Day, provides a general analysis of the function of war aims from which to evaluate the policy. Carroll appraises its effects after the European war had ended.

Next we turn to a set of chapters on "The German Case," which illustrate several kinds of intelligence required for enlightened propaganda strategy. The studies by Dicks illuminate the basic structure of attitudes among various German personality types and social groups. Padover's "Folio of German Types" shows how the basic data can be enriched, and focussed to current intelligence needs, by continuing interrogation of individuals. The Gurfein-Janowitz chapter reports a pioneering trend study of Wehrmacht morale, as revealed by masses of comparable data quantified on selected indexes to morale. The intelligence value of systematic study of German communications, by the method of Content Analysis, is shown in the Speier-Otis chapter. The "Standing Directive" by Crossman, which actually governed SHAEF Sykewar operations against Germany, is a brilliant demonstration of how propaganda strategy can make maximum use of the terrain bounded by policy directives and audience predispositions.

Readers interested in following out other detailed cases, for example "the Japanese case," could match the Dicks study of basic personality-ideology correlates by such an analysis as Geoffrey Gorer's "Themes in Japanese Culture." Data of intelligence value on Japanese communications are given in Peter de Mendelssohn's book *Japan's Political Warfare.* An evaluation of intelligence findings for propaganda strategy, parallel to Crossman's, is the Foreign Morale Analysis Division's memorandum "Current Psychological and Social Tensions in Japan" (reprinted in A. H. Leighton, *Human Relations in a Changing World,* Appendix B).

Chapter 4

POLICY AND THE INTELLIGENCE FUNCTION *

By

HAROLD D. LASSWELL

THE INTELLIGENCE function adapts itself to changing conceptions of policy and to innovations in the procedures by which facts are gathered, analyzed, and presented. New policy ideas are today resulting from the vast transformations that are taking place in the structure of society, state, and government. New methods of observing, analyzing, and reporting data have arisen as an outcome of the growth of modern social and psychological sciences. So swift is the stream that we may fail in every effort to chart the banks within which it flows; yet the importance of seeking to understand the complex relationship of policy and intelligence is great enough to justify the risks involved. Greater clarity may reduce the amount of fumbling that is invariably associated with new efforts to adapt old functions to different conditions.

A canvass of the existing literature reveals that very little systematic and unified treatment has been given to the intelligence function. In limited spheres, notably in relation to military policy, there are theoretical discussions and practical manuals.[1] It has long been an axiom that command depends on adequate intelligence of the resources and plans of the enemy. In the realm of diplomacy there are valuable hints on how information may be obtained.[2] Concern for the internal security of the state [3] and aspirations toward revolutionary action [4] have both inspired contributions to the intelligence problem. The literature of democracy has reiterated the need of an intelligent public opinion; however, there has been a minimum of advance

* Reprinted from *Ethics*, (vol. LIII, No. 1) October 1942.

toward specifying the criteria by which relevant intelligence for the citizen and the official may be recognized.[5]

It is possible to fathom some of the factors that have contributed to the comparative neglect of the intelligence function as a whole. In preliberal, predemocratic states, ideological policy was simple. The aims of policy in this field were to detect sedition at home and conspiracy abroad and to encourage the reverent acceptance of state-friendly religions. In liberal, democratic states, however, there is nothing simple about the ideological goals, if we take these aspirations literally. Democracy means respect for human dignity. This implies a commonwealth of mutual deference. (To be deferred to is to be taken into consideration; in a democratic government or state this calls for participation in the making of important decisions.) Policy is democratic when it is consistent and compatible with human dignity. Obviously this calls for deeper knowledge of reality than the simple recording of momentary approval of contemplated lines of action.

Although the ideal of human dignity is positive, it entered the stage of the large-scale modern state clad in the scanty garments of negativism. Private businessmen were out to get government out of the market. The expanding business society expressed itself through the competitive market and representative government. The focus of attention of the businessman was limited to the market; the focus of attention of the government man was restricted to auxiliary functions. The postulated pre-established harmony of profit-seeking and national gain was accepted as a moral gloss on the business way of life. "The pursuit of profit is the salvation of the world." [6] No positive conception of the relationship between the parts and the whole of a democratic state was sought. It was not missed.

In recent times the re-expansion of government has redefined the focus of attention of the policy-makers of liberal, democratic states. More and more they are compelled to try to find a unified set of positive objectives, to "reconcile" business and government. At the same moment that the internal structure of the state is changing, the key symbols and symbol elaborations of the state are under attack. Communist revolutionaries deride the democratic aspirations of such states as hypocrisy; Nazi revolutionaries deride them as decadent and contemptible. The

Nazis reject both symbols and practices; the Marxists reject only the practices.

The sheer intellectual task of clarifying the goals and instruments of democratic idealism has gone largely by default. If we look back to the seventeenth and eighteenth centuries in England, we are impressed by the strength of the intellectual currents that were running toward unity of state aim. When David Hume wrote about social processes, his contributions included not only essays on the balance of trade but on the balance of power. The doctrines of mercantilism [7] were a rather coherent body of policy ideas: states were conceived as succeeding or failing in terms of power (by which was meant political fighting effectiveness); power was believed to depend on stimulating exports in return for precious metals. Goals were so clearly defined that intelligence operations could count goods and weigh bullion and apply this practical meter stick to the measurement of policy success and failure.

The liberal, democratic state did not succeed in harmonizing professed ideal and effective policy, partly because the democratic elements in the ideal were left undeveloped. Intellectual life showed the effect of the bifurcation of market and government, and "political economy" became preoccupied with the routines of the market. In the liberal, democratic state men spoke of "prosperity," not of "power"; yet prosperity was not their ostensible goal. The cardinal value was the dignity of man, but prosperity was not translated in terms of human dignity. Bentham's calculus of felicity was pointed in this direction, but it was not specified in terms capable of being operationally applied to an extremely complicated division of labor.

Some shortcomings of liberal, democratic states have been failures of policy and intelligence; the urgent question of the moment is how these deficiencies can be surmounted. Can the policy-makers who profess ideals of human dignity learn to specify what they mean in operating terms? No doubt the intelligence function can aid, to some extent, in the task of clarification; unquestionably the intelligence facilities of modern society can provide relevant knowledge when goals are put in definite terms.

Modern procedures do make it possible for the first time in the history of large-scale social organization to realize some of the aims of democracy. Social and psychological sciences have developed procedures that are capable of reporting the facts about the thoughts and feelings of our fellow-men. In the Great Society, with its thousands of specialized material environments, its enormous geographical spread, and its instantaneous communication, special measures must be taken to learn the significant facts of life. By means of quick interviews, we can supplement some of the guesses that are made about what men think; and by prolonged interviews and participation we can probe more deeply into the texture of experience. By disciplined methods we can locate the zones of poor democratic performance and determine the factors that contribute to their continuation. We are accustomed to think of production goals for wheat or pig iron and to graph the facts about goal and performance. By using our new instruments of mutual understanding, we can specify our goals and report on their state of realization. The very act of specifying the meaning of human dignity disciplines both our policy-makers and our scientists. The gathering of knowledge can be synchronized with the needs of policy and with the formal standards of science.

We can actually study the thoughts and feelings of each of the major divisions of modern social structure and perfect means of making them fraternally intelligible to one another. Certainly we professional people need to be reminded constantly, and concisely, of the point of view of skilled and organized labor, of farmers, of unskilled laborers, of small and middle businessmen, of party and government leaders and administrators, of monopolistic and basic businesses. Policy decisions need to be tempered in the light of racial, confessional, and other group attitudes. If democracy includes a decent regard for the thoughts and feelings of others, our procedures can and should be applied to the enormous task of making these facts available to the various components of our society.[8] By examining the contents of the channels of public communication,[9] we may determine the degree to which even the opportunity exists of taking the other fellow into proper account. Up to the present time, it must be conceded, our press, film, and radio channels of mass communication have not adequately performed this task.[10]

Each public policy calls for two types of intelligence: ideological and technical. By ideological intelligence is meant facts about the thoughts, feelings, and conduct of human beings.

Other facts are technical. It makes no difference whether the policy goal is phrased in ideological or technical terms; both kinds of information are involved in any complete consideration of goals or alternatives. Ideologically phrased objectives are to strengthen the will to victory of the home population; to demoralize the fighting will of the enemy; and to win allies. The attainment of these objectives depends upon many technical considerations, such as geophysical factors affecting radio reception. If goals are phrased in technical terms (tanks, guns, planes), they depend upon data about the thoughts and feelings and conduct of factory workers and of many other elements of the population. It is evident that we are compelled to pass back and forth between ideological and technical facts in contemplating each and every line of policy.

Whatever scheme is used to classify policy, each policy and each category of policy must be properly integrated with every other. By policy we understand the making of important decisions. A decision adds energy and determination to preference; it is part of an act of striving. Values, therefore, are not only indorsed; they are sought by mobilizing a significant part of the values already at hand. The importance of decisions may be appraised according to the magnitude of this potential mobilization of resources. In the most vital personal decisions, character, material goods, friendship, and life are at stake. In the realm of public policy the stakes are comparable: moral integration, material assets, diplomatic position, and continuity.

For any personality, individual or collective, policy is concerned with total value position. Within the field of total policy, distinctions may be drawn that aid decisions by classifying ends and means. In the realm of high policy a fourfold classification has often been serviceable, according to which the four fronts of policy are military, diplomatic, economic, ideological. Each sphere of policy is to some extent an end and to some extent a means; successful policy proceeds by continuous integration. Thus every proposed military policy must be evaluated with reference to other objectives in the sphere of military policy and to goals in the sphere of diplomacy, economics, and ideology. If the specific military goal is indorsed as consistent and compatible with other objectives, it becomes an end of integrated policy. Other spheres then become integrated to it as means to end. In turn, the military sphere must be integrated with policy initiatives that arise in every other sphere. A diplomatic proposal, designed to aid in the successful negotiation of a trade treaty, may be to offer the inducement of allowing a complement of foreign officers to be trained in American military schools. Perhaps this is consistent and compatible with military objectives; hence the military facilities may be made promptly available as means of carrying out the policy. In the economic sphere it may be proposed to conserve our metal resources by increasing imports. The conservation program may be indorsed on military grounds, and the co-operation of the Navy may be needed to intercept cargoes bound for foreign ports. In the ideological sphere the cultivation of friendship with a foreign power may lead to the suggestion that radio broadcasts be increased to foreign countries from adjacent territory. If the Navy controls bases in adjacent territory, its co-operation is an essential means.

For purposes of brief definition we may sum up the four fronts of policy as ends and means. The end of military policy is predominance over enemies in battle; the distinctive means are instruments of violence. The end of diplomatic policy is favorable agreement, whatever the substantive character of the agreement; the distinctive means is negotiation. The end of economic policy is production; the distinctive means are productive instruments. The end of ideological policy is favorable attitudes; the most distinctive means are symbols. We may subdivide each policy front into internal and external. If this is done, some clarification is needed about the internal diplomatic front, since usage has limited diplomacy to external relations. In our expanded sense of the word, diplomacy includes offer, counteroffer, consent, dissent, mediation, conciliation, arbitration, adjudication, legislation. Hence it is appropriate to speak of the internal diplomacy of a state. At present, there is no consensus on how these internal processes are classified. Sometimes they are assigned to the internal ideological front. Often what are here called diplomacy and ideology are bracketed together as "political" policy—despite the patent advantages of reserving the term "politics" for the overall term. A threefold division thus results: military, economic, political. Nearly every other thinkable breakdown is sometimes made and is often useful. If a two-term classification is desired, the most satisfactory is the one hinted at above: ideological and technical.

In the former the emphasis is upon thoughts and feelings and upon the symbols that circulate through the channels of radio, film, press, and conversation. In the latter the starting-point is material objects. The usual instruments of ideological policy are speeches, news conferences, news releases, magazine articles, photographic stills, newsreels, film shorts, feature films, leaflets, books, cartoons, charts and tables, broadcasts, plays, rumors, maps, exhibits, demonstrations, letters, telephone messages. Propaganda is the positive guidance of such material; censorship eliminates. Personnel selection for symbolic rather than technical reasons also comes within the field of ideological action. In this theater of operations personnel choices need to be made in the interest of democratic integration. Army and civilian cadres are made up of varying ratios of persons answering different specifications as to age, sex, size, income, education, residence, religion, party (and the like). Some combinations aid democratic attitudes; others militate against them.

What the intelligence function can contribute to policy may be exemplified in certain simple instances on different policy fronts. The contributions can be summed up in three points: intelligence can (1) clarify goals, (2) clarify alternatives, and (3) provide needed knowledge. First, a military example: Reconnaissance reveals that hill 46 can be enveloped by routes 1 or 2. If orders are not clear, instructions may be requested. It may be pointed out that liaison would be easier to maintain along 1 than 2, but that 5 per cent more casualties could be anticipated. This statement of alternatives could be supported, if challenged, by facts about the deployment of enemy forces in the immediate sector and by facts about losses under comparable conditions. Second, an example from diplomacy: Policy instructions may be to negotiate a trade agreement, but the time period may be left vague. Intelligence may report that peaceful persuasion would produce the result in about six months; that an opportunity to receive stock in American business concerns would diminish opposition so much that success could be hoped for in three months. The supporting facts include knowledge of the attitudes of influential leaders. A third example is economic: If available steel is used to reach the tank quota, the shipbuilding quota will suffer by one-fourth. Intelligence may therefore ask for clarification of goal and support the estimates by data about present stocks and production ratios. A fourth example is ideological: Are atrocity stories to be played up more in the future than in the recent past? Intelligence may report that if more atrocity stories are circulated among the wives of skilled workers, it may give them a more vivid sense of what war is and stimulate their aggressive interest in helping their husbands keep on the job. This estimate of the probable result may be supported by interview data collected in the field and by the results of an experiment in which more interest in the war is indicated after reports of Japanese atrocities.

These instances have deliberately been selected on a low level of abstraction, but they show the essential interrelations between policy and intelligence. In practice, decision-makers of every level are finding new goals and subgoals, contemplating new alternatives, asking for new information as a means of evaluating future probabilities. Policy thinking is "forward" thinking; it is manipulative and responsible. It is always guided to some extent by knowledge; and a recurring problem is to perfect the intelligence function so that it brings to the focus of attention of the decision-maker what he most needs to think about and what he most needs to think with.

We may classify the types of knowledge needed for ideological policy as follows: (1) distribution of attitudes, (2) trend of attitudes, and (3) comparisons of available alternatives with past situations and with scientific findings. In the example above the distribution of attitudes in the homes of war workers is obviously pertinent to war production; knowledge of whether the trend had been more or less favorable would highlight the seriousness of the problem; comparison of the results of exposure to atrocity news would be relevant to decision.

Attitudes are hypothetical patterns of reality; the terms used to name attitudes must be given operational definitions from the standpoint of many different observers. In giving instructions for the identification of carbon, we have no trouble in choosing a definitive index. But this is not true of an attitude, like hatred of the President or of Hitler. We must work with many indices and construct rather arbitrary rules to govern the inclusion or exclusion of the resulting profiles.

Attitudes may be inferred from many kinds of data: (1) what people say and do; (2) what is said to people; (3) what is done to people. We may record what people say and do when they are unaware that they are being interviewed or when they are unaware that they are being observed for scientific or policy purposes. Our observer may be so situated that he may affect the result by influencing the attitude of the subject, or he may not. An example of the former case is the interviewer or participant-observer; although the subjects do not know the full significance of the participant-observer, they respond to a definite person in the situation. A spectator-observer may be buried in the grandstands and have no effect on the conduct he is watching. In the same way the reader of an intercepted message may have no personal effect.

By examining what is said to people, we may be able to foresee their responses. Policy-makers are accustomed to rely upon inferences that they make from what is brought to the focus of public attention in the media of mass communication. Many decisions are affected by inferences about public response that are made when the policy-maker reads a newspaper or listens to a broadcast on the way to the office. Inferences may also be based upon knowledge of what has been done to people and of how they have responded in the past. Thus, if we hear of acute housing congestion, of speed-up, of rising prices of consumption goods, of shortages of consumption goods, of rapid introduction of groups against which there is a local bias (racial, religious, partisan), we may construct many plausible inferences that are often confirmed by additional data.

The terms used to describe people are of cardinal importance, since they imply hypotheses about the factors that significantly affect response. We are concerned both with position in the social structure and with personality structure.

The organization of the intelligence function calls for the proper articulation of many specialists with policy-makers. Some problems arise because of the novelty of the procedures involved. Since the science of communication is itself in its infancy, the opportunities now open stimulate both imagination and ambition. Specialists who have become associated with the development of one specific procedure of observation are often prone to exaggerate its place in the total picture. Hence they may "oversell" one group of policy-makers on the results that can be expected from polling or psychiatric interviewing or content analysis or organizational analysis. Acceptance of a given skill group may be followed by disillusioned rejection, and the growth of a mature and well-developed intelligence operation may be retarded.

Policy-makers in business and government are well acquainted with the idea of describing the distribution of attitudes in a given group. They are also familiar with the idea of describing the distribution of politically significant symbols at the focus of attention of a group. The former has come from the counting of votes in elections and in poll interviews. The second has come from the practice of clipping the press of selected groups. Clipping bureaus are long-established institutions inside and outside government. The opinion poll has made rapid progress since the appearance of the American Institute of Public Opinion.

Although the idea of quantitative summaries of significant material is widely accepted, their interpretation is capricious. If you believe in the importance of world-organization after the war, you will probably be less critical of data that purport to show that a great many Americans look forward to such an outcome. If, on the contrary, you reject this goal, you may dismiss entirely the procedure by which the data were obtained or you may engage in vigorous methodological controversies about it. It is not generally recognized that, while the words recorded in brief polling interviews are highly valid in predicting elections, they are of indeterminate validity in forecasting how people will respond in situations that are as yet unorganized. The focus of attention of the group is in an advanced state of organization with respect to action when mid-election polls are taken; but remarks about price regulation may have no more significance than showing that the term itself is a negative word to most of the responders. Hence if something is to be done, it may be useful to reselect the validating symbols.

Another difficulty arises from the task of selecting and presenting certain kinds of information in a form deemed useful by policy-makers. Policy-makers are usually poised toward action. They want to choose between clear-cut courses of action. Hence intelligence material must be processed in a way that commends it to decision-makers.[11] Now scientists are accustomed to think in intervariable ("equilibrium") terms and to appraise their data as pertinent or not if they confirm or disconfirm a general proposition that is part of the systematic structure of their science. Hence they are not accustomed to consider the timing of their results in terms of policy objectives. If they find that experimental animals show more scratching and biting behavior when they are put on short rations than when they are cut down in sexual opportunities, they may take it for granted that these results are pertinent to policy. But what policy? Do they expect policy-makers to cut down on sex opportunities rather than rations? If so, when and where? Notice that there may indeed be policy implications; my only point is that the act of processing intelligence material must find an acceptable relationship to the policy-maker's conception of his policy alternatives.

Scientists who are accustomed to long interviews are faced with the problem of cutting their results down to a form that is valuable for policy and yet preserves something of the depth perspective of their data. From brief polling results we may know that 60 per cent say "Yes," 20 per cent say "No," and 20 per cent are noncommittal in reply to a question. If we look at the replies in the perspective of intensive knowledge, we may rearrange them in many different ways. Ten per cent of those who say "Yes" may do so because they want to bring about a negotiated peace; 20 per cent may say "Yes" because they want to block a "peace without victory." But the 10 per cent may own and affect by advertising newspapers that reach millions of people. It is a sterilizing process to limit the description of how people feel and think to an overterse bar chart; yet the busy executive may be impatient of the time it takes to read a set of qualifying riders.

Intensive procedures can be most effectively used when they are guided toward the "sore spots" or the "success spots" revealed by quick, extensive procedures like polling or brief content analysis. Also, intensive procedures can be pointed toward policy problems that can be dealt with at rather long intervals. The effect of withdrawing husbands and fathers from the home needs to be studied, and these investigations are best done by intensive methods. The policy alternatives may grow out of exploratory investigations; they may, for example, result in vigorous measures to increase the time spent out of the home and in selected community activities.

We are able to adapt to the needs of ideological intelligence many of the presentation forms developed for limited use in our society. In some ways the best and the most characteristic intelligence report is the prospectus offered to potential investors in new undertakings. The prospectus may rest on a foundation of vast research conducted by production engineers, market analysts, and many other technicians. No matter how elaborate the factual groundwork, the final results are put in clear-cut and inviting synoptic form. Photographs and charts illustrate the text, and the text is arranged freely to aid clarity, brevity, and emphasis. Good prospectus writers have successful careers because of the exceptional utility of the function they perform as go-between, uniting promoter, technician, and investor.

Documentary reports cannot take the place of personal presentation if full advantage is to be taken of research and planning. Ideological material is less definitive than technical reports, and, if it is to be correctly related to policy, the head of intelligence must be a member of the inner policy councils. Only by constant emphasis can policy-makers come to recognize the full degree of their reliance upon certain facts for basic clarification of their task.

The intelligence operation constantly asks for new specifications of objectives. Policy-makers often leave goals phrased in ambiguous language, hence open to misunderstanding. One function of the intelligence branch is to point out any handicapping ambiguousness and to bring about authoritative declarations. Often the goals enunciated by makers of policy are inconsistent or even contradictory; hence the policy branch must often call for new directives at every level of decision. Often, too, authoritative statements are entirely missing in reference to many zones of action; one duty of an intelligence branch is to call attention to these omissions.

When the process of goal discovery has been carried to the most inclusive objective, we come to the key ideals of the state. The specialists on integrating the flow of fact cannot bring about goal clarification unless the need of integrated policy is widely felt. Intelligence specialists who try to force rigorous proclamation of purpose may fail to carry the policy group along with them. During our present period of transition from a business-dominant to a government-dominant state, the relationships between those who formulate authoritative declarations of policy and those who perform the intelligence function will be in a constant state of redefinition. To push ahead too far and too fast will often lead to the rejection of disciplined fact-gathering. And yet failure to keep the need of clarity at the focus of attention of policy-makers is to delay needed adjustments to reality.

At present the nontotalitarian states have difficulty in formulating war and peace aims. As a result of World War I legalistic and diplomatic aims were revealed as obviously insufficient to the needs of policy. Of course, we stand for legal order; but what is the form of social structure that will sustain the sense of justice capable of sustaining a legal order of the type we want? The influential elements of nontotalitarian states reveal their policy confusion when they are reluctant to put their objectives in basic terms of social structure. We still hear of "victory" as a goal; but "victory for what?" is not made manifest.

The crux of the matter is that deep timidities complicate the task of translating democratic aspirations into compelling institutional terms. Slogans like the "Four Freedoms" are not enough unless they are completed by slogans that point to the operating rules of a society that puts freedom into practice. We are in a war of ideas, but we have not found our ideas. It is essential to face our timidities without fear and to deal with them directly. Some of the reluctance of our leaders of wealth and government springs from basic pessimism about the possibility of maintaining the fundamental characteristics of our pattern of state and society. In one sense, Marxist predestinarianism has conquered the world, for there is deep distrust of the prospects of any order save one distinguished by total governmentalization of organized activity. Our intellectuals have not even clarified in operational terms the meaning of a social order compatible with human dignity and safeguarded by a balanced structure. A striking example of this hiatus concerns the middle classes. For centuries it has been an axiom of much political philosophy that freedom depended upon perpetuating a flourishing middle group between the extremely rich and the extremely poor. This means that the condition most favorable to a free society is a balanced income structure. Despite the fundamental need of clarity in this vital matter, our thinkers and decision-makers have not succeeded in specifying rules of balance. Despite our quantifying tendencies in production and in the intellectual life, we have not chosen critical ratios of balance and defined in clear terms the fundamental conditions and goals of policy. At present we do not clearly and vividly stand for the principle of dynamic balance versus despotism and anarchism. In these years of stress, however, we may succeed in discovering a unifying conception of democratic policy. When this unity is found, the ideological intelligence function will be smoothly articulated with policy. In the meanwhile there can be a persistent and clarifying interplay between such branches of the intelligence function as can be perfected and those who share in the making of important decisions.

Chapter 4. Notes

1. Concerning World War I see Maximilian Ronge, *Kriegs- und Industrie-Espionage* (Vienna, 1930).

2. See especially James Westfall Thompson and Saul K. Padover, *Secret Diplomacy: A Record of Espionage and Double-dealing, 1500-1815* (London, 1937).

3. See Book I of *Kautilya's Arthasastra*.

4. Refer to the secret literature of the Communist International, such as A. Neuberg, *Der bewaffnete Aufstand: Versuch einer theoretischen Darstellung* (Zurich, 1938). (False bibliographical data.)

5. An effort like that of Charles E. Merriam in *The New Democracy and the New Despotism* (New York, 1939) is most exceptional. The leads suggested by Graham Wallas in *The Great Society* (London, 1914) have never been adequately followed up (chaps. x-xiii).

6. From my notes of a speech delivered by an American businessman on his return from negotiating the "Dawes Plan."

7. On the full range of mercantilism consult Eli F. Heckscher, *Der Merkantilismus* (2 vols.; Jena, 1932).

8. See Bruce Lannes Smith, "Propaganda Analysis and the Science of Democracy," *Public Opinion Quarterly*, V (1941), 250-59.

9. Representative recent contributions to this emerging science include: Douglas Waples (ed.), *Print, Radio, and Film in a Democracy* (Chicago, 1942); Paul F. Lazarsfeld, *Radio and the Printed Page* (New York, 1940); George Gallup and Saul F. Rae, *The Pulse of Democracy* (New York, 1940); Gardner Murphy and Rensis Likert, *Public Opinion and the Individual* (New York), 1938. On content analysis see Harold D. Lasswell, *World Politics and Personal Insecurity* (New York, 1935), chap. ix; "World Attention Survey," *Public Opinion Quarterly*, V (1941), 456-62.

10. See Harold D. Lasswell, "The Achievement Standards of a Democratic Press," in *Freedom of the Press Today*, ed. Harold L. Ickes (New York, 1941).

11. A classical discussion of "Thought at the Level of Planning" is in Karl Mannheim, *Man and Society in an Age of Reconstruction* (New York, 1940), Part IV.

Chapter 5

WAR AIMS IN POLITICAL WARFARE *

By

HANS SPEIER

I

A REALISTIC DISCUSSION of the use of war aims in political warfare perhaps starts best from a clear understanding of the fact that propagandists do not make foreign policy; they talk about it.[1] They inform the world about the policy of the country for which they speak. They interpret this policy. They translate its meaning into language that will be understood by people who are not experts on foreign policy. They point up its successes and conceal its failures. And they try to disparage the foreign policy of the enemy.

The propagandist enjoys more freedom when he informs his audience than when he interprets. He has the least freedom when he needs it most. His interpretations have to stay within narrow limits and are, as a matter of routine, subject to clearance by policymaking agencies. Sometimes the use of a single word or the translation of a phrase must be approved beforehand. This situation prevails in all countries at war.

Because the propagandist depends on the policymaker, effective liaison between their agencies is of great importance in political warfare. But liaison between the statesmen and the top personnel responsible for propaganda is not institutionalized in any country. Unlike experts in foreign, military and naval affairs, experts in propaganda are seldom among the participants at international conferences. In fact, the more important the parley, the less likely it is that there will be propagandists among the attending advisers.

There is nothing wrong with this arrangement. Propaganda

* Reprinted from *Social Research,* (vol. XIII) May 1945.

campaigns are neither so important nor so final as military campaigns, and the plans of men experienced in foreign policy, while less final than the plans of the military, anticipate results far more important than the results the propagandist may hope to achieve. For this reason the worst propaganda schemes are usually less harmful than moderately bad designs of statesmen.

The cooperation between the statesman and the propagandist can in some regards be compared with the relations between a husband who wants to save and a wife who likes to spend. Propagandists are usually inclined toward short-range considerations. A policy that is focused on enduring interests, future conditions and long-range objectives may restrict the propagandist's daily operations, and when this happens the propagandist has to comply. He complies, but is sometimes dissatisfied. The sense of frustration that he feels may be caused by the prudence of the statesman, but the training that is most valuable in the work of a propagandist is no education for appreciating political prudence.

War aims are integrally related to foreign policy. To the extent that foreign policy is public it becomes part of the ammunition to be used in political warfare against the enemy. The propagandist wants to talk about war aims primarily in order to precipitate victory or to delay defeat. If the war is going well for his side, the propagandist, like the general, wants to shorten it. Statesmen have the same objective, provided that shortening the war does not conflict with the more important aim of obtaining a desirable peace. Should such a conflict arise, the statesmen may decide to do what Richelieu did during the Thirty Years War and what neither generals nor propagandists can be expected to do on their own initiative: they may subordinate the objective of shortening the war to that of obtaining a more desirable peace.

II

The most obvious aim of war is victory. As Mr. Churchill once remarked: "You asked, what is our aim? I can answer in one word: It is victory, victory at all costs, victory in spite of all terror, victory however hard and long the road may be . . ." [2] This is a clear statement. It ought to be remembered at every discussion on war aims in times of war. At the same time, Mr.

Churchill's answer is a definition of war aims merely in terms of war, and one that holds true for all possible war aims in very many, if not all, wars of the past and the future. It does not tell us what the victor will do with his victory, and in particular what he will do with the vanquished. But nothing less than that is what we mean by war aims as distinguished from declarations of a strong determination to conquer.

What, then, is the function of war aims in the wider sense of the term? Obviously, they give a political meaning to the war. If they are defined by great statesmen they help to clarify the minds of lesser men; they are meant to strengthen, or at least not to impair, your will to fight, and to weaken the enemy's will to fight you back.

War aims affect the expectations of the enemy. They may influence his political calculations; they may reduce or intensify his fears and raise or stifle his hopes regarding the consequences of defeat. The way in which war aims are defined and used depends on the nature of the war.

In certain circumstances war aims are addressed to the enemy government, and state the political sacrifice it will have to make if it decides to discontinue the struggle. In this case war aims are used in order to attain a triumph of diplomacy over war. They enable the enemy to compare the cost of defeat or a renunciation of victory with the cost of delaying or preventing defeat. The enemy is expected to reason about the issue of peace.

Despite the state of war and despite the normal wartime expectation of enemy ruses, a measure of common understanding and mutual trust must exist even in the noise of battle, if war aims are to be employed in this manner. In order to induce the enemy government to reason about the issue of peace it must be not only politically desirable but also socially possible to sit down with the enemy and talk peace. Obviously, such a situation does not prevail in absolute wars. Genghis Khan did not state war aims. He always began his campaigns with the ominous warning, "We know not what will happen; God knows," and ended them with the wholesale slaughter of men, women and children. A triumph of diplomacy over war is possible when there is a balance of power in international politics—when wars are waged to gain a relative advantage within the balance rather than for the sake of upsetting it. In such circumstances the status of the enemy as an enemy is a temporary one, and war aims are means of persuading him to resume his role as a partner or associate in a balanced system of power.

One of the most striking illustrations of the triumph of diplomacy over war was the peace that ended the Thirty Years War. The triumph was great because it was slow in coming. Diplomats got together in Münster and Osnabrück—towns that had not suffered too much from the ravages of war and were declared neutral. After having agreed on how many wars were raging at the time, the diplomats began to talk and write about agreeable terms of peace, gauging the remaining wealth and prestige of each country by the display of its diplomats, and using the outcome of the lustily continuing battles as bargaining points in the negotiations. Seven years after the Preliminary Articles for the Universal Peace Conference had been drawn up, the diplomats concluded the Peace of Westphalia.[3]

In modern times the triumph of diplomacy over war is perhaps even more elusive, because of the participation of large masses of the population in the military and political conduct of wars. On the other hand, precisely this situation increases the importance of political warfare. War aims may appeal over the head of the government to the people, a course adopted by French statesmen in the French Revolutionary wars, by Trotsky at Brest-Litovsk and by Woodrow Wilson. In this case your war aims are addressed to certain parts of the enemy nation in an efforts to induce them to overthrow their government in your interest or, if they cannot do this, at least to further your interest by disloyalty to their government. If your interest coincides with the larger interest of mankind, it will be useful to stress this fact, because it lends the strength of universality to your appeal. If it does not so coincide, it will be good strategy to pretend that it does, because the enemy cannot be expected to act only in your interest. Such revolutionary war aims are most effective if they split the enemy by convincing a part of the enemy nation that it has a common interest with mankind at large, rather than with you, against the enemy government. The enemy government must appear contemptible, criminal and, in any case, no longer acceptable as a partner in diplomatic negotiations.

The temptation to adopt such a revolutionary course waxes with the moral indignation about the enemy government, and wanes with aversions to civil disorder. It also grows when the chances of defeating the enemy without the help of treason in his country are slim. Finally, revolutionary war aims may recommend themselves by other incidental advantages. For example, at the time of the Lusitania crisis in 1915 Colonel House advised President Wilson to place the responsibility for war between Germany and the United States, if it became inevitable, upon the German emperor and his military clique, and to make it clear that the United States was fighting for the liberation of the German people as well as for the liberation of Europe. Colonel House saw an incidental advantage of this policy in its good effect upon the German-Americans.[4]

Regardless of the nature of war and the use to which war aims are put, the task of defining them in the best possible way appears rather easy, if it is assumed that they are defined merely for the purpose of political warfare. It is in the interest of political warfare to have the country's statesmen talk a soft peace while its generals wage a hard war, but it does not matter to the propagandist whether the statesmen talk a soft peace because they sincerely believe in it or because they merely want to trick the enemy into believing in a soft peace while he is still fighting.

If one assumes that war aims are defined merely for the purposes of political warfare, it is difficult to understand why statesmen are sometimes reticent on war aims or why they do not always talk soft peace in times of war. For this reason there will always be people who, though they have no axe to grind, are very insistent that their government ought to adopt less severe or more specific war aims.

The lack of resounding British war aims at the beginning of the war in Europe was often criticized in Britain. Many men in public life, including members of the House, tried to get the British government to talk soft peace. In February 1941, for example, a motion before the House of Commons called for a debate on peace terms, which would include among other things "provision of food to Continental nations . . . ; opportunities for the German and Italian people to choose for themselves whatever form of self-government they think fit . . . ; the removal of unemployment, undernourishment, bad housing and the lack of educational opportunities so that all races and creeds may live together in peace, liberty and security, enjoying

the good things of life, both spiritual and physical and rendering service in return." Mr. Churchill replied: "The terms of
the Motion standing in the name of my honorable Friend illustrate the very large measure of comprehension of British peace
aims which prevails in this country and elsewhere. I do not
think there is the slightest need for a Debate on this subject at
present." [5]

Or take the more recent case of Senator Wheeler, in this
country, attacking the severity of the demand for unconditional
surrender and advocating in its stead encouragement of a democratic German government in order to shorten the war. Mr.
Stettinius, reaffirming the policy of unconditional surrender,
replied promptly that the Senator spoke for a small and discredited minority.

In totalitarian countries there are only official war aims. In
democratic countries there are official war aims, unofficial war
aims, unofficial opinions on official war aims, unofficial war aims
of prominent individuals and groups, polls on unofficial war
aims and polls on polls. Unofficial aims and opinions can be
used in political warfare against the enemy if they support the
foreign policy of the government. In this case they help to
create the impression abroad that the nation is united behind
its government. If unofficial war aims are more severe than
official aims, they are used by the enemy in his domestic counterpropaganda to negate the possible effect of official war aims.
If they are less severe than official aims or if they openly reflect
enemy propaganda, they are not quoted by the enemy, as their
only advantage to him is that they may impede the domestic
war efforts of his opponents.

The same holds true of secret war aims, official or not, which
leak out to the public. A case in point is the publication in 1917
of the secret treaty promising to Italy certain territories in return for her participation in the first World War. Similarly, the
recent discussion of the so-called Morgenthau plan in the American press gave more ammunition to Dr. Goebbels than was
foreseen by the American journalists who availed themselves of
the leak. If they had foreseen it, they would have kept quiet.

The American, Theodore N. Kaufmann, who in 1941 advocated the sterilization of 48 million male Germans, is very well
known in Germany; [6] but the Germans do not know that many
of the main aims of Nazi propaganda are openly pursued in

certain German language papers in this country, such as the *Wanderer,* the *Detroiter Abendpost* or the *Abendpost Chicago;* nor do they know that certain English language newspapers follow a similar editorial policy. One may be sure, however, that the German government is well informed about these facts.

If one looks more closely at responsible domestic criticism of official war aims, and at the reasons for its rejection by responsible statesmen, one does not necessarily find that the critics are always wrong and the statesmen unfailingly right. One will notice, however, that war aims are defined not only for the purposes of political warfare but for many other purposes as well. These purposes often conflict with those of political warfare. Statesmen in times of war cannot with impunity afford to be angels of peace merely for the sake of propagandists, or to be cynics in the guise of angels. There are too many disillusioned people in this world who distrust angels, and too many moralists unwilling to forgive cynics. Nor is it possible for statesmen to speak to the enemy without being overheard by others.

III

The weapons used in political warfare differ in many respects from the arms employed in military fighting. They hit widely different targets at the same time. A politically important statement may aim at one particular group, say the enemy government, but will reach at the same time other groups as well, for example the neutrals or the domestic critics of the man who made the statement. The statement may also miss the intended target altogether and reach only others instead. There is no fire in political warfare without the possibility of backfire, no percussion without its repercussion, and duds sometimes blast the wits out of the gunner. All this deprives the laws of political warfare of the imposing simplicity of ballistics.

Statements on foreign policy are meant to influence, in different directions, various audiences with different predispositions. At home a declaration of war aims must brace national unity in such a way as to further the war effort. Instead of giving useful arguments to the opposition it must maneuver the opposition into a place where it cannot show its displeasure about the government's leadership without discrediting itself.

The same war aims must serve the function of pleasing

neutrals or of intimidating them—as the case may be—in order to strengthen one's own cause, materially and morally.

War aims must meet with the approval of allies as well, especially of those allies who might want to conclude a separate peace. War aims must give the impression that the unity in fighting the common enemy is buttressed by a measure of common understanding about the desirable state of international affairs at the end of the war. Fighting a common enemy creates a stronger bond among friends than do endeavors which lack this reminder of the usefulness of cooperation. But to look ahead with confidence to a constellation of postwar interests that will admit of cooperation and compromise is to acquire an additional incentive to fight the war without reservations. The different objectives based on this constellation of interests need not form a pattern of harmony, but if they do, this pattern can easily be marred by demands that it include the means of reducing enemy fears and raising enemy hopes. Thus it is difficult to define war aims satisfactorily, and it is possibly dangerous to follow the advice of propagandists.

Wars of coalition, with attendant differences in national interest and tradition among the allies, present especially noteworthy obstacles to the definition of war aims. These obstacles do not exist in wars waged without powerful associates.

Marshal Stalin once remarked: "It would be ridiculous to deny the difference in ideologies and social systems of the countries composing the Anglo-Soviet-American coalition. But does this preclude the possibility and expediency of joint action on the part of the members of this coalition against the common enemy who threatens to enslave them? It certainly does not preclude it. More, the existence of this threat imperatively imposes the necessity of joint action upon the members of this coalition . . ." [7] Undoubtedly Stalin was right. But the speech in which he stressed the necessity of joint action against the common enemy contained also his famous statement on the future of the German army: Stalin declared it "not only impossible . . . but also inadvisable" to destroy all organized military force in Germany.[8] At that time there was, in the coalition against Germany, unity regarding the war aim of victory over Germany but flagrant disagreement on the war aim of German disarmament.

By the time of the Moscow Conference, about a year later,

disagreement on this particular war aim seemed to have vanished. The old aim was now voiced only by captured German officers in Soviet Russia, who expressed their gratitude to the Soviet authorities for enabling them to convene according to Article 129 of the Soviet Constitution. This article grants the right of asylum to those who wage a war of national liberation. The Union of German Officers and the older and larger organization, "National Committee 'Free Germany,'" amply contributed to nationalistic anti-Hitler propaganda from Russian soil. Official Russian policy, however, underwent a change. At the Yalta Conference the leaders of the three major powers were united in their determination "to destroy German militarism and Nazism . . . to disarm and disband all German armed forces; break up for all time the German General Staff; remove or destroy all German military equipment; eliminate or control all German industry that could be used for military production."

The intentions of Marshal Stalin's earlier policy are obscure. It is possible that he was merely waging political war against Germany, with the intention of weakening the loyalty of German military chiefs to their leader. It is also possible that Stalin engaged in "a propaganda maneuver . . . designed to hurry up the too leisurely effort of the British and Americans to create a 'second front.'"[9] Finally, it is possible, and indeed likely, that the statement had both purposes—that it was intended both to weaken the German war effort and to warn Russia's allies.

On other occasions statements on war aims have been used for encouraging rather than warning friends. The two most important instances in modern history are President Wilson's Fourteen Points and the Cairo Declaration.

President Wilson's speech before Congress on January 8, 1918, in which the Fourteen Points were enunciated, was not only a declaration of American policy but also a bold and futile attempt to keep Russia in the political camp of the coalition against the Central Powers at a time when she was about to conclude peace with Germany. Wilson introduced the Fourteen Points by a long statement on Russia. "The voice of the Russian people," he said, called for "these definitions of principle and purpose." The sixth of the Fourteen Points dealt with "The evacuation of all Russian Territory and such a settlement of all questions affecting Russia as will secure the best and freest cooperation of the other nations of the world in obtaining for her an unhampered and unembarrassed opportunity for the independent determination of her own political development and national policy and assure her of a sincere welcome into the society of free nations under institutions of her own choosing and, more than a welcome, assistance also of every kind that she may need and may herself desire. The treatment accorded Russia by her sister nations in the months to come will be the acid test of their goodwill, of their comprehension of her needs as distinguished from their own interests, and of their intelligent and unselfish sympathy."

Wilson's attempt failed, despite the energetic efforts of the Creel Committee in Petrograd to give wide publicity to the speech. The German authorities were in a position to impose their peace upon Russia. It deprived the country of 89 percent of its coal mines, 54 percent of its industrial enterprises, 32 percent of its agricultural land, and 34 percent of its population; also it cut Russia off from the Black Sea and almost from the Baltic Sea as well.

The Cairo Conference of November 1943 is another noteworthy instance of the use of war aims for cementing alliances. President Roosevelt, Prime Minister Churchill and Generalissimo Chiang Kai-shek declared jointly that "all the territories Japan has stolen from the Chinese, such as Manchuria, Formosa and the Pescadores, shall be restored to the Republic of China." American comment was very favorable. Barnet Nover spoke of "an act of faith and a gesture of friendship . . . in view of China's present weakness." [10] Few observers discussed the question to what extent obliging our Chinese ally would further or impede our political warfare operations against Japan. Hanson W. Baldwin warned, however, that the declaration would increase Japan's will to fight and was "likely to be more of a handicap than a help to our Pacific war." [11]

Let us consider this instance for a moment. Let us assume that an expert in our political warfare against Japan had been present at Cairo and had agreed with Mr. Baldwin. When this expert was shown the draft of the declaration ought he to have been in the position to advise against it on the grounds that he expected it to create difficulties in his political warfare operations against Japan? Obviously his advice could be taken seriously only if he had arrived at his decision after consulting his colleagues on China and other Japanese-occupied areas in the Far East. Let us disregard the fact that they would have violently disagreed with him. Let us concede that it would not have been harmful and that it would have been possible to consult, concerning the declaration, with a group of experts in matters of political warfare.

It certainly would have been folly to base a decision on their advice, for the political perspective of propagandists is exceedingly short. As experts in political warfare they would not have taken account of the traditions of our foreign policy in the Far East, the lasting interests of this country, the political relations, both at that time and after the defeat of Japan, between Britain and the United States, China and the United States, Russia and the United States. In short, the data and the considerations on which they would have based their advice would have been grotesquely inadequate in view of the great political issues that were affected by the declaration. Statesmen, not propagandists, must make policy. Historians may yet tell us that one of the reasons for Hitler's failure as a statesman was his being too much of a propagandist.

IV

The fact that this war is a war of coalition cannot possibly be overlooked in studying the history of political warfare against Germany. The most important and probably the most effective aim in political warfare against Germany has been the liberation of the countries overpowered by the Nazis, and the restoration of sovereign rights to those peoples who were forcibly deprived of them. Without this aim there would not be any United Nations. As early as September 20, 1939, this aim was stated by Neville Chamberlain. It was repeated by Churchill after the fall of France and after the fall of Yugoslavia and Greece. The list of countries to whose liberation Britain was pledged had grown long. There can be little doubt that British, and later American and Russian, determination to liberate the subjugated countries was a most important reason for Germany's complete failure to rally Europe behind her idea of a New Order.

The desire of Britain and the United States to restore sovereign rights to the enslaved peoples of Europe was restated in the Atlantic Charter, to which the Soviet Union declared her adherence on September 24, 1941, at the conference of the Allied governments in London. This war aim has again been restated in the Declaration on Liberated Peoples, which is part of the Report on the Crimea Conference. On the other side of the globe, the repeated solemn pledges to restore the freedom of the Filipinos and to establish and protect their independence have served a similar purpose.

Regard for allies, or for prospective allies, was also the reason for the reticence of British leaders on war aims other than liberation, during the period preceding the Atlantic Charter. Considerations of this kind were naturally much more urgent than any intensification of Britain's political warfare against Germany by the announcement of more specific war aims. When Churchill spoke about the Atlantic Charter in the House of Commons on September 9, 1941, he made this unmistakably clear: "I have, as the House knows, hitherto consistently deprecated the formulation of peace aims or war aims—however you put it—by His Majesty's Government, at this stage. I deprecate it at this time, when the end of the war is not in sight, when the conflict sways to and fro with alternating fortunes and when conditions and associations at the end of the war are unforeseeable. But a Joint Declaration by Great Britain and the United States is an event of a totally different nature." [12]

Perhaps the most important instance of the influence of coalition warfare upon the definition of war aims is the demand for unconditional surrender.

The principle is not a new one in American history, not even in wars with Germany. It was advocated by Senator Lodge, Theodore Roosevelt and very many other critics of President Wilson's policy of 1918, both in this country and in Europe. On October 7, 1918, Colonel House, commenting on Wilson's difficulties in replying to the German plea for an armistice, remarked that Wilson did not seem to realize the nearly unanimous sentiment in this country against anything but unconditional surrender.

If the assumption is correct that generals surrender more easily when their honor or at least their face is spared, the formula of unconditional surrender is clearly of little value in political warfare. If one demands unconditional surrender one must expect determined resistance as an answer. Thus from the point of view of political warfare it would appear sensible to speak of unconditional surrender when enemy resistance is definitely broken, but until that moment to hide one's intention to demand unconditional surrender. But the demand for unconditional surrender was made public at Casablanca in January 1943. There may therefore have been reasons for its publication which outweighed its apparent disadvantages to the conduct of political warfare.

Various reasons have been advanced for the insistence on the principle, perhaps the most interesting one by Mr. Churchill on May 24, 1944. "That principle," said Churchill, "wipes away all ideas of anything like Mr. Wilson's Fourteen Points being brought up by the Germans after their defeat, claiming they surrendered in consideration of those Fourteen Points." [13]

I find it difficult to see the merit of this argument. It is true that between the two world wars the Germans were past masters in distorting the meaning of the Fourteen Points, their contribution to Germany's military defeat and their relation to the Treaty of Versailles.[14] The Germans displayed considerable skill in mendacity, both in creating a legend that they had not been defeated on the field of battle and in breeding hatred of the western democracies. But I submit that Germany's unconditional surrender will not in itself prevent the Germans from indulging once more in such pernicious flights of fancy. The foundations for various new legends have already been laid by Hitler and other Germans who have blamed Italian treachery, the treachery of German generals, and various other treacheries for what in German propaganda is known as "the crises" or "the trials" of this war. It will not be difficult for the Germans to connect such alleged treacheries with alleged Allied bribery and satanic designs, and then we would have the new legend.

To illustrate, on September 11, 1944, the Berlin correspondent of *Aftonbladet* quoted an article by Dr. Ley in *Der Angriff* as follows: "The grave military and political reverses are entirely due to treachery, which reached its climax with the attempt on Hitler's life. The German forces were never defeated during the last World War, but were betrayed by reactionary politicians. Without internal and external treachery we would have settled the enemy long ago. The African, Sicilian and Italian campaigns were one series of acts of treachery. We would have conquered Egypt, Suez and the Near East if our Italian Allies had done their duty. All the prerequisites existed, but were destroyed by Victor Emmanuel and Badoglio, who foiled the efforts of the Italian Army and Navy. The treachery of the Badoglio troops was noticeable also in the Eastern front. North of Stalingrad they caused the Stalingrad catastrophe, and thus a series of defeats from Stalingrad to the Vistula was started by men like Generals Höppner and von Treskow." [15]

Insistence before victory on unconditional surrender and its long-range political effects will be no substitute for measures that may have to be taken to prevent the rise of new legends in Germany after her defeat. Nor does it appear reasonable to me to suppose that the Allied conquerors will be less hated this time for defeating, occupying and disarming Germany than they were last time for considerably less drastic measures.

It is possible, however, that the political and military situation which prevailed in this war of coalition at the time of Casablanca influenced President Roosevelt's decision to issue a statement on unconditional surrender as early as January 1943. Those were the days of the smashing Russian victory at Stalingrad. Almost a year and a half had to pass before a Second Front was established—a year and a half of an almost uninterrupted series of Russian victories. The men and women in the occupied countries who were resisting Nazism were hoping for a Second Front. Uninformed public opinion in this country and Britain had followed Stalin's lead in relentless propaganda for an earlier establishment of a Second Front. The political arrangements accompanying the landing in North Africa had not created the impression that the United States would refuse to conclude other deals in Europe if they should become militarily advantageous. There may also have been ignorant people abroad who doubted in January 1943 the determination of this country not to falter until Germany was finally defeated—not to change its policy in any circumstances, including the election of a new president in the fall of 1944.

No evidence is available that considerations of this kind actually played a part in formulating the demand for unconditional surrender, but obviously the demand was a heavy political bomb thrown onto the battlefields in Europe, where very many Russians but no American or British soldiers were dying at the time. Mr. Churchill went on record with a statement that the strong words "unconditional surrender" were put forth by President Roosevelt and endorsed by him, Churchill, "in days of our comparative weakness and lack of success." [16]

Nor should it be forgotten that only a little more than two months before the Casablanca Conference Stalin had reiterated war aims which betrayed a disquieting concern for German militarists, in the event they turned anti-Nazi. I have already quoted Stalin's statement on this issue. It was in line with earlier official Russian statements which favored revolutionary war aims during the long initial period of German victories in Russia. The day Russian soil was invaded Molotov had said in a radio address: "This war has been forced upon us not by the German workers, peasants and intellectuals, whose sufferings we well understand, but by the clique of bloodthirsty fascist rulers of Germany." Stalin repeatedly spoke in the same vein. For example, on July 3, 1941, he said: "In this great war we shall have loyal allies in the peoples of Europe and America, including the German people, who are enslaved by the Hitlerite despots."

The formula of unconditional surrender which Stalin adopted with a slight modification in his Order of the Day of May 1, 1943, cleared the political atmosphere. In wars of coalition it is always easier to agree on negative war aims than it is to reach an understanding on affirmative ones.

In Allied propaganda to Germany the demand for unconditional surrender is treated as follows.

First, it is repeated and stressed as the main message of the United Nations to Germany today. I am inclined to think that its effect upon Germans must have been particularly great early in 1943, when no Second Front existed as yet, when the American air offensive against the German war economy had not yet out-distanced the German blitz against Britain, and when Germans had been thoroughly indoctrinated by Dr. Goebbels to believe that this time the bragging Americans would be too slow and too much preoccupied in the Pacific for making their power felt in Europe.

Second, unconditional surrender is presented as the end of misery and destruction and death, which the German people suffer in consequence of the policy of their government. It is presented also as the only alternative to more misery and destruction and death on German soil, if the Germans continue a war which everybody in his senses knows to be lost by the German armed forces.

Third, it is made clear that unconditional surrender entails the destruction of Nazism from which the German people suffer: the end of Gestapo persecution and Nazi lawlessness. Unconditional surrender is the prerequisite of the punishment of the men who have committed indescribable crimes all over Europe and in Germany herself.

Fourth, it is made clear that unconditional surrender does not mean the destruction of the German people or their enslavement. President Roosevelt and Mr. Churchill have clearly and repeatedly stated that the unconditional surrender of the vanquished does not relieve the victors of their obligations to humanity and their duties as Christians. Freed of the burden of arms, the German people will be able to earn their way back into the comity of nations. There are probably few nations in Europe better prepared than the Germans to understand that there are imperative duties to which no rights correspond.

V

Allied statesmen have not talked soft peace during this war. Is there any evidence that softer war aims, if this expression may be used, would have shortened the war? In order to answer this question it is necessary to distinguish clearly between those Germans who hold power and those who do not. Obviously, it would have been possible to shorten the war by concluding a compromise peace with the German government in the second period of this war. As long as Germany's military position was favorable, the German government would not have been willing to conclude a compromise peace, because, naturally, it wanted something better than that: a victor's peace. When Germany's military situation deteriorated the German government would probably have consented to a compromise peace, since it would have meant political victory and personal escape from punishment for the chief criminals in the German government.

There is a lesson to be learned from the response to Wilson's Fourteen Points in Germany during the last war. Those Germans who hold power during this war not only have tried to ridicule the Atlantic Charter but also warned before the conferences at Teheran and Yalta that another "Wilsonian swindle" was in the offing. By "Wilsonian swindle" they meant any statements by Allied leaders offering to the German people anything less than destruction, enslavement and physical annihilation after the defeat of the German armed forces.

It is difficult to decide whether the German leaders have fallen victim to their own legend about Wilson and his Fourteen Points or whether they have merely used anti-peace propaganda for whatever it is worth, in order to support by words the physical terror exercised against those Germans who have become weary of war.

In any case, large masses of the German people during the first World War understood Wilson to mean that peace was unobtainable as long as Germany was ruled by men who in their domestic policy were reactionary and in their foreign policy imperialistic. These masses and their leaders had no power. They could not prevent the imperialistic peace treaties of Brest-Litovsk and Bucharest which Germany imposed upon Russia and Rumania respectively. Nor did they succeed in overthrowing the government before Germany was decisively defeated on the field of battle.

The men who held power in Germany during the first World War hoped to win a victory which would strengthen Germany's military and economic situation by aggrandizement in the West and in the East. Ludendorff's war aims were oriented toward the requirements of a new war.[17] When Germany's military situation deteriorated, it became evident that the German Supreme Command had no clear idea of the "fateful conditions" which, according to Prince Max von Baden, were outlined in Wilson's Fourteen Points.[18] The request for an armistice was forced upon Prince Max by Ludendorff when he realized that the war was lost. Ludendorff was in a hurry to obtain an armistice. The high pressure methods which he used against the reluctant Prince Max did not include the argument that an appeal to the Fourteen Points should be made.

The most interesting reference to the Fourteen Points, from a military source, was made almost three months before Ludendorff urged Prince Max to end the war, by Major Alfred Niemann in a memorandum of July 20, 1918. This memorandum was approved by Ludendorff and earned the author a position of special trust in the Kaiser's entourage. It read in part: "Use Wilson's idea of a League of Nations through the mediation of a neutral state, not for the purpose of realizing this utopian scheme but in order to begin negotiations. The slogan that an end must be made to the massacre of peoples possessing highly valued cultures appeals to most nations. Wilson's hypocrisy must become a means of entrapping him." [19]

When the first German note was dispatched to Lansing, early in October 1918, Walther Rathenau, a man later murdered by German fanatics, opposed it publicly and criticized the harshness of the Fourteen Points. He felt in particular that Point Six, dealing with the evacuation of Russia, was tantamount to unconditional surrender.

It would be difficult to maintain that the men who rule Germany in this war are more reasonable than Ludendorff or Tirpitz. The men who do not hold power in Germany today may be more reasonable than Hitler, and perhaps even more reasonable than Rathenau was in October 1918. But they do not hold power. In fact, it is much more difficult for them to seize power than it was for the powerless opponents to the reactionaries and imperialists during the first World War.

Still, the argument has been advanced that it might have been possible for an anti-Nazi opposition in this war to overthrow the Nazi regime if the United Nations had indicated their willingness to grant a better peace to a German government formed by anti-Nazis. In view of the terroristic nature of the Nazi regime, which renders a seizure of power difficult—war aims or not—only the German army could conceivably overthrow the Nazi rule. Thus the decisive issue centers around the status to be granted to the German army. Better terms than unconditional surrender would have had to include, as a minimum, discussion with the enemy with arms in his hands. At this price, too, the war could possibly have been shortened, since many German generals must have known for quite a while that they have not succeeded in their attempts to realize Hitler's plans of conquest.

In brief, it appears that "softer war aims" might have shortened this war if a more compromising policy had been adopted either toward the leaders of the National Socialist party or toward the leaders of German militarism. It is difficult to conceive that anything but compelling military reasons, which do not exist, could speak for such a policy.

The nature of this war, determined, as it is, by German aggression; the nature of the coalition which Germany has mobilized against herself for a second time in a generation; the respective national contributions to the defeat of Germany by the forces allied against her—all these factors have gone into the making of our war aims.

VI

In wars that last long it often happens that the constellation of interests which prevails at the beginning undergoes a change as other vital interests become involved during the war. Germany began this war with her rear protected by a treaty with Russia. She is ending it with the desperate prophecy that her defeat by Russia and the western democracies means the Bolshevization of Europe.

"Of course," Goebbels said on February 1, 1945, "it is correct that we fight for our life in this war, but it cannot be disputed that our life is the nucleus of Europe's life, and the husk would drop off and fall to the ground if the kernel were to wither away. By refusing to recognize these facts the political bourgeoisie is inviting its downfall. How many more proofs are needed to corroborate the prognosis, after almost the whole of eastern Europe and southeastern Europe have started on the path to hell for lack of political instinct . . . Historical facts have allotted to the Reich the role of natural leader on the Continent, for better or worse. The Continent draws its life from our strength, and our impotence and our downfall would cause it to sink defenseless to the ground."

Thus, according to Goebbels, it shows a lack of political instinct to wage war against Germany and to defeat her. Toward the end of the last war Colonel Häften, with the approval of Ludendorff, suggested an anti-Bolshevist propaganda campaign to support the failing German arms. In this war the German government has been convinced ever since Stalingrad that its last and only hope lies in splitting the United Nations and in turning the western democracies away from and against Soviet Russia. Ever since Stalingrad the insistent cry of German propaganda has been, "Change your enemy or you are lost!"

After the last war the importance of war aims in political warfare was much overrated, especially by the Germans. After this war we may be led to conclude that war aims and the foreign policies of the great powers behind them are of importance primarily in affecting the duration of the peace to come. At the present stage of the war one may indeed say that the duration of the peace depends upon the foresight, articulateness and compatibility of the foreign policies of the great powers.

It must be remembered that the official war aims of the United Nations reflect an agreement among nations whose foreign policies do not coincide, and that the interests of these nations cannot all be reconciled without difficulty, unrelenting effort and willingness to make compromises.

In this war, which transcends any possible European balance of power system and in which no attempt has been made to persuade the enemy to become a partner in peace talks, the total defeat of Germany is an aim, an end. Soon, however, that defeat will be a new fact in the constellation of national interests within which great and small powers will pursue their policies. Similarly, liberation of the countries temporarily subjugated by Germany is a common war aim of the United Nations, but after this end has been attained it becomes apparent that liberation from the fear of Nazi rule is not identical with liberation from want. Continuing want is partly a result of Nazi exploitation and war, and partly a consequence of our global strategy. For logistic and other reasons freedom from want in Europe presupposes victory in the Far East. Political and economic life in Europe is likely to be hard and bitter for perhaps years to come.

The noblest aim of nations at war is to gain through victory the right to determine the course of history. Let us hope that the statesmen of the victorious nations will show prudence, and will act with remembrance of the men and women who gave their lives for peace when their nations were united against their common enemy.

Chapter 5. Notes

1. Text of an address delivered at the New School for Social Research on March 4, 1945, at a Discussion Evening conducted by the Institute of World Affairs.

2. House of Commons, May 13, 1940.

3. For a brief description of the negotiations see R. B. Mowat, *A History of European Diplomacy 1451-1789* (New York, 1928), pp. 104 ff.

4. See *The Intimate Papers of Colonel House*, arranged by Charles Seymour, vol. 2 (New York, 1926), p. 466.

5. Both statements quoted from *Peace Aims*, British Official Statements, A Chronological Record, from September 2, 1939, to September 24, 1941 (British Information Service), pp. 18-19.

6. On Theodore N. Kaufmann's book, *Germany Must Perish,* see my remark in *Social Research,* vol. 8 (September, 1941), p. 325: "The book is so violent that it might have been written in the German propaganda ministry in order to launch a really successful anti-American hate campaign in Germany." In the meantime a collection of excerpts from the book, together with slanted passages from speeches by President Roosevelt, has sold several million copies in Germany. Wolfgang Diewerge, the compiler of this collection, has had a brilliant career in the propaganda ministry. See Ernst Kris, Hans Speier and Associates, *German Radio Propaganda,* Studies of the Institute of World Affairs (New York, 1944), pp. 485-86.

7. November 6, 1942. Quoted from *Soviet War Documents,* Embassy of the USSR, Washington, D. C., Information Bulletin, Special Supplement (December, 1943), p. 39.

8. *Ibid.,* p. 41.

9. Carl L. Becker, *How New Will the Better World Be?* (New York, 1944), p. 196.

10. Washington *Post,* December 4, 1943.

11. New York *Times,* December 4, 1943.

12. *Peace Aims* (cited above), p. 26.

13. Quoted from text published in New York *Times,* May 25, 1944.

14. See Harry R. Rudin, *Armistice 1918* (New Haven, 1944) and Lindley Fraser, *Germany Between Two Wars. A Study of Propaganda and War Guilt* (New York, 1945).

15. For Hitler's leading contribution to this legend in his speech of September 10, 1943, see Kris, Speier and Associates, *op. cit.,* pp. 276 ff.

16. In his speech of January 18, 1945, quoted from New York *Times,* January 19, 1945.

17. See the official inquiry by the German Reichstag into the causes of Germany's defeat, *Die Ursachen des deutschen Zusammenbruchs,* vol. 2, pt. 1 (Berlin, 1925), pp. 106 ff.

18. See Lindley Fraser, *op. cit.,* p. 46.

19. Quoted in Appendix to *Ursachen* . . . (cited above).

Chapter 6

WANTED: A DECISIVE IDEA *

By
WALLACE CARROLL

[Mr. Carroll has just concluded a review of the political
and military situation in the fall of 1944. D.L.]

THIS WAS the situation on November 20, when Eisenhower sent
his appeal for a new idea which would speed the advance of his
armies.

In London, the British Chiefs of Staff immediately appointed
a committee of officers and civilians and invited the United
States to send representatives to collaborate in the drafting of
plans. In Washington, the American Chiefs of Staff appointed
a committee of officers, most of whom had been unaware of
psychological warfare until that moment, and put them under
the direction of a colonel whose chief qualifications were a
155-mm. mouth and a .22 caliber brain. All along the Western
Front the men of America, Britain, and France were dying in
the snow and mud, and the long shadow of winter was falling
on the people of a continent which had already known too
much torment. But the air in the Pentagon was warm and fil-
tered—and sterile. The American Committee met, and one of
the officers said: "Let's not stick our necks out. Let's let the
British stick their necks out." The Committee agreed, and
adjourned to await the British plan.

In a few weeks this plan arrived in Washington. The British
invited the Americans to make criticisms and amendments and
to join in the execution of the plan. Unfortunately, it was not
a good plan. The British were tired—after more than five years
of war they had run out of ideas. Like almost everyone who had
tackled the problem before them, the British planners conceded

* Reprinted from *Persuade or Perish*, published by Houghton Mifflin Company, Boston, 1948.

that the Casablanca principle should not be impaired, but they recommended that the Germans should be shown that unconditional surrender did not mean extermination. They proposed to do this in a number of ways—by infiltrating reports into Germany that the Allies, in order to rehabilitate Europe, would want to keep German industry and German labor employed after the war; by encouraging the belief among German religious groups that organized religion would have an important part to play in the restoration of Germany; by making greater use of German prisoners-of-war to give the Germans at home an impression of Allied benevolence; by creating the impression in Germany that another conspiracy against Hitler was making progress.

The American Committee examined this plan and sent its amendments to London. All through December and the early part of January, the exchanges across the Atlantic continued until the plan with its amendments and annexes was as thick as the Washington telephone directory and every bit as meaty. On January 20, the completed plan went to the American Joint Chiefs of Staff. Two days later, Admiral Ernest J. King, Chief of Naval Operations, proposed that the Joint Chiefs send a memorandum to the President on the entire problem raised by Eisenhower. The memorandum, as drafted by King, recognized that only the leaders of the three principal Allies could do anything effective to counter German propaganda on unconditional surrender. It conceded that the unconditional surrender principle could not be modified "without detriment to the prosecution of the war and the establishment of acceptable peace conditions." Still, it suggested that a declaration by the three principal Allies that Germany would be allowed to retain her political and economic independence might weaken German resistance.

The next day, January 23, the Joint Chiefs of Staff decided that King's proposal was not practicable. They knew what the President would say. Nothing ever came of the British plan with its American amendments.

But the propagandists at Supreme Headquarters had not waited for inspiration to come from London and Washington. Earlier in the autumn, the American Chiefs of Staff had sent Eisenhower the draft of a directive on the military government of Germany—the celebrated Directive 1067. Using this document as a guide, Noel Newsome, who had left the BBC to join the Psychological Warfare Division, drafted a series of thirteen statements on Allied Military Government and what it would mean to the German people. On December 4, Radio Luxemburg, the BBC, the American Broadcasting Station in Europe, and the Voice of America in New York began to broadcast these statements to the Germans in the name of the Supreme Commander.

The statements were clear, terse, and to the point. If the German people permitted the Nazis to carry out their scorched-earth policy, no one but the Germans would be the sufferers. The Allies would bring their own supplies into Germany, but not for the benefit of the Germans. Any supplies which were not required for the Allied armies would go to the victims of Germany. The German people, therefore, would have to provide their own food, fuel, and clothing. The Allied Military Government would uproot National Socialism, dissolve all its organizations, arrest and try its leaders. Germans would be required to help apprehend the Nazi criminals. All government officials, judicial authorities, and employees of public utilities would be required to remain at their posts unless the Allies instructed them to the contrary. All those who had not compromised themselves by National Socialist activities would be permitted to keep their jobs, but Nazis would be ruthlessly purged from all key positions. The rule of Military Government would be a rule of law. All Nazi courts would be abolished, but the German criminal and civil courts would be allowed to reopen under Allied supervision once they had been purged of undesirable elements. Freedom of religion would be guaranteed and the churches purged of Nazi influence. German currency would continue to be legal tender, together with Allied military marks. German officials would continue to collect taxes and to enforce measures against inflation, such as rationing and price control. Banks would be closed only if this became absolutely necessary. The right of Germans to hold lawfully acquired property would be respected. The property of the Nazi Party, however, would be seized, and the Military Government would try to find the rightful owners. When circumstances permitted, German workers would be allowed to establish democratic trade unions. Collective bargaining would be restored, but strikes and lockouts which threatened military security would be prohibited. All schools would be closed until the teaching staffs had been purged.

These statements described Allied intentions—they made no promises or commitments to the Germans. Their tone was stern and uncompromising. Yet they conveyed the impression that the Allies knew exactly what they were going to do and that they would bring to Germany the kind of rule that appealed to the German character—a rule characterized by order, discipline, efficiency, and authority.

The thirteen statements appeared to me to be a godsend. They certainly came close to that definition of unconditional surrender which we had been seeking since the spring. It seemed that they might well provide an antidote to the *Strength through Fear* propaganda of Goebbels, for while they were stern enough to be a credible expression of Allied intentions, they presented a picture of Allied rule which was attractive in comparison with the picture he had been painting. But we realized it would be necessary to repeat them over and over again to erase the impression he had presumably made on the German mind.

Once again we moved into a major campaign. Each day, together with the British and the Psychological Warfare Division, we broadcast one of the statements. In mid-December, we started to repeat them and explain their meaning more fully to the Germans. Then, suddenly, we were brought to a halt.

On December 16, the Germans launched their surprise counteroffensive in the Ardennes. For several weeks the outcome was not clear. But German hopes rose with the progress of their armies and German minds were not receptive while the Allies were being driven back from German soil, so the broadcasts of the statements were suspended. At the same time, Murphy, who had originally approved the statements, began to have qualms about them, and officers in the Civil Affairs Division of the War Department demanded that they be dropped. It was their fear that in summarizing or amplifying the original texts, broadcasters might unwittingly give assurances or promises which the Germans would seize upon and use to embarrass Military Government officials during the coming occupation. The conflict between propagandists and the Civil Affairs officers had not been settled when the Battle of the Ardennes Bulge was over. It dragged on all through January—right on, in fact, until the three-power declaration on the future of Germany was issued in February at the Yalta Conference. That declaration was less concrete than the thirteen statements, but as a three-power agreement, it was more authoritative. The statements were quietly dropped.

That was the end of the many efforts to define or modify unconditional surrender in the case of Germany. In the closing months of the war, the German civil and military leaders tried by every means in their power to evade the Casablanca dictate. It was of no avail, for though President Roosevelt was no longer there, the end was the end he had wished. But when Germany had surrendered, the Secretaries of State, War, and Navy quietly got together and agreed that it would be wise to give propaganda a little more leeway in the case of Japan.

And did the demand for unconditional surrender prolong the war against Germany, as its critics feared? There is no good reason to believe that it did.

We are always prone to forget the dangers which threatened us once we have left them behind. There were many dangers threatening the United Nations when the American and British leaders met at Casablanca. Many of those dangers were within the great coalition itself. Yet in spite of everything, the alliance of the three Great Powers was maintained until final victory; the resistance movements continued to expand until they played a worthy part in the liberation of their countries; the neutrals were induced to make a contribution to the Allied victory and the home front in America and in Britain was able to resist all the shocks and temptations of war. The Casablanca decision had something to do with all that.

If it had done nothing more than cement the coalition of America, Britain, and the Soviet Union, the policy of unconditional surrender would have justified itself. I know I have presented evidence that it caused some friction within the coalition. But that was of a minor nature. The three leaders were agreed on the basic policy, though two of them at times questioned the wisdom of insisting on that policy in public. And what was the policy in its barest essentials? Eden put it in one sentence: "What we mean by unconditional surrender is that we are not prepared to make a negotiated peace with Germany." At Casablanca, the Western Powers renounced what was really their more favorable position for dealing with the

Germans in order to maintain solidarity with the less-favored Russians. The Russians may later have protested that talk of unconditional surrender was "bad tactics," but if America and Britain had not publicly bound themselves, they would have been hounded day after day by Russian suspicions. Even in the very last days of the war, after the western Allies had given numberless proofs of their good faith, Stalin and Molotov raised cries of treachery when America and Britain proposed to accept the surrender of the beaten German armies in Italy. What would have happened if the western Allies had left themselves open to a bargain with a German Badoglio and had actually made such a bargain? An agreement of this kind would presumably have involved the surrender of the German armies in the West. And what would then have happened in the East? We may be sure that the reaction of the Russians would not have been mild. They had shown in 1939 what they could do when they suspected the Western Powers of trying to foment a Soviet-German war, and there were plenty of high German officers on the Eastern Front ready for a bargain with the Russians if they could get it. Whatever the difficulties we have encountered in making peace in Europe, they are nothing compared with what we might have faced if we had made a questionable bargain with the Germans. In facing the Russians in the post-war world, we have had clean hands and a clear conscience, and those are assets which we must not underestimate.

Without the Casablanca formula the western Allies would have had no respite from Soviet suspicions and accusations of treachery and double-dealing. With it, they exposed themselves to a few gentle complaints that they were being unnecessarily stern in their propaganda. Anything which so effectively kept Soviet suspicions in check for more than two years was nothing less than a stroke of genius! [1]

So much for the benefits of the Casablanca dictate within the Allied coalition. What was its real effect on Germany?

The war might have been shortened in one of three ways— by action on the part of the Nazi leaders, by action on the part of the German generals, by a mass uprising of the German people. Did unconditional surrender deter any of these three groups from yielding to the Allies?

With regard to the Nazi leaders, it must be said that not even the critics of the unconditional surrender policy wanted to negotiate with them. Even without the Casablanca decision, no one among the Allies would have proposed an appeal to Hitler, Himmler, Goering, and Goebbels. The policy thus becomes irrelevant to their case. But even if it did apply, no one can contend that it made the leading Nazis fight any harder or any longer than they otherwise would have fought. There is, indeed, some documentary evidence of an indirect kind which shows that they did not take unconditional surrender very seriously. Up to the very end, they believed they could come to terms with the West. Himmler, after making his offer to surrender to America and Britain, but not to Russia, in the closing days of the war, solemnly asked himself whether he should bow or shake hands when he met Eisenhower, and he actually believed that Eisenhower would keep him in office!

If the Allies had not adhered to the Casablanca dictate but had made an offer to Germany, they would simply have played into Goebbels' hands. In the period between the two wars, he and Hitler had drilled into the Germans the belief that Germany had been tricked into surrender in 1918 by the offer of the Fourteen Points. He would, therefore, have had no difficulty in convincing the Germans that any Allied proposals were another trick; that the Allies were making such proposals because they could not defeat Germany in the field, and that they now wanted to trick her again. For this reason an attempt to relax the unconditional surrender formula might very well have had the effect of prolonging German resistance.

Did unconditional surrender discourage the German generals from yielding to the Allies? Did it prevent the generals from rising against the Nazis? Some German Nationalists and militarists certainly tried hard to convince American intelligence officers in Switzerland that it did. But a German army surrendered to the Allies in Tunisia less than five months after the Casablanca Conference, and from that time to the end of the war German generals surrendered by the hundreds on the different fronts. Other German generals, who were fully aware of the Casablanca dictate, led the rising against Hitler on July 20. It was their own incompetence which spoiled that effort, not the policy of unconditional surrender. And it was the fear of Hitler, Himmler, the SS, and the Gestapo which kept other German generals from joining in that effort or from making a subsequent attempt. Many of them were quite candid about this fear.

And what of the German people? The Allied investigators who combed Germany after the hostilities heard only one excuse for the failure of countless "anti-Nazis" to rise against the Nazis. The Nazi controls were too strong. It was impossible to do anything without being caught by the Gestapo. When the United States Strategic Bombing Survey went to work in Germany in 1945, its public opinion specialists, using the best indirect techniques of interrogation, sounded out the Germans on unconditional surrender. After questioning a representative sample of five hundred Germans in the American, British, and French zones, the specialists concluded that only nine per cent of the German civilians in the bombed areas and thirteen per cent in unbombed areas had been unwilling to accept unconditional surrender before Germany's final defeat.[2]

Although I believed in the fundamental soundness of the Casablanca decision, I felt during the war years that Roosevelt was mistaken in not agreeing to a definition of unconditional surrender or a statement of intentions toward Germany. Yet I must confess I can find no reason to believe today that such a pronouncement would have had an appreciable effect on German morale. What could we have offered these politically apathetic people which would have given them the moral and physical courage to face the machine guns of the Nazi régime? We could—and did—achieve lesser effects with our propaganda, but that was beyond our capabilities. The Free Germany Committee in Moscow did hold out the prospect of a rosy future for Germany, but its propaganda was no more successful than the austere propaganda of the Western Allies.

Since mine is definitely a minority view, let me quote the supporting opinion of the British historian, H. R. Trevor-Roper. In *The Last Days of Hitler,* Trevor-Roper wrote:

> It is sometimes said that the Allied insistence on "unconditional surrender" frightened the Germans into continued obedience; but if this implies that they would otherwise have revolted, I do not think it is true. Of those Germans who preferred the rule of the Nazis to unconditional surrender, how many would have been inspired to rebellion by an Allied assurance of moderation? Conditions can only be made with power-holders, or alternative power-holders, otherwise they are

not conditions but promises; and what German was influenced by promises after twelve years of Doctor Goebbels? Of alternative power-holders, the Army leaders might perhaps have been ready to bargain; but conditions which included the destruction of the German Army would have seemed no conditions to them; and anyway, even the Army failed in its politics. As for the "democratic opposition," invented by virtuous journalists —it is a creature as fabulous as the centaur and the hippogriff. No doubt many Germans quietly grumbled about the Nazis and have since claimed to have been their enemies; but in time of war, bargains can be struck only with real political forces, not with whimpering shadows. Who of these "democrats" ever concerted a program or approached the Allies with concrete proposals? A few high-minded aristocrats, a few disappointed officials and dismayed parsons—were these really more promising than the Schellenbergs and Schwerin von Krosigks? If we wish to explain the docility of the German people, we must look for some other explanation, and find it, perhaps, in that most discouraging German characteristic: the despair of politics.[3]

No, the policy of unconditional surrender did not prolong the war against Germany. But—and this is the important question today—will it prolong the peace, as its author hoped? That depends on how well we remember its meaning. Americans and their allies should remember that they offered no bribe to the Germans, but subjected them to overwhelming military defeat.[4] They should remember that they took what appeared to be a hard course and accepted whatever sacrifices it entailed, so that German militarism and fascism should have no chance to rise again. Americans should remember that their allies stayed with them on this course, even though they sometimes doubted that it was the right one. Those Britons who were later so free in accusing Americans of a lack of principle should remember that on the principle that counted most America stood firm. And those Russians and others who so lightly accused America and Britain of Fascist sympathies should remember that the Americans and British might easily have made a settlement which left the German Fascists a free hand in eastern Europe. They chose, instead, the way of unconditional surrender.

Chapter 6. Notes

1. In the interests of historical accuracy, I must record that one of the men who played a leading rôle in Soviet-American relations expressed doubts to me that President Roosevelt ever considered unconditional surrender as a check on Soviet suspicions. He said that the President never discussed with him the effect of unconditional surrender on relations between the Western Powers and the Soviets, and that the President would presumably have done so if he had given much thought to the matter. On the other hand, Elliott Roosevelt, in his account of the Casablanca meeting, says: "Father, once his phrase had been approved by the others, speculated about its effect in another direction—Russia."

2. The complete statistics follow:

	Unbombed (per cent)	Bombed (per cent)
Unwilling to accept unconditional surrender before the end	13	9
Willing to accept	51	57
No personal admission of willingness but think surrender inevitable	20	18
Indifferent, never heard or thought about it	16	16
	100	100

3. From *The Last Days of Hitler*, by H. R. Trevor-Roper. Copyright 1947 by H. R. Trevor-Roper. Used by permission of The Macmillan Company, publishers, and Macmillan and Company, Ltd.

4. The General Board of the United States Army which studied psychological warfare operations in the European theater after the war verified the fact that Allied propaganda made no promise or commitment to the Germans about their future treatment.

Chapter 7

GERMAN PERSONALITY TRAITS AND NATIONAL SOCIALIST IDEOLOGY *

A war-time study of German Prisoners of War

By

HENRY V. DICKS

Introduction

THE OBJECT of this paper is to report, rather belatedly, a war-time study on German prisoners of war which served to throw some light on the connections which exist between character structure and political ideology, and to illustrate the methods used in investigating both these sets of data. In this way it may contribute by way of example or prototype to future work in the integration of clinical psychiatry, social anthropology, and political science. In brief, the study consisted in contacting a random sample of German Prisoners of War passing through a certain British Collecting Centre, and subjecting them to prolonged interviews according to a schedule presently to be described in detail, drawing up a "personality profile" which was then compared with the political ideology of the same man as ascertained (in the greater part of the sample) by another interviewer, and finally, subjecting this comparison to a test of statistical significance. Concurrently a much larger random sample was being subjected to a political interrogation alone, from which a general distribution of political attitudes among the German Prisoner of War population could be derived.

The writer happens to be bi-lingual and partly educated in German schools. On being posted to the Directorate of Military Intelligence he was instructed to undertake any suitable studies which might help in the understanding of the enemies' mind

* Reprinted from *Human Relations* (vol. III, No. 2), June 1950.

and intentions and in the conduct of psychological warfare. The study which is about to be described was a by-product of other work, more directly relevant to the War, which the writer was briefed to do between 1942 and 1946. The main effort during the period in question was directed to a running survey of enemy morale which enabled us to plot fluctuations in the expectations and preoccupations of German prisoners during various phases of the war for purposes of propaganda. It was from this part of the work that we derived, amongst other things, our data on the distribution of political attitudes in the sample population.

The second piece of work consisted in the description and evaluation of the human relations and morale structure within the German Armed Forces as seen through the eyes of a British Army psychiatrist. (2), (3). It seemed of some practical importance to devise, if possible, a psychological technique by which selectors in the future Allied Administration of Germany might be helped to distinguish Nazis from non-Nazis without recourse to the very crude and falacious criteria of reference to formal membership of the Party and the like. It also occurred to the writer at that stage, that here might be a method which, if further refined, could find general application in that branch of Social Science concerned with the study of the relation between culture and personality. Some practical use was in fact made of the correlations of personality and political attitudes obtained and presented in this paper, when, early in the organisation of the Control Commission for the British zone of Germany, a Selection Centre was set up for potential high-level German personnel in which both the technical and the general frame of reference of this study formed part of the criteria used in the screening procedure.

During many informal conversations with some two thousand German prisoners of various ranks and arms, and as a result of the study of captured documents both of an official and of a purely private character, a broad picture of the general recurring regularities of German mental behaviour became gradually apparent.

It is not the intention in these pages to pillory the German people. The study required concentration on the origins of their recent mass behaviour. Many aspects have not been covered. When speaking of "national character" we mean only the broad, frequently recurring regularities of certain prominent behaviour traits and motivations of a given ethnic or cultural group. We do not assert that such traits are found in equal degree, or at all, in all members of that group, or that they are so conjoined that the extreme is also the norm. Neither do we assert that the traits are found singly or in combination in that group alone.

It should also be emphasised that this study was not concerned with the historical, political, or economic conditions which might have brought about the emergence of what we have called the "national character" or its manifestations in German Nationalism, Militarism, and National Socialism. It confined itself to psychiatric findings in present living individuals and endeavoured to test certain hypotheses concerning their mental make-up in relation to their political beliefs and convictions at the time of the interview. Nothing in this paper must be taken to imply that the economic and historico-political field forces are in any way under-rated by the writer.

Hypotheses

This paper then will be limited to that part of the work which consisted in an attempt to compare and show the interdependence of personality structure and political ideology in the population studied. Before proceeding to the detail of the method and its results, a statement of the assumptions and preliminary hypotheses which underlay it is called for.

The basic assumption made was that a political ideology was only in part a function of intellectual indoctrination or automatic group-conformity and that the sincerity with which men held various views on social and political matters was part of a Gestalt in which their personality structure was more or less deeply involved. Hence, for the adequate appreciation of a social or political movement it was essential to appraise the psychological structure of its participants, grading them in some way in terms of intensity of identification with the ideology and aims of the movement, and of consequent dynamism as carriers or infective agents. It was thought that the more an ideology fitted unconscious need systems of an individual, the greater would be the cathexis given to it by him.

The second assumption was, in brief, that the child is father to the man, and that the life history of individuals provides a clue to later character structure and to the ways in which the main infantile conflicts and emotional vicissitudes had been transformed into what have been called character traits, seeking expression in social behaviour.

The third assumption was that a national culture was likely to produce certain recurring regularities in the pattern of meeting the frustrated need systems consequent upon the socialisation of children through educational influences. It might, therefore, be possible to describe and define more precisely a configuration of personality traits which was shared by a large number of representatives of a given cultural group over and above regional, social-economic, educational, or other sub-group differences. Then, any desired sub-group of the culture could be subjected to comparison with the "norm" in respect of the presence and intensity of the traits or variables by which the main group had been described.

The processes of arriving at a working hypothesis to be tested grew slowly out of impressions left by previous participation in German life, which was not at that youthful time subjected to any critical or scientific evaluation, but which nevertheless formed an important part of one's experiences. In 1941 the writer was detailed to take over for some six weeks the psychiatric care of Rudolf Hess, then recently arrived in Britain. The description and evaluation of Hess' personality appears elsewhere.[1] Here it is mentioned only as one of the factors contributing to the selection of certain psychological variables to be looked for in the German and in particular in the Nazi personality. (It will later be seen that some of the traits looked for on strength of contact with Hess did not in fact prove to be significant in distinguishing one kind of German from another.) A third important preliminary to the setting up of a working hypothesis was the unrivalled opportunity for informal conversations with a heterogeneous group of German Prisoners, together with "mass observation" of their behaviour amongst themselves, and the study of a great variety of documents already alluded to. Some six weeks or more after this process of steeping oneself in the current German idiom, a series of pilot interviews was begun, branching out from a routine political interrogation already practised at the camp before the writer's arrival. During these pilot interviews both ideology and something of a personality assay were attempted together, and the conviction grew that the following hypotheses would repay more careful study.

1. That the German prisoners who held Nazi or near Nazi beliefs and ideology with conviction and fanaticism, had a personality structure which differed from the norm of German national character in the sense that they embodied this structure in more exaggerated or concentrated form.

2. That Nazis or near Nazis were likely to be men of markedly pregenital or immature personality structure in which libido organisation followed a sado-masochistic [2] pattern, based on a repression of the tender tie with the mother and resulting typically in a homo-sexual paranoid (extrapunitive) relation to a harsh and ambivalently loved and hated father figure, with its attendant sadism towards symbols of the displaced bad portion of this figure; in increased secondary ("defensive") narcissism; in libido splitting *vis-à-vis* female love objects; and in tendencies toward hypochondriacal (internal persecutor) and schizoid or hypomanic (guilt denial) features.

Description of the Study

1. Distribution of Political Attitudes

To test these hypotheses, it was necessary to turn on, as it were, a higher power of the microscope on a statistically adequate sample of the prisoner population passing through our hands and to devise a method of examination of these selected men by which their personality structure on the one hand, and their political attitudes on the other, could be as clearly as possible examined in parallel. Ideally, a team of at least three should have been required for doing the job thoroughly. There should have been a psychiatric interviewer, his clinical observations and inferences should have been supplemented and corrected by the use of projection tests and other quasi-normative personality evaluations by a clinical psychologist, whilst political attitudes should have been examined by a third interviewer, working blind in relation to personality factors, but skilled in interviewing and in the appreciation of German social and political outlook.

This would, however, have turned the study into a formal laboratory set piece of very doubtful value, considering the setting. Few of the subjects would have reacted as spontaneously as in fact they did. Only one of these desiderata could in practice be obtained; very soon the work was divided between the writer covering the entire aspect of personality study and a number of "lay" interviewers who conducted almost all the political interrogation after a period of tuition and supervision by the writer in accordance with the schedule reproduced as *TABLE 1*. Naturally, political ideas and emotions were often expressed in the course of the psychological interview, and personal life stories were equally frequently given to the political interrogators. This was a limitation on the "purity" of the "experiment" which is hard to remedy in what is essentially a piece of "fieldwork."

TABLE 1

Name of P/W	Age	Rank ....
Unit	Domicile	Education ....
Profession	Parents' Religion......	Own Religion ....
Class		

A. OUTCOME OF THE WAR

Germany wins ....   Compromise Peace...   Doubtful ....
                                     Germany loses ....

Germany wins:—

  Within one year ....   Within two years ....   In over two years ....

Notes on views (e.g. (i) World Dominion, (ii) "United Europe," (iii) Restoration of Independence to Occupied Territories (which?) (iv) How Germany will win).

Compromise Peace:—

  With Western Powers........   With Russia........   "All round"........

Doubtful:—

Notes:—

Germany loses:—

  Western Powers invade first..................   Russia invades first..........

Where will Germany stabilise her defence line in (a) France, (b) Italy?

B. ATTITUDE TO REGIME

Complete loyalty ....*(FI)* Believer with reservations............*(FII)*
Divided............*(FIV)* Anti-Nazi............*(FV)* Unpolitical............*(FIII)*

Believer with reservations:—   Doubtful:—
Notes:—   *Notes:—*

Anti-Nazi:—   Unpolitical:—
Notes:—   *Notes:—*

Attitude to Hitler personally:—
Notes (e.g. Worship, Acceptance, Doubt, Hostility, Any substitutes?)

C. HOME FRONT

Confident .... Doubtful .... Pessimistic ....
Doubtful and Pessimistic:—
Notes on topics discussed (e.g. Food, Clothing, Sabotage, Foreign Workers, Effect of Losses, Women's call-up)

Effect of Air Raids:—

Very dangerous.... Dangerous .... Ineffective ....
Notes:—

D. ATTITUDE TO UNITED NATIONS

(i) BRITAIN

Hostile .... Divided .... Admiring ....
Notes:—

(ii) U.S.A.

Hostile .... Divided .... Admiring ....
Notes:—

(iii) RUSSIA

Hostile .... Divided .... Admiring ....
Notes:—

German defeat of
Russia:— Yes .... Doubtful .... No ....
Russian occupation:—Feared ..... Indifferent .... Welcomed ......
Western Powers
preferred:— Yes .... Indifferent .... No ....
Notes:—

E. PROPAGANDA

(i) GERMAN

Hostile .... Divided .... Admiring ....
Notes:—

(ii) B.B.C.

Listened to:—   Yes.............. Heard quoted.............. No............
Notes on opinions:—

(iii) SCHWARZSENDER (Freedom Stations)

Listened to:—   Yes.............. Heard quoted.............. No............
Notes on opinions:—

(iv) MOSCOW

Listened to:—   Yes.............. Heard quoted.............. No............

(v) LEAFLETS

Read........ Seen, not read........ Heard quoted........ No knowledge....

F. POST-WAR EXPECTATIONS IF GERMANY LOSES

German people exterminated.... Square deal and reconciliation..
Germany will rise in new war.... Other ....

G. SERVICE CONDITIONS

Satisfied: G.A. .... Dissatisfied: G.A. ....
           G.N. ....   G.N. ....
           G.A.F. ....   G.A.F. ....

Notes (Subject matter of grouses: e.g. awards, Officers, rations, etc.)

H. FIGHTING QUALITIES

High .... Fair .... Poor ....
Notes:—

A few words of explanation as to the way in which the above
schedule was employed may be useful. It will be seen that there
are certain items which were simply checked, but that for each
item there were spaces for notes (larger than the reproduction
shown here) in which the interrogator would write qualitative
observations on his subject's responses, noting especially striking phrases, clichés culled from Nazi propaganda, fervid declarations of faith, accusations against the Allied Powers, all
manner of expressions of opinions or doubt on the political side,

which influenced the interviewers' judgement. Some of the headings and material had of course more value to psychological warfare and morale themes than to the mere assessment of these men's political attitudes. That was especially true of our recording of the numbers who listened to or were familiar with Allied radio transmission and later with Allied leaflets, and of conditions inside Germany. Even in the responses to such enquiries, however, the political temper of a man was laid open or substantiated.

The schedule was never filled in in the presence of the subject, but was completed later. Any data from other sources were added to the notes, and finally the man was placed by the observer, frequently after case discussion between several interrogators who knew the subject well, in one of five categories as follows:—

F.I. *Fanatical, whole-hearted Nazis (the hard core);* people who had thoroughly identified themselves with the ideology, aims, and attitudes of the Nazi leadership, as stated and propagated in the written and spoken pronouncements of the N.S.D.A.P. and its affiliated organizations.

F.II. *Believers with reservations* (camp followers and near Nazis); a fraction which was more nearly identical with former German Nationalists, and not infrequently better educated than the fanatics; who were ready to admit certain shortcomings of the Nazi regime and its methods of waging war, but usually on the grounds of inefficiency rather than on ethical or political grounds. The veneer of Western culture was usually somewhat thicker than in the zealots.

F.III. *Unpolitical men;* the group composed of men essentially concerned with private motives such as subsistence and security, who usually also passively accepted the current social and political conditions. The repetition of a number of Nazi-political clichés without emotional conviction was discounted.

F.IV. *"The divided"* (later called *passive anti-Nazi* by Norman Brangham); were men in conflict, disillusioned, not knowing where they stood. They had often supported Hitler in the past because of the promise of economic benefits and political order, but they had a general bias against Nazism and war. They were often recruited from former believers with reservations, and were mostly loyal patriots.

F.V. *Active convinced anti-Nazis;* men who had maintained opposition in feeling, thought and sometimes in deed to the regime on religious, ethical, political, or individualist grounds.

It must be stressed that these were classifications which had been made on empirical grounds before the beginning of the study here described. In practice it was a useful division which corresponded to the realities of political interviews and attitudes of the German forces towards the war and it was accordingly retained as the basis for political classification of the population studied. It must be emphasized also that at this stage the F rating stood merely as a code for a set of political attitudes and had as yet no connotations as to personality structure. It was precisely these connotations which the subsequent study set out to discover.

Taking the main items in the political schedule, the $F.I$ group tended to expect German victory usually in a short time and to be followed by world dominion, or at least dominion over a united Europe from which all non-Germanic influence would be excluded. They expressed complete loyalty to their regime and its leaders, and were ready to testify dramatically to the rightness of their beliefs. They usually equally readily minimised difficulties on the home front; regarded even our later air-raids as ineffective; professed unwavering hostility to and contempt for the three major Allied nations, and in particular expressed what came to be called the "Bolshevik Bogey." It followed that they usually dismissed with contempt our radio transmissions, or staunchly professed never to have heard them. Under "post-war expectations" they most readily thought that in the "purely hypothetical" event of an Allied victory the German people would be exterminated, or alternatively that Germany would rise in a little while to try world conquest once more. Their opinions were expressed with emotional fervour and in Goebbels' language.

The believers with reservations $(F.II)$ tended in general towards similar scores and the difference between them and the fanatics was usually one of emphasis, degree, or conviction; but sometimes such men would admit criticism of one or more Nazi leaders or their policies; would tend to grant the seriousness of the threat from Allied bombing, and would find something to admire or be ambivalent about in their enemies.

The unpolitical group $(F.III)$ would tend in the main to give replies of the "don't know" type. Characteristic of what the unpolitical subject might say is the following—'First we had the Kaiser, then Mr. Ebert and Mr. Hindenburg, and now that Hitler, but we still have to milk our cows.' Such men were readily worried about the home front and their dear ones and were usually indifferent as to the outcome of the war or the resulting political situation, provided that they retained some security, property and means of keeping themselves and their families alive. Their attitude was summed up in a recurrent sentence: 'All this is far too difficult for me, I am only a small man.'

The passive anti-Nazis *(F.IV)* tended to score in the doubtful headings much more often than not, but sometimes made gallant attempts to profess their loyalty and belief in victory and a great future for Germany, in order to cover up their lack of faith. Their remarks on Nazi leaders usually tried to stress the constructive and beneficial aspects of the regime, while regretfully admitting that all was not well. Their doubts were often shown in gestures, hesitancies and modes of expression rather than by the substance of their remarks.

The anti-Nazis *(F.V)* tended to favour German defeat, from which alone they hoped a better world could be reconstructed. They wished to make amends all round. They would express freely, although sometimes with anxiety, their hostility to the regime, its ideas, and its leading personalities. They would tend in general to be admiring either towards Britain or the U.S.A. or Russia, not always towards all three, but would tend to have more objective political views about the comparative merits of Germans and non-Germans than other German prisoners, except when they were doctrinaire Marxists or "anti-German" renegades. They would equally reject German propaganda and admire the truthfulness or efficacy of ours. They would expect a square deal from the Allies and discount German atrocity propaganda of the "strength-through-fear" type.

Such, briefly, were the ways in which these five categories tended to score and answer the schedule. The interview was by no means stereotyped, but was conducted in an informal manner.

The sociological data of all men undergoing the questionnaire were carefully recorded under such headings as age, regional affiliations, urban or rural, bombed or non-bombed area, occupational and economic status, educational level, arm of service, service rank, and parents' and man's own religious beliefs or affiliations. These data were incorporated in current reports to Psychological Warfare agencies, together with the assessment of and reasons for the men's satisfaction or dissatisfaction with their service conditions and with subjective assessments on the part of the interrogators of their fighting qualities and with a note of the type of military unit from which they stemmed. For purposes of correlating such social data with political and military morale, preparations were made in 1944, with the collaboration of Edward Shils, Hazel Gaudet, Elmo Wilson and others of the SHAEF Psychological Warfare Division, to review these data and make them capable of being compiled and worked over on a large scale. This was, however, not completed at the time and the records passed out of the writer's hands.[3] Some impressions might, however, be worth giving. The fanatical Nazis were usually under 35 and of lower-middle class origin, with an admixture of intellectuals and working class youths, the latter often of the tough bully type. The believers with reservations tended to be of better education than the fanatics and were drawn from the class of regular soldiers, more solid intellectuals and business men, but contained a considerable sprinkling of working-class men in the upper income brackets. The unpolitical group was mostly composed of small town artisans, country folk, unskilled workers, enlisted regular service personnel and minor civil servants. The divided or passive anti-Nazi category contained much the same population as the F.II's, with whom there was two-way traffic. The anti-Nazis (F.V.) comprised many sorts of men, from working-class Trade-Unionists and Marxists to convinced Catholics and Protestants, intellectual liberals, men with an international outlook, and not a few aristocratic conservatives of the "good old" sort. The young sons of these types of people were a not inconsiderable ingredient. In short the F.V's contained the same kind of collection of persons and types as would have formed any continental Resistance movement. In no case was formal membership of this or that Nazi party branch made the basis of classification. To many professions such membership was a condition of employment and signified little.

In all some four hundred unselected prisoners were subjected to the political interrogation at the centre where this study was carried out. In addition, from the summer of 1944 onwards the field interrogation teams and the Psychological Warfare Division of SHAEF and its Army representatives were conducting

TABLE 2

AVERAGE DISTRIBUTION OF POLITICAL ATTITUDES
In a Sample of *ca* 1,000 German P.O.W.s

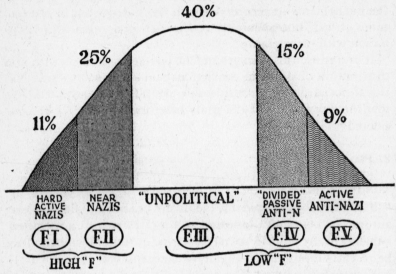

11%	25%	40%	15%	9%
HARD ACTIVE NAZIS	NEAR NAZIS	"UNPOLITICAL"	"DIVIDED" PASSIVE ANTI-N	ACTIVE ANTI-NAZI
F.I	F.II	F.III	F.IV	F.V
HIGH "F"		LOW "F"		

SAMPLES   September 1944   (1) 600 unselected GERMAN P.O.W.s
Captured in Cherbourg Peninsula
(All foreign-born, etc., excluded)

October 1942 to July 1944.   (2) About 400 unselected P.O.W.s
(German and a few Austrian).

analagous interrogations based on this method on a large scale. Some of these teams passed through an intensive course of instruction and role playing given by the writer and by his now experienced colleagues. The consolidated figures may be conveniently expressed as a graph sufficiently accurate over the period September 1942 to July 1944 to bring out the salient distribution of the five types of political attitude. These are shown in *TABLE* 2.

It will be noted that during most of the period in question a large proportion of German soldiers, sailors, and airmen did not yet feel that the war was lost. It should be noted that all foreign-born levies were excluded, and only citizens of the German Reich and a few Sudeten Germans and Austrians were

admitted into these samples. It should also be noted that the
F.I, F.III and *F.V* figures remained practically constant up to
the very end of these opinion checks, whereas the *F.II* category
tended to change towards the *F.IV* as the outcome of the war
became more certain. Naturally the *F.III*'s tended to colour
their statements in accordance with the fluctuations of the fortunes of war, but essentially retained their dominant preoccupation with private aims.

It is against this background of our acquaintance with the
distribution of political convictions and attitudes towards National Socialism of a considerable sample of German P.O.W.
that the second part of the study here dealt with must be considered.[4]

2. Personality Studies

1. THE SAMPLE

The sample consisted of 138 men, examined between the
autumn of 1942 and the spring of 1944. They were unselected
—that is to say we had to rely on what prisoners happened to
be recently captured by sea, air, or land and sent to the collecting centre in question. The period of the war accounts for the
relative shortage of "Army" in the sample, and for the relative
preponderance of the upper educational brackets among avia-
tors and skilled U-boat crews, and later, among the *élite* of the
Afrika Corps. From the list of prisoners in the camp names
would be selected by the camp duty office because the subjects
happened to have a few hours to spare from other interviews
or prior to removal from camp, which was small and had a large
turnover. General treatment and living conditions in the camp
were good, and a welfare service in accordance with the provisions of the Geneva Convention was in being.

In no sense could the sample be described as accurately re-
flecting the composition of the German male population or even
of the Wehrmacht. One had to do the best one could. The
group in fact included people from 18 to 55 years old at various socio-economic levels, and from private to Lt. Colonel in
rank; from farm labourer to University lecturer in the educational scale, with a high proportion of regular soldiers especially
among the naval fraction of the sample.

The composition of the sample is shown in *Table 3*.

2. THE METHOD OF EXAMINATION

The method of examination consisted of prolonged, personal, non-directed interviews in a quiet room, an informal atmosphere being maintained; in not a few instances several inter-

TABLE 3 †

SERVICES

Navy	60
Army	48
Air Force	32

RANK

Officers	26
Non Officers	112

AGE GROUPS *

17—21	44
22—28	43
29—35	25
36+	26

* These groupings were decided on by reference to ages of subjects at the beginning of the Nazi regime.

EDUCATION

Primary	9
Post-Primary	50
(Secondary and Tech.)	
"Higher"	79
(University and Techno-	
logical graduates)	

OCCUPATIONAL

1. Professional, Higher Executives, land owners and University students	17
2. Managers, business clerks, "White collar" workers	20
3a. Big factory skilled workers	6
3b. Small factory skilled workers	16
4. Unskilled labourers ...	4
5. Independent tradesmen (tailor, cobbler, small shopkeeper, etc.) ...	19
6. Small farmers, etc. ...	6
7. Merchant seamen, fishermen	2
8. Regular services ... (Many ex-skilled operatives among these, e.g., electricians and mechanics).	48

REGIONS OF ORIGIN

Seaboard	4
Berlin	1
Rest of Prussia	4
"Rhineland"	1
Bavaria	
Württemberg	
Thuringia (Saxon) ...	

† The breakdowns in Table 3 do not all sum to 138, "Services" totaling 14 and "Regions of Origin" totaling 137. It was not possible to adjust these discrepancies before publication. D.L.

views, the average time per man being about two hours. It was an essential condition that the subject was willing and ready to converse. No kind of pressure was used, as it would have been fatal to the whole spirit of the study. No psychiatric or medical status was disclosed, the interviewer merely representing himself as an officer privately interested in the prisoners as men. The main skill consisted in preserving a heart-to-heart rapport, so that formal test procedures, filling up of schedules in the men's presence and similar evidences of specialist investigation had to be avoided. Rough notes were sometimes taken at the interview, but the case record was written or dictated immediately afterwards, from memory.

At times it was possible to obtain a Matrix Intelligence Test on the grounds of the man's wish to know how he should use his period in captivity to fit himself for post-war life, but this added little to the kind of data interesting for the purpose in hand. Murray's T.A.T. came into the writer's hands too late to make it worthwhile using without experience.

The aim of therapeutic closure was achieved with scarcely any exceptions. It was possible to verify that the individuals so interviewed had enjoyed their talk, and were at worst left slightly non-plussed by the purpose of such a prolonged "chance encounter." In the main they felt helped by someone taking time to interest himself in them as human beings.

3. THE SCHEDULE OF PERSONALITY VARIABLES

Though the conduct of the interview was non-directive, the data it sought to obtain were arranged in a schedule previously worked out, to test the hypothesis above defined, by reference to a *personality profile*. The Schedule was divided into (a) Social background data, consisting of the details already listed under *Table 3;* (b) psychological background data and (c) present personality traits.

The two latter will now be delineated, as originally conceived and defined. Their choice and the use that was made of them represents the crucial point of the whole study. They are based on the psycho-analytic hypothesis of personality development. The variables represented by the categories used are, of course, open to challenge by other schools of thought, while the skill or accuracy with which they were assessed at interview and in the light of additional data about each subject remains unverifiable, like any clinical psychiatric diagnosis not tested by long observation and by the criterion of therapy.

4. PSYCHOLOGICAL BACKGROUND DATA

These data are selected items of the early personal history of the individual. The time factor and the reality situation, which forbade more than a certain degree of contact with each subject, imposed necessary limitations on what could be ascertained. This part of the examination restricted itself to getting a general picture of the life history, emphasizing the parent-child relationships as recalled by the subject or as readily inferred from the account given by the subject. No attempt was made, for example, to collect systematically feeding and toilet-training data. It was felt to be practicable only to record the following as variables:—

(i) PARENTAL PREDOMINANCE IN CHILDHOOD

(*a*) Father dominated
(*b*) Mother dominated
(*c*) Equal harmonious influence of both parents
(*d*) Equal conflicting influence of both parents
(*e*) Broken homes: deaths, divorce, orphanages, foster-homes, etc.
(*f*) No inference made [5]

The criteria for the above were defined by data on the description given by the subject to such questions as: Tell me about your people—which of them do you resemble—who had most influence? Who made the major decisions? Who had the money bags? Who wore the trousers? Who did the punishing? In more tricky cases these enquiries might be phrased as general questions referring to what the man felt was typical of a good German home, and how he would behave if he had such a home. The data under this head were recorded without attempt at evaluating intensity.

Much qualitative detail, in varying degree of depth and clarity was naturally obtained, but this did not lend itself readily to coding.

(ii) RELIGIOUS ATTITUDES

A simple set of alternatives, without finer discrimination, but subsuming obvious major differences in parental cultural and social value systems to which the subject would have been exposed. Scored separately for each parent.

(*a*) Observing, sincere Catholic.

(*b*) Observing, sincere Protestant.

(*c*) Easy-going, tolerant indifference or nominal adherence.

(*d*) Consistent atheism, rationalism, secularism, materialism.

(*e*) *Gottgläubig*—This last category represents the peculiar Germanic-Nazi deism, hostile equally to traditional Christianity and to the attitudes under (*d*) above.

The same categories were also used to differentiate the subject's own current religious attitude under "Traits" (below), and will not be repeated in the description.

(iii) SOLUTIONS OF THE OEDIPAL PHASE

This was the heading under which information concerning the course of emotional development from the infantile Oedipus phase was recorded. The inferences were drawn both from the history and from present attitudes. This category is to be considered as transitional between historical background and present character structure. From it several other variables are derived, as will appear below.

Under this heading Father and Mother cathexes were dealt with separately as follows:—

MOTHER CATHEXIS

Intended to record whether a man's love bonds with the infantile mother-figure were judged

(*a*) to be still attached to his actual Mother or to a mother surrogate of his childhood, or

(*b*) to have been transferred to a female love-object of the man's own generation in the manner considered the "normal" state of affairs, i.e., to his wife, sweetheart, or mistress.

Against these scores there were three sub-categories provided for cases in which the Mother cathexis was judged to be predominantly transferred to symbolic objects:—

(*c*) the *Führer* (or similar male authority figure) as the protecting, nourishing figure loving all his children. This heading was introduced on empirical grounds after pilot interviews.

(d) The State or the man's service (e.g. his unit), or other "secular" institution fulfilling a similar substitutive nurtural, maternal role, it having been found on pilot interviews that a number of German P.O.W. felt their service *milieu* to function as a mother which protected, clothed, fed, and paid them.

(e) A church, or similar "spiritual" institution. (Mother Church, etc.) The five alternatives so derived were scored, but not rated quantitatively.

FATHER CATHEXIS

Through this variable it was tried to get a supplementary picture of libido vicissitudes, and classify the major possible outcomes of the tie to the father. It was assumed that the relationship to male leader figures is modelled on, and draws the subject's libido from the Oedipal, father relationship. Evidence related to these secondary figures was included in the total appraisal, in addition to expressed and inferred attitudes towards the actual father or childhood father surrogates. The following categories were drawn up as alternatives to be scored about each man.

(a) Mature Object Choice: This score was intended to show that the personality had largely overcome infantile attachments to the father symbol and was regulated by a mature ego-structure, free from major influences of an introjected father-image in the super-ego. This information, and that for the subsequent subvariables, was obtained both from evidence in regard to relationship with paternal figures and by probing of attitudes relating to guilt, authority, submissiveness, and towards the upbringing of sons.

(b) Persistent Father Identification: This heading records the direct form of immature "fixation," in itself a normal transition phase in the male child, from which a boy derives a certain continuity of male cultural traits ultimately absorbed into his own ego-structure. The theory underlying this variable as here used is that a boy, faced with his ambivalent feelings towards his father, normally introjects the father and comes to identify himself with him, behaving towards his super-ego as if it were the punishing and rewarding father, and towards the environment with a mixture of omnipotence phantasy resulting from having his father as his ego ideal, and of inferiority and submissiveness due to re-projection of the super-ego into other authority figures. The quality of this identification is important. In so far as it is wholly benign it tends to its own supersession by maturity, and to the disappearance of ambivalence towards authority figures cf. score (a) above. Its persistence is therefore always a symptom of some degree of guilt, ambivalence, and unresolved conflict over the Oedipus situation. This situation is conceived as the nucleus of subsequent attitudes towards freedom and authority; of guilt; of inhibitions on spontaneous tenderness, and on full maturation in heterosexual relationships; consequently of homosexual trends, inferiority feelings, and various mechanisms expressive of defences against castration threats from within and without.

(c) Equivocal or Partial Identifications: This score, as the name implies, is a form of divided Oedipus solution, where the individual has incorporated contradictory ("heteronymous") elements from both parents into his super-ego, has an unstable, split ego-ideal, with consequent contradictions in character, as for example in a man who followed his father into a military career but really always hankered after being a painter like his mother, uneasy in all social relationships involving these antagonistic inner forces.

(d) Rebel Attitude: This self-explanatory score represents a persistent immature rejection of paternal (or perhaps parental) authority. It might be termed a negative Oedipus solution, in which the subject clings to an attitude of defiance, covering a deeper castration anxiety and need for submission and dependence. It is the opposite of (b) above, in so far as it displays the hate aspect of the ambivalence towards authority, whereas in (b) the loving aspect of the ambivalence is uppermost.

(e) Mother Identification: This score records the result of an evasion of the father situation, in that the child adopts the mother's attitude towards the father in dealing with the threat from a severe father figure. When the mother tie has to be surrendered, it is dealt with by introjection. It involves the personality in a passive, feminine alignment to love problems and often in overt behaviour, the extreme of which would be passive homosexuality and feminism. There is overlap, but not identity, with "Mother-fixation" under the heading of Mother Cathexis above. In the latter the mother is still the overt love object; in the present case no such tie is manifested in conscious behaviour, though at a deep level this is the case. In Mother identification the Mother may be devaluated, and females regarded as rivals to the love of father-figures. As compared with identification, the simple persistence of attachment to the mother is a more naive and uncomplicated thing, implying different ways of dealing with Oedipus guilt. In "Mother fixation" (Score (*a*) under "Mother Cathexis" above) it is permissible to postulate a father tolerant of a boy tied to his mother's apron strings.

GUILT INCULCATION

This category, in contrast to the mere classificatory and qualitative scoring used above was rated on a three-point scale.

(*a*) Overt, grossly obvious guilt (Persecutory or depressive anxiety)

(*b*) Heightened guilt shown by inner drive, over-precision, obsequiousness, self-justification (Murray's "blamavoidance")

(*c*) Normal limits.

This was intended to rate super-ego pressure as shown up in the life history. It is the weakest part of the study. There was lack of clarity in the original formulation, which did not for example differentiate between shame and guilt patterns or between felt ego-ideal pressures and defended, unrecognised super-ego pressures (such as manic denial). For this reason it was found to be non-discriminating. It failed to differentiate, say, between a projection and an acceptance of personal or group responsibility, both being lumped together as evidence of "*guilt*." In fact, varieties and levels of guilt are better brought out directly by the other variables employed.

TENDERNESS TABOO

This "background" category is based on Ian Suttie's ideas on the importance of tender love, especially in the maternal relationship, for the development of security and the integration of the personality of the child. It was scored as present or absent. Since we were primarily concerned with a delineation of the harsh, sadistic Nazi personality, we set up the quality in its negative aspect, i.e., a taboo, or prohibition on tender relations in the family culture of the subject. It will be seen that this also is closely bound up with the Oedipus situation, i.e., the degree to which the subject felt free or forbidden to have a tender mother-baby relationship. No attempt was made to seek out different possible antecedents for tenderness taboo, e.g., whether it was related chiefly to fear of the father or to a rejection by the mother on strength of the latter's acceptance of the harsh, "masculine" patterns of child upbringing. The assumption made was that a tenderness taboo signified repression of the internal loving mother in the personality, both as "need" and as "object."

The variable was looked for in the same topics as the general atmosphere and quality of parent-relationships, supplemented by data relating to present attitudes towards babies, young animals, artistic and humanitarian values and religious formulations. So much for what was recorded under "Background." The rest of the data were grouped under "Traits."

5. TRAITS

These were defined as aspects of personality and behaviour discernible as major themes to the psychiatrist at the time of examination, and less dependent on an exploration of early history. They were listed on empirical grounds after pilot interviews and from general discussion and contemplation of the German character. They are all to some extent overlapping or complementary and, psychologically, dependent on such nuclear experiences as the Oedipus situation. In contrast to background data, an attempt was made to rate most of the traits on a three point scale on clinical grounds. The following were the traits looked for as variables together with the scores, or other values, assigned to them:—

AMBIVALENCE

The presence of irrational contradictory affects of love and hate towards one and the same object—in practice and under the circumstances of our enquiry often a "political" object, e.g., the *Führer* or The British. Another criterion of ambivalence was the need to balance overt or unrecognised hated objects with a good object, e.g., the dramatic transference of good qualities to one, and bad qualities to another of two British officers at the camp.

Three point scale:
1. Gross, obvious
2. Perceptibly heightened (or "clinically observable")
3. Normal limits or absent.

EXAMPLE:

Score 1. *Gross:* Case 106, Age 32

'I am a German and cannot be a traitor,' while offering to do propaganda against the Germans.

'My sole happiness is my children,' when in fact he was always away.

Always belonged to two camps—Jesuits and Nazi Party; later Nazi party and an opposition group. A conspirator who looked both ways at once.

Score 2. *Perceptibly heightened:* Case 107, Age 20

Considerable pull in two directions: 'When one is at home one thinks what a good place school is: one always wants to be somewhere different.' Went into Air Force because Father was veteran Pilot of World War I, but he hates discipline and military life. At school he wanted to join in the fun but also keep people at arm's length.

Score 3. *Normal:* Case 110, Age 22 (citation of record)

Father was just and not very stern. 'Everybody admired my Mother. She was loved by us all.' Tolerant towards all the farm hands, Polish and Russian: 'I love my own land and feel animosity to nobody.'

SPLIT LIBIDO

This concept is used to describe the dichotomy of tender and of sensuous love in relation to heterosexual love objects. The extreme case would be the man who marries an idealised frigid mother-figure with whom he is impotent, but who has promiscuous relations with prostitutes or similar "debased" women.

The connection of this trait with the oedipal conflicts over mother-cathexis are obvious. There is also evidence from analytic practice that this trait is the outcome of a defence against homosexual impulses. Its conclusion was suggested by the personal histories of several Germans, and by perusal of German novels. Three point scale as previously.

EXAMPLES OF SCORING:

Score 1. *Gross:* Case 128, Age 22 (excerpt from Diary)

'I cried like a child for I' (his fiancé). 'Why is everything in life so double-edged? . . . I's picture looks so strange.' 'It was a lovely night with that little girl in barracks . . . but don't lower class women seem ugly? . . .' 'I can't do without some erotic experience . . . a whore-monger after all!' (gives list of casual pick-ups and dates during a fortnight's absence) etc.

Score 2. *Perceptibly heightened:* Case 201 Age 20

Note reads: Frequent allusions, with interested disapproval, to morals of Hitler Maidens, naked dancers, etc. Yet his idea of a wife is dull and demure. Cannot see full comradeship of sexes. 'Women must be kept out of politics' too.

Score 3. *Normal limits:* Case 110, Age 22

Note reads: He took a very sane view of the wife he wants. Not interested in getting mixed up with some glamorous, expensive, useless film star type . . .

SADISM

This trait was intended to describe the presence or absence in the personality of direct primitive aggressive traits derived from what is called the "pregenital phase." It was taken for practical purposes to imply the impulses to dominate, bully, hurt or kill. It was felt from the beginning that rating such a quality would be almost impossible, as no man, except an occasional fool, would admit to an enemy officer such impulses even if he were conscious of them. Reliance was placed on circumstantial or indirect evidence (cf. known record of Kramer at Belsen) and on the impression made by the subject on the psychiatrist in the light of the latter's insight into psychological mechanisms. Means of confirming this evidence were at hand owing to the set-up of the centre.

There was no rating, only scoring under one of the following:—

1. Overt, gleeful, apparently guilt free—the tough killer sort, i.e. (no intropunitiveness).
2. Stern, incisive, aggressive personality.
3. Indifference—calm acceptance of sadism in other ("impunitive").

The above three were classed together as anti-social forms of sadism.

4. Averagely aggressive, "normal" by British standards. (Loves a fight, but essentially kindly, tolerant, without need to kow-tow).
5. Gentle, submissive, over-conciliatory, smooth.
6. Horror, condemnation or guilt over sadism in others, squeamishness over atrocities, blood-phobias, etc.

These latter three were classed as social sublimations or reaction formations to sadism, No. 4 being regarded as the most mature disposal of initial aggressive trends, in an ascending degree of intro-punitiveness.

EXAMPLES OF SCORING SADISM: (Excerpts of notes)
Score 1. Case 90 (Bomber Pilot) Age 25

Thrusting, prognathous face and manners. Bites his nails as he says: 'When we have liquidated Russia—then mercy on this Island! . . . Coventry will be child's play.' 'We had to break out, a nation of 100 million will not be ground down . . .' (thumps fist on table) 'We have not yet avenged ourselves for the way the French treated us in the Ruhr . . .' (About resistance men): 'If these fools will cut our cables they must go against the wall . . .' Further conversation discloses his delight at the fate of Jews . . . talks about 'draconic hardness.' Picks his spots on face and says 'I won't let them heal.' Gives impression of whipping one with his stream of bitter words.

Score 2. Case 89. Quartermaster (U-boat), Age 26.

Hard, depressed eyes. 'I grew up in misery' . . . 'No time to laugh' . . . 'I gladly went to the service and my mother laughed when she saw me off—one is schooled there' . . . 'you should see our little boys march, heart and soul' . . . 'The German *must*—Frederick the Great's "damned duty and obligation" rules everything' . . . 'Those who differ are outsiders and do not count . . .' etc.

Score 3(*a*). Case 105. Midshipman, Navy, Age 21.

The outstanding feature is the almost incredible indifference when he describes the drowning of his own shipmates before his eyes only a few days earlier.

Score 3(*b*). Case 84. W/T rating, U-boat. Age 22.

Calmly relates how he has put a girl in trouble. Has watched his mother being 'sat on' by Father and approves. 'Can't help what the S.S. do—not my affair.'

Score 4. Case 82. U-boat, Stoker, Age 20.

Fresh, friendly boy, full of stories of boyish pranks, skiing and fisticuffs. Father beat him when he was too cheeky. 'Can't understand why we have to have a war—always the decent fellows who belong to sports clubs are killed' (said to a comrade).

Score 5. Case 91. Leading stoker (U-boat), Age 23.

A simple, innocent fellow who excites protectiveness in all who deal with him. Ex-featherweight boxing champion. Early responsible for his young brothers, because mother was weakly. Hopes war will be over soon because it is so silly. At first timidly, but with growing confidence, criticises atrocities against Jews, and fears as result Germany will be terribly dealt with. Is polite, meek and agrees with all the kind officers who have had the interesting 'technical talks' with him.

Score 6(*a*). Case 81. Bomber crew W/T operator, Age 24.

'I was never athletic and was over-protected, but joined because friends' taunts stung me.' Objects to stupid bombing raids. Can see only chaos and destruction resulting from war. Dreads reprisals for all the bad things done.

Score 6(*b*). Case 107. Sgt. Pilot, Age 20.

Shut-in, thoughtful person, keen on philosophy and art. Hates uniform. Hates it when people quarrel, hates rough horse play and isolated himself from his comrades in the unit. Condemns any but the most chivalrous conduct, and winces at German and Russian barbarism.

It should be noted that the trait of "submissiveness," which has loomed so large in all discussions of the general pattern of German behaviour, appears in this schedule only as a subvariant of the ratings for sadism. Psychologically this is justifiable in view of the close association of sadism and masochism. It was decided not to give submissiveness the status of a variable in this study. The aim was to distinguish Nazi types from others, and the trait of submission was held to be so widely distributed in the culture that it would fail in its purpose as a discriminating factor. (The omission has been rectified in later refinements of technique when we were able to invent suitable criteria for rating and distinguishing types of submissiveness separately, but this was achieved by team work after 1945 and cannot be included in the present paper.)

HOMOSEXUAL TRENDS

Under this trait were classified not only the comparatively rare perverts, but, more importantly, marked tendencies in the direction of male preference: depreciation of women, idealisation of male anatomy and beauty, advocacy and interest in male dominance and male associations, the cult of hardness and "manliness," hence the prizing of such obvious "phallic" virtues as male prowess, erectness, thrusting and daring, and condemnation of softness, yieldingness and laxity, the contempt for tender, feminine interests and objects, preference for sons, etc. The usual three point scale was used.

EXAMPLES OF SCORING:
Score 1. *Gross and obvious.* Case 108, L.A.C., Age 21.

Father a neurotic who drank and deserted Mother when P.W. was aged 1. Mother out at work. Lonely childhood. 'Terribly fond of young people.' 'All my feelings are in the comradeship of the Unit and of Hitler youth.' (Asked about women in public life) says vehemently 'No—their place is in the kitchen!' Incontrovertible evidence of passive homosexual episode with another prisoner, six weeks only after capture. No interest in girls.

Score 2(a). *Perceptibly heightened.* Case 77. Lt. Fighter-Pilot, Age 21.

'A father must train his son to his own liking and rescue him from his Mother's apron strings.' 'If I have childern, I could of course devote myself to my son—but a daughter, no, unless she was beautiful.' 'I love being an officer because it is beautiful to educate young men.' Uncritical worship of Hitler. Was 'his Mother's all.'

Score 2(b). *Perceptibly heightened*. Case 126. Lt. Observer, Age 20.

'My father shaped my education.' 'I have to thank his firmness that I was pulled out of the bad state (pampering owing to childhood illness, &c).'

Submission to stern discipline and bullying regarded as his salvation. Idealization of taking charge of young men, as youth leader and officer. He saw his greatest reward in their love and trust. 'But not as schoolmaster—only in the living emotional comradeship of the Hitler Youth or the Service.'

Score 3. *Normal limits:* Case 112. Lieut., Infantry, Age 22.

This man has straightforward self-valuation, deprecates all this nonsense about good comradeship. Though experienced campaigner, was warm in his feeling about 'going to marry his girl.'

NARCISSISM

The criteria for this trait were self-centredness, touchiness in self-esteem (Murray's "infavoidance"), preoccupation with own bodily prowess, appearance and self-adornment, pride, vanity, etc. It included concern about personal status (rank, exhibition of War decorations) as well as the displacement of personal narcissism to the military or national group. The derivation of this sort of narcissism is held to be a reaction to insecurity feelings—the result of not feeling loved and of feeling rejected, hence having to withdraw libido from outer objects and bestow an undue proportion on the Self (secondary narcissism). Three point rating scale.

EXAMPLES:

Score 1(a). *Gross:* Case 56. Major, Paratroops, Age 35.

Aloof, conceited, pleased with himself, under which is great fear of showing his despair and emptiness. His recipe for living (abridged): 'A woman always looks first whether a man is polite, correct and properly dressed . . . Every woman gets angry if a good-looking man does not show her attention . . . You must play tennis well—correctly, surely—let the girl do the running about . . . and dance well—but miss a beat in a quick step if it maintains your dignity. . . . I have never been completely in love or drunk—never let your blood get the better of you.'

Score 1(b). *Gross:* Case 87. C.P.O. U-boat, Age 25.

Revolted from 'unhealthy' life in a bakery where he might contract lung trouble. Spent all his spare time in open air swimming pools and gymnasia, and became an 'ace' among his admiring club-mates. No time for serious relationships. Found all the girls wanting—he sees through people so quickly. Kept himself aloof—how could anyone lower himself to get drunk like a swine! Touchy to 'insults' by interrogators. Fastidious, manicured, conceited. Defensive head mannerism when talking.

Score 2(a). *Perceptibly heightened:* Case 109. Lt. Artillery, Age 22.

Cocky, conceited. Despises the common herd. Boasts of his feats of strength and toughness. Intolerant of criticism or differing opinions.

Score 2(b). *Perceptibly heightened:* Case 83. Captain—Pilot, Age 30.

A swell. Enquires rank of interviewer. Asking for better face-cream and bothers welfare officer daily for nail-file. Apologetic he has not shaved when visited unexpectedly. Contempt for all inferior races. Personal charm, very open to flattery by remarks about his chestful of medals.

INFERIORITY FEELINGS

This trait overlapped with narcissisms of which it is an aspect. It was listed separately in an attempt to rate evidence of disturbed narcissism, as expressed in the gap between level of aspiration ('a person like me ought to be capable of so much') and subjective self-valuation. Personal inferiority and its displacements to the group are both included as evidence. Unequivocal over-compensations are rated as part of the symptoms. Three point scale:

EXAMPLES:
Score 1. *Gross:* Case 81. Wireless Operator, Air Force. Age 24.

Anxious, and touchy about only having elementary schooling. Feels unwanted by his stepfather. Weak and delicate, decided to become a flyer and hero. (Covered with combat medals). 'As a soldier one does not feel fear.' Deeply hurt by a "high British Officer' who offended his soldierly honour. 'I must not be thought a cad.' 'I could not survive the disgrace of defeat, I would commit suicide rather than become a Russian serf.'

Score 2(a). *Perceptibly heightened:* Case 93. Stoker Petty Officer
    (Reserve), Age 42.

'I am only a small man.' 'I did my duty, nobody can blame me.' 'We are desperate, poor little Germany' (marked personal identification).

Score 2(b). *Perceptibly heightened:* Case 123. Sgt. Flak, Age 29.

Felt a weakling, owing to games prohibition—outgrew his strength. Refused a commission as not 'fitted enough.' Very defensive about the superiority of German institutions, but also said 'The German is so silly and impressionable, he cannot be allowed to think for himself.'

PROJECTION

This trait category included paranoid mechanisms, from the upper limit of gross clinical systematised persecution symptoms and suspicion to emotionally charged, extra-punitive scapegoat devices, self-exculpation, bitterness, innuendo, and touchiness. Rating took into consideration the degree of insight present. An attempt was always made to allow for social stereotypes and for recent experiences. Three point scale:

EXAMPLES:

Score 1. *Gross:* Case 205. Lt. Cdr., Engineer, Age 34.

Father always felt to be an overpowering man. Felt he was his weak Mother's most difficult child, different from the siblings. Always shy. As a boy felt others were laughing at him. Felt unappreciated as a human being and only valued for his technical ability. Had acute terror episode when he felt he was being influenced by British secret rays to become a traitor. Also felt sure the British were bent on annihilating Germany. Reacts to political interrogation with *tu quoque* arguments, and is on defensive before he is even attacked by argument.

Score 2. *Perceptibly heightened:* Case 106. Lt. "Special duties"
    (German Propaganda Service), Age 33.

Scents division, intrigue and secret plotting everywhere. Felt he was envied his post at the Ministry of Propaganda. An undermining, intriguing type who offered his services to British psychological warfare, he is full of specious rationalizations of his conduct and blames his duplicity 'on the way they have treated me.' He felt 'there was a spirit of revolution abroad' among the German people (1943), which was unfounded and clearly a projection of his own renegade, anti-father feelings. A hint of messianic flavour in his intention to found a new movement of national regeneration.

Score 3. *Normal limits:* Case 110. W/T operator. Air Crew. Age 22.

Even standard propaganda displacements (e.g., to Jews and Slavs) are much reduced as compared with many POWs. He carefully distinguishes between 'the man who looks much like himself' and economic theory, and recognised that Slav and German could live well together. No personal animosities or suspicions. Optimistic about his personal future.

HYPOCHONDRIA

This term denoted morbid preoccupation with minor complaints, fear of disease or of the serious nature of trivial ailments; fads and anxieties about the purity and wholesomeness of food and drink, about vitamins, etc., but excluded any fears of being poisoned, etc., by the captors. Anxiety states, hysterical symptoms and true "somatic paranoid" hypochondriases were included. The rating, on a three point scale, was in terms of the severity of clinical picture and of the depth of aetiology.

The postulated psychological basis for including this variable is the interplay between projection and introjection mechanisms found in relation to a "bad object," in Klein's sense. This bad object introjected may become an "internal persecutor" (like a cancer or T.B. phobia)—or projected, when it is phantasied as an "external persecutor"—as under "Projection" above.

In view of the purely clinical nature of this well-known symptom, examples are scarcely required.

PSYCHONEUROTIC ANXIETY

This trait category was used as a "blunderbuss" term to cover a variety of more than transient, overt neurotic symptoms, short of projection or hypochondria above, such as free-floating anxiety, psycho-somatic conversions and phobic or compulsive states including stammers and tics. No attempt at exact clinical differentiation was made in the scoring, but a three point scale rated degree of severity and involvement of the personality in the symptoms.

Examples would cover the familiar syndromes and are omitted.

DEPRESSION

This variable includes the usual sense of that term in psychiatry, to denote the presence of any degree of affective disorder characterized by hopelessness, morose introspection, self-blame and self-destructive trends, associated with observable physical and behaviour symptoms such as "flexion" and retardation. A three point scale was used. Examples are scarcely required.

Unfortunately, the complementary trait of mania was omitted. Neither were of any significance as it turned out. Only one distinctly hypomaniac individual was observed.

SCHIZOID TENDENCIES

This heading covered only those cases in which a clinically morbid degree of personality split or thought disorder was observed. It overlaps to some extent with ambivalence and split libido, which also represent some degree of dissociation or instinct diffusion, and of course with paranoid trends. Here we included such phenomena as loss of reality sense, depersonalisation; increase in the phantasy content of thinking; extreme shyness; asocial withdrawal tendencies; stereotypy; and "simplicity" and immaturity not warranted by level of general intelligence, especially when associated with the classical bodily configuration. It was found possible to score this category only in terms of presence or absence. The point was to try to differentiate between a personal psychopathy and the almost endemic German cultural split between affective and thought processes and between private and collective standards of value.

Apart from the social data recorded under *Table 3*, there were thus 17 main variables, with a provision for sixty different scores under their heads, either as qualitative distinctions or intensity ratings. In addition there was provision under each main variable for the "No inference made" score.

6. RECORDING OF DATA

As stated, case histories were recorded at first by hand, later by dictation, immediately after the interview(s). Looking through these records after a lapse of some five to seven years, it is clear that in this respect technique varied a good deal from bad to good. Scores were assigned immediately, and reviewed in the light of other known data (documents, testimony of camp-mates, ex-shipmates, other interrogators, and special modes of observation). In most cases the record was a long narrative, but in some of the later cases the relevant material was recorded under the "17 variables," with a general rounding off of the personality history and description at the beginning and end of the record. In four cases it was possible to obtain near-ver-batim records (in German) of the interviews: these were in addition written up as above with relevant passages of the verbatim notes marked and referenced for the relevant variable.

There was, of course, no way of keeping the men off political topics, and some of this necessarily formed part of the evidence. In such events an attempt was made to gauge the personal emo-tional involvement in the political or military views expressed. The F-rating was copied from the Political Schedule Item B (See *Table 1*).

Next, a set of "hand Hollerith" cards of standard format were obtained, round the margins of which all scorable items of the social data, political variables (including F rating) and psycho-logical variables were represented by a coded box. The scores were marked in the appropriate box on a separate card for each subject and re-checked for accuracy.

7. TREATMENT OF DATA

Mr. Edward A. Shils, then serving in the United Kingdom with a branch of the U.S. War Organisation, was acting as un-official adviser to the writer during this investigation, and the coding and statistical treatment of the data were his contribu-tion. In view of pressure of other work we decided that 138 was a sample just adequate for the χ^2 technique.

For purposes of testing the significance of our data against the F ratings, the scores were grouped in conformity with the preliminary hypothesis.

The political scores were divided into a Nazi and near-Nazi

group comprising the *F.I* and *F.II,* and a non-Nazi group composed of the *F.III, IV* and *V.*

The Mother Cathexis data were divided into those where the Mother-bond was given to an actual real female love object (scores (*a*) and (*b*)), and those in whom it was transferred to an ideal figure, human or institutional (scores (*c*) and (*d*)). Score (*e*), the religious displacement, was not included as it was felt to belong to the "religion" variable. The Father Cathexis data were divided so as to include all scores indicating an alignment with the father on one side, and the alignment against the father on the other. Therefore scores (*a*), (*b*), and (*c*) were lumped together, and (*d*) and (*e*) formed the counter-grouping.

Under Sadism the three so-called "anti-social" scores (1, 2, 3) were grouped together, and the three "social" scores were joined (4, 5, 6).

The "man's own religious attitude" category scores were so grouped as to contrast Church-adherence (*a*), (*b*) with militant non-church adherence (anti-Christianity) (*d*), (*e*) and both these with easy-going indifference (*c*).

The remainder of the scores under each main variable were divided into groups in whom the characteristic studied was absent or present. In the case of three-point scale ratings the "gross" and "perceptibly heightened" data were joined against the "normal limits" scores in respect of each variable.

It will be seen that this enabled us to recast the question of our hypothesis into a statistical form. The original question, it will be recalled, might have run: 'Is the Nazi a person who has had to reject his good mother-object in favour of submitting to a threatening father to whom he is fixated, so that he remains to a clinically distinguishable degree ambivalent, split in his libido, unconsciously homosexual, guilt-laden and unable to let his sadism mature into socially acceptable (loving or restitution-making) form, defensively narcissistic in order to protect himself from his guilt and inferiority which nevertheless betray themselves in heightened tendencies to project and to suffer neurotic anxiety, with special liability to hypochondriacal preoccupation with bad internal objects, and does he show any marked psychotic personality traits? And does he in this sense differ markedly from his non-Nazi compatriots?' The statistical expression of these two questions was cast into the tetrachoric formula, and calculated as shown in *Table 4*. By good fortune,

TABLE 4

	F rating			F %			χ²	Probabi...
	High (I+II)	Low (III, IV, V)	Total	High (I, II)	Low (III, IV, V)	Total		
Parent dominance								Unreliable
1 Equal	31	41	72	·43	·57	1.00		
2 Mother +	23	26	49	·47	·53	1.00		
3 Father +	54	67	121	·45	·55	1.00		
Man's religious adherence							27.8	Between 0 and 0.001 Statistically significant
1 Roman Cath. (strict)	17	26	43	·40	·60	1.00		
2 Protestant (strict)								
3 Nazi (Gottgl)	30	5	35	·86	·14	1.00		
4 Atheist etc.	18	40	58	·31	·69	1.00		
5 Indifferent	65	71	136	·48	·52	1.00		
Father Cathexis Father							10.3	0.00137 approx. Statistically significant
1 Mature object choice	58	52	110	·53	·47	1.00		
2 Persisting father identification								
3 Partial identification								
Anti-Father								
4 Rebel	4	20	24	·17	·83	1.00		
5 Mother identification	62	72	134	·46	·54	1.00		
Mother Cathexis							21.5	Less than Statistically significant
1 Still attached to Mother	32	62	94	·34	·66	1.00		
2 Transf. to female partner								
3 Transf. to Führer	33	10	43	·78	·22	1.00		
4 Transf. to State or Service								
	65	72	137	·47	·53	1.00		
Guilt Feelings							1.5	0.22067 Unreliable
1 Gross	44	42	86	·51	·49	1.00		
2 Perceptibly heightened	21	31	52	·40	·60	1.00		
3 Normal limits	65	73	138	·47	·53	1.00		
Tenderness Taboo							6.7	0.00964 Statistically significant
Present	37	25	62	·60	·40	1.00		
Absent	23	40	63	·37	·63	1.00		
	60	65	125	·48	·52	1.00		
Ambivalence							2.4	0.12134 Unreliable
1 Gross, obvious amb.	51	49	100	·51	·49	1.00		
2 Perceptibly heightened	13	23	36	·36	·64	1.00		
3 Normal or absent	64	72	136	·47	·53	1.00		

TABLE 4 (contd.)

	F rating			F %			χ^2	Probability
	High (I+II)	Low (III, IV, V)	Total	High (I, II)	Low (III, IV, V)	Total		
dism*							12.63	
ati-Social (1, 2, 3)	42	26	68	.62	.38	1.00		
cial (4, 5, 6)	21	46	67	.32	.68	1.00		Less than 0.01
	63	72	135	.47	.53	1.00		Statistically significant
mosexual trends							4.1	0.04288
Gross ⎫ Perceptibly heightened ⎬	46	39	85	.54	.46	1.00		Statistically significant
Normal	18	32	50	.36	.64	1.00		
	64	71	135	.47	.53	1.00		
rcissism							1.7	0.19229
Gross ⎫ erceptibly heightened ⎬	49	46	95	.52	.48	1.00		Unreliable
Normal	17	26	43	.40	.60	1.00		
	66	72	138	.48	.52	1.00		
eriority feelings							1.3	0.2541
Gross ⎫ erceptibly heightened ⎬	41	39	80	.51	.49	1.00		
Normal	24	34	58	.41	.59	1.00		Unreliable
	65	73	138	.47	.53	1.00		
jection							.88	0.00301
ross ⎫ erceptibly heightened ⎬	45	30	75	.60	.40	1.00		Statistically significant
ormal	21	40	61	.34	.66	1.00		
	66	70	136	.49	.51	1.00		
iety							4.2	0.04042
ross symptoms ⎫ erceptible symptoms ⎬	49	43	92	.53	.47	1.00		Statistically significant
ormal	16	30	46	.35	.65	1.00		
	65	73	138	.47	.53	1.00		
ression							0.24	0.6242
ross symptoms ⎫ ilder symptoms ⎬	23	28	51	.45	.55	1.00		Unreliable
ormal	42	43	85	.49	.51	1.00		
	65	71	136	.48	.52	1.00		
zoid features							.050	0.4463
esent	4	7	11	.36	.64	1.00		
sent	61	65	126	.48	.52	1.00		Unreliable
	65	72	137	.47	.53	1.00		

ꜱ: (1) Any distribution-probability of 0.05 or less is statisically significant.
   (2) Split libido and Hypochondria were omitted from the table as unreliable.
   (3) Where numbers in the first total column add to less than 138, the difference shows the number of cases in whom "No inference made" was scored for a given variable.
dly recalculated as above by Mr. J. L. Boreham.

there were, as it turned out, roughly equal numbers of high *Fs* (I and II) and low *Fs* (III, IV and V).

Discussion

These statistical tables show that under the conditions and with the method of study used the following variables showed significant relationship to the political attitude or *F* factor:—

(i) A man's religious alignment; the solution of the Oedipus situation in respect both to (ii) the Mother and (iii) the Father cathexes; (iv) Tenderness Taboo; (v) Sadism; (vi) Homosexuality; (vii) Projection; (viii) Neurotic anxiety.

Within the limits of a paper in a periodical the discussion of these correlations will have to be confined to the narrow context of the study here described, and the temptation to enter fully into the relationship of German culture, institutions and character with the Nazi movement resisted.

It must be remembered that *in this study* it was only proposed to test the hypothesis that certain variables, abstracted from a Gestalt which for short could be termed "German national character" would be found in greater amount or concentration in more Nazi personalities than in other Germans. The scoring was designed for this purpose and is otherwise meaningless in that it includes major characteristics of the entire human race as viewed from the psycho-analytic position. Its meaningfulness arises from the conjunction or cluster of variables to form a syndrome which emerges as having significance from the statistical assay.

1. The German Character

For the sake of readers not familiar with this field, a very brief abstract of the formulation of the basic adult male German character (disregarding finer shades due to subgroup variation) must therefore precede the main argument. This outline is culled from the writer's *Psychological Foundations of the Wehrmacht* (2), supplemented by references to Kecskemeti and Leites's study. (11). There are several studies on the German character written from the psycho-dynamic angle which should be consulted (1), (2), (4), (8), (9), (11), (13), (14), (15) and which are borne out by the findings of this report.

The "average" member of the Wehrmacht can be described

as tense, earnest, industrious, meticulous, over-respectful to authority and anxious to impress. He is a martinet in his dealings with his social inferiors and his subordinates. He is very touchy about status. He requires uniformity and order, and is uneasy in unforeseen situations. He suffers from the *sentiment d'incomplétude*. In contrast to his striving for clarity and efficiency is his tendency to value, and search for, the depths of experience, that richness of emotional satisfaction he feels to be unattainable except by flinging away bourgeois restraints and fetters. He idealises his women in their role as mothers and as objects towards whom libidinal aim-inhibition is demanded; but he also depreciates them socially and sexually on the plane of reality: the typical German home is patriarchally structured.

Conformity and "loyalty," as of a servant to his master, are rated among the highest virtues, and demonstratively stressed in home and institutional life, almost as synonymous with "honour" on the one hand and with unquestioning obedience on the other. The emphasis on persevering toil as the goal of a burdensome life patiently if ostentatiously borne, is part of this pattern. Of a dominant person severity, imposingness, and hardness are expected, and love and admiration reactions towards it vary directly with the severity and punitiveness of the authority figure. A weak authority is despised, and hostile feelings towards it break surface. This associates the typically weaker, yielding mother with contempt, as one of those under paternal domination.

The mother-seeking tendencies, whether of sadistic or of passive colouring, are banned from personal awareness and form the background of guilt which the ready acceptance of "manly" father-submissive attitudes covers. The German mother, indulgent and over-protective especially to the favoured male baby in his early years, yet also connives at this "masculine" build-up of her son. She provides no adequate counter-weight to the father, but by culturally imposed inconsistency increases her son's guilt and confusion by furtive rewards behind the father's back.

Allegiance to paternal authority is furthered by the projection of the German's own repressed aggressive feelings to the authority itself, thereby increasing the estimate of that figure's punitiveness. Typically, non-conforming aggressive trends against authority are dealt with by identification with the authority and by counter-cathexis or reaction formation against the offending impulses. This leads to a kind of "surrender of the ego" in favour of authority, with the result of "externalising the super-ego." This is demonstrated in a reliance on social norms and clearly defined duties rather than on inner conduct regulation. Ego deficiency creates a sense of weakness or emptiness with consequent craving for depth and completeness.

The widespread impairment of personal autonomy leads to over-compensatory stress on secondary narcissism. This is shown on the personal level not only in status anxiety but also in brooding concern over individual "problems," in attempts to preserve areas of strict "privacy" in the personality, and in the cultivation of a "distinctive character" façade. On the group level we see the well-known national self-inflation of "Germanism" as much richer and "Kultur"-giving than lesser, shallower, un-understanding breeds of men, hence as entitled to lead and to gain the lead by any means.

The uncertainty of self-valuation leads Germans to the need to define status *vis-à-vis* all persons and groups and to violent fluctuation in "total" omnipotence and "total" impotence feelings; between the magical powers of their will and their self-assumed "efficiency" and sudden caving-in when confronted with "overwhelming facts" against which even titanic, "colossal" efforts are vain. While it is manly to struggle with hard "fate," it is useless to defy "inscrutable, inexorable destiny."

Direct return of repressed aggression is manifested in the handling of weaker persons, as, for example, children or inferiors in rank. In this situation the identification with a stern authority is given full play accompanied by a sense of moral rectitude. It is also frequently shown as touchiness, quarrelsomeness, and more importantly as an expectation of aggression on the part of others (individuals or outgroups) against whom one must be on guard. Germans seem to be readily insulted. This reaction is likely to be a mixture of id projections and displaced super-ego (authority) re-projections.

Displaced or vicarious satisfaction for aggressive needs which had undergone early repression is found in collective power symbols, or in support of projects for group aggrandisement, which promise fulfilment of forgone instinct gratifications in a millennium of plenty and of harmony.

A revalued return of masochistic longings is also typically

exhibited in the stereotyped idealisation of "loyalty-conformity" *(Treue)* as the acme of "manliness"; the image being that of an obstinate, unruly boy who is hammered into shape and "tempered" into dogged virility by a strong father-figure, represented for example by military induction. Repressed anti-paternal tendencies used also to have some degree of sanctioned outlet in the "adolescent revolt," when the young German would go "wandering" in search of "freedom," pseudo-adventurously, communing with Nature, flinging away sexual and urban restraint, but in reality evading rather than facing the conflict with authority. Fathers often secretly connived at this adolescent procedure, in the knowledge that it was the prelude to later conformity. It is in this wanderlust stage that conformity itself is often shown in the formation of gangs with "older brother" leaders, the whole group then defying "senile" authority without fears.

For the rest, "freedom" needs have mostly been transferred to the national group which, characteristically, should have no restraints or limits to its omnipotence, precisely because the personal ego is experienced as weak, helpless and the sport of inner and outer forces. Here an id projection is clearly at work. Against this infantile greed and omnipotence, now displaced to the needs of the group and moralistically rationalised as *Lebensraum* or as the inescapable consequences of *Machtpolitik* inherent in the struggle for existence, there militate the sated, rich, or covetous older rivals who want to keep the poor little German from his rightful heritage ("a place in the sun" as Kaiser Wilhelm put it). The German oscillated between virtuous, meek acceptance of deprivations inflicted by his own authority and the impatient rejection of the sense of inferior status in the eyes of sibling-nations.

The picture is thus mainly one of an ambivalent, compulsive character structure with the emphasis on submissive/dominant conformity, a strong counter-cathexis of the virtues of duty, of "control" by the self, especially buttressed by re-projected "external" super-ego symbols. In this norm bound, burdened pattern there occur episodic "release" symptoms. Individually they are—attacks of rage, as when "unauthorised" encroachments are made on the jealously guarded ego-core. The release symptoms on the group level we have witnessed between 1864 and 1945. Both are often rationalised as "the end of the tether." Group "outbursts" are exculpated chiefly by projective mechanisms either as defensive wars justified by the danger threatening from dangerous (potency or status-menacing) external forces, or else as leading to "rewards" or "dues" for patiently borne deprivations implicit in excessive intra-group and personal self-control. Courage is drawn for these aggressive outbursts from group sanctions in joint loyalty to a good super-ego leader figure (Bismarck, Kaiser, Hitler) who takes responsibility and so incidentally shoulders the guilt of failure.

Hierarchical pyramidal patterns for social institutions with the Army as the model and apex were created as the most appropriate to meet the needs of such a character structure.

2. The Significant Variables

Returning now to an attempt to evaluate the data obtained from the personality studies in more detail it will be convenient to change slightly the order of the variables which were found to be significant as differentiating high-F-scoring German soldiers from their low-F-scoring compatriots.

1. *Father Cathexis*

By definition of this variable, and from the general outline of the German character in Section 1, it was expected that the type of person active in promoting the Nazi regime would show a high degree of identification with a harsh, authoritarian father-object, with all that this implies in the way of defence against feelings of "weakness" i.e., against making demands for indulgences on the mother. The successful maintenance of the father figure as good demanded the sternest counter-cathexis against doubt or criticism, and led to fanaticism or dogmatism, "total" conformity and "obedience" exalted as "loyalty" (*Treue*). The emergence of the militant Nazis in leadership roles favoured their assuming the characteristics of *successful* father or older brother behaviour in relation to less-ranking people towards whom the exercise of command and power was expected by the culture pattern. It was remarkable that even in cases where the real father was described as indulgent, the culture, through various secondary father figures, managed by the time adolescence was reached to turn the balance towards the identification with (or incorporation of) the collective stern, male super-ego norm, through which authoritarian, aggressive behaviour receives its group sanction. Aggression could operate without conscious guilt by this direct, super-ego permitted path. Part of the aggression connected to the bad fraction of the Father object was utilized in wielding stepped-down *Führer* power over subordinates. The rest of the "bad father" complex was displaced to various outgroup symbols, especially "rich old men" images such as the British (John Bull) or the Americans ("Jewish financiers").

Untransformed id aggression against the parents is persecuted partly in "weaker" people who become the bearers of repressed needs, such as the "greediness," "secret plotting" or "dirtiness" of Jews, Russians, and other scapegoat figures who "contaminate" the purity or ferment disunity by their "hyper-critical" liberal ideas. German civilians fared hardly better than nationals of occupied countries in these men's esteem. The allied leaders were felt to share fully the destructive punitive characteristics of bad fathers, and this was taken as a matter of course. Another part of id aggression found outlet through the "revolutionary" *élan* of National Socialism, purporting to be the uprising of the young, iconoclastic builders of the millennium of the blond supermen against the weakening corrupt Christian-bourgeois rule of "arterio-sclerotic" *(verkalkte)* elders. In this phantasy-system Hitler played the role of the ever-young rebel older brother, himself a self-avowed oppressed "little man," and received the full positive father-cathexis.

Those who scored "equivocal Oedipus solutions" had histories of suppressing their regressive longings for indulgence or their artistic natures associated with mother values.

2. *Mother Cathexis*

The chief inference from the prevalence in the high-F class of scores indicating gross transfer of mother-significance to political or institutional symbols is this: passivity and affection can only be expressed in relation to objects sanctioned by the Nazi sub-culture. To be tied to a female was the equivalent of being feminine or weak oneself. One could be married, but this bond counted for less than the State, the Party or the Service. The possibility of a false skew in the high F results under this variable exists in that the sample contained an undue proportion of naval personnel serving regular engagements, sometimes motivated by bad home background. It is not unusual for men in any country to "go to sea" under the deeper pressure of "prodigal son," restless, security-seeking impulses and to attach maternal values to the ship in which they serve. Even Germans call their ships "She." Even so, the withdrawal of libido from real women, and the co-existence of father identifications in the same group shows the nature of the process at work, laying the subject open to acceptance of Nazi authoritarianism.

Equally significant in this variable is the correlation between low F ratings and the capacity for frank loving relationship to female objects. German prisoners with good object relations to a loved, and presumably loving woman were less prone to libidinize military or political institutions with excessive cathexis, in disregard of other human values and relationships. It is well known how anxious the Nazi leaders were to win more citizens over to a "We" consciousness, away from private allegiances, toward investing most of their love in the metaphysical "National community" with strongly emphasized "Mother Earth" attributes.

3. Religious Adherence

The table supplements what has just been said. The Churches, more especially the Catholic church, formed the one remaining counter-weight to state totalitarianism in Germany, opposing it with their own claims on the individual. "Mother cathexis" (and it usually was the mother of the subject who had had the religious influence) transferred to a religious body was less likely also to flow towards Party or other "man-made" groups. This is not the place to go into the details of the interesting differences between German Catholic and Protestant attitudes in respect of the demands of the State on the individual or of the influence on individual or group structure.

What is perhaps even more significant in the table is the high correlation between high F and the vague deistic mumbo-jumbo which was professed by the FI and II. Essentially this was a creed of fatalistic belief in a Higher Providence modelled on the German Super-ego, a tribal deity which had placed Germany in the centre of the Universe and had sent trials of strength to this unique nation, destined for leadership. The *gottgläubig*, or God-believer, was at one and the same time rejecting "effeminate" pacifist Judaeo-Christianity and "godless" Marxist materialism. A number of the latter with some of the toughest nihilistic Nazis made up the "Atheist" scores.

It was not unexpected that the "easy-going indifferent" group correlated on the whole with low F scores as here defined. In other contexts religious puritanism and secular political fanaticism might well form a joint group to be contrasted with this category.

4. *Tenderness Taboo*

The result throws additional light on the fate of dependent and passive love needs in men who have remained identified with a punitive father-image, in which hardness was a virtue and softness a failure. Softness was equated with impotence, surrender and femininity; hardness with steely nerves, potency and manliness in crudest metaphor of childish evaluation of parental roles. To behave like a poor frightened, soft-hearted mother would also be to give way to tender, passive desires towards the father. Any awareness of such tendencies becomes tabooed, together with those activities, objects, and interests which associate with feminine values: love of the arts, protective tenderness to weaker things, expressions of sensitivity, affection or *finesse* in relation to life. Expressions of tenderness would also be unconsciously equated with regression towards a favoured state of infancy in which sphincter-control was not yet demanded, nor an ascetic check placed on the enjoyment of the maternal body and caresses. To betray such a weakness would thus signify a treason against the father and a preference for the mother. The picture is that of the "affectionless character," with affinities to the tough delinquent personality.

5. *Sadism*

The results of the correlations are in keeping with expectations. It was interesting that the people scoring under "overt, gleeful" were of three kinds: the "elegant pansies" who demanded hair-nets and face cream from their captors; the innocent "baby-face" boys; and the thin-lipped film villains. We may see in the sadistic attitudes of the first two the operation of reaction formations against passive tenderness-seeking trends in "spoilt-boys," who have turned their frustration rage resulting from deprivation into a pattern of revenge. One also gained the impression that the need to recoup oneself for a sense of weakness by exerting power over something had a kind of therapeutic value to the subject—e.g., as in discharging machine-guns at distant victims or kicking elderly Jewesses, de-humanized symbols of repressed primary good objects that had to become bad. The slight displacement of sadistic power-needs to phallically or anally-invested weapons ensured conformity with the militaristic norm of the "100 per cent. thoroughgoing soldier." The lack of permitted good objects in the world of the over-sternly educated, wooden-faced disciplinarians makes other people either objects of abject devotion if they are in dominance over them, or else into unreal, faecal part-objects to mould, destroy, attack or bully as the sole means of feeling reality and "emotion." The Nazi-German tendency to speak of people as "human material," as "racial groups" or as "flocks of sheep" was of a piece with this depreciation of human values. Here is another aspect of the affectionless character who has been forced to repress his good objects and gain the approval of the sadistic super-ego by compulsively "going one better" in the persecution of bad objects.

By contrast the so called "social" transformations of aggressiveness by maturation or by reaction-formation of a restitutive or "depressive" pattern (accepting inner control and responsibility) betoken a much less disturbed even if ambivalent, relation to early objects which is reflected in the concern shown to preserve them.

As a curious antinomy to the prevalence of aggression, there is in Germans of all types a squeamishness and dislike of avowing or of facing aggression, as shown by their submissiveness in the face of strong or imposing behaviour, and in their avoidance of direct reference to aggressive acts. No military vocabulary has such a wealth of circumlocution to express brutality; few armies have taken greater pains to make war impersonal and out of sight of the enemy's face. Germany took the utmost pains to keep the enemy at arm's length and away from the homeland. This would seem to be an effort at warding off assault and castration fears from the self. The "Sadists" (as herein defined) had identified themselves with a castrating authority expected to do terrible things to one if he got within range, and did these horrible things themselves. If results on oppressed victims were not as they expected, they would say, "we have not been hard enough."

The non-sadists felt the "enemy" to be placatable by "good"

behaviour on their part, and in any case sufficiently potent for good to preserve and cherish, mostly by typical compulsive re-action formations. Their ambivalence was less and not so rigor-ously polarized into "Black" and "White."

6. Homosexuality

The scores in this variable confirm the expectation that passive subordination to a severe, punitive father whom it is necessary to love, should result in the heightening of uncon-scious homosexuality. Its significance for the subject tended to be disguised or countered by the already mentioned revaluation of such submissive feelings as "manly," if they concerned au-thority or leader figures. Being beaten in childhood, being drilled and bullied during military training were socially and individually valued as pleasant and fortifying experiences. Such experiences held in common cemented the typical "adolescent gang" comradeship of the Armed Forces and especially its *élite* units filled with Nazis, their bonds strengthened by common devotion to a leader (Hitler especially but also many subordi-nate heroes of the "ace" type). Such leader worship was often expressed in highly lyrical, barely desexualized terms.

Homosexual traits, as signifying a "masculine protest" de-fence, have already been related to the depreciation of "fem-inine" values and interests, and to the glorification of manly strength. It is a well-established psychoanalytic finding that the homosexual's fear of women is at bottom the dread of being like them. The trait thus links up with tenderness taboo and its antecedents. It is one way in which ambivalent love needs of affectionless characters can be expressed in clumsy, adolescent fashion as an institutionalised "cult of manliness" akin to Spar-tan practice. This way was institutionalised by German milita-rism.

7. Projection

The finding indicates that the high *F* scorers had typically managed to re-project their super-ego, i.e., their father image highly charged with punitive and destructive qualities. In so far as the culture norm and indeed individual situations de-manded an emphasis on the positive or love aspect towards such an authority, the negative or hate aspect of the ambivalence had to be displaced away from the personal and the in-group authority in order to preserve these as good. In these people both primary hate and later criticism or rebellion against the super-ego-authority had to be warded off. In this way the self and the authority could remain blameless and loveworthy. The attribution of hostility to any stranger, common enough in German culture, becomes a necessity for sadistic individuals, so that they can justify their aggression as counter-aggression and self-defence. Nazi propaganda has shown many examples of this tendency and has provided the group with images for this purpose. The scapegoats were split further into Id-images (the greedy Jew or the blood-thirsty Bolshevik), and "disappointing" near ingroup images, such as the treacherous British "Nordic" brothers who had created the Versailles treaty and now further betrayed Aryan solidarity by fighting on the "Id" side. The reader is referred to the remarks made in this connection under Father cathexis above.

In a written record it is not easy to convey the difference between those who were merely believing the Nazi version of recent history in a country with a controlled press, and those to whom guilt projection, self-justification and narcissistic touchy bitterness about the necessity to be brutal in order to make the world safe from "inferior vermin" was a dire need of preserving their personality. Perhaps the most stereotyped attitude ran like this: "all these scheming sophisticated enemies around us have abused our notorious unsuspecting simplicity, goodness, and softness. But if they think us such fools as to submit to their will to destroy us, we will know how to defeat their evil intent with the greatest ruthlessness; now we shall act without mercy or scruple . . ." Lack of insight into the effect on their neighbours of prior aggressions committed by the Germans themselves followed the pattern of *"Cet animal est très méchant; quand on l'attaque il se defend,"* whereas this very same idea was often used by high F Germans in self-justification. The cognate stereotype was: 'I cannot understand why we nice Germans, of all people, should be hated by everybody.' The frequent expectations of annihilation, castration, etc., at the hands of the Allies in case of their victory have already been referred to as the responses of high F scorers in the political interview.

8. Neurotic Anxiety

That high F scorers should have reacted with neurotic symptoms twice as frequently as their compatriots was at first sight a surprising result. So far as combatant stress was concerned, the risks and experiences of the high and the low F scorers had been similar. Most of the POWs belonged to service units where both physiological and personality screening might have been expected to weed out predisposed men, such as Flying personnel, U-boat crews and armoured corps. In this respect the high Fs tended to be "better" specimens. On reflection, however, the finding was consistent with that conception of the outbreak of neurotic symptoms which stresses the importance of social factors on the integration of personality. The difference between the high and low F scorers must have been in the meaning of capture and of the loss of their combatant status and service *milieu* to them. We already know that the high F personality is strongly extrapunitive, heteronomously regulated and supported in his morale by the combination of leader and comrades. The very fact of capture not only arouses paranoid fears about his captors' intentions. In doing so it also activates the deeper ambivalency conflicts which give rise to this persecutory anxiety. Passive impulses of surrender and admitting submission to the now proven stronger enemy (see above under German character) are no longer counteracted by the inner effects of all the forces of the Nazi-military brotherhood and leadership, but have to be fought off by the poor little ego alone, suddenly faced with a change from an armed potency role to a disarmed impotence role.

Looking over the case histories, somatic conversions of a hysterical type predominated in the clinical pictures. This accorded with the general impression by the writer and other observers that German soldiers in general tended to be terrified of admitting to "nervousness"; 'the German soldier has no nerves' ordained Hitler, who himself suffered from what was almost certainly hysterical blindness in World War I. The favourite alibi for moral weakness or "collapse" was physical, i.e., projected to the somatic sphere. The genesis of these neurotic symptoms was thus a way of canalizing guilt at capture ("weakness") and anxiety at being abandoned by supporting authorities and faced by hostile authorities whom they now wanted to be loving authorities. Self-punishment, quasi-medical self-justification and a veiled but demonstrative appeal for sympathy and succour were expressed in these terms.

By contrast the less tensely super-ego-ruled and less internally persecuted characters of the low *Fs* were able to adjust more easily. In some cases psycho-somatic disorder was present in them before capture when it signified anti-service protest. For the rest it occurred chiefly in the conflict-torn "good-soldier but-not-a-Nazi" *F III* personalities whom it was decided, as will be recalled, to class with non-Nazis for statistical stringency.

3. The Non-Significant Variables

Despite the fact that some of the selected variables, which were included on the strength of the preliminary hypothesis, did not discriminate between the high and low *F* scorers, a few words about these are in place. No more need be said about *guilt* which was sufficiently criticized in the Section on Psychological Background Data.

Parent Dominance was too crude and superficial a concept, and invited such descriptions as 'When I was small it was Mother but later it was Father,' or 'each in their proper sphere,' etc. The observation by field workers, or else the inferences from other data among our material, would have been more informative on this point. Most observers are in fact agreed on the regularity of father dominance in the great majority of German homes. Even the partially dissentient Rodnick (13) brings much evidence in favour of this situation, though he is apparently not fully aware of the ambivalent depreciation-idealization split governing the status of women in German society.

Ambivalence was evidently too generalised a trait in the culture to use as a discriminating variable in this study. The numbers were too small to justify re-combinations. By definition the most divided men were the *F III* rated as non-Nazis. Even so, it is the writer's impression that the pattern of ambivalence was different in the high *F* scorers and the low *F* group. Whereas the low *Fs* tended to be torn between the good and bad qualities of their own authorities (Nazi regime, trust in their propaganda) and hence also to be partly disloyal and favouring the Allies, democracy, etc., the high *Fs* had polarized their good and bad objects rigidly: divine Hitler-Germany versus satanic enemies. The split was more extreme, there were no shades of grey.

Libido split failed completely as a discriminating factor. There were many unmarried men, the majority of the sample had spent three or more years in service conditions and so on. The impression remains that the attitude to the mother which brings about this phenomenon is widely dispersed in German culture. The psychological factor really tested for was affectionless sensuality and this emerged more clearly in the data about Tenderness taboo, sadism and homosexuality.

Narcissism and its closely co-varying inferiority feelings were a "disappointment," as can be seen by referring back to the formulation of the working hypotheses. Possibly, by sub-dividing "Gross" scorers from "perceptibly heightened" and normal, a different result might have been achieved, but that may be true of the other variables. The prevalence of narcissistic features as shown especially by touchiness about status and evidences of vanity and conceit seemed as independent of political attitude as possible, though the transfer of inflated ego needs and claims to the national group tended to be more common in the high F's. This possible differentiating factor, i.e., the displacement of secondary narcissism to group symbols was not followed up in this study.

The reason for the non-discriminatingness of *Inferiority Feelings* is easier to understand *a posteriori*. In this variable were recorded many such plaintive expressions as 'Who am I to judge such things? I am only a little man' or 'We Germans are everywhere disliked.' Some of these stereotyped statements by F III, IV and V were of a simpler "humble-pie eating," submissive character than the boastful, over-compensatory assertions of superiority by the F.I and II, which could be easily "cracked" to reveal very similar doubts about worth and potency. It might have been better to discriminate "compensatory superiority" and straight "inferiority" as variables, than to lump them together.

Depression and Schizoid tendencies were included without great expectations, but rather as a safeguard, especially as there was much talk of "madness" of the Nazis at that time. As regards depression, the table would seem to show merely that any loss of objects (through being captured) whether these be real people

or symbolic substitutes, was liable to cause depressive reactions
in a certain proportion of German prisoners of war.

4. The High *F* Syndrome

An attempt must now be made to formulate a coherent picture of the character structure of the high *F* scorer. Such a picture must be an abstraction, a genotype composed of the
essential trends and behaviour patterns of a large number of
individuals. To the writer such a delineation would have the
reality of experience as a frequently recurring stereotype of life
history, attitudes and views in persons he has known. To the
reader not already familiar with German and Nazi mentality
in living persons, a typical case is likely to be more acceptable,
and will now be quoted exactly as noted within a few minutes
after leaving his room seven years ago. Translations of German
terms have been added in parentheses. The method of recording
was that of grouping notes under the relevant variable headings.
These are somewhat condensed since a magnificently revealing
private diary formed a valuable source of detailed evidence, as
well as the frank comments of a group of Non-Nazi fellow-
P.O.W.'s whom the subject had managed to offend.

*Case 128, Junior Lt. "W.," German Army Signal Corps, Age 21.
Single. Captured Tunisia 15.3.43. Interview 15.9.43. 2½
hours*

Although only in Tunisia for a short time, W. appears to
have managed to be wounded twice and spent most of his service time in hospitals where he was eventually captured. He has
a few mild grouses about treatment by French and Americans
but not against the British.

Background. He is an *Auslandsdeutscher* (German domiciled
abroad). His father was a business man in Belgium, where W.
also went to a German *Oberschule* (High School) for six years.
At the *Umsturz* (Hitler's accession) in 1933 the father transferred to a German State Service and W's home has been in
various foreign cities. For two years he was at a N.S. *Politische
Erziehungsanstalt* (National Socialist Political Training College). Then, for some reason, he was taken away and went to a
private *Internat* (Boarding School) where he tried to do his
Abitur (University Matriculation Examination), but, according
to his diary, failed. After this he joined the Army. He does not

yet know what he wants to do in after-life as he has not got a regular commission.

Parents. Father and Mother German. Father was always the head of the house. He compared this arrangement with the authoritarian state of which the family was the prototype. It would not do for the husband to be *"unter dem Pantoffel"*— (hen-pecked). It was uncomprehensible to him that there could be equal partnership of the parents. He appears to have been somewhat spoilt and evinces no particular attachment to either parent. The impression received of both of them is dim. The mother is a staunch Lutheran churchwoman but when W. resigned from the Church on typical Nazi grounds she was not allowed to interfere and the father said: 'You must do as you think right, my boy.' He had one sister, whom he regards rather as a little toy (diary). Score: *F.+*

Guilt drive. As will be seen from the diary, he considers himself rather a roué and makes a frantic effort to appear as hard as nails. In his adventures with various girls there are emotional sentences of pseudo-remorse rather than genuine concern, e.g., *'Bin ich denn ein Schwein?'* (Am I really a heel?) and there is an elaborate façade of self-justification by the new Nazi "Darwinian" paganism and compensation can be seen in his taking the point of view that one has to be above reproach in one's conduct as an officer. The guilt sense is, however, repressed and on the surface it is absent. A certain self-justification is constantly in evidence during the interview. Score: *G.D. 2.*

T.T. His attitude towards the opposite sex is a somewhat hectic and forced one and he seems to depend very much on constant sexual adventures and makes a great show of yearning for kisses, etc. Essentially the tender element seems to be lacking in his personality. He was at pains to point out that no such nonsense as house matrons or feminine influence was tolerated at his Nazi school. His mother and sister were just brushed aside, although he admitted that the mother is the *Mittelpunkt* (centre) of the family. Score: *T.T.+*

Religion G.G. Although he admitted the existence of a higher Direction of the world, he emphatically rejected the Christian ethic as being too soft and could not agree with the Sermon on the Mount as being un-German and unbiological. Consequently he had joined the majority of the "new" Germans who stood aside and preferred to work out their own salvation. He did not admit that religious philosophy should play any part in *Weltanschauung* which he interpreted as being merely the order of this world and nothing to do with the supernatural order, in which politics and the State were not concerned. It was a mistake to mix the two. Score: *G.G.*

Mother Cathexis. It is difficult to come to a definite conclusion. This is a case where some analysis would need to be done. The psychopathological picture as it presents itself is of a pathetic need for erotic reassurance, whilst the main allegiance is given to the State and the regime. It does not seem as if successive girl friends are fulfilling other than narcissistic reassurance functions, whereas his essential anchorage is in Germany itself as a conception. Score: *4.*

Father Cathexis. He is very much on the side of authority, and, in fact, considers it his duty as an officer to upbraid those who do not support authority and the established order (see his letter of complaint to a superior officer). There has been displacement from the actual father to the Nazi hierarchy which he accepts as the natural order, but he states also that his actual father was a very strong Nazi. Score: *2.*

Ambivalence. As appears from the diary, his relation to some of his girl friends is marked by duplicity and ambivalence. The same is true of his attitude towards his comrades whom he is ready to report and get into trouble if they do not agree with him. His attitude during the interview was one of exaggerated politeness and apology for the many uncomplimentary references to England and British policy. The attitude to England itself is one of envious and two-faced admiration. In this case the personality itself is thoroughly identified with this split. Score: *1.*

Split Libido. This is gross and the best evidence is his own diary which need hardly be amplified. He was quite pleased to convey the impression that he was a *roué,* a breaker of hearts, but that somewhere a girl worthy to marry him was awaiting him, (he was engaged to an idealized girl), but that the series of naughty little adventures was part and parcel of a German gentleman's mode of living. (Cf. also Section in this paper, Split Libido, for extracts from his diary). Score: *1.*

Sadism. M.C.: (another informant) says: "A great bully, full of stories of life at school when he was delighted, with some assistance, to bully and kick those weaker than himself. Very proud of these stories."

He could not, of course, in an interview, be brought to relate such stories, but it was very clear that his attitude was one of naked use of power which he justified and considered as the right biological attitude. This applied in his whole-hearted approval of the means used by the State for dealing with inferior races. He is thoroughly and joyously identified with the view that might is right and that the need, i.e., achievement of power, justified the means which would be hallowed by success. Score: *1*.

H.S. He is quite consciously identified with the view of the predominance of the male. His attitude is devoid of tender aspects and rather of the conscienceless gang sort. At the same time, his complete subordination to authority and the voice of the master appears from his attitude towards his school. The relegation of woman to an inferior status is very marked. He is ambivalently devoted to a young man in the same P.O.W. party and has several sentimental entries about him. Score: 2.

Narcissism. He is an entirely self-centred and pitiless young poseur in whom object relationships are of the nature of narcissistic identifications. He is conceited, preoccupied with his self-regard and "face" as an officer. His introspections reveal morbid preoccupation with his own reactions and his dependence on entirely autistic erotic gratification. The essential shallowness of feeling which has always got to be whipped up by erotic experience is expressed by *"Ich glaube ich könnte mit dem Mädchen glücklich werden"* (I think I could be happy with that girl). Another entry: *"Ein langer Tag zusammen; sie ist ja so verliebt"* (A long day together; she is so much in love). *"Wenn die Frau weint und mich anfleht muss ich lachen."* (When the woman weeps and implores me I have to laugh). There are a number of allusions in his diary to possible continuing masturbation which would be very likely. Fairly purrs when he thinks he is treated with due respect by the British. Score: *1*.

Projection. There is some evidence of projection apart from the customary Nazi foreign political views in which Jews and Freemasons play a big scapegoat part. Two personal traits that might be mentioned are his resentment at any rough treatment on the part of Transit camp authorities such as the remark in his diary; *"Behandelt wie Verbrecher und Gesindel"* (Treated like criminals and rabble), which is an accurate reflection of his own attitude, and further his undue suspicion of the motives of many of his fellow prisoners. He is very ready to pounce on critics of the Nazis with accusations of disloyalty and is up in arms over minor pilfering in the German-run camp kitchen, etc. Despite his own obvious police-dog attitude, rationalized as watching over "German honour," he remarks that the other officers are not comradely towards him. He is incapable of seeing that he himself has an essentially anti-social priggish, tell-tale attitude. Score: 2

Inferiority Feelings. The whole personality is full of over-compensations. He is a little, rather weedy youth who fancies himself as the paragon of soldierly virtue and obviously tries to hide behind a very thin façade of polite correctness to pose as the upholder of Nazism in the camp: *"Man kann manchmal zweiflen, aber wir glauben, weil wir Deutsche sind"* (One can sometimes have doubts, but we have faith because we are Germans). He is also very touchy where his own status is concerned and has a great feeling of satisfaction that the shame of his failure of the *Abitur* is compensated by his now being an officer. His national inferiority towards the British is openly expressed. His sexual life is also a compensation for an essential shallowness of feeling. Score: *1*.

Hypochondria. There is slight pre-occupation with his health but in view of two wounds and dysentery this is not above normal. Score: *3*.

Anxiety. In the sense of neurotic symptoms enough evidence has already been adduced to show that this boy has a very profound anxiety state. He is restless, has an inner drive and a few days at a station are enough to make him enter in his diary that he has *Budenangst,* i.e., claustrophobic symptoms. He is dependent on constant distraction and change and the above mentioned erotic gratification, interspersed with occasional bouts of drunkenness. There are repeated entries about: *"Das Warten ist schrecklich—ein ulkiges Gefühl im Bauch."* (This waiting is frightful—such a queer feeling in the stomach). He has, however, a capacity to tolerate some anxiety and speaks of a dread of flying; he refused to be flown again in an air ambulance. He appears to have little capacity for making friends. His bearing during the interview was nervous and over-deferential for a boy of good education. His clinging to his officer status and his extreme nationalism also have an anxious and compulsive character. Score: *1*.

Depression. Apart from a certain amount of military pessimism there is no evidence of true depression. Score: *3*.

Schizoid Split. The high degree of narcissism, the incapacity for deep affect and the almost frantic clinging to the reality of officer "face" and N.S. *Begeisterung* (fervour) betoken a schizoid personality which is further supported by his appearance and physique. He is a small man with a tight cynical mouth with an incongruous petulant protruding lower lip, hostile, questioning, suspicious eyes behind horn-rimmed spectacles, dark hair which grows low on his temples. The personality makes a most unpleasant impression and one cannot warm to him. In no direction was any warm human feeling discovered. He is full of *ad hoc* arguments and has a very ready intelligence. One feels that if his Nazi faith were taken away from him, the personality would break asunder as there is no other central integrating factor. In my opinion a schizoid psychopathy: "affectionless character."

F Rating. It is not necessary to describe his political views in detail as they are absolutely standard and marked by a cynical ferocity. The only deviant feature is that he thinks that Germany is still so immature that she needs to be bullied into a sense of unity. Score: *1*.

The rabid, compulsive quality in this young Nazi was perhaps that which made him the most typical embodiment of the high *F.* syndrome; he was selected as one kind of polar extreme of the species: the spoilt, insecure, restless type from a comfortable home, but not daring to love or be ordinary.

A sense of split and disunity, only held together by fanatical identification with symbols of group power, runs through the personality. It would not be true to say that other individuals rated as *F*I in the series could have been diagnosed as suffering from so marked a character disorder as to justify the term psychopathy; but the same elements were there.

It is the contention of the writer that the character disorder it is proposed to call the "High *F* syndrome" is a cultural artifact and not a genetic or constitutional affliction of the individual. It belongs rather into the same order of phenomena as "the Puritan character" or "the Public School Type." All these represent in their own time and place behavioural and motivational patterns easily derivable from the larger cultural area in which they are embedded. The derivation would seem, at least in the case of the Nazis, to be explained in terms of a selective reinforcement of behavioural traits, defence mechanisms, etc., typical of the German norm, brought together to form a logical extreme, almost a caricature of these norms. Each trait or variable was, in its way, a German virtue, inculcated and socially admired as attributes of a leader personality among them. The ideal of being a heroic, virile nation of soldiers has been held before German youth for at least a century. To be modelled on the pattern of the masterful commander who has learnt to subdue all weakness or "irrelevant" moral softness in others by first having it beaten out of himself by an "iron" authority was the proudest aspiration. Fathers would reinforce the trend in their sons in both directions—submission and need to dominate. The unrecognized damage to the personality had to be shored up by a number of culturally generalised defensive patterns which, because of their function of sustaining or containing the repressed, were themselves of the nature of reaction formations, rigidly held and socially highly valued.

Of such a character were some of the other constituent traits of the Gestalt we have called the High F syndrome. This is true of the stress on minimizing the influence of mothers and women, on the glorification of male dominance and friendship visualized as a dare-devil, but disciplined, cameraderie of front-line soldiers. The brittleness and deeper vulnerability of the norm demands rigid definitions of status both in interpersonal and in inter-group relations, with prescribed or expected arrogant or submissive behaviour *vis-à-vis* status-inferiors and status-superiors in accordance with the hierarchical principle, jealously guarded and enforced.

Even the adolescent revolt was patterned and condoned as a safety valve, channelled towards homosexual rivalry, combativeness and tests of strength, (duels, alcoholic tolerance, etc.), with concessions towards sexual licence, in the confident expectation that the powerful pressure of group norms would in due time bring the wheel full circle towards conformity. It was quite smart to be thought a young conscienceless rip.

In any culture there will be some more and some less complete representatives or active carriers of the pattern. Once the "Prussian authoritarian" pattern above outlined had become the dominant trend in Germany, those who were most efficiently displaying its characteristics were likely sooner or later to 'reap the social advantages of going furthest along the approved path of behaviour—group produces recognised example; recognised example influences group: group produces more extreme example——' (1).

The case-history cited, and some of the extracts adduced as examples of scoring in the preceding section, support the view that in the case of Germany the bearers of the more extreme traits were those whose character development had most suffered the distortion implied in the process of personal assimilation to demanded norms. It is as if in their anxiety to placate their super-egos, the high *Fs* had fallen over backwards. In psychiatric terms this would imply a higher than average level of persecutory anxiety, with more desperate need to dissociate, project, and even regress. There is surely a direct connection between the degree of felt harshness of internalized parent objects and the level of badness of the inner world, i.e., repressed aggression. It is likely that the relation between a harsh cultural ego-ideal and this repressed aggression is that of reciprocal aggravation, according to the formula 'character moulds institutions, institutions perpetuate character.' Thus the two inter-war generations, in an era of rapid social change, appear to have had the effect of accelerating the cumulative effect of this field relation: personality ⇌ culture.

The level of anxiety which the defeat in World War I and its consequences must have produced in characters of this kind can be imagined, economically threatened, socially displaced and with their influence reduced as they were. The records suggest maniac denial and regression to magical restitution and vengeance phantasies. The now weak and therefore despised nation had to be rescued from its shamers and traducers by the romantic hero-gang. Narcissistic identification with Germany demanded a sharpening of split in the ambivalence. Germany *must* be good and powerful—outgroups alone were evil and attackable. It only required Adolf Hitler's considerable gifts of verbalizing these phantasies and giving them coherence to bring many birds of a feather together round the hero-leader they required. In this sense many of the detailed responses and imagery of objects of love and hate in our sample were copied direct from Hitler and his chief lieutenants. But these in turn were really nothing more than the previously acclaimed *clichés* and symbols, adapted and formulated into a paranoid system: the narcissan megalomania and group solipsism, the guilt denial by rationalizing all aggression as counter-aggression sanctioned by group status and "survival" claims; the homosexual self-surrender by the sworn gang of brothers to the worshipped "Man of Destiny" who took all responsibility; and the persecutory projection of all infantile weakness, hate and greed impulses to the various outgroups who could thus become the target of total destructive attack. Maternal good object values, as represented for example by Christianity, were pushed aside and persecuted as "sissy." Though the activist Nazi felt himself in this as a member of the *élite,* he also acted as a mere passive agent of the now substituted "Higher Destiny," carrying out, automaton-like, the promptings of his id, coming to him as the Führer's doctrine, his super-ego safely in the care of those above him. It seems as if id and harsh super-ego had here achieved a fusion of direction or aim.

We have seen that in the section on the distribution of political attitudes towards National Socialism that there were, among the active male population of the *Wehrmacht,* never less than 35 per cent of active carriers of this ideology with verbal or implied support for its associated practices, with a hard fanatical core of some 10 per cent. It is not therefore surprising that National Socialism, despite its internal irrationality and self-contradictions, already implied in its name, had the success the world has witnessed. It was so close to the personal dynamics and phantasy needs of a considerable proportion of the cultural group and had formulated them in such culture-syntonic terms that resistance was ineffective. Even for those not sharing the high F syndrome personality, there was something to assimilate from the models of successful high F behaviour held up before them by the *élite* of German society preponderantly composed of the type we have described here. The vast majority of those not classified as FI and II were submissive and apolitical. In other words they possessed, at least, one set of the attitudes shown by the more extreme types, namely that of subordination to strong authorities, but they lacked the aggressive paranoid activism, probably because their inner object world was of a kindlier nature. The ideals which the Nazis claimed to incarnate were however so widely and pervasively preached in German institutions that even persons of "non-authoritarian" personality accepted them. Only the small group who might be called compulsively anti-Authoritarian (as some sub-varieties of the *FV* class) could bring themselves to real rejection of the Nazi pattern, and then usually because they had cathected some other system—e.g., Catholicism or Marxism.

Concluding Reflections

The writer is aware that the publication of work seven years old may strike his readers as now somewhat naive and elementary in a field which has since the end of the War been much studied. It may, however, stand as an example of a method of enquiry into the motivations in political ideology and behaviour, just because it was carried out under field conditions and without the refinements and rigours of a completely planned piece of research. Despite its length, this paper has had to restrict its persuasive illustrative material to a minimum. Nor is any *a posteriori* criticism attempted—this is left to the methodologically trained reader with the object of eliminating errors in future work of this type.

Considerable refinements in method were, in fact, made in the subsequent applications of the method by the team responsible for the screening centre under British Control Commission auspices in 1945-6. It is to be hoped that at some future time the now scattered members of that team will be able to publish the sequel. Similar work in a U.S. Control Commission screening centre bears traces of having been influenced by the study here described. (12), (14).

It cannot be denied that political currents of recent years have tended to wash away a clear awareness of the deeper character structure possessed by the leading *elite* of one of the most cataclysmic movements in the history of Western Society. A reminder may not come amiss. What is being done in Germany or elsewhere to protect society from the dangers of the "High *F*" in places of power, and to ensure a change in the pattern of parent-child relations, educational policy, and social mores according to a more loving, tolerant code of human values to prevent his like being perpetuated in civilized communities? And what studies are going on, based on the psychodynamic concepts, to enquire into the host of politically significant group phenomena now challenging the wisdom of our epoch? [6]

Acknowledgments

The writer's thanks are firstly due to the War Office, London, for the opportunities to carry out these studies and for permission to publish, and especially to the then Director and Staff of the Department of Army Psychiatry and Biological Research, among whom Drs. G. Ronald Hargreaves and A. T. M. Wilson gave him special encouragement and help. Special gratitude is owing to Edward A. Shils for his aid, advice and management of the treatment of data, and to the skilled, insightful, and devoted collaboration of those connoisseurs of German mentality who carried out political interviews and furthered the study in countless ways: Norman S. Marsh, George A. Thompson, Walter Gumbel, and Norman Brangham, all at the time officers in the British Army.

REFERENCES

1. Brickner, Richard M. *Is Germany Incurable?* New York, 1943.
2. Dicks, Henry V. *Psychological Foundations of the Wehrmacht,* War Office Research Memorandum, 1944.
3. ———. "The German Deserter" id. 1944.
4. ———. "German Political Attitudes" id. 1944.
5. ———. "National Socialism as a Psychological Problem" id. 1945.
6. ———. "The Ten Categories." Internal Memorandum, German Personnel Research Branch, Control Commission for Germany (British element) 1945.
7. ———. "Why the Germans became Nazis" (B.B.C. Broadcast). *The Listener,* June, 1947.
8. ———. "The Psychological Approach to the German Problem," The Royal Institute for International Affairs, Private Memorandum, 1947.
9. Erikson, E. H. "Hitler's Imagery and German Youth," *Personality.* ed. Kluckhohn and Murray, New York, 1948.
10. Fromm, Erich, *The Fear of Freedom,* London, 1942.
11. Kecskemeti, P., and Leites, N. "Some Psychological Hypotheses on Nazi Germany," The Library of Congress, Washington, D.C., Document No. 60, 1945.
12. Levy, David M. "The German Anti-Nazi: a Case Study." *Am. Jl. of Orthopsychiatry,* July, 1946.
13. Rodnick, David. *Post-War Germans.* New Haven and London, 1948.
14. Schaffner, Bertram. *Fatherland.* New York, 1948.
15. "Germany After the War." Report of a Conference held at Columbia University, New York, mimeographed 1944.

Chapter 7. Notes

1. See *The Case of Rudolf Hess*, ed. J. R. Rees, London. 1947 (Heinemann).

2. Cf. Fromm, E. *The Fear of Freedom*, London, 1942. This book and Fromm's views were not at that period known to the writer.

3. Some details of these studies may be found in Shils, E. A., and Janowitz, M. "Cohesion and Disintegration in the Wehrmacht," *Public Opinion Quarterly*, XII, No. 2, 280 (1948).

4. A full treatment of the morale and political attitude studies during the SHAEF period in World War II will be found in Daniel Lerner's book *Sykewar* about to appear as this goes to press.

5. The score "No inference made" was provided for every variable, but will not be repeated in the text.

6. As if in answer to this concluding question, the writer has just received the large volume, *The Authoritarian Personality*, by Nevitt Sanford and associates, which on first reading seems to embody nearly all the concepts of this present paper, and which describes just the kind of refinements of technique not available to the writer.

Chapter 8

A FOLIO OF GERMAN TYPES *

By

SAUL K. PADOVER

1. A middle-aged school teacher: Agnes F

FRAU AGNES F, 56, is an elementary-school teacher from Aachen. In April 1944 she was bombed out and moved to Roetgen where she began to teach 2d and 3d grade classes. She has been a school teacher since 1909.

Frau Agnes is a motherly woman, bespectacled, smiling, and unnervous. She expresses herself in a pedagogical tone, with the clarity of one who spent a lifetime explaining simple things to children.

Late in life, at the age of 41, she married a man without work or profession. Her husband suffers from anemia and she has always supported him and the household. Frau F is, therefore, a woman of considerable, if quiet, self-confidence. Her husband, who helped the maid in the house, is a member of the Nazi party and, it appeared from Frau Agnes's naive account, was in the habit of explaining to her the Nazi *Weltanschauung* in some detail. During the interrogation Frau Agnes always prefaced her comments with the disarming remark—"I don't know, of course, whether it's so or not, but they say . . ." *They* clearly meant the Nazis as represented by her housebound husband.

Frau Agnes F told us she knew nothing about politics—she was merely a simple teacher, she said—but she was a veritable storehouse of Nazi political lore. All the Hitler arguments, viewpoints, and cliches had somehow found an echo in this "unpolitical" school teacher. It goes without saying also that

* The interviews in this chapter are reproduced, without change (except omission of last names), from photostats of Professor Padover's original reports to Psychological Warfare Division, SHAEF.

she, too, claimed to be "anti-Nazi." In proof of that she informed us that before 1933 she used to vote Centrist.

Did she ever teach political subjects or tell her pupils political stories? Why, heavens, no! she exclaimed. She only taught reading and arithmetic, she said. What did she read to the children? Nothing political, she said: only such stories as the life of the Fuehrer. What did she say about the Fuehrer? Frau Agnes became enthusiastic and genuinely eloquent as she retold the tale of the Fuehrer's early life. "I told the children how the Fuehrer [she never said Hitler] was born in a small town in Austria, how even as a little boy he already interested himself in German history, how he dreamt of being a painter-artist, how his father did not permit him to study art, how his loving mother helped him to become a painter after his father died, how he had no great genius to be a painter, how his mother died and how he was forced to give up his studies and become a housepainter, and how he came to Germany . . ."

We asked Frau F whether the Nazi party interfered with the school system. She said oh no: "There was absolute freedom of teaching," and added that, of course, all the textbooks were changed. She was quite familiar with the new books and when we asked her to explain to us Germany's post-World War I history she became fluent and even eloquent:

"Wilson did not keep the 14 Points. So Germany had to find an escape [Rettung]. Then came Ebert, a Socialist, and times got worse. Then came the inflation and times got even worse than before. The people yearned for better times and so Hindenburg came. The Marshal got old and older and suddenly there appeared Hitler who brought a new idea. He promised the workers improvement [Besserung]. So Hindenburg made him Chancellor of the Reich, and when Hindenburg died they made Hitler Fuehrer. Hitler won over the workers because he gave them work, vacations, and Kraft durch Freude. This attracted the mass of the German people to the Fuehrer. And when industry saw how the Fuehrer brought deliverance [Erettung] to the workers, industry also joined the ranks of the workers and embraced the new idea. So everybody was with the Fuehrer."

Since Frau F was so well informed and so anxious to enlighten us, we asked her to continue with her discourse, particularly on the subject of the present war. She said:

"In 1935 the Fuehrer started to build up the *Wehrmacht*. He did it in order to make Germany great. This idea appealed to the German workers because it abolished the class fights. I personally believe that although all men should be considered as fellow men, there must be some distinctions. The Fuehrer wanted to abolish all distinctions, but I am afraid this noble idea didn't penetrate as far as the Fuehrer dreamt. Maybe his subordinates didn't carry out his noble wishes.

"Anyhow, the war came and we were very disappointed. We were afraid that it might turn out to be terrible for us. Some people said: '*Hitler konnte den Hals nicht voll kriegen*' [Hitler could never get enough]. But still there was great enthusiasm for the war at first. There were great successes. Then came Stalingrad. We lost confidence. We began to think that maybe the war won't end in our favor. That made us mad at the Italians because they should have helped us and they didn't. The front was too big for Germany alone."

We asked her to explain to us the causes of the war and she agreed readily. At first she said that one of the causes of the war was, unfortunately, the Fuehrer. "He always wanted something more." But when she warmed up to the subject she informed us that the "war was started by England." England, it seems, got tired of allowing Hitler to take more countries and more territories and so she started war against Germany.

How did the war with Russia start? Frau F explained that the Russians began to arm a long time ago in order to invade Germany. "So we defended ourselves by attacking them. We said that we don't like Bolsheviks and we don't want them to come to our country; so it is good to fight them first before they are ready to attack us, because they are a big country with lots of materials."

Why did Germany attack Poland? "That," Frau F explained to us, "was a pure *Verteidigungskrieg*. Germany had to defend herself against the Poles."

She was convinced that now the war is lost for Germany. When we asked why, she said with a gentle smile: "*Viele Hunden sind des Hasen Tod* [Many dogs cause the death of the hare.]" That, she added, is an old German saying. Among the biggest "*Hunden*" causing the death of the innocent hare is the United States. "America," Frau F told us, "is too big and rich for us to overcome. When America entered the war we all lost hope."

We asked her whether she ever listened to the foreign radio. She said that she did not but that she did occasionally hear news that was not in the Nazi programs. The treatment of the Jews, for example. She had heard people say that the Germans had "murdered" Jews in Poland and she did believe that the SS was capable of such deeds. When a few years ago they burned the Aachen synagogue she was so upset that she could not teach that day. "It was unjust to destroy the sanctuary [*Heiligtum*] of the Jews. Moreover, one has no right to destroy what doesn't belong to one."

What did she think of the Jews? "They are the enemies of the German people and of mankind," she replied, and added: "But I don't know whether it's true. They say so." Did she ever know any Jews? Yes, she once had a Jewish friend, Selma Bloch, daughter of the well-known orchestra conductor. "She was a fine and able lady" [*eine patente Dame*]. As for other Jews, "they did a lot of good for the German people, but the party did not like them and so they destroyed them." Frau F did not think that was right or just. "Without war we have no right to destroy people. Moreover, there is the religious injunction: Thou shalt not kill."

Frau F takes an uncheerful view of the future. She said: "Germany is *kaputt*. She lost the war and will, therefore, be partitioned. I would prefer our part to become an American republic or *colony*."

As for the Nazis, they should not be allowed to remain in power. "They have lied to us and deceived us [*belogen und betrogen*]. They should be deposed. The German people must renounce them. They are not good leaders." The young Nazis must be told that what was told to them hitherto was not quite true. All the German people must be informed that they were "*belogen und betrogen*" by the Nazi leaders. The latter promised to win the war and they didn't.

Frau F was even ready to chide the Fuehrer.

"Why," she asked, "doesn't he make an end of it now that the war is hopeless? If he were a real patriot, he would say: 'The war is lost, save what you can.' But he continues the war out of self-prestige and obstinacy. He made up his mind, '*Wir kapitulieren nie*' [we never capitulate], and he sticks to it. He is the kind of man who once he makes a decision never gives up. He should now sacrifice himself—as leader of the people—for the German nation."

On the way out Frau F, convinced that she had made a deep impression upon us, said with a genial smile: "May I shake your hand in friendship?"

2. A Socialist who did Nazi occupation work in Russia: Franz E

It is said that the Russians believe that all Germans who occupied Russia were equally bad and that German workers, including former Socialists, behaved just as brutally as the other Germans. Confirmation of this can be found in conversations with young Russian workers in Germany who claim that during their slave-labor period in the Reich nobody showed them any pity except German communists.

In territory occupied by us, however, many Germans, especially Social Democratic workers, claim that they were friends, supporters, and helpers of the poor Russians (a claim which the Russians, who should know, vehemently deny). A case in point is Franz E, 31, a quick-witted Social Democratic miner from Würselen. E, now employed in the Würselen city administration, has also had the unique experience of being an administrator in Russia under the Nazi occupation. He is, of course, full of praise for the Russians and claims to have been their friend and protector in Russia.

Like so many miners in this area, E is the son of a miner. He went to work in a needle factory at 15 and 4 years later he changed jobs and became a miner. Like his father, he became a Social Democrat; but unlike his father, he rose in the miners' hierarchy to become a *Fahrhauer* (in charge of 12 men) and a *Steiger* (150 men). To this day, E wears a white collar.

He knows all the anti-fascist arguments and has the anti-fascist cliches at his finger tips. But there is something smooth about his manner that does not carry conviction. Under Hitler, he said, the miners earned about 200 RM a month—"not enough to live on and not enough to die on." As a *Steiger*, he earned from 350 to 400 RM, but, he says deprecatingly, "I was only the puppet of the *Fahrsteiger*, who was usually a Nazi." He speaks of the Nazi-created mine officials as "drones," and of the miners who joined the Nazi party (about 1/3d of all former Socialists and Communists became Nazis) as "parasites."

E presents himself as an undefiled anti-Nazi fighter ("We could form no organization, however; to do so, meant death or 20 years in concentration camp"). He even claims to have carried on sabotage in his section of the mine. Between 1939 and 1941 the Nazis asked the miners to produce more and more coal (*um die ganze Welt zu eroberen*). He, E, was not going to help Hitler conquer the world, however. As a *Fahrhauer,* he saw to it that his 12 men made "a good vein become a poor one —only experienced miners know how to do that." Instead of producing 7 or 8 wagons of coal from a vein, they produced 2 or 3. This meant no loss to the miners because they were paid a minimum wage of 6.70 RM. He explained to his miners that the vein was dangerous, and that if they worked too hard they would wear themselves out and become sick. Thus they worked only about 2 hours a day and the rest of the time they played match games.

Such is E's story of sabotage; but knowing E and the conditions of labor and supervision, one may dismiss it as a pious fraud.

E says he used to get up at 2 AM to listen to the BBC; it was too dangerous to listen during the day or evening. From the BBC he gathered facts and figures that persuaded him that Germany could not win the war, especially after the United States became a belligerent. "I thought through the implications of conquering the world for a country like Germany, having to fight Russia, Britain, and the United States; and I realized it could not be done." Still he was willing to do his bit.

In 1942 the Nazis issued a call for experienced miners to work in Hitler's great new colony, Russia. E responded to the call. He says he did it out of curiosity. "Here was my chance to see and to study the Soviet Union." (A Communist miner in Würselen, a man who knows E, told us that no decent Communist or Socialist worker would accept such a job that involved helping Hitler exploit a conquered country; he views E with considerable suspicion and some contempt.)

E was sent to the Donetz basin, to a village named Schistyakovo, where, as a German representing the occupying power, he became the sole administrator of the community. In this mining village he had 250 Russian workers under him. He treated them beautifully, he says. They also loved him. From E's account, it was love almost at first sight. They admired each other mutually. The Russians taught him *Gemeinnutz vor Eigennutz*. They also showed him the virtues of a genuine communist life.

E, whom the Nazis paid 7,000 RM a year (double his salary in Germany), plus an allowance for his wife in Germany, came to appreciate communism as practiced in his village. First, he found a Russian mistress—a 20-year-old school teacher. Second, he had fine living quarters. Third, he ate as he never dreamt of eating in Germany. The first morning he was in the village, Vera prepared the breakfast table and set 10 boiled eggs before him. He thought the eggs were for a whole week, but he greedily ate 3 (in Germany eggs had been a luxury, like caviar). When Vera returned to the room and saw that he had left 7 eggs on the table, she exclaimed in surprise and wondered whether the German gentleman (he wore a *Wehrmacht* uniform) was sick. "Russian men," she explained in broken German, "eat 10 eggs. What's the matter with German men!" Such was E's introduction to communism in Russia.

At first the villagers were cold and aloof, but when they discovered that the new German *Herr* was their friend they warmed up, E says. He used to go visiting their homes (one suspects that, in view of Russia's famous hospitality, his visits may not have been without gastronomic motivation). When they got to know him better, he says, they discussed politics and they told him that they were "absolutely convinced" the Germans would be forced out of Russia. Some of the villagers were members of the communist party; others were sympathizers. There were many intelligent men among the miners. "The most intelligent man I ever knew was Nicolai Lubtschik, the manager of the mine (*Betriebsfuehrer*)." He spent much time with Lubtschik, to whom he confessed (secretly) that he was a Social Democrat. In the mines the Russians carried on sabotage, a form of anti-Nazi activity which might have cost Superintendent E his head but which, he claims, he cheerfully condoned. The Russians did not know that he knew that they sabotaged. He was able to cover up for them because it was up to him to set production estimates, and he usually set them low. Early in September, 1943, E left Russia—the Red Army was coming uncomfortably close. And the villagers wept at

Herr E's departure! Asked why he did not remain among his Russian friends, E replied smoothly that he was afraid that the Soviet Government would not take the time to investigate his lofty motives but would shoot him out of hand.

When he returned to Würselen, the director of his mine, a man named Aschke, refused to give him the job of *Steiger* because he was not a Nazi party member. So E had to content himself with being a modest *Fahrhauer*. Then Russian workers —about 500 out of a total of 2200 miners—were brought to the mines and he, as a Russian specialist and as one who could speak some Russian—was given charge over them. He did what he could for them, which was not much. "What they suffered is indescribable." They were given half the food rations of the German miners; they were mistreated, robbed, and deprived of all human rights. Always hungry, they used to come to E and pour out their grievances. They liked him so much that they called him by his first name (as Russian workers do at home). He helped them by registering their output higher than it actually was.

E says he is not a communist but a Social Democrat. He thinks, however, that German Socialists should take over the best features of the Soviets. The latter is really a workers' state. If certain communist measures were applied in Germany, he says, the standard of living in the Reich would double. He thinks that after the war the German communists and Social Democrats will merge into one workers' party. Members of both parties are now "waiting" to see what the United States will do; they are biding their time, observing and saying nothing. "America is the master; what it orders will be done."

The workers, he says, have learned plenty from Hitler and they will see to it that they do not repeat the same mistakes as before 1933. They will uproot the Nazi evil by applying the same tactics to the Nazis that the latter used against the workers. Fanatical Nazis, he says, should be put to hard work; that will transform them quicker than any other kind of punishment. E and his friends have a list of Nazis in the community and they are keeping a sharp eye on them. When MG first appointed Nazis to municipal jobs, this list came in handy. Now there are few if any Nazis in the city administration.

E thinks that partition would be a good thing for Germany. He hopes that the Rhineland would become American. "If that happens, we'll have a better future. If nationalistic agitators should start trouble, I hope that the United States will suppress them. We'll help. We'll set up our own Gestapo; it will be as hard as Hitler's, and it will uproot all agitators. For us an American occupation could only better, not worse."

[A few days ago we happened to be talking to a group of young Russian workers in Würselen, when E saw us and he came over and tried to insinuate himself into the group. The Russians were stone cold to him. Then he tried to put his arms around a Russian woman; she shoved him away. He tried this playful gesture once more and she threw off his arm with a gesture of dislike. Rebuffed, he finally went away. We asked the Russians whether he was really a friend of theirs. They smiled sarcastically. One said in broken German: "He no good. No German is good."]

3. An ex-SS Man: Helmut K

Helmut K is a well-bred, well-mannered youth of 21 from Bockum, a Krefeld suburb. He has a haughty nonchalant air and is quite proudly conscious that he has been a *Waffen-SS* man for 3½ years. He tries hard to create the impression that he has cut himself off completely from his long Hitler-inspired past. "When I took off my uniform in December," he says, "I became a civilian for all time." Indeed, it is pathetic and infuriating to hear this seemingly good-natured son of a middle-class professional man speak of reorienting himself and then mouth all the cliches of Nazism and SS-ism. K knows that he has become implicated in a criminal institution; but he is unable to conceal his callousness and brutality simply because his values have been distorted through long indoctrination and actual participation in SS atrocities. During the long conversation, he blandly admitted this participation.

We met K accidentally. We were standing outside the Military Government building when he came up to us and asked where he could obtain a pass to circulate in the *Stadtkreis*. Without any fear, he produced a paper signed by an *Oberfeldarzt* that he had been released from the SS in December, 1944 (lung trouble). The paper gave his rank as an SS-*Standarten Oberjunker* [Senior Warrant Officer] in the 600th Paratroop Bn.

The conversation was conducted in a friendly informal manner in a room adjoining the CIC. As a boy, K belonged to a special Hitler Youth troop engaged in police and patrol duties. At 17 this "elite" troop was inducted into the *Waffen*-SS. K says all this activity was *muss*—"compulsory." He described his father, a university graduate and chemist in the I.G. Farbenindustrie, as a "completely unpolitical" scientist who had never expressed a single political idea to his son. It was not until much later in the conversation that K casually revealed his father left the Catholic Church in 1935 and encouraged the 12-year-old Helmut to do likewise. When we asked why the father had taken such a drastic step, K smiled with amiable contempt and said, "The Church? But gentlemen, does one really need such a thing?"

It was clear to us that the father was the son's first Nazi influence. K maintained he had no fear of remaining behind and making himself known to the authorities. "You are not like the Russians," he said. "You are not animals. I have been a soldier and I knew you would treat me honorably as such." He said that obviously there are many higher party officials walking around the streets who are not molested. He cited Herr Tümpen, Nazi Mayor of Bockum, who is still Mayor of the town. K's comment was: "If somebody fights *politically* for his country, he doesn't change his opinions overnight. Yet you leave him in peace." Therefore, K implied, why should not he, a soldier, be treated fairly. From other statements he made, K also figured that if he had evacuated with the troops, he might have been inducted again into the SS and been killed or captured by the Russians. Since his long stay in an army hospital last summer recovering from his third wound, K seems to have been obsessed by a fear of death.

Probed on his knowledge of German culture, he merely shook his head and said, "I know very little about German history. I made my *Abitur* (Junior college), but all I have ever learned is the history and the personalities of National Socialism." After asserting that he is now a "democrat," he said that "one must admit Germany was wonderful up to 1939. Life was pleasant and you could do what you wanted to do. It was much better than what we had before 1933 when there was chaos and communism. From 1918 to 1933, a different regime came into power every five minutes. There were 40 or 50 parties at least. It was the worst period in history. Under the Fuehrer we were building peacefully when the whole business started. The war came because we wanted to build a highway to Danzig through the corridor. Poland would not allow it and began to persecute the Germans living in her territory."

K, the "democrat," raises his voice slightly when he talks of Jews. Jews engage only in "dirty business deals, exploiting the little man by lending him money, charging enormous interest and then foreclosing on his property." He does not consider the problem a "matter of religion but of race." Germans, for example, "could never do such things." K was personally present in his Hitler Youth role when the Krefeld synagogue was razed in 1938. "Everyone was overjoyed to see the burning," he said. "It meant we were getting rid of the Jews. It had to be done. They were opponents of the regime." K said he had never known a Jew personally outside of an elderly man who ran a store in Neuss where the K family used to shop long ago. The elderly man looked like a "typical rascal of a Jew."

He described his life in the SS with enthusiasm—the splendid comradeship, "pure and absolute," the excellent relationship between officers and men, the strenuous training, the "select elite" of students and "better people" who made up the SS, their pride, devotion to obedience and gentlemanly behavior. "Your propaganda says much about our officers," he said, smiling. "But it's not like that at all. We mistreat no one." The only point where he showed any trace of bitterness is when he explained that he would have been an officer long ago (he had completed OCS) if it had not been for an affair with a French girl.

K took part in the Russian campaigns of 1941 and 1942 as an artillery signals man. He was in the Ukraine and deep in the Caucasus. Before Kharkov in 1942, his unit used *Pressluftgranaten* (compressed air bombs) for the first time. "It was an excellent weapon," he said. "When we advanced later, I saw 60 Russians sitting in a cellar. They were all dead, but they had no wounds and they were sitting there just as if everything was normal." He said the Red Army brought up loudspeakers and warned that gas would be used if the air bombs were employed again. K said an order came from higher up to stop using the air bombs. (It was in this connection that

K said he is "convinced Hitler would use gas on the Allies as a last salvation.")

K told how the SS forced *Wehrmacht* infantry back into the line in Russia. "Sometimes the *Wehrmacht* soldiers shot their own officers or the officers deserted to the Russians, and the infantrymen would fall back for lack of leadership. We were there to put them back into the line. I know what they say about us, but that is all exaggerated. We just put our officers into their ranks and encouraged them and that was all there was to it. If there were any murders committed, it was the *Wehrmacht* and not us that did it. They were always discontented, but our morale was always of the highest."

Of the Red Army, he said with contempt, "The Russian? That's no soldier. That's masses." The Russians could have been beaten easily, had it not been for the bad winters of '41 and '42 that fouled up the supply lines. K chided the Führer at this point. "Hitler should have been content with what he had in 1942. He had to attack in the east in '41 because of Russian preparations, but he should have been content with what he had."

As a signals man, K listened often to Allied radio stations. SS men were frequent listeners, but skeptical ones. He said it was "mostly out of curiosity" and had little effect on them. "Propaganda is propaganda. Yours is better, more varied, but it's still propaganda." He lacks any clear idea of the Allied attitude toward the war. "I'd like to ask a question. I have always wondered what interest America has in Europe. Is it out of friendship or what? You have everything, a big rich land, everyone is happy there. Why did you come over? Because you wanted to help England perhaps?" When he was told that Germany declared war on America, he seemed genuinely surprised, even skeptical. Obviously, he wanted to say that he believed America "came over to Europe" out of financial interest, but the level of frankness had not yet reached that extreme. He was, however, convinced that America's natural enemy is Russia and war would break out between the two countries in Germany itself at some time.

After telling of his unit's participation in anti-Partisan activity in Russia behind the lines, he described how he completed his Paratroop training and toward the end of 1943 joined the 600th Paratroop SS Battalion in fighting the "terrorists and bandits" in Jugoslavia. His last jump was made on Marshal Tito's headquarters in May, 1944. Their mission was to capture Tito and his staff and hold the area until an SS tank unit could break through. He said they failed to capture Tito because of the "betrayal" of two captured *Blitzmädel,* who tipped off Tito's intelligence men. They did capture two Partisan generals, many documents and lesser officers. What did they do with them? He was not very convincing when he brushed off the question with, "Oh, we interrogated them and treated them like ordinary prisoners." Later, he intimated they were shot.

K often referred to the time he lay in a hospital all during the summer of 1944, convalescing from his third wound. Apparently, it was then that his faith and loyalty in victory and the Führer were somewhat shaken; it was then that he began to fear death in a losing cause and a *verlorener Mann* ["lost man"] as he described Hitler; it was then that he began to feel "oppressed" because he could not marry a French girl. The latter feeling, however, was obviously influenced by the hope that if he insisted on marrying her, he would be released to the *Wehrmacht* from the SS and thus he would escape being forced to die by "holding out to the last."

"I had a great deal of time to think things over," he says of this period. I came to the conclusion that those of us who are dying are dying in vain. There was no chance of winning. Invasion in the West, Russian masses in the East. I thought the whole thing out, but I knew that we would go on fighting because we *must,* because we are ordered to. I, personally, wanted to end my part in the war. I did not want to die in the last five minutes. But I knew that I *must* continue fighting if I am ordered to." He also thought over the affair he had had with a girl of French parentage who had been raised in Düsseldorf. He met her in Metz in 1941 when he was in training, and when he revisited her in early 1944, he found he had a son. He asked for permission to marry her. The application went all the way to Berlin and was refused. He threatened to leave the SS and enter the *Wehrmacht.* This was forbidden. Finally, he married the girl anyway in a secret civil ceremony in France. The marriage was discovered and declared null and void; his commission as an officer was blocked. This affair had considerable influence on him. It was the first time he had personally experienced his loss of freedom. This came out later in the conversation; he was asked why he suddenly became a "democrat." His answer was prompt—"I decided that when they forbade me to marry whomever I wanted." His wife, whom he is not very attached to now, is at present a volunteer in the *Flakmaedel* [Women's Ack-ack].

K's admission of his part in SS atrocities and brutality came when we steered the conversation to the behavior of American and Russian troops. He was amusedly tolerant when he spoke of the American occupation of Bockum, his home town. "As a soldier, I understand perfectly. They gave us a couple of hours to move out, then settled down comfortably in our homes, tore everything out, drank anything they could get hold of. We did the same thing. You know, a soldier is curious . . . he sees something he likes and he takes it with him, watches or anything. A soldier likes to tear things up. That's clear to me. We did the same thing. . . ." He waved his hand knowingly as if he wanted to say, 'I was in Russia, after all, and you know what happened there.'

We asked about the Russian soldiers. Were they really as "wild" and "criminal" as they say? He said slowly, "I don't think they took many of our men prisoners."

"And you reciprocated, of course?" we asked.

He nodded his head. "We took no Russian prisoners all during 1941. They were questioned and then we got rid of them."

"How could you get rid of so many of them?" we asked offhandedly.

He pointed to the nape of his neck. *"Nackenschuss,"* he said. "Right here in the back of the neck. It was an order [*Befehl*] and *Befehl ist Befehl*. All terrorists and bandits were also shot like that."

Would he shoot *anyone* on a *direct order*? He hesitated an instant, and then hunched his shoulders. "If it is an order, one *must* do it. Most of those we are ordered to shoot are criminals anyway. Otherwise, we would not have received an order to shoot them."

We asked if he had heard of Maidenek in Lublin. He said yes, he had been in Lublin in 1943, recovering from his second wound. Had he heard of the 850,000 gassed and cremated there? He corrected us quickly. . . . "That is an exaggeration. I only knew of 16,000 and they were all shot in the back of the neck. The SS *Totenkopf* unit did most of the work there. They had to do it on order. Yes, it was repulsive . . . but it had to be done. . . . It *is* true that we cremated the bodies. . . . We didn't want another Katyn, you know," he said with a clever smile. He described Katyn as a massacre of Polish officers by Russians. "We did not make their mistake of burying the dead. We cremated them."

Asked how this affected him from the humanistic point of view, he said: "We never thought much about it. Most of them were Jews or were in a concentration camp. Everyone in such a camp is probably a criminal. Otherwise, how could he have got into the camp in the first place? You must understand that it is not a personal thing. The man who receives an order to shoot a civilian cannot take time out to find out who is and who is not a criminal. We leave that to the higher authorities."

How "high" is a "high authority"? He said the "order comes from way up. It is not up to our Battalion or Regimental commanders. They are little men. My God, as a matter of fact, even the Generals are little men. They get "their orders from the political higher-ups."

During this admission of shooting civilians and prisoners in Poland, Russia and Jugoslavia, we (Lt. Peter H was present) showed no sharp reaction, and K himself demonstrated no uneasiness about his own participation in the shootings. His attitude was that it was all in the past, that he had merely obeyed "orders," and that the victims were "criminals" and thus deserved execution. His standpoint was that he is now a civilian and wanted to study in peace and his military past was honorable and forgotten.

While still in his frank mood, he spoke of the war "lasting a long while yet." He said the Reich Government "has been in Munich for some time now, and it is there where the last battles will be fought. After the Russians and Allies meet in Central Germany, they will have to fight for South Germany. You will not be able to use tanks in the Alps and the Tyrol and so it will go on for a long time."

"Hitler," he said, "will fight to the last. He *must* because he has said it repeatedly. The troops will also fight until there are no more of them left. Probably Hitler at the last minute will go to the front and die on the battlefield. Then they will be able to say he died fighting. I, personally, would not fight anymore if I had the choice. I don't want to die for a *ver-*

lorener Mann (Hitler). I realized that when I was in the hospital last summer. But if I were in uniform, I would *have to* fight. I take it for granted the SS will be the last to stand around the Führer."

Of Hitler himself, K said: "He is a good man. He means well. But he wanted to be a second Napoleon. He thought he was strong enough to achieve success in his plans. But I wouldn't like to see the whole thing start over again. The Führer failed."

What will be done with Hitler? "I don't think you will kill him. I don't think you are capable of that." K startled us then by saying, "But I would hang all the leaders. I, myself, would kill Hitler because he has not given up and saved what is to be saved. The men of July 20 were men of reason. They understood the situation." (On July 20, K was in the hospital "thinking things over.") K may think he has deserted his Führer, but the Führer's ideas and the crimes are still with him.

4. A Nazi real estate broker: Arthur K

Arthur K, 52, is a *Treuhaender* [real estate broker, or property trustee] from Aachen who joined the Nazi party in 1933, made money handling confiscated Jewish property, and now speaks unfavorably of Hitler and his works.

K had been in the real estate and tax assessment business for 3 years when Hitler came to power. He became a member of the Nazi party because it was good business to do so. "Otherwise," he said, "I would have been *brotlos*" (without employment). There were, he said, 8 *Treuhaender* in Aachen and all of them joined the party in 1933. All of them made money during the Hitler regime, but more especially during the war.

As a practical businessman, K had no aversion to profiting from Hitler, but neither was he enthusiastic about the regime. He is certainly no admirer of it now that it has lost the war and caused inconveniences to comfortable people like himself.

He told us how in the latter part of September he was hiding in Aachen in order not to be evacuated by the Germans, and all the time the *Wehrmacht* was looting houses and stores. At first he, a German patriot, was astonished at this banditry committed by the German Army, then, he said, he realized that it was quite natural. The *Wehrmacht,* he said, was full of Nazi youth and "the youth corrupted everything."

K was tense and nervous during the interview. His conscience was uneasy both because he was a *Treuhaender* and a German. As a *Treuhaender,* he had at his disposal much Jewish property and he knew every detail of how the Jews had been robbed. As a German, he knew of the atrocities committed in Europe, especially in the East, and he was plainly disturbed at their consequences. When he first heard soldiers telling of horrors committed against Frenchmen in France and Jews in Poland he "could not believe it." Later he heard persistent tales of "shooting, gassing, and mass murders" and he reluctantly assumed that it was all true. He could not doubt what was told because he had seen what the Nazis did to Jews in Aachen. "I know how they treated Jews in my city; I know it from my Jewish clients."

Jewish businesses and property, he explained, was disposed of by the city which set a price on every item. The price was, of course, as low as possible, but even then the Jewish owner did not get it. The money was put in the bank—only 7% or 8% of it was allowed to the seller. "The government, or the party, kept the rest." The *Treuhaender* earned 3% to 4% of every transaction. He also received an "Aryanizing" fee of 5%. In short, K implied reluctantly, being a *Treuhaender* for Jewish property was quite a racket.

Herr K regretted the whole thing. He never was anti-Semitic. In fact, he had never heard the word "Jew" until 1923, when some Nazi agitator began to throw it around. In Aachen there was no anti-Semitism. The city had but few Jews "and they were colossally liked because they were fine people."

And the results of this whole "Aryanizing" swindle and finagling? Jews had owned the textile factories at Aachen. Then came the Nazis and "Aryanized" the factories. Then came the war and the factories piled up paper profits, while the machines wore out and could not be replaced. Then came the Allied bombers and knocked out the factories. Then came the *Wehrmacht* and looted what was left. Now there is nothing but ashes and ruins and rubble. Herr K shook his head at it all.

He recalled the tricks one had to employ to get along in the real estate business under the Nazis. You had to have a friend in every government office, but you dared not bribe openly. So you invited the particular *Beamter* to a good dinner and treated him to excellent drinks. One entertained a good deal in those days, Herr K explained, and usually one frequented the same *Kneipe* where the party officials with their wives or girl friends were to be found. Thus one became known as a "regular fellow" among those who wielded power under the swastika, and thus one obtained commissions for jobs or tips about property sales and exchanges. K told us how for several weeks he went to eat and drink at the tavern where the Aachen *Kreisleiter* was a regular guest, and in this way he finally managed to make his acquaintance. To know and be known by the *Kreisleiter* of a city was an invaluable asset to a man in the real estate business.

Herr K's business was not confined to real estate, but also involved advice on taxes, property evaluation, and foreign money exchanges [*"Devisen"*]. During the war, but particularly since 1941, the real estate business was not good. People, K said, had lots of money and wanted to spend it on concrete things, such as houses and lands, but there were few sellers. In the last few years K could not recall the sale of a single house in Aachen! So great was the lack of confidence in German paper money that nobody would exchange a solid piece of property for paper currency. Those who could, bought diamonds, paying 25 times the normal price. "The middle classes," K said, "had no confidence in money because they did not believe Germany could win. To us, only goods and property were 'gold.'"

Since K's contacts were largely with property-owning people, we asked him what, in his opinion, was their attitude about the future; whether, for example, they feared Communism. He replied that so far as he knew Germany had never been threatened by Communism and that the Nazi claim to have saved the country from the Reds was a plain lie. As for the future, people did think there was a possibility that Communism may become a force in the Reich. He himself had never met a Communist, but he often did hear people on the street and in streetcars say, 'We'll come to power some day.' He always assumed as a matter of fact that those who spoke like that were Communists. Everybody knows that there are a lot of Communists in Germany. As for fearing them, K said that he did not. 'There is a lot of drivel about Communism in the Press, but it's nothing but lies. I have no idea what Communism is; I have never lived under a Communist regime. It may be bad or it may be good. I don't know."

K observed that the *"Vaterlands Gefuehl"* [feeling of patriotism] was vanishing in Germany and that only the big industrialists are supporting the regime. Hitler was "the salvation of capitalism," and the capitalists made millions out of the war. Even the workers, who at first "were orated into intoxication," now are sobering up and are becoming lukewarm in their support of the Nazis. Incidentally, K's assertion that the chief supporters of Hitlerism were the capitalists and workers is a favorite one with the middle class. Others, especially professional people, have made similar statements. (This is a point that deserves further investigation and development. If such a split between middle classes, workers and capitalists does exist, our propaganda could take advantage of it by divisive tactics.)

Now that the factories and buildings lie in ruins, neither K nor his middle class friends has any use for the Nazis. He does not blame the Allies for the Aachen shambles; he blames Hitler and his party. Anything, even Communism, would be better than *"These"*—meaning the Nazi "scoundrels." He spoke of *"Diese"* with hate in his voice. "Nazism," he said contemptuously, "is not a polity; it is a tyranny [*"Zwangsherrschaft"*] of a few."

He recalled also with tenderness the days of the Republic, that unfortunate Republic which had been so relentlessly maligned by Nazi propaganda. Under the Republic, which was run by the Social Democrats, Germany *"hatte eine anstaendige Regierung"* [a respectable government]. The government was so good and decent that "we didn't even notice that we had a government." To be sure, there was unemployment, but that was a purely economic, not a political, question. Anyhow, Bruening was beginning to solve it.

He hoped that now that *"alles ist kaputt"* [everything is ruined] it will be possible to rebuild Germany along middle-class, democratic lines. Perhaps America would lend money. Perhaps Bruening would take over the government and rule with "goodness" and not with "severity." But he was pessimistic. The picture of Aachen lying in ruins was too vivid in his mind to permit an attitude of hopefulness.

K denied that the German people were guilty of the atrocities committed by the Nazis in Europe. The people, he said, were ignorant of the crimes, at least of the extent of the crimes. Ger mans simply could not believe that fellow-Germans were capable of perpetrating such horrors. He hopes that the guilty will be punished, but not the whole nation. He felt the same way about the Generals. The latter, even the biggest ones among them, only obey higher orders. "They are professional soldiers, not politicians. They don't think of politics." In short, only Hitler and the higher Nazis are responsible for everything. The German people, the German Generals, German businessmen are innocent victims of the bad, bad Nazis.

5. A German communist: Josef M

When we inquired in mine-infested Würselen how many civilians had been killed by mines, MG referred us to the "Grave Digger," a German who daily risks his life digging out victims and making mines innocuous. We were told that the "Grave Digger" does his dangerous work voluntarily and without compensation.

He came into the room, a powerfully-built young man with brooding eyes and said his name was Josef M and his job de-mining booby-traps. We were eating lunch and we offered him a sandwich. He shook his head—"Why do you do that; don't you know I'm a German?" And he added slowly—"A German wouldn't offer bread to a foreigner."

That day and the next we spent many hours with M. He took us through the town, which he knew intimately. He guided us through the Ravensberg battle field, where scores of German soldiers still lay where they had fallen, cut up, broken. He led us through bunkers where American soldiers had died and through mine fields which he had not yet de-mined. And throughout all these expeditions M made comments that were biting and bitter, and sometimes as brutal as the environment.

His story is not only that of a strong personality; it may also be revealing of the state of mind of other Germans like him— of men who profess allegiance to a political party that was once Hitler's most aggressive enemy and that may yet emerge as a power in Germany.

M, 30, is a miner, the son of a miner who was a communist. When he was 14 he left home and went wandering through Germany. In Berlin, at the age of 15, he fought on the barricades on "Bloody Sunday" (May 1929), when the Social Democratic chief of police fired on the radical workers. M still remembers that with some bitterness. Next to class violence, he was most shocked by the slums [*Elendsgebiete*] and poverty around Berlin. In Wedding he saw 500 to 600 families crowded into one tenement, while in the richer suburbs of Grunewald one family occupied 30 rooms. "I saw that some lived in luxury and others had nothing to eat. I asked myself *warum* [why]? As a human being, don't I have the right to live too?"

In Würselen, M, at the age of 16, organized about 60 youths into the Young Communist League. The Nazis dissolved the group in 1933 and threw M into concentration camp. His father and an aunt were likewise imprisoned. Because of his youth, he was released after 4 months. He continued his anti-fascist activities, this time underground. Of the 60 youths in his group, he said, the Nazis succeeded in winning over only about half a dozen.

In 1934 M helped organize the *Kampfbund gegen den Faschismus* [Combat Union Against Fascism] in Aachen, whither he went nightly. The *Kampfbund* listened to the Moscow and the Basel radios and distributed miniature editions of the *Rote Fahne* which was printed in Belgium. Within a few months the Gestapo ferreted out the *Kampfbund* and destroyed it by incarcerating its leaders. One leader, Radermacher, was sentenced to 12 years; an uncle of M's was given 5 years; a 60 year old aunt, 3 years; and a cousin, 4 years.

Despite the increasingly efficient Gestapo terror, M pursued his anti-Nazi activities in Würselen. Any formal organization was out of the question. Anti-fascist workers, especially those who were friends, met in small social groups, listened to the foreign radio and discussed politics. M's favorite radio was not Moscow but London. He still remembers with pleasure the broadcasts which Thomas Mann made over the BBC. "Mann is the kind of person lacking in Germany today—an honest man." In general, M prefers the BBC to the American radio. He criticizes the latter (despite his admiration for everything American) for its "nervous tempo" and for its lack of political analysis. The BBC, on the other hand, was calm and thoughtful. "London knew how to entertain its listeners." When he listened to Peter Peterson, for example, "I had a feeling as if he were sitting in my room and speaking to me."

M does, indeed, show an intimate knowledge of large world

political events of the last 5 years, a knowledge he gleaned from the Allied radio. He can quote at length from Roosevelt, Churchill, and Stalin. He knows about the Moscow Conference, about Teheran, about the Atlantic Charter, about the Four Freedoms.

Throughout the Nazi era, M's group collected money for political causes. Collections were made for *Rot Spanien* [Red Spain] and for the families of Nazi victims. When a Christian Socialist named Bock was sent to concentration camp, M's communist friends collected money for Bock's wife. "Bock," he said, "was not of our party. But what mattered was that he was an honest anti-fascist. Formerly we had been emenies, but we became friends in need."

Until 1939, the *Wehrmacht* disdained to take M. He was considered "politically unreliable" and was given a pass showing that he was not worthy of the honor of serving in the German army. When the war broke out, the *Wehrmacht* decided that he was eligible for the *Wehrgemeinschaft des deutschen Volkes* [Defense-Community of the German Nation], but he declined the honor of serving in Hitler's army (as a miner he was in a deferred occupation). "Honor?" M said sarcastically, "what kind of honor—the honor of serving in a fascist army? I told them what Liebknecht had said to the reactionary judges when he was tried by them—'You talk of honor, Gentlemen. But my honor is not your honor [*Meine Ehre ist nicht ihre Ehre*]. And your honor is not my honor.' "

In the mines, M said, there was little sabotage. Workers were "not even allowed to be sick." One Dutch miner, ordered by the doctor to stay in bed for 2 weeks, was sentenced to 3 months in an *Arbeitslager* [work camp]. Some miners did heed the BBC instructions to slow up their work, but on the whole this "passive resistance" did not amount to much. "The Germans," M said in slow, contemptuous tones, "are the cheapest and most cowardly people—a *Misthaufen* [manure-pile]."

For the German people M has boundless contempt, a contempt that he expresses in searing language, as if he were castigating himself. He loathes the Germans for their self-pity, their docility, their cowardice, and their slavish obedience. *Knechtseele*, he calls them. "There are no good Germans," he kept on repeating; "even the workers are corrupted and without guts." The Germans, he said, must be made to pay for their crimes; they must be made to suffer deeply before they are permitted to live among civilized nations. M's voice trembled as he spoke of what "they" did in Poland—when he said "they" he meant Germans, not just Gestapo or SS. "What they perpetrated in Poland puts the Middle Ages to shame." His cousin, a *Wehrmacht* soldier stationed in Warsaw, saw how the SS shot 2 Jewish children, then clubbed them to pulp with their butts.

"They," he exclaimed with tears of rage in his eyes, "they are not human. They are *Vieh*—cattle. They have no right to be considered human. Only a German, a *schweinische Deutsche* [swinish German] could perpetrate such horrors. Never should the United States, England, and Russia forget or forgive. I know the German people; I know what swine they are. I'm ashamed to be a German. I know no Fatherland that is called Germany. I want to see the German nation give its last drop of blood to build up what 11 years of Nazism have destroyed."

He said that the Germans are now trying to curry favor with the Americans by claiming that they have never been real Nazis at heart, that they were only *Muss-Nazi* [Nazis-by-compulsion]. M dismissed such claims as specious hypocrisy, as typical German crawling. "Must?" he exclaimed. "There is only one *must*—death. One must only die, but one cannot be compelled to do anything against one's convictions. Those who joined the Nazi party did so in order to profit from it. I know one blacksmith, a member of the Centrist party; he refused to join, and for many years he hungered. I take my hat off to him. He didn't profit from fascism, but he didn't lose his soul either."

When he and his comrades used to talk about the "brutality of fascism," they were laughed at. Only now do the Germans begin to realize that fascism means death and destruction. "They see that Würselen is a pile of debris, destroyed by the *Wehrmacht,* and they realize what Germans are capable of. But now the innocent must suffer with the guilty. Let every German city be destroyed like Würselen. Then the people will perhaps learn to cast out from their souls this swinish militarism."

M took us through the Ravensberg battle field, just outside of Würselen, where scores of dead German soldiers were rotting in the mud. As we made our way through the mine-fields, he pointed to the decaying cadavers and muttered, in a voice of inexpressible scorn, "Fascist dung." Before a rotting group of corpses, lying in a twisted heap, he stopped and pointed—"Look at them—the fascist swine. That's the end-product of fascism: death, death in a mud-hole." He picked up the corpse of a young officer by the scruff of the neck and said: "You see this thing—it was a particularly objectionable fascist swine; it used to strut and boast about its Fuehrer . . ." And he cast the cadaver from him with a gesture of loathing—"*Misthaufen* [manure-heap], pfui . . ."

Always Nazi-fascism was to him a horrible disease and even in the darkest hours, when Hitler was sitting on top of almost all of Europe, M did not give up hope that the disease would be eradicated. Only once in all these years did he lose his communist faith for a moment, and that was in 1939 when Hitler and Stalin made their famous pact. "When I heard of their alliance," he told us, "my heart sank into my stomach and I trembled all over." In his despair he talked to his communist father, and the parent restored his faith. "Son," the old man (who died 2 years later of silicosis) said, "you don't understand. You are only a *Staubkorn*, a particle of dust in the process of history. When the Russians do something, they do it with a purpose."

Ever since then, M has had complete and unquestioning trust in the Soviets. He is frankly cynical about Moscow's use of General von Seydlitz and his Free Germany Committee. He is convinced that after Stalin has used the Generals for his purpose— the overthrow of fascism—he will get rid of them. To M the Generals are no better than the Nazis. After the attempt on Hitler's life on July 20, M for once found himself in agreement with the Fuehrer—when the latter shot the Generals. "These gentlemen had supported Hitler in all his fascist adventures; they marched into Poland with music and drums; they devastated France; they ravaged Russia. Hitler loaded them with crosses and medals. Then Hitler was good enough for them. Now that they know they cannot win, they are turning against him. And such people talk about a Free Germany!" M is sure that Stalin will know how to treat the Generals as they richly deserve.

As a communist, M rejects scornfully all the standard German heroes from Charlemagne to Bismarck. To him the only heroes are those who fought and died for their ideals, especially proletarian ideals. He mentioned the "communist martyr" Etia Andre who was condemned to death by the Nazis in 1934. He spoke of 5 other martyrs, boys under 18 who were executed in Cologne. One of these boys had said to the Nazi judge—"My honor in a prison uniform is higher than yours in a judge's robes."

Although a communist and an admirer of the Soviet system, M categorically rejects all idea of dictatorship. "We have had 11 years of dictatorship, and that's enough," he said bitterly. He wants to live in a land where the Four Freedoms reign, "like your President said in a speech." For him personally, "spiritual freedom is more important than food." He knows, however, that this view is not a German view. "Give the German people bread, and they will cry *Heil Hitler*. As for me, I want democracy."

He is so grateful to the Americans for having come to liberate the Germans that he is willing to sacrifice his life in the Allied cause. If given a chance, he would "immediately" put on an American or any Allied uniform and "fight the Germans." The latter, he said, are too cowardly to free themselves; therefore he wants to show "a little gratitude" to those who bring freedom. He quoted a 16th-century saying from the period of the Peasant Wars:

UND SETZT IHR NICHT DAS LEBEN EIN
WIE KANN DIE FREIHEIT GEWONNEN SEIN
(If you don't stake your life,
how can you win freedom?).

M's hatred for Germans is equalled in intensity by his admiration for Americans. Even before the Americans entered Würselen he did what he could to help them. There was one battery in town which he wanted to seize from the Germans, but he needed the help of 10 comrades. The latter, however, refused to take the chance, and now M refers to them bitterly as "true German *Knechtseele* [slave-souls]." After their refusal, he broke the gun he had kept hidden for 11 years in the cellar; with Germans being what they are, no revolution was ever possible in Germany, hence there was no need for a gun. He managed to help the Americans in another way. One day, during the 6-weeks' siege of Würselen, 10 members of the SS *Leibstandarte* asked him to help them desert. M's motto, being *Ein guter deutscher Soldat ist ein toter Soldat,* [a good German soldier is a dead soldier], he assisted them in a venture that could easily cost them their lives. He put them in a cellar and scrounged food for them. In the end they were caught. Whatever happened to them, to M they were as good as dead; he did not care—he had achieved his purpose of keeping them from fighting the Americans. Incidentally, the 10 deserters were all Austrians in their early 20's; one was the son of a bank director from Krems.

Würselenites, M said, were waiting for the Americans to come and deliver them, waiting as if for the messiah. Daily people asked: *wo ist der Amerikaner? Warum kommt er nicht? Warum ist er nicht hier?* [Where is the American? Why doesn't he come? Why is he not here?]. On the morning of November 17 the deliverers came. M was sitting in his room with 4 comrades when his mother announced that German Panzers were on the street. Then neighbors came in with the news that the tanks were American, not German. M took out a bottle of Schnapps and toasted the liberators. A few days later he offered to pick dead bodies out of the mine fields and booby-trapped houses. He developed a method of removing the delicate wires from the mines. "Not everybody can do it," he said with some pride. Asked why he endangers his life like that, he replied that he wanted to show his gratitude to the liberators. As for danger, he shrugged his shoulders—"you can die only once."

In the first 3 weeks, M picked up 132 dead German soldiers and 32 Americans. From German booby-trapped houses he removed 14 German civilians, of whom only 8 were recognizable; the others were just pieces.

At this point our German-speaking driver, Pfc Joseph Frauendorfer, who had been listening to M in absorbed fascination, interrupted him to ask his opinion of the fighting qualities of the American soldier. M replied that the American is a *sport Soldat* [a soldier who considers war a sport] and that he is right in being a cautious fighter. Why should the American needlessly sacrifice his life to liberate such rotten people as the Germans? "I am sorry for every drop of American blood that is shed for our freedom. Americans should not die; they have something to live for. They live *wie Gott in Frankreich* [like God in France], whereas Germans have not much to live for and are no good anyhow." M said that at first he thought American infantrymen were afraid. But in the Ravensberg battle, the

Americans sent patrols in the dead of night through the German lines. "Men who have fear don't do that."

M wonders whether this is not, after all, the American Century. He and his comrades have frequently discussed this subject and they think that the United States has something to offer to the world. It would be a good idea *das Volk geistig zu amerikanisieren* [to Americanize the people spiritually]. He is sure that the Americans are not imperialistic, because they are now fighting fascism *aus Ueberzeugung* [out of conviction]. His favorite American authors, by the way, are Upton Sinclair and Zane (he pronounced it Tzahne) Grey. The latter's novels have convinced M that Americans are gentlemen—"they treat women like ladies even in the most primitive surroundings."

Young M is bitter without being cynical. He is a communist who does not seem to know much of Marx and does not accept the idea of dictatorship. There is in him a passion for righteousness and justice, and this sets him apart from most Germans with whom we had any contact. His intense bitterness at his own people derives from his frustration, from his knowledge that the Germans have taken a path that has led them to self-destruction and has earned them the contempt and hate of the civilized world. He is driven by a tremendous urge to atone for the follies and the crimes of the German people.

6. *An "Old Socialist": Georg T*

Georg T, 47, comes from Ehren near Trier. He had a grocery at Saarbrucken and a wine shop at Saarburg. At Saarbrucken he was a member of the League for Human Rights and helped hundreds of Jews and other Hitler victims escape by means of false papers. In 1939 he moved to Danzig where he worked in the administration of docks for 1 year and in a stocking factory for 1 more year. In 1942-43 he was head of a section in the Foreign Property Office [*Haupttreuenstelle Ost, Grundstueckverwaltung*] at Dirchau near Danzig. Afterwards he returned to his home region: Bittburg in the Eifel. Here he worked as personnel manager in a motor factory which employed 150 workers, 65 of whom were Russian women. When he heard the Americans were approaching the area, T began to prepare for flight. First he helped the 65 Russian girls, for whom he had profound sympathy, escape into the mountains near Luxembourg (he and

2 friends, one from Cologne and one from Holland, made all the preparations, including the provision of food and blankets); then he obtained guns and grenades from *Reichswehr* soldiers (in exchange for food). On September 17 he ran over to the American lines and gave the U.S. officers important military information, for which he was warmly commended.

Two influences had moulded T's life—his brother and the Social Democratic ideal. The son of a Catholic merchant, Georg T studied music as an avocation (he plays all instruments) and commerce as a profession. Early in life he became a Social Democrat, and he has remained one ever since. Now, after 11 years of Hitlerism, the Socialist ideal is for him more sacred than ever. He never compromised with Nazism, but fought it with all the means at his disposal. Nazism had, in fact, steeled him in his determination and made him oblivious to self and ambition. He has the thin, intense, thoughtful face of a man whose mission is more important than his life. He speaks quietly and one feels in him an emotion that just barely is held in check.

His brother Matthias is still an influence with him. Matthias has been in Sachsenhausen concentration camp (No. 67411) since 1933. During these 11 years Matthias's spirit has remained unbroken. Matthias, his brother told us, was a Communist leader before Hitler came to power. From 1928 to 1933 he was Communist member of the Reichstag (from Duisburg). Twice a month Matthias writes to his brother; in these cryptic letters (Georg read, and explained, one of these letters to us) he informs his brother that he is still hopeful, still unchanged, still expecting to fight fascism and build a decent society on its ruins. And regularly, during all these years, Georg T sent packages of food to his brother in concentration camp, and these gifts and exchanges have kept alive the body of the one and the spirit of the other.

It was not easy. In 1936 the Gestapo decided that Georg T's correspondence with his brother was an act of treason. So Georg was thrown into concentration camp, Lager 6 in Emsland. Here he remained until 1938.

T had always disagreed with his Communist brother on the question of dictatorship. Georg, the Social Democrat, favored the "democratic life," while Matthias insisted upon the dictatorship of the proletariat. Now Georg, too, has come to the conclusion that one must use "dictatorial methods against the Nazis." Moreover, he is convinced that a "democratic Germany is impossible."

All the old Social Democratic leaders are either dead or in concentration camp. T claimed that some 3,000,000 Socialists are in concentration camps—unquestionably a fantastic figure. There is no Socialist organization in Germany, neither open nor secret. There are still millions of old Socialists, but each man is for himself, each man distrustful of his neighbor. Consequently, T believes, Social Democracy "has no future in Germany."

T observed a new tendency among the intellectual classes, particularly in the Rhineland with which he is most familiar, a tendency towards the Left. He said that intellectual and professional people have swung towards a socialist ideal and that now there are more "socialist-inclined people" than ever before. He believes that Thomas Mann's broadcasts have had a great influence on the intellectuals. "Mann has given them a new hope."

This new tendency, however, does not mean the restoration of the Social Democratic party. It may mean some form of national communism.

T denounced as *"grundfalsch"* [fundamentally wrong] the notion that Germans are incapable of self-government or of resistance to tyranny. There are, he said, plenty of leaders among the older generation; and many will emerge from the youth. Was then not Germany's youth poisoned by Nazism? He denied it categorically. He himself had spoken to many young *Wehrmacht* soldiers. Generally he found them eager to hear what he had to say, anxious to follow something better than war and killing and dying. Many, from his personal knowledge, have already "recognized the Nazi swindle." He always said to the young soldiers: "If you keep your heads and save your lives by surrendering, then you have won the war, because then you will be alive to fight Hitlerism." And many of them would nod. In any case, he was never denounced by them for such speeches.

His voice quivered slightly as he denied the charge that the German people never resisted Nazi oppression. Thousands of Germans, he said, are still in prisons and concentration camps, suffering from their convictions. "If you ever will look at the court and criminal records you will be surprised at the amount of resistance that existed in Germany." Talk to lawyers and judges, he said; then you will find out how great has been the resistance.

Vaterland? For him the old type of patriotism no longer exists. "I recognize no Germans; I recognize only Nazis and anti-Nazis."

We asked him how one could differentiate a Nazi from an anti-Nazi; so many now claim to be anti-Nazi. That, he replied, is not difficult. Ask a man what he thinks of the social question; a real Nazi will have no social ideals. Ask him what he knew of the concentration camps and the treatment of Jews. If he denies knowing anything about it, then you ask him why he never interested himself in the suffering of his brothers. Ask him what he did when he heard about the murder of the Jews in Poland. If he claims to be "unpolitical," then you know he is untruthful—the Nazis permitted no "unpolitical" people.

The German people themselves must begin with "a thorough housecleaning." All Nazi leaders and officials, beginning with the *Blockwart,* must be interned. The guilty must be ruthlessly destroyed. The young must be "reeducated."

But can the Germans do it? T exclaimed: "You will talk to many, you will hear many sides. But always you will recall what I tell you: There is a sound core in Germany. There are good people in Germany. Help the good people exterminate the evil."

Despite his age and frail health, T, who is childless, pleaded for a chance to fight Nazism. He is willing to be returned to Germany to work underground. He has a thorough knowledge of the area between Trier and Cologne and knows all the reliable and Nazi elements. He is willing to do anything: either organize anti-Nazi Germans outside the border or go into Germany gun in hand. "Every hour," he said, "is lost. I am ready to go with you to death, if necessary."

Before he left, T made one request. We thought it would be the usual request for cigarettes, but we were mistaken. He asked for a book to study the English language.

7. *An Artillery Lieutenant: Rudolf K*

Rudolf K, 21, was interrogated at the PWE at Henri Chapelle one day after capture. Since we were primarily interested in his attitudes and reactions, we did not examine him for military information except in the sketchiest manner. He attended the *Mittelschule* in Berlin until the age of 16; then he studied to be an electro-technician; then, at the age of 18, he entered the army (March, 1942). From March, 1943, to February, 1944, he was on the Russian front near Chelm. He came out of Russia a *"Faehnrich"* [ensign] and later in the year became a lieutenant (artillery). He was captured by the Americans on the Monschau front on December 17 when the bunker, in which he and 60 men were stationed, was smashed by tanks and the air vents sealed off. Rather than choke to death, "we had no choice but to surrender." Asked why he, a German officer, did not fight to the last bullet, he replied bitterly: "To die in the bunker was senseless; it would not serve the fatherland"—the implication was that he wanted to live in order some day to fight again.

K is a slow-spoken young man, without animation and with tense obstinacy. He does not express himself freely, and he is so unused to conversation on the level of ideas that many of our questions not only surprised him but also made him admit: "You asked me questions I never asked myself."

He is a man without education or knowledge; in place of convictions, he has obstinate verbal patterns which revolve around "fatherland," "Germany," "nationalism," "army" and similar word-clusters. From the German Army's point of view, K is probably an ideal officer—unimaginative, unpitying, unquestioning. He is not a Nazi; he is an obedient soldier. Hitler is the government, and K obeys and fights for the government. The aims and cliches of the "eternal" Germany are the aims and cliches of Lieutenant K.

This is the more surprising in that K is not a *"Junker"* or a member of the upper or middle classes. He is the son of a carpenter and in his boyhood he had known starvation and misery. His father, who lived in Neu-Koeln, the "red" suburb of Berlin, was unemployed under the Republic, and this is one reason why K has no use for the Republic. His father must have been a Communist (K would neither admit nor deny this) and never joined the Nazi party. Throughout the whole Hitler period K senior neither discussed politics in his home nor ever mentioned the Fuehrer's name. Why was that? Lieutenant K shrugged his shoulders. "People," he spoke in the third person but obviously referred to his own home, "didn't talk politics at

home if they knew the children had different opinions from
their own." Then he added as an afterthought: "In Germany
when people have different thoughts, (i.e., different from what
is official) they don't make them known. They would be *dumm*
to admit them publicly." He explained that Germany is a big
country with a lot of people, and they cannot all agree. When
he was on leave, he eschewed politics or social contact completely; he would stay by himself and keep silent. Incidentally,
the last time he saw Berlin, when he was on leave, was October.
The city, he said, "is practically completely destroyed." One sees
people on the streets, however. "I don't know where they come
from or where they live."

K was unhappy at his captive state. He and his soldiers in the
bunker did not want to surrender because they feared being
separated from their families for a long period of time. "Everybody wants to see his home from time to time. When one fights
on one's home soil one has an opportunity to visit his brothers
and sisters. That's why we don't like to be captured."

He had, moreover, been mistreated by the Americans. He
showed us, in great indignation, where the insignia were torn
off his tunic by the Americans. He was struck with a shovel
once. He was given a shovel and asked to dig his own grave. All
this was "not decent." Germans do not treat American prisoners
that way; it is *"verboten"* in Germany to mistreat American
PW's. Why was he maltreated? Because, he explained angrily,
the Americans wanted him to give away the German artillery
positions. He refused, and so did his colleague, a captain. The
latter was then struck in the face with fists and pistol butt. "If
we had given away our artillery positions, English and American planes would have been over the spot within an hour and
our comrades would have been killed. Therefore we were willing to sacrifice ourselves for our comrades."

We asked him whether the Germans had never mistreated
prisoners of war; he denied it vehemently. We asked him
whether the Germans had ever mistreated Russians, Poles, or
Jews. No, he had never seen Russian PW's mistreated—this he
said haltingly, uncertain of himself. What kind of people are
the Russians? He himself had never had any contact with them
during his whole year in Russia. He had never spoken to a Russian—Chelm, where he was stationed, was empty of people. But
he had dogmatic opinions of the Russians. They never retreat.

They are *Stur* (obdurate, bovine); they fight to the death. They are silent, non-urban fighting men. They have a different concept of *"Vaterland"* from the Germans. He saw Russian prisoners and they looked to him *"stumpfsinnig"* [stupid, idiotic], indifferent to their fate, fatalistic; whereas German prisoners always think of their families and entertain "human" thoughts. As fighters the Russians are *"zaehe und verbissen"* [tough and sullen]. Still the Germans are better soldiers. The Russians drove the Germans from the Soviet Union only because the *Wehrmacht* had to fight on 2 fronts. "I am convinced, however, that we can and will stop the Russians at our frontier."

As for mistreatment of Poles and Jews, K reluctantly admitted that he had "heard" of atrocities committed in Poland. He was not in favor of such atrocities. At first he did not believe what he heard. Then he thought that people who did such things were *gemeine Leute"* [mean people] and he "despised" them. He does not believe that a real German officer would ever give an order to kill "defenseless" people. SS officers might— "but I have never had any contact with SS officers and know nothing about them." Would he, Lieutenant K, obey an order to shoot civilians? He hesitated a long time before answering, then he said he would not shoot "defenseless" women and children. "But, then, a German officer would *not* give such an order." He refused to grant such a possibility even theoretically.

K was not lucid about the origins of the present war; his utterances came out disjointedly and hesitantly. "I have long pondered over the causes of the war," he said. "It came about through Poland. The Corridor cut off East Prussia from the Reich. We had to unite the Reich. If the Poles had yielded, there would have been no war." How did the war with Russia start? "For me the war in the East came as a surprise. I don't know why it started. You ask me why, then, I fought against Russia? I fought because every German has a duty to be a soldier and as a soldier one has to obey."

The war with the United States was equally puzzling to K. He thought for a long while before he formulated his thoughts. "America declared war on Japan and as an ally of Japan we had to declare war on America. One has to keep one's word. Why should I know such things? As a soldier I have nothing to do with such decisions. I cannot judge whether or not it was a mistake to attack America. I only obey. I only fight for the fatherland. I am not concerned with politics. In my opinion, it makes no difference as to who rules the Reich, so long as the conditions are *menschlich* (humane)."

Under Hitler conditions in the Reich were *"menschlich."* Before Hitler, many people did not have enough to eat and there were street fights everywhere. He himself remembered the time when there was not enough to eat in his parents' home. Hitler came and gave people work and bread. "Hitler had the right idea. What was his idea? It was that everybody should have work and that there should be no hunger. The trouble was that the Fuehrer lacked the assistants to carry out his idea. The Fuehrer is humane. I am sure he would never have ordered the killing of women and children. Nor would Goering. Nor would Himmler or Goebbels. I heard that such orders were issued, but I am sure Hitler did not issue them."

Asked whether he knew the word democracy, he thought for a long time and said: "Democracy is the same as Nazism or Communism. It is an idea. What idea? I never experienced it personally, so I can't say. Germany had it in 1933. America has it. In Germany it caused bad times, or maybe the economic situation did it. In America I don't know what it is like; I have never been there. All these big words—Nazism, Communism, Democracy—are the same at bottom. I can never get any clarity on such things. And what difference do they make anyhow? So long as the people have bread and work, it is all the same."

Would he, then, not care if Germany became Communist, for example? K stared us fixedly, an obstinate line around his mouth. "If Russia occupies us we would become a *Sklavenvolk* [slave nation]." If Germany loses the war to the other powers, there would "certainly be poverty for years to come."

But he was convinced that Germany was not going to lose the war. "I don't know how long it will take to achieve victory, but it will be achieved. I am convinced of it, or I would not have fought." He absolutely refused to consider the possibility of defeat. "I am firmly sure of victory; I have never entertained thoughts of losing." He did not know how victory would become, but come it would. "They—the Generals—must have good reason to fight on. They believe in the *Endsieg* [final victory]. Otherwise they would not sacrifice German blood."

The putsch of July 20 puzzled him and he frankly could not explain it. He could not believe that German Generals could be so disloyal as to attack the head of the government. He insinuated that General von Witzleben must have had some private, rather than patriotic, motive for his conspiracy against the Fuehrer. "What surprised me, however, was that Hitler was caught so unawares."

K admitted hearing about Paulus and Seydlitz and their Free Germany Committee. He refused to express an opinion on the subject, not wishing to give the impression that he had the temerity to criticize high German Generals. He made it clear, however, that he did not approve of them. "On the other hand," he said, "we have Vlasov who organized a Free Russian Committee on our side. It is possible that Paulus was bitter on account of Stalingrad, where he sacrificed so many German soldiers and didn't win through."

The German army, K said dogmatically, will never give up. "It did not give up in the last war either. Only the civilians gave up. I am convinced the American army will never reach the Rhine. I cannot even imagine being defeated."

The Germans will continue to fight to the end. K said he had never heard of the order proclaiming a "scorched earth" policy, but it did not surprise him. The fight will go on for every German city, town, and village. There is no point at which he, or his colleagues, would cry halt. Didn't that necessitate having to shoot and kill German civilians in places occupied by the Allies? "Yes," said K slowly; "but we ask civilians to evacuate when we have to retreat. If they don't, what can we do? As an artillerist, I know it is not a pleasant feeling to have to destroy German homes, but for the defense of the German fatherland it is necessary to do so."

8. A race-conscious and Nazified girl: Trude S

An Aachen school teacher once told us that the young students in his school fell into 2 categories—"verkraenkelt" [sickly, infected] and "vergiftet" [poisoned] with Hitlerism. The majority, he said, are merely "verkraenkelt" and can be redeemed with some effort.

Trude S, 17, a Würselen student, belongs in the category of the "verkraenkelt." The daughter of a locomotive engineer, she considers herself one degree higher than the working class and displays the symptoms of a petty bourgeoise. If Germany had won the war, and if Würselen were not a solid proletarian community, Trude S would certainly have grown into a full-fledged Nazi. As it is, she can probably be deflected into another course.

She joined the BDM when she was 10 and enjoyed the frequent meetings, specially the sports (she likes swimming, track, tennis). Once a week she met with her *Schaar* of 10 girls and they discussed politics. Trude was bored with that. The Fuehrer, she said, "talked politics *bis zur vergasung*" (to the point of asphyxiation). Political lectures were in the form of a catechism. The Fuehrerin asked: "What did the Fuehrer do for Germany?" The girls replied: "The Fuehrer abolished unemployment. He built roads. He constructed factories. He made cities flourish." Trude was cynical as she told us about it. "It's all *quatsch* (nonsense)," she said with a grin.

Trude's friends at school were enthusiastic for the war. She was enthusiastic too. They basked in the glory and in the conquest of the world by the mighty *Wehrmacht*. The young boys, she said, used to boast: "Wait till we join the *Wehrmacht*—then it'll be over quickly: we'll show them."

Her father, the locomotive engineer, served in Russia where he was wounded, and when he came home he cursed the campaign, cursed the war. "Our soldiers," he said, "had to fight against tremendous odds. The war is lost." Trude did not believe what her embittered father said. Only now does Trude realize that the war is lost and she thinks, quite cheerfully, that she was *"belogen"* [lied to]. Asked in what sense she thought herself *"belogen,"* she said: "Take, for example, V-1. Goebbels lied about that. He said to us that the enemy will beg us on his knees to give him peace. The V-1 will force the enemy to his knees. And what happened? When we heard of the V-1, we hoped and hoped for victory, and in the end nothing came of it. Thus we were lied to."

Up to 1943, at least ¾ths of the youth of her acquaintance were Nazi: now most of them have "melted away." The realization of defeat undermined their patriotism. "Losing the war," she said, "meant losing also our *Vaterlandsliebe*" [love of fatherland].

We asked her to define what in her opinion constituted a young Nazi. She described him as a person who (1) believes everything the government says, (2) believes in victory, (3) says

Heil Hitler, (4) is *Gottglaeubig,* and (5) goes to party meeting Sunday morning during mass time.

In her disappointment at Germany's losing the war, Trude has turned against everything that is openly Nazi. Asked if she would marry a Nazi, she exclaimed: *"Um gottes willen, neh!"* [For God's sake, no]. Would she marry a Frenchman or a Russian? Her answer was an equally vehement No. "Everybody knows that they are so crude." This led her to discourse on the subject of race, which, it turned out, was her favorite study.

Germans, she explained, must marry only Germans. "It is not right to marry a non-German." She might marry an American because "most Americans are of German race." When we hinted that the German race is mixed, she denied it indignantly. She could not answer what race Goebbels and Hitler belonged to. All she knew was that the Nordic race, to which the Germans (and she too: she is big and heavyish) belonged, was "the superior, the most valuable" [*wertvollste*]. A Nordic, she defined as if memorizing the whole sentence, is 1.70 meters high, big, has grey-blue eyes, and is earnest. Originally these Nordics, "the best racial and spiritual type," were members of the SS. The Nordic SS were the ideal males of girls like Trude S.

Who, we asked, were the lower races? Russians, Poles, Italians, Frenchmen, Jews, she said. The French are inferior because "they are small, temperamental, excitable [*hitzig*], and changeable." The Italians are also "temperamental and changeable." German soldiers in France and Italy were forbidden to have any contact with the women of those countries, Trude told us with some pride. Of Jews, Trude said that there were "many intelligent ones among them," but that they weren't perhaps good for Germany. Still she thought that since the German race was made up of 6 (Nordic) racial tribes, she saw no reason why there should not have been a 7th race, the Jewish.

Among the Nazi youth, especially between the ages of 16 to 18, Trude told us, about half had close relationship with the opposite sex. This was particularly true of the little Fuehrers and Fuehrerinen who "harmonized together."

Trude said that she likes to read books, mainly love stories about the gentry. She also claimed to be a student of history and we asked her what she knew of Germany's past. Her knowledge was not extensive. Of the Republic she knew nothing. In this connection she mentioned "Bismarck, who wanted to solve the German question." Wilhelm II? "He was a cowardly fighter; he ran away."

We wanted to know how the present war came about and Trude explained that it began with Poland. "The Poles mistreated Germans. The German government would not stand for it and sent in German soldiers. This was the right thing to do, but Hitler should have made an end with the war after he took the corridor." Then Germany had to fight France because the latter had an alliance with Poland. "As for Russia we had to go to war with the Soviets because they began to transport troops and munitions, so we went there first."

How, we asked, did Germany get involved in war with America? Trude said that she heard Hitler's declaration of war on the U.S. and she told a friend: "This is stupid [*Bloedsinn*]. America is too big and produces too much." But her friend laughed at her.

Trude expects Germany to be divided up among the powers, the left bank of the Rhine to go to France and England, and the right bank to be taken over by Italy, Poland, Czechoslovakia, and Austria. Then, she said, "everything will be over with race and fatherland," and their heroes—and Trude's too—will be Charlemagne, Frederick the Great, and Bismarck. Did she not count Hitler among the heroes? No, she said. "If Hitler were really a great man, he would make an end of this war."

Maybe, Trude thought, communism would come to Germany. What is communism? "It is against Nazism. Communists say that wherever you're well off, there is your fatherland. I think that's true. This was said by Jew Marx. He incited the workers which wasn't so good. Am I a communist? Now everybody wants to be a communist. I personally would like to see a government like we had before 1918, a government with a Kaiser at the head of it, and not an ordinary man of the people (like Hitler)."

Trude's mind is thus a portrait of monumental confusion—at the same time a Nazi and anti-Nazi, an anti-Semite and a pro-Semite, a Communist, a monarchist, and a snob.

Chapter 9

TRENDS IN WEHRMACHT MORALE *

By

M. I. GURFEIN AND MORRIS JANOWITZ

In ORDER to guide combat propaganda teams in their leaflet and loudspeaker missions and to direct strategic psychological warfare against the Wehrmacht, the Psychological Warfare Division of SHAEF, under Brigadier General Robert A. McClure, undertook a continuing study of the fighting morale of the enemy's troops. The study, expanding the work started in North Africa and Italy, represented, perhaps for the first time in warfare, an attempt to evaluate trends by procuring and analyzing comparable data.[1]

Main reliance was placed on the systematic analysis of front line interrogations of captured prisoners as well as detailed psychological interviews gathered in rear areas, the results of which were systematically evaluated. Materials gleaned from captured enemy documents, reports of secret agents, recaptured Allied military personnel and the observations of front line combat observers were also evaluated. As an adjunct, a monthly statistical survey of attitudes among captured German soldiers was undertaken. This article summarizes the main trend conclusions of this statistical opinion poll.[2]

The main findings underlined the conclusion that the ideology of the "average" German soldier remained singularly steadfast. Hitler—personification of evil to the democratic world—for example, held the loyalties of more than 50 percent of his army through the defeats of 1944 and until March 1945, two months before V-E Day. Belief in secret weapons was also a source of vital strength. On the other hand, although the German army fought hard until the end, as early as June and July 1944 less than half of the prisoners of war thought that they

* Reprinted from *Public Opinion Quarterly*, Spring 1946.

could eject the Allies from France. Reverses in the fortunes of battle and the deterioration of the conditions of life at the front were reflected in further depression in the German soldiers' expectation of victory. This pointed to the wisdom of non-ideological lines of attack on the psychological warfare front.

Stimmung vs. Haltung

Aside from the technical difficulties involved in measuring prisoner of war opinion, it has become a commonplace among those who worked in psychological warfare against the Germans, that attitudes encountered before or after capture bore only a limited relationship to fighting behavior under combat conditions. The practical difficulties of surrender in modern battle, the habit of automatic obedience and the Nazi terror sustained a fighting effectiveness often unrelated to morale. The Nazis themselves emphasize the sharp distinction between Stimmung [Attitude] and Haltung [Behavior]. It was felt, however, that in strategic terms, sharp deviations from the established norm of attitudes would give the clue to distintegration. And, in fact, the clue was found prior to the last spring offensive, before which there had been no sharp deviation in attitude and, correspondingly, few large scale surrenders.

The conclusions from the attitude data gathered through statistical polling procedures, which this report sets forth, should not, however, be taken as the pattern of the collapse of the Wehrmacht. These polls must be viewed in conjunction with the more important mass of documents collected and prepared on the Wehrmacht as an integral fighting organization and as a social and psychological entity. The evaluation of this material still remains as a future task.

Method Employed

A write-in questionnaire, preceded by a standardized introductory talk, was administered to periodic random samples of prisoners of war collected at transit cages. This was necessitated by limitations of personnel, and by field conditions. Such a procedure gave continuing samples of prisoners, rather than of the enemy army itself.[3] But, since the results of the questionnaire were considered only on a trend basis, it was possible to analyze important shifts in opinion, which should reflect important changes in attitude in the Wehrmacht itself.

The validity of the replies was dependent on two unique factors. First, the prisoners were almost wholly unfamiliar with the procedures of write-in questionnaires. Second, they who had been living for twelve years under Nazi controls might have become psychologically inhibited from stating their true opinions. Thus, Nazis might tend to hide their Nazism, and members of the non-political center might tend to exaggerate their anti-Nazism. To meet these difficulties, (1) a standard set of detailed instructions for filling out the questionnaires was administered to each sample. Spot checks revealed that the prisoners were making only an inconsequential number of errors in the completion of the forms. (2) Extreme care was taken to overcome resistance to expression of genuine opinion by the use of a standardized introductory talk which emphasized that the poll sought after free independent expression of opinion in line with American traditions and that the identity of the individual prisoner would be protected.[4] Although exact scientific tests were not undertaken to determine any significant differences between answers obtained through direct interrogation techniques with those obtained from questionnaire surveys, extensive matching of the results revealed a high degree of similarity.

The Theory of the Questionnaire

The questionnaire generally contained about twenty questions, most of them of current interest for psychological warfare. To measure basic attitudes on a trend basis, however, five key questions were used. These questions were selected on the basis of psychological evaluation of the patterns of German thought developed by interrogation. The aim was to select questions which would give not detached, objective answers but which would, rather, reveal a relative adhesion to the German ideological position and propaganda line, both in current belief and in longer term trends.

The key questions were thus selected to reflect: (1) Expectation of Victory, (2) Confidence in the Battle Situation, (3) Belief in Secret Weapons, (4) Fear of Revenge by the Allies (a favorite

Goebbels' theme "Strength through Fear") and (5) Faith in Hitler. (See Table No. 1)

Pattern of Collapse

When viewed as a whole, the five key questions represent strikingly the long term, relative stability of Wehrmacht attitudes until the beginnings of the final collapse in March 1945. Expectations as to the outcome of the war fluctuated with the success of Allied advances. As to ideological attachments, there was no significant break until February and March 1945, at which point of time significantly large scale surrenders began to occur.

Expectation of Victory

The hardships of battle, the shock of capture and the sight of vast quantities of military stores and mobile equipment behind our lines limited "after capture" belief in victory among prisoners of war even during the first phases of the Normandy campaign. In June and July only about 40 percent of samples of prisoners of war thought, "It is possible to eject the Allies from France."

But as the campaign progressed expectations of success among prisoners of war deteriorated as the Germans were pushed back across France until a low point of widespread and almost utter defeatism was reached in mid-October. The question naturally presents itself whether the group of prisoners captured in mid-October who were surveyed presented an atypically low morale group or whether the objective situation had deteriorated so as to affect attitudes in this fashion. (Col. 6 of Table 1) Observations at this time indicated no serious divergence in the type of prisoner in this randomly selected sample from earlier or later samples. The events of the late September drive which took the Allied armies to the borders of Germany had apparently caused this serious fall in German expectations.

The sharp rise in November troop morale similarly reflects the stabilization which set in after we failed to follow up what theretofore appeared a vast strategic retreat of the German army. (Col. 7, Table 1) This feeling grew in large measure out of the relative security of a temporarily stabilized front, and a sky partly free of Allied aircraft grounded by bad weather.

TABLE 1

Trends in Wehrmacht Morale Based on Write-in Questionnaires

Date of Capture		(1) June 26-28 1944	(2) July 1-17 1944	(3) Aug. 1-10 1944	(4) Sept. 1-10 1944	(5) Mid-Sept. 1944	(6) Mid-Oct. 1944	(7) Nov. 15-30 1944	(8) Jan. 1-14 1945	(9) March 1945
Number of Prisoners		363	155	160	643	634	345	453	324	388
Place of Capture		CHER-BOURG	CAREN-TAN to ST. LO	ST. MALO to LE MANS	METZ-NANCY REGION	WEST FRONT	WEST FRONT	AA-CHEN-METZ	WEST FRONT	WEST FRONT
QUESTION		%	%	%	%	%	%	%	%	%
Do you trust the Fuehrer?	Yes	67	57	68	65	60	42	64	62	31
	No	18	27	17	19	24	43	22	30	52
	N.A.	15	16	15	16	16	15	14	8	17
Do you think it is possible to eject the Allies from France?	Yes	42	37	49	27	—	—	51	39	10*
	No	38	49	29	51	—	—	30	47	83*
	N.A.	20	14	22	22	—	—	19	14	7*
Do you believe that Germany is winning the war?	Yes	—	—	52	38	46	28	50	44	11
	No	—	—	11	39	33	57	27	42	78
	N.A.	—	—	37	23	21	15	23	14	11
Do you believe that revenge will be taken against the population of Germany after the war?	Yes	16	13	36	28	21	18	—	—	—
	No	75	81	51	61	67	74	—	—	—
	N.A.	9	6	13	11	12	8	—	—	—
Do you believe that Germany still has war decisive "Secret Weapons"?	Yes	37	44	66	49	48	33	53	47	14
	No	35	37	15	37	32	52	29	40	77
	N.A.	28	19	19	20	20	15	18	13	9

Note: *Question on March 1945: "Do you think it is possible to eject the Allies from Western Germany?"

Their conceptions of victory also underwent revision and meant in large measure an absence of total defeat. Nevertheless the degree of recovery reflects faithfully the Wehrmacht's ability to effect as complete a defense as was technically feasible.

In January (Col. 8), expectation started to decline when the tonic of temporary advance after many months of retreat began to wear off. When the failure of the offensive was clear to the troops, Germany's psychological reserves became exhausted. In the spring of 1945, critical defeatism set in as the final combined two-front assault against the Fatherland developed. It was a defeatism which failed to develop into any positive efforts among large groups of soldiers to remove themselves from the battle. Group surrenders were relatively few. However, the troops and even their junior officers once cut off by our armored thrusts surrendered at the first opportunity.

In March, about 10 percent of the prisoners of war sampled still persisted in their belief of continuing the war. They were the fanatical "hard core" on whom events made no impression and who would have retired into the Bavarian Alps for a last ditch stand if they had been called upon or if it were technically feasible. They were the minority who had held the Wehrmacht intact during the constant defeats of the last months by their willingness to apply sanctions short of nothing.

Early in the Normandy campaign the approximate size of the fanatical "hard core" was first established at this figure of between 10 and 15 percent of the total Wehrmacht. Subsequent events proved that this figure was accurate. Although in the initial period of the Western campaign, the success of Nazi indoctrination gave the impression of much more widespread fanaticism, detailed interrogation made it possible to separate out the minority of "total Nazis." They not only held the full pattern of Nazi ideas—many more than 10 percent did—they held these concepts with a deep religious fervor. They were men who were profoundly shocked by capture, unlike their weaker comrades who, though hopeful of victory, were glad that they themselves had survived the battle.

Faith in Hitler

Throughout the entire Western campaign, faith in Hitler was expressed by well over fifty percent of the Wehrmacht, with the exception of one particularly low morale group. Many a German soldier although personally despairing in ultimate victory continued to resist vigorously, in part because of devotion to Hitler. Hitler was a man who had done so much good for Germany. He had so clearly shown his affiliation with the interests of the common man, that he would not have continued the war had he not believed it to be to the best advantage of Germany, politically at least. This ideological prop remained intact throughout the ups and downs of the battle situation and the corresponding changes in optimism as to the outcome of the war. It was only in March, 1945, when the German armies were cut up and at the verge of disintegration that the figure dropped below fifty percent.

Yet thirty percent still professed confidence in Hitler under these conditions. This was the group composed not alone of hard core Nazi fanatics, but also of devoted followers, who clung to the hope that Hitler in the final moments of the war would produce a political formula which would soften defeat. A clash between the Western Allies and Russia was their main hope. What sort of citizens these soldiers are likely to make under American occupation is easy to estimate.

Belief in Secret Weapons

Related to ideological faith in Hitler was the positive contribution to morale arising from the belief that Germany *still* had a decisive "Secret Weapon." Belief in the secret weapon reached a peak in August (the V-1 had been employed in June) and propaganda, both official and word of mouth, among the German troops raised expectations for more powerful weapons. Naturally the failure of the secret weapon to materialize during the critical months of the early fall undermined faith. However, it was maintained and even restored once the Wehrmacht made a stand at the borders of Germany. About half of a sample of November prisoners of war professed their faith in secret weapons.

Hope and faith in secret weapons for many of the rank and file soldiers were merely irrational wishful thinking. During the fall and winter, front line life became unbearable. An understanding of the growing strategical hopelessness was dawning in the minds of all but the most unthinking soldiers, or at least, daily operations at the front were demonstrating the hopelessness of his own unit's position as far as replacements, armament and supply were concerned. Under these conditions, the hope of a secret weapon was the only factor that could translate ideological attachments and the unwillingness to face reality into some sort of plausible explanation for continued resistance. As a result many a German soldier held to this belief with fanatical fervor.

For many of the more educated soldiers belief in secret weapons supplied the same need, but was explained on some sort of a rational basis. It reflected their confidence in German industrial genius and inventiveness which would produce the weapons of war—new ones as well as the traditional ones—in such high quality, if not in numbers superior to the Allies, that the tide would ultimately turn.

Fear of Revenge

In general, fear of revenge against the population of the home front by the Allies was not widespread among captured German soldiers. Affirmative answers given to the question, "Do you believe that revenge will be taken against the population of Germany after the war?," seldom reached more than about 20 percent of the prisoners. Correlation to other key questions showed that they were confirmed Nazis whose opinions never varied on the subject. Clearly their opinions were fashioned by fear of revenge not only against Germany but also against themselves personally. Countering the German propaganda line, the traditional respect of the broad masses towards the American and British as people of dignity and fair play was at work. To be sure, the figure of expectation of revenge may have been somewhat decreased by the circumstance that the Germans were captives in American hands. This lack of fear of revenge after the war indicates again that an important aspect of motivation for continued resistance came not merely out of the negative fear of defeat and its consequences, but rather an acceptance of the positive elements of National Socialist doctrine which sought for victory.

The techniques employed, although subject to limitations as indicated, were undertaken for the purpose of determining psychological warfare output to the enemy. The steadfastness with which the German soldier held to his loyalty to Hitler, for example, indicated that a frontal attack on this particular ideological symbol was less likely to succeed than appeals based on non-ideological considerations, e.g., as promise of good treatment and survival through capture. In general, it was found expedient to concentrate on such primary appeals and on the hopelessness of the battle situation.

Chapter 9. Notes

1. The systematic study of Wehrmacht morale for psychological warfare purposes owes its origin to the work of Lt. Col. Henry Dicks, psychiatrist, Royal Army Medical Corps, and Prof. Edward Shils, Department of Sociology, University of Chicago. Early in 1944, they prepared basic papers on the subject and outlined the goals of research which were followed up during the military operations in Western Europe.

2. Elmo Wilson, Heinz Ansbacher, Hazel Gaudet, of the Office of War Information, and Major Donald McGranahan were active in launching this survey. Max Ralis was largely responsible for the collecting and processing of the data.

A similar survey was undertaken by Lt. Col. Martin F. Herz in Italy, for the Psychological Warfare Branch, 5th U.S. Army.

3. Professional statisticians would certainly be amused at the prospect of being called upon to draw a representative sample of the enemy army from prisoners of war. The exact size and composition of the enemy army was unknown, nor could it be assumed that all those taken prisoner were equal in fighting quality to those who were not captured.

4. The stage of their imprisonment at which to administer the poll was not easy to determine. Theoretically, it might have been immediately after capture, or a long time after capture. There was no firm data on the point, but researchers in North Africa and Italy had indicated a marked difference in response depending on the time of questioning. It seemed that the shock of capture tended to obscure prevailing attitudes. On the other hand, long incarceration tended to create new post-capture attitudes which were of slight interest. Either Nazi convictions were often strengthened as a result of the persistence of Nazi leadership in the camp or life in a static camp eliminated, among some, all political attitudes. Pragmatic tests indicated that by a week to two weeks after capture the shock of battle had worn off, while the effects of prison camp life had not yet taken root.

Chapter 10

GERMAN RADIO PROPAGANDA TO FRANCE DURING THE BATTLE OF FRANCE *

By

HANS SPEIER AND MARGARET OTIS

A. Categories of Analysis

THE RESULTS obtained by a quantitative content analysis of verbal propaganda are dependent on the way in which the propagandistic statements are classified. A given propagandistic text contains many individual statements, while the scheme of analysis consists of a limited number of general categories under which all individual statements must be subsumed. The construction of the scheme of analysis is not only a matter of *comprehensiveness* (so that all statements can be subsumed under one of the general categories). Nor is it only a matter of *mutual exclusiveness of the categories* (so that each statement can be subsumed under one category only). It is also a matter of *analytical purpose*. Evidently, the content of propaganda can be analyzed in very many ways, each requiring a special set of categories appropriate to a specific end. Which classificatory scheme is used is a matter of choice among the questions and hypotheses which the analyst formulates *before* he begins to define the categories of his analytical scheme. In other words, the strategy of an analysis of content depends on clearly formulated hypotheses as to what the analyst should try to discover.

The main objectives of the following study of German radio propaganda to France before, during and after the Battle of

* Reprinted from *Radio Research 1942-1943*, edited by P. F. Lazarsfeld and . N. Stanton, published by Duell, Sloan and Pearce, New York 1944.

France have been derived from a general theory of propaganda to the enemy in total war.

The Function of Propaganda to the Enemy in Total War

If one tries to analyze the function of propaganda in total war, one must have an understanding of what is meant by total war. For our purposes it is sufficient to bear in mind that total war is not *merely* and not *always* a matter of physical violence. Mr. Cyril Falls has recently said that total war can be defined as *"a state of hostility independent of acts of violence, which are called forth only when the circumstances favor them."* [1]

This definition is both appropriate and orthodox. As a matter of fact, it is a restatement of Hobbes' understanding of war:

> . . . Warre, consisteth not in Battell onely, or the act of fighting; but in a tract of time, wherein the Will to contend by Battell is sufficiently known: and therefore the notion of *Time,* is to be considered in the nature of Warre; as it is in the nature of Weather. For as the nature of Foule weather, lyeth not in a showre or two of rain; but an inclination thereto of many days together; *So* the nature of *War,* consisteth not in actuall fighting; but in the known disposition thereto, during all the time there is no assurance to the contrary. All other time is *Peace.* [2]

Thus war, according to Hobbes, has its periods of "phoneyness," when there is no overt fighting and when propagandists can pretend to be the friends of their enemies. Certain Nazi writers clearly realized this nature of modern war and described in detail the techniques of various kinds of non-military warfare in those periods of total war in which the caissons are not rolling. [3]

What, then, is the function of propaganda to the enemy in total war? *Propaganda to the enemy is an attempt to realize the aim of war—which is victory—without acts of physical violence, or with less expenditure of physical violence than would otherwise be necessary.*

Consequently, one may distinguish two functions of propaganda to the enemy in war, depending on the relation of propaganda to the specific stage of total war: in periods of "phoney war" (when the weather is foul although it does not yet rain) propaganda is a *substitute for physical violence,* whereas in periods of actual fighting propaganda changes into a *supplement to physical violence.* Before actual fighting starts, the propagandist may succeed in persuading the enemy that it is expedient for him to negotiate rather than to fight, to wait rather than to arm, to reconsider rather than to act, etc. In particular, the propagandist may succeed in terrorizing the enemy with words—or so we say when we mean that he terrorizes him with the threat of physical violence. In all the territorial conquests of the Nazis before the invasion of Poland propaganda was successfully used as one of the substitutes for physical violence. In the period of the "phoney war" in the West, i.e., before the invasion of the Low Countries, German propaganda served again this function of a substitute for military action.

The situation changes when actual fighting begins: bombs become more important than words, and military success more significant than the activities of propagandists. Doing something is always more important than saying that something will be done or has been done, or that it means this or that. A situation arises in which the "enemy is not beaten by radio communications but by heroism and valor" [4] and by superiority of arms.

In view of these considerations we have decided to divide the whole period under analysis into sub-periods of foul and rainy weather respectively, not dividing according to length of time but according to stages of the total war. This "periodization" enables us to study the dependence of German propaganda on the general "event structure" of the social process of which propaganda is a part. The following periods have been distinguished:

Period   I: April 26 to May 9, 1940: preceding the campaign in the West. (*Phoney War*)

Period II: May 10 to May 28, 1940: from the invasion of the Low Countries until the surrender of King Leopold of Belgium. (*Invasion*)

Period III: May 29 to June 4, 1940: from the beginning of the evacuation of Flanders to the completed evacuation from Dunkerque. (*Retreat*)

Period IV: June 5 to June 20, 1940: from the second major offensive (*Battle of the Somme*) to the armistice.[5]

Period V: June 21 to July 3, 1940: after the Battle of France. (*Post-Armistice*)

The "Natural Aims" of Symbol Warfare

If the propagandist's cause is to be victorious without acts of physical violence or with less expenditure of physical force than would otherwise be necessary, the enemy must do something foolish. Propaganda to the enemy is thus an invitation to foolishness, to do anything but fight, which, in war, is reasonable.

The first aim of symbol warfare is therefore the enemy's surrender without fighting it out: this we call *submission*.

The second aim is fighting the wrong opponent. Ally may turn against ally, civilian against soldier, the rank and file against the officer, labor against capital and vice versa, Gentile against Jew, citizens against their government: this we call *subversion*.

The third kind of foolishness may be called *co-operation* with the enemy when he is erroneously regarded as a friend, protector or partner.

Fourth, people may come to think that their individual safety and gain and comfort are more important than the defense or power of their country. This is foolish, because it works only as long as not many people think and act in terms of what we call *privatization*.

Finally, the soldiers cannot fight and the workers do not work when there is *panic*. Panic is therefore another natural aim of symbol warfare.

Submission, subversion, co-operation, privatization and panic, then, are natural aims of symbol warfare—being those actions of the enemy which spell his defeat. Submission is military and political non-action against the enemy; subversion is politically inverted action against parts of the collective self; co-operation is politically reversed action *with* the enemy; privatization is non-political action *for* the private self; and panic is socially undirected action.

Types of Symbol Warfare

How do those who engage in symbol warfare try to induce these foolish actions? Obviously, they may either *suggest them directly,* in which case we speak of *agitation.* Or they may merely present such a picture of the situation that their listeners are induced to act foolishly, without being told explicitly what to do. In this latter case we speak of *propaganda* in the narrower sense of the term, which may be distinguished from and related to agitation by regarding it as implicit or concealed agitation.

For purposes of content analysis, then, all agitational statements will be so classified as to correspond to the five types of foolish action of the propagandee. The "natural aims" of symbol warfare are types of agitation.[6]

Different from the types of agitation, the main classes of propagandistic statements cannot be derived from the natural aims of symbol warfare, because propaganda consists of news and opinion pertaining to the situation in which the propagandee is to act, whereas an agitational statement suggests a specific action to the propagandee. And seldom can a situation be so described, propagandistically or otherwise, that only one course is open for action. "Throw the British out of France!" is subversive agitation. "The British have a jolly good time behind your lines" is propaganda which may possibly dispose the French toward doing something *against* the English, but may also induce them to co-operate *with* the Germans or to act *for* themselves.

What connection then exists between agitation and propaganda? The *ultimate* goal of the propagandist coincides with that of the agitator; both of them want to contribute to victory by means other than physical violence. In other words, there is an ultimate connection between the main directions of propaganda and the types of agitation, but there is not necessarily a correspondence between each specific direction of propaganda and each specific type of agitation. We have constructed a scheme for the classification of propagandistic statements whose categories correspond *logically* to the types of agitation (in a way to be indicated presently). This scheme permits us to study how far there is an *actual* correspondence between the directions of propaganda and the types of agitation.

It seems to us that the principal ways in which propagandists in war may hope to induce the enemy toward submission, subversion, co-operation, etc., are these:

1. They *may attack the enemy's confidence in victory* by pointing out that the odds are against him; because he is weak or has failed, while the propagandist's side is strong or has had success.
2. Similarly, propagandists may point out that the enemy is socially divided or that the propagandist's side is really united with that of the propagandee.[7]
3. They *may attack the enemy's conviction of the right to victory* by telling him that he is guilty of all sorts of immorality, whereas the propagandist's side shines in the glory of a just cause and is generally angelic.
4. They *may confuse the enemy's understanding of the complex world he lives in,* in particular by presenting certain groups and leaders on his own side as his real enemies, i.e., as internal enemies or exploiters. Correspondingly, propagandists may make every effort to present their own side, the external enemy, as a partner, real friend or protector who is going to treat his misled foe with consideration.
5. Finally, propagandists may depoliticize their audience not by confusing the roles of enemy and friend, but by presenting non-political values and loyalties as more important than the political ones. Statements pertaining to exploitation by internal "enemies" and good treatment by external "friends" may be said to split the listener socially, while statements on the senselessness of the war and appeals to the listener's private safety and comfort may be said to divide his soul: they divide the French citizen from the man who happens to be French.

On the basis of these considerations we distingiush five general classes of propagandistic statements or *main directions* of propaganda. Each propagandistic statement is either a nonmoral or a moral statement, and any statement "discourages" or "divides" the listener. In addition, each propagandistic statement can be classified according to *"subject reference"*: it is positive when the subject is on the German side, negative when it is on the enemy side. Therefore, within each main (general) direction there are two *supplementary* (specific) directions. Thus, the following directions can be distinguished:

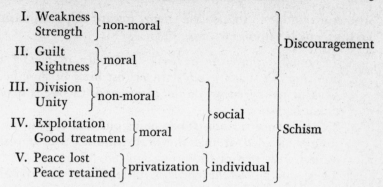

Directions I-IV are interrelated in three ways:

First, (a) weakness, guilt, division, exploitation, are directions of statements referring to the *enemy* side, whereas

(b) strength, unity, rightness, good treatment, are directions of statements referring to the *German* side.

Second, (a) weakness, division, strength, unity, are directions of statements *without* any moral evaluations, whereas

(b) guilt, rightness, exploitation, good treatment, are directions of statements *with moral evaluations.*

Third, (a) weakness and guilt are directions of statements referring to the *enemy side* as a whole or to some internal group of that side with which the listener is *identified;*

(b) strength and rightness are directions of statements referring to the *German side* as a whole or some internal group on that side from which the listener is entirely *excluded;*

(c) division and exploitation are directions of statements referring to the *relation* between the *listener* or a group with which he is identified *and the enemy side* or an internal group on that side;

(d) unity and good treatment are directions of statements referring to the *relation* between the *listener* or a group with which he is identified *and the German side* or an internal group on that side.

It appears thus that each propagandistic statement can be classified [8] when the following questions are answered:

1. What is the subject reference of the statement, both general and specific?

2. With what group is the listener identified or to what group is he opposed?

3. Does the statement contain a moral evaluation?

The general relation between the natural aims of symbol warfare (our "types of agitation") and the "directions of propaganda" can be stated as follows:

1. To submission correspond statements in the direction of *discouragement;*
2. To subversive actions correspond statements in the direction of *division* (from internal enemies) and *exploitation* by internal enemies;
3. To actions involving co-operation with the enemy or the conqueror correspond propagandistic statements in the direction of *unity* (with external friends) and *good treatment* by external friends;
4. To actions increasing privatization correspond propagandistic statements in the direction of *peace lost* and *peace retained;*
5. To panic no single type of propagandistic statement can be said to correspond.

The Elasticity of Propagandistic Reasoning

In addition to our main purpose of discovering how the aims of propaganda vary with the structure of events we were also interested in discovering how the Nazis used various types of arguments in their propaganda. Thus, besides classifying propaganda statements according to direction, we have distinguished between different statements within each of them. That is, we have distinguished between the different sorts of attributes and actions [9] given as reasons of enemy weakness, guilt, division or exploitation, and own strength, rightness, unity or good treatment. These attributes [10] do not exhaust all actual meaning found in the material analyzed. They were listed by us, after several preliminary codings, as being the most important ones.[11] For example, in the statement, "Frenchmen, you must save your beautiful country from ruin," we would not code beauty as an attribute of France.

Each statement containing an attribute which is included in our final list is regarded as a unit for purposes of coding and counting. If two attributes occur within a single sentence, that sentence constitutes two units, and, conversely, if a number of sentences all pertain to a single attribute, they only constitute one unit. The one exception to this general rule is in the case of a single attribute having more than one subject reference, in which case it is counted as a corresponding number of items.

In thus listing attributes within the directions it was soon found that the same attribute often appeared in more than one direction. In other words, an attribute would be put to different argumentative purposes in different contexts. This dependence of the argumentative purpose of an attribute on its context is true of discourse in general. My bravery may be your foolhardiness. It is particularly true, however, of any wartime propaganda, where it is expedient to present similar attributes as both praiseworthy or reprehensible, depending on whether they refer to the self or to the enemy. It may thus be said that a wartime situation favors the *elasticity* of reasoning. Thucydides wrote of Greece during the Peloponnesian wars that "even the common meaning of words was changed arbitrarily." (III.2) It is possible, however, that the extent and pattern of this elasticity should differ, depending on the philosophy of the propagandist concerned. We classify attributes in such a way as to show within the framework of our scheme the extent and pattern of their elasticity in Nazi propaganda.

Attributes are classified as pairs of opposites: a positive attribute and the corresponding negative attribute, such as successful-unsuccessful. Each attribute may appear with the German or the enemy side as subject reference, which gives us four initial versions of the same general attribute:

1. You have the positive attribute
2. You have the negative attribute
3. We have the positive attribute
4. We have the negative attribute

Each of these versions can be put to many argumentative purposes, i.e., many different conclusions can be drawn from each of them. These possibilities we have reduced to six major classes. According to our scheme, each attribute may be used as a reason for:

1. Non-moral weakness
2. Non-moral strength
3. Immorality connected with strength

4. Morality connected with weakness
5. Immorality connected with weakness
6. Morality connected with strength

There are thus 24 possible meanings for every attribute listed. As our coding system allows us to identify an attribute as having any one of these meanings, we are able to study the elasticity of reasoning in Nazi propaganda in terms of this scheme.

B. Findings

AGITATION

German symbol warfare against France was predominantly propagandistic rather than agitational in character. Out of a total of 2,309 entries for all periods (from April 26 to July 23, 1940), 2,209 or 96 per cent were propagandistic statements, and only 100 or 4 per cent were agitational ones. These statements, taken from a sample program of a news bulletin and commentary for each day whenever possible, were distributed over the five periods as indicated in Table 1.

TABLE 1

DISTRIBUTION OF PROPAGANDA AND AGITATION
(in per cent of total references)

	Period					
	I	II	III	IV	V	Total
	%	%	%	%	%	%
Propaganda	100	93	93	94	98	96
Agitation	0	7	7	6	2	4
Total per cent	100	100	100	100	100	100
Total references	364	395	260	790	504	2,309*

* The actual total for this row is 2313. The error of 4 references, however, is clearly insignificant. D.L.

There was practically no agitation in the period of phoney warfare (I) and in the period following the armistice (V). It thus appears that in periods where symbol warfare is a substitute for violence it does not take a direct form; in periods where it is a supplement to violence it sometimes does.

We distinguish between agitation in the form of suggestions and agitation put in the form of commands. Within each of these categories we further distinguish between agitation for attitudes and agitation for actions. As might have been expected, very little agitation was found in the form of commands, as this would be more suitable for a conquered country than for an enemy country. Also, agitation for action predominates in all periods except the last. Only after the armistice (Period V) do the Nazis become more concerned with attitudes than with actions.

Agitation is used mainly for submission and subversion, less for co-operation and privatization, and not at all for panic (see Appendix G, Table 1).** The continuance of subversive agitation after the armistice (Period V) can be explained by the fact that although it was no longer necessary for the Nazis to preach revolt against the French Government, they continued to preach revolt against England. Since the French had no longer any immediate contact with the British, this would naturally take the form of agitation for attitudes rather than for actions.

DIRECTIONS OF PROPAGANDA

In their propaganda as distinguished from their agitation the Germans talked much more about the enemy than about themselves. This is in line with the principle, expressed by many Nazi leaders, that also in symbol warfare the offensive is preferable to the defensive.

TABLE 2

PERCENTAGE DISTRIBUTION OF PROPAGANDISTIC STATEMENTS ABOUT OWN AND ENEMY SIDES AT DIFFERENT PERIODS
(in per cent of total propagandistic references)

	Period					
	I	II	III	IV	V	Total
	%	%	%	%	%	%
Own side	28	31	23	35	30	29
Enemy side	72	69	77	65	70	71
French	5	33	32	43	32	29
English	45	19	31	17	32	29
Allied	22	17	14	5	6	13
Total per cent	100	100	100	100	100	100

** This Table and others cited can be consulted on pages 572-3 of *Radio Research 1942-1943*. D.L.

As indicated in Table 2, for the average of all five periods only 29 per cent of all statements pertained to the German side, while 71 per cent had the enemy side as subject references. The distribution of attention given to the two sides in the five different periods did not vary much. The Nazis talked least about themselves (23 per cent) in Period III (during the retreat), and talked relatively more about themselves in the last two periods, i.e., during the Battle of the Somme and after the armistice.

French—English—Allies

The attention given to the French, the English and the Allies (French and English undistinguished) by the German radio in the five periods affords some insight into the dependence of German propaganda on the specific stage of the war.

As the war progresses, the Germans refer less and less to "the Allies" when talking about the enemy. In other words, the statements about the enemy become more *specific* with regard to nationality as the war proceeds. In addition to the steady decline of references to the Allies, the Germans talked more about the English when they talked less about the French and vice versa. The highest percentage of references to the English was of course the period of the phoney war (Period I), when these references were nine times as frequent as references to the French.[12] This was the period of the war in which German propagandists were trying to persuade French listeners that Germany had no quarrel with France, and that the English were the trouble-makers. In this period, propaganda was a substitute for military action, and the main effort of Germany's symbol warfare was directed to divide the Allies. The function of propaganda changed with the invasion. Now, with symbol warfare relegated to a merely supplementary function, the French are attacked by words as well as guns, and French listeners now hear more about the French than the English. This was found to be true even during the retreat (Period III), when references to the English were of course more numerous than they were before and after Dunkerque. After the armistice, however, when France was down, German propagandists became again more eloquent about the English. In fact, they talked as much about the former allies of the French as about the French themselves. Propaganda, freed from its merely supplementary role, tried to focus French attention on British, rather than German, villainy.

Country vs. Countrymen

In coding subject references we have also differentiated between *impersonalized and personalized designations,* such as "France" as distinguished from "the French." The content of the statement that "France" is going to lose the war seems hardly different from that of the statement that "the French" are going to lose it; but we thought that the difference between these forms of subject references may be significant in propaganda and provided for specific coding in our scheme. The results, presented in Figure 1, have borne out our hunch.

It is not primarily important that the country references are generally more frequent than the countrymen references. What is important is the different ratio of these two designations as we compare France, England and Germany.

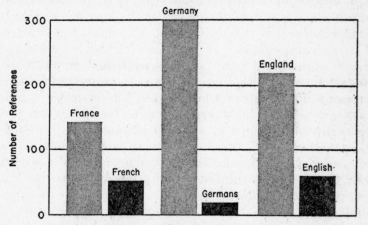

FIG. I.—References to Country Versus Countrymen

The ratio is highest for Germany. The German propagandist when speaking of his own side refers only once out of 18 times to the *Germans* and usually prefers to speak of *Germany.* Obviously he is of the opinion that the designation "Germans" is more likely to arouse antagonistic feelings on the part of the listener than the designation "Germany." Furthermore, the majority of the German statements refer to strength, and it is plausible that Germany, rather than the Germans, is presented as strong.

In the case of *England* the situation is different. When speaking about England, references to the English rather than the country are made once out of five times. As we shall see, exploitation and guilt are relatively more important than weakness on the English side, while on the German side strength is relatively more important than the good treatment and rightness. Exploiters are likely to be personalized; we should expect, therefore, relatively more references to Englishmen than to Germans.

The ratio is lowest for "Frenchmen vs. *France"* (the former being referred to once out of every four times), which is again partly due to the fact that exploitation plays a considerable role on the French side. In addition, we may suspect that in German broadcasts to French listeners the difference between country and countrymen as designations is less important in the case of France than in the case of Germany or England: both "Frenchmen" and "France" are presumably of equal appeal to a French audience.

Distribution of Directions

The relative importance of both main and supplementary directions for all periods taken together is shown in Table 3. To recapitulate our definition: "main" direction refers to the total class of statements irrespective of whether they pertain to the enemy or the German side; "supplementary" covers these two respective sides. Thus "weakness" would be a supplementary direction for the enemy and "strength" for the German side. Both types of statements are summarized in the main direction "weakness-strength."

It appears that by far the most important direction is that of weakness-strength, under which almost one-half of all propagandistic statements could be subsumed. Within this main direction, statements conveying the impression of enemy social division amounted to only 2 per cent of the total.[13] Interestingly enough, the supplementary direction, own strength, is of much greater importance in the total of all statements pertaining to the German side than is enemy weakness on the enemy side. While 7 out of 10 statements pertaining to the German side are statements on own strength, only approxi-

TABLE 3

DISTRIBUTION OF MAIN AND SUPPLEMENTARY DIRECTIONS OF
PROPAGANDISTIC STATEMENTS FOR ALL PERIODS
(in per cent of total propagandistic references)

| Supplementary directions | | | | Main directions | |
| Own | | Enemy | | Total own and enemy | |
	%		%		%
Unity	0	Division	4	Unity-division	2
Other strength ...	71	Other weakness ...	34	Other strength-weakness	45
Rightness	18	Guilt	24	Rightness-guilt	22
Good treatment ...	11	Exploitation	30	Good treatment-exploitation	25
Peace retained	0	Peace lost	3	Peace retained-lost	2
Residual [a]	0	Residual [a]	5	Residual [a]	4
Total per cent...	100		100		100
No. references...	679		1,350		2,209

[a] See the discussion of this category in the text.

mately 3 out of 10 statements pertaining to the enemy side
refer to enemy weakness. Thus the pattern of German propaganda is not "We are strong and you are weak," but rather
"We are strong and you are immoral." The German morality-
statements (rightness plus good treatment) constitute 29 per
cent of the German total, whereas the corresponding directions on the enemy side (guilt and exploitation) amount to no
less than 54 per cent of the enemy total.

Like unity-division, the direction peace retained-peace lost
was quantitatively of little importance, amounting to only 2
per cent of the grand total. The fact that we found no single
statements to be subsumed under "peace retained" may be
partly due to the scarcity of *talks* in our sample. It is however safe to say that the Nazis, when talking about the comforts
of peace, tend to stress those which the enemy has lost more
than those which the Germans have retained in spite of war.[14]

As *residual entries* we have listed all statements which, contrary to expectations, stressed *French* strength or morality.
Most of these statements occur in the last period, when France
is defeated. We found no such statements on the German side
("admissions" of deficiency), so that the small percentage of

4 per cent for residual statements is entirely made up of *"concessions"* to the (defeated) enemy.

The Three Main Directions at Different Periods

The relative importance of the three most frequent directions—strength-weakness, rightness-guilt, good treatment-exploitation—amounting to 94 per cent of all statements is shown in Figure 2 for each period. While the specific propa-

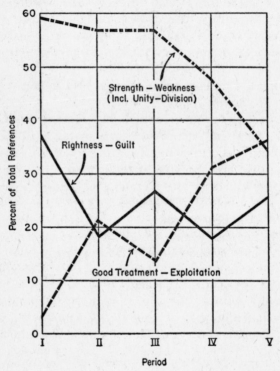

FIG. 2.—Distribution of Three Main Directions for Each Period [a]

gandistic meaning of this graph requires an analysis of the *supplementary* directions—as shown in Figure 3—even the trend of the *main* directions (i.e. class of statement regardless

[a] The percentages shown by the three curves do not add up to 100% for each period because the direction Peace retained-Peace lost (Privatization) is not shown on the graph.

of subject reference) reveals a few general characteristics of German propaganda in its dependence on events.

The direction strength-weakness is highest in the first period, before the actual fighting begins. It remains high until Dunkerque, drops sharply during the Battle of the Somme and is slightly lower than the direction good treatment-exploitation after the signing of the armistice. Statements pointing out that Germany will treat (treated or treats) France (and the Frenchmen) well and especially all assertions to the effect that the English (or French leaders) take advantage of the French by exploiting them, were designed to drive wedges into the enemy's social structure and paralyze his will to resist. Such statements were rather infrequent in the period of the phoney war, but they rise to one-fifth of all statements in the invasion period and to more than one-third in the last two stages of the conflict.

The direction good treatment-exploitation comprises all statements involving an immoral (or moral) attitude *toward France*. Assertions of the enemy's guilt or Germany's just cause in this war are also morality statements, but the enemy's immorality is directed *towards Germany* and, conversely, German morality is not specifically related to France. Such assertions have been classified as statements on rightness and guilt.[45] Except for the last period under analysis, the frequency of these statements is in inverse relation to statements on good treatment and exploitation. Especially during the phoney war, when Nazi propagandists did not talk much about exploitation on the enemy side or on the good treatment of Frenchmen by Germans, they did talk a great deal about enemy guilt.

The Dependence of Propaganda on Events

The *logical* opposites which we have distinguished as supplementary directions in each main direction, viz., strength *vs.* weakness, rightness *vs.* guilt, good treatment *vs.* exploitation, are not *factually* interdependent. As is evident from Figure 3, Nazi propaganda manipulates supplementary directions independently, stressing either weakness *or* strength, guilt *or* rightness, etc., rather than both weakness *and* strength, guilt *and* rightness, etc. Thus the development of the *main* directions from period to period as shown in Figure 2 somewhat obscures the strategy of Nazi propaganda.

A comparison of the supplementary directions in Figure 3 shows that weakness, guilt and exploitation, the enemy directions, fluctuate more than do strength, rightness and good treatment, on the German side: *the dynamics of propaganda is determined by the presentation of the enemy rather than by the presentation of the self.* Or to put it differently, the way in which German propagandists talk about Germany is less dependent on events than is their talk about the enemy. The fluctuations of the main directions as shown on Figure 2 are chiefly the result of fluctuations of the *enemy* directions.

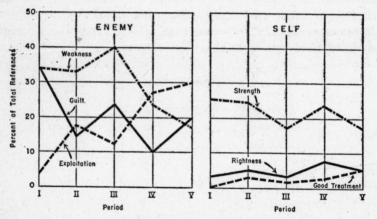

FIG. 3.—Distribution of the Three Supplementary Directions on Enemy and German Sides
(in per cent of total references)

The fluctuation of a trend curve can be stated in terms of *range* or of *amount* of fluctuation. The range of fluctuation is the distance between the highest and lowest points of a curve. For example, the curve for guilt, Figure 3, reaches its peak (34) in Period I and its trough in Period IV (10); its range is 24. The amount of fluctuation is the sum of all distances between adjacent points of the trend curve. The amount of fluctuation displayed by the curve for guilt in Figure 3 is very high (54) because the curve, within its range of 24, fluctuates considerably from period to period. Two trend curves can have the same range, but if one of them moves up and down more frequently, its amount of fluctuation will be larger. If a curve goes steadily in one direction without reversal, range and amount of fluctuation will be identical. If a curve shows reversal, amount is higher than range of fluctuation. The difference between amount and range is a measure of smoothness, zero meaning no reversal in direction.

The *range* of fluctuation for the supplementary directions (see Table 4A) bears out more precisely the contention that the dynamics of German propaganda to France are determined by the presentation of the enemy rather than by the way in which the Nazis talk about themselves. The range for statements on the enemy (enemy directions) is about three and a half times as great as that for statements on the self (German directions). More specifically, assertions about rightness show the smallest range, statements on exploitation the widest range of fluctuation, with guilt as a close second.

TABLE 4A

RANGE AND AMOUNT OF FLUCTUATION

Directions	Range [a]		Amount [b]	
Exploitation	26		38	
Guilt	24		54	
Weakness	16		30	
All Enemy		66		122
Strength	8		22	
Good treatment	6		8	
Rightness	5		11	
All German		19		41

[a] Range expresses difference between highest and lowest proportion of references to each direction at any of the five periods.

[b] Amount expresses sum of differences in proportion of references to each direction from period to period.

The *amount* of fluctuation is a better index of the dependence of German propaganda on events than the *range* of fluctuation, since the former does not obliterate reversals of the curves within the range. Generally speaking, the amount of fluctuation of all statements on the enemy is four times as large as that for all German directions. As to the individual directions, guilt (which has only the second highest range) is the direction with the largest amount of fluctuation. It may therefore be said to constitute the direction with the greatest sensitivity to events. Since statements on exploitation too show a high amount of fluctuation from period to period, it appears that *the German propagandist readjusts his propaganda strategy primarily by changing the frequency of specifically directed immorality charges (guilt and exploitation) to changes in the total situation;* secondarily he does so by changing the frequency of assertions of enemy *weakness.* In comparison with these adjustments, all others are definitely of subordinate importance.

It would be erroneous, however, to conclude from this result of our study that German propaganda is less concerned with the adjustment of its "factual," non-moral statements (on strength and weakness) to the changing scene than with the adaptation of its charges of immorality to such changes. This conclusion is correct only as long as guilt and exploitation are distinguished as they have been in the preceding discussion. An inspection of the trend curves for guilt and exploitation in Figure 3 shows, however, that the conclusion must be revised when the two curves are combined so as to obtain the trend curve for the *combined* immorality directions. With the exception of Period V, the *specific* assertions of enemy immorality (guilt and exploitation) are inversely related: when guilt rises, exploitation drops. However, if all immorality statements are taken *together,* regardless of whether they indicate guilt or exploitation, a much smoother curve results for the five periods. Consequently for *all* immorality statements (guilt and exploitation combined) range and amount of fluctuation are smaller than they are for either guilt or exploitation statements [16] (see Table 4B).

Thus, once the number of propagandistic directions is reduced to four (viz., enemy weakness and enemy immorality, own strength and own morality), it appears that enemy *weakness* is the direction with the highest amount (though not with the widest range) of fluctuation. Similarly, the relative emphasis on German strength varies (within a rather small range) almost as much as that on enemy immorality.

In other words, while Nazi propaganda does not altogether live up to its avowed principle of letting the facts speak for themselves, it certainly tries to make the most of the military defeat and weakness of the enemy.

TABLE 4B

AMOUNT AND RANGE OF FLUCTUATION OF NON-MORAL AND
COMBINED MORAL DIRECTIONS

Directions	Amount [a]	Range [b]
Weakness	30	16
Immorality	24	18
All enemy	54	34
Strength	22	8
Morality	15	9
All German	37	17

[a] Amount expresses sum of differences in proportion of references to each direction from period to period.

[b] Range expresses difference between highest and lowest proportion of references to each direction at any of the five periods.

As to *incisiveness of certain events*, it is rather interesting that Dunkerque had a greater impact upon German propaganda strategy than the beginning of the actual fighting war. The total amount of fluctuation from Period III to Period IV was 59 points for all specific directions as over against 41 points for the differences between Periods I and II. In Period III (from the surrender of Belgium to the completed evacuation of Dunkerque) Nazi propaganda was particularly concerned with stressing the *weakness* of the enemy. In this period 40 per cent of all statements were assertions of enemy weakness, the highest percentage of any direction for all five periods. Clearly, Dunkerque was presented by Nazi propaganda as an Allied defeat rather than as a German victory, while the period leading to the Fall of France (Period IV) was as much of a German victory as an Allied defeat (see Figure 3).

Own Morality vs. *Enemy Immorality*

As has been said, Nazi propaganda talks more about the enemy than about Germany (see Tables 2 and 3). This is true for each period. A breakdown of all propagandistic statements into moral and non-moral assertions shows that the denunciation of enemy immorality is a particularly urgent concern of the Nazis: the ratio of statements about the enemy to statements about the self is higher for morality assertions (4.2:1)

than for non-morality statements (1.2:1) or for all statements
(see Appendix G, Table 2).

Thus, *own morality is less important than enemy immorality
in German symbol warfare*. And while it is true that also own
strength is regarded as less important than enemy weakness,
the predominance of statements about the enemy is far greater
in the category of morality assertions than in the category of
factual statements (weakness and strength).

To the extent that own morality is mentioned, the Nazis
present themselves as both right (just) and generous (promising good treatment). As Figure 3 shows, the directions rightness and good treatment reinforce each other. By contrast,
enemy immorality is not always presented the same way regardless of what happens. Rather, it is presented by the propagandist with a view to the event structure.

When Nazi propagandists make statements about German
rightness they commit themselves less than when they promise
good treatment. One should therefore expect a higher proportion of rightness statements than of statements in the direction of good treatment. The figures, as shown in Figure 3, seem
to fulfill this expectation, but the differences are not statistically
significant. The relation of assertions of guilt to assertions of
exploitation on the enemy side is clearer. During the period of
the phoney war, Nazi propagandists tried to discourage their
French audience by impressing upon it the war guilt of the
Allies. With the start of the real war, exploitation, the more
aggressive, more dramatic and more provocative of the two
types of moral accusations, became more important than guilt.
Only Period III presents an exception to this generalization:
during the evacuation of the British Expeditionary Force general immorality charges outweigh specific exploitation statements.

French vs. English Weakness, Guilt and Exploitation

In order to understand these shifts in emphasis more fully,
it is important to consider the relative weight attributed by the
Nazi propagandists to *French* and *English* weakness, guilt and
exploitation, respectively, in the five periods. We have shown
before (Table 1) that statements about the English and the
French develop inversely, while statements about both of them

("the Allied") drop steadily as the war goes on. Table 5 contains the breakdown of statements on the three main directions for English and French subject references.[17]

It appears that in the period of the phoney war (Period I), when Germany pretended not to be really at war with France, the overwhelming propaganda attack in broadcasts to French listeners was directed against *England*. Not the French were weak, but the English; not the French were immoral (guilty) but the English. The picture changes with the outbreak of actual fighting. Now violence speaks its own language and propagandists are relegated to perform a function which is distinctly

TABLE 5

DISTRIBUTION OF FRENCH VS. ENGLISH WEAKNESS, GUILT AND EXPLOITATION

(in per cent of total references on enemy side, excluding neutral countries)

Directions	I	II	III	IV	V
Weakness					
French	2	25	25	26	9
English	30	9	19	8	12
Guilt					
French	5	6	6	8	8
English	29	5	8	2	10
Exploitation					
French	0	10	8	24	19
English	4	14	12	17	24

subordinate to that of the soldiers. In Period I, when the propagandists "fight" alone, they attack the *British* by pointing out their weakness. In the three battle periods (II-IV), however, German propagandists have the task of echoing the language of bombs and pointing out *French* weakness (to their French audience) becomes their major concern. Even during the evacuation from Dunkerque (Period III), when statements on English weakness rise considerably, they are outnumbered by assertions of French weakness. The propagandistic meaning of statements about enemy weakness varies therefore with the amount of actual violence in war and correspondingly with the function of propaganda.

The propagandistic *intent* of German statements about enemy weakness during the period of the phoney war may be said to be closer to the meaning of statements about exploitation than in any of the actual battle periods, since most of the weakness statements point out *English* lack of strength to a *French* audience. Likewise, the rise of anti-English assertions *after* the Battle of France was decided (Period V), which contrasts so sharply with the drop of statements on French weakness, invites a similar comment. In order to disrupt whatever bonds between France and England still existed, and in order to destroy whatever was left of loyalty to the former Allies in the hearts of the French, German propaganda spoke more about English exploitation, guilt *and weakness* than about the immorality and weakness of the French.

As to all accusations of immorality—guilt as well as exploitation—German propagandists were concerned with England more than with France in all periods except during the Battle of the Somme (Period IV). This predominance of charges against the *English,* rather than the French, was particularly great again in Period I (phoney war).

Military vs. Political Weakness and Exploitation

Within each direction we have classified and coded all propagandistic statements in such a way as to be able to analyze the particular relation between each direction and particular *spheres* of life, such as military, political, economic, cultural, etc.

As Figure 4 shows, *weakness is a predominantly "military" direction, while exploitation may be called a "political" direction.* One might expect this in times of war. What one might not necessarily anticipate is the fact that in the period of phoney war (I) German propagandists went so far in concealing Germany's belligerent intent as to stress the enemy's political weakness more than his military lack of strength.

A somewhat more general inference may be drawn from Figure 4. German propaganda charges the armed forces of the enemy with weakness rather than immorality, while the enemy politicians, political groups and institutions are accused of immorality rather than inefficiency (and other kinds of weakness). Or to relate this generalization to the intelligibility of the complex world in which the listeners live, military defeat, which affects the structure of this world more incisively than anything else, is reported factually, in non-moral terms. *Political matters, which are more obscure in the sense that their factual meaning is less evident, are presented by propagandists*

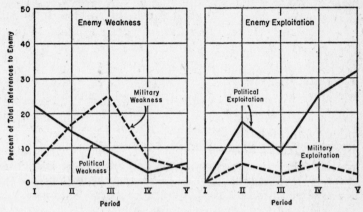

FIG. 4.—Military Versus Political Weakness and Exploitation

in moral language, so as to define targets for indignation. If one does not shun a simplification, he might say that propaganda to the enemy merely communicates existing military facts, but tries to create (or may try to create) a political world.[18]

ELASTICITY

The Pattern

The most popular instance of the "elasticity" of German propagandistic reasoning pertains to air raids. When German planes raid enemy towns they smash military objectives with unfailing accuracy, whereas enemy planes are equally accurate in destroying hospitals, schools and churches. Thus, air attacks are given the meaning of strength in the one case and that of immorality in the other. Toward the end of the Battle of France the Germans went so far as to boast of their raids on the open city of Paris. "The bombing of Paris has created a deep impression in the Italian Press which says that Germany has scored once more and that she is taking the initiative every day" (June 3, 1940).

The elasticity of propagandistic reasoning is not only a result of a different evaluation of one's own and one's enemy's conduct and characteristics. Elasticity may also result from a different evaluation of the same action by the same actor at various periods. Finally, the propagandistic objective to prove that the enemy is immoral (or the self moral) may influence "reasoning" to such an extent that an action is interpreted in the same way in which the failure to act is interpreted. Thus, in propaganda to France, German broadcasters sometimes presented the enemy's success as well as his lack of success as reasons for his immorality. The charge of lack of success was used chiefly after June 1940, for instilling a sense of guilt into fallen France. On the other hand, "success" was attributed to the enemy (and given the meaning of immorality) almost exclusively with reference to their victory in 1918, as for instance:

> A nation (i.e., Germany at the time of the first World War) which has given its blood on the battlefield for four years but was undefeated in arms, had to bow its head and to submit to a regime of force imposed by the conquerors (June 30, 1940).

Such instances of the elasticity of propagandistic reasoning could be multiplied. This elasticity follows a definite pattern with only a small residual percentage in the use of attributes which does not conform with it. The pattern may be illustrated with reference to the attribute "attacking—not attacking." The following six meanings of this attribute are given overwhelming preference by the propagandist:

1. *If you (the enemy) attack,* this is likely to mean immorality associated with strength, for example, brutality (c).[19]
2. *If you do not attack,* this is likely to mean plain (non-moral) weakness (a) or
3. Immorality associated with weakness, for example, cowardice (e).
4. *If we attack,* this is likely to mean either plain (non-moral) strength (b) or
5. Morality associated with strength, for example, bravery (f).
6. *If we do not attack,* this is likely to mean morality, for example, considerate saving of lives (d).

Generally speaking, the elasticity of propagandistic reasoning is not schematically perfect. The pattern of the six preferred meanings represents a selection from twenty-four logically possible meanings, as is illustrated by the following scheme:

SCHEMATIC PRESENTATION OF THE TWENTY-FOUR MEANINGS WHICH
THE FOUR VERSIONS OF ANY ATTRIBUTE MAY HAVE

		Non-Moral		Moral			
		Weakness	Strength	Immorality (strength)	Morality (weakness)	Immorality (weakness)	Morality (strength)
Your (Enemy)	Positive [20] attribute		c				
	Negative attribute	a				e	
Our (Self)	Positive attribute		b				f
	Negative attribute				d		

Schematically perfect elasticity of propagandistic reasoning would exist if the meanings of each version of all attributes were evenly distributed over all six schematically co-ordinated meanings, giving about 16 per cent of all cases for each version to each meaning. As has been said, a distribution approximating such schematic perfection, which would be indicative of a complete arbitrariness in the use of words, does not exist. No less than 97 per cent of the attributes used in Nazi propaganda to France, when classified according to the preceding scheme, fell in the six categories (a) to (f). The remaining eighteen possible meanings were assigned to attributes in only 3 per cent of all cases extending over all periods. In the last period (V), however, this *residual* percentage—referring to meanings outside the pattern—rose to 9 per cent. After the armistice, the Nazis inflated the *strength* of the defeated nation—for purposes of flattering the "enemy" when he was going to be "converted" to a "partner," as well as for purposes of heightening the glory redounding to the self. In Periods II and III, the residual percentage was as high as 6 and 5 per cent respectively, because during the invasion and at the time of Dunkerque, Nazi propagandists attempted to split the British and the French by praising the second at the expense of the first ("You fight, the British retreat").

The pattern of the six preferred meanings may be said to reflect the Nazi views on propaganda efficiency in reasoning. From it the following rules pertaining to the elasticity in propagandistic reasoning may be derived:

I. *Rules That Support the Elasticity of Propagandistic Reasoning*

An attribute shall have a different meaning depending on whether it is used:

(1) With regard to myself or with regard to my enemy;
(2) Positively or negatively;
(3) With regard to the enemy as a whole or to some subgroup on the enemy side (i.e., whether it is used for purposes of discouragement or creating schism);
(4) At one time or at another in the course of events.

II. *Rules That Limit the Elasticity of Propagandistic Reasoning*

(5) Seldom can generally recognized indisputable facts be convincingly interpreted as having two opposite meanings. Thus an attribute having a non-moral meaning (i.e., strength) should not also be given the opposite non-moral meaning (i.e., weakness).
(6) It is only rarely expedient to speak of my enemy as either strong or moral and of myself as either weak or immoral.

The *residual* percentage of meanings which do not fit into the pattern of propagandistic reasoning may be considered, in a sense, as violations of the above rules.

The criticism might be made here that the rules and the pattern itself are typical of *all* war propaganda in general, from the time of Thucydides to the present day. This is probably true to some extent, for there is no doubt but that war favors opportunistic reasoning according to the "rules of elasticity." Under this heading would come the exploitation of the "fifth column" to explain all early reverses of the war, and the preference given in democratic countries to denunciatory words where neutral ones would be more appropriate. Thus, the *New York Times* of October 26, 1942, wrote:

There are two words in the American war vocabulary that have been overworked and should be deleted for the duration.

The first is "treachery," which always applies to a successful Japanese attack. . . . The other word is "sneak." There have been too many sneak raids popping into our naval vocabulary. . . . Let's forget "treachery" and "sneak" and talk about attack.

Even the skeptic who is inclined to attribute the "elasticity of propagandistic reasoning" to the wartime situation at large rather than to the Nazis, will have to admit that warnings like the one just quoted are not possible in present Germany. Ultimately, however, a comparative study of Nazi war propaganda and democratic war propaganda is needed in order to determine conclusively whether or not the elasticity of propagandistic reasoning is a specific Nazi-phenomenon or a general war-phenomenon. Most likely, the question is not one of "whether" but one of "how much." It is in this regard that our study of the elasticity of propagandistic reasoning in German propaganda to France provides some insights which may be useful: we have found that *attributes most intimately connected with Nazi philosophy are more elastic than attributes more generally used by all propagandists in times of war*. This result of our study is briefly discussed in the following, concluding, pages.

Elasticity Within the Pattern

While the meanings of the attributes used fall almost wholly in the pattern of the six preferred classes, there are significant variations in the distribution of meanings within the pattern. One type of attributes classified under the three groups "successful—unsuccessful," "affected by war—not affected by war," and "confident—not confident," were given predominantly non-moral meanings of "weakness" or "strength" respectively. The percentages of such meanings lay between 70 and 80 per cent for the groups. (See Appendix G, Table 3.) These attributes may be called *"non-moral* attributes." Another types of attributes, classified under the three groups "unjust—not unjust," "belligerent—not belligerent," "inflicting—not inflicting suffering," were given predominantly moral meanings, the percentage ranging between 83 and 88 for these groups. (See Appendix G, Table 4.) These attributes may be called the *"moral attributes."* It can be seen from the tables that *the Nazi propagandists used the moral attributes less often in a non-moral sense than they used the non-moral attributes in a morale sense.* In the hands of Nazi propagandists, morality is handled more rigidly than the world of facts.

There is a third type of attributes which may be called *"ambivalent"* because the meanings attached to them are neither predominantly moral nor predominantly non-moral. Instead (as can be seen from Appendix G, Table 5), they are more evenly distributed, not only between non-moral and moral categories, but between all six categories of the pattern which we found to exist within our scheme. Also, the residual percentage of meanings outside the pattern is much higher for ambivalent attributes than it is for either the non-moral or the moral attributes. (14 per cent as over against 5 and 2 per cent, respectively.)

These ambivalent attributes comprise again three subgroups: "effective—not effective," "taking—not taking the initiative in war" and "young civilization—not young civilization." Of these three groups, the last one is the most elastic. Assertions pertaining to national "age" and its evaluation are an important concern of Nazi propagandists. They shift freely the meaning of "age" with relation to events. Until the outbreak of the war with Russia, the Nazis presented themselves as a vital young nation at war with the decadent democracies of Europe. After this event they assumed the role of an old and cultured nation defending the European heritage against Asiatic barbarism. Then, in his speech of November 8, 1942, Hitler went so far as to call English civilization "infantile." In propaganda to France, however, the specific attribute of national age was *not* yet elastic. But other attributes within that group which are associated in Nazi propaganda with national age were so. Thus, for example, "democratic methods" (which is associated in Nazi propaganda with old civilization) is used to signify enemy weakness and enemy immorality. However, "undemocratic methods" (associated in Nazi ideology with young civilization) is also used to signify enemy immorality.

> The democracies react to a crisis with democratic methods, namely a change of government. (May 9, 1940)

In this statement, "democratic methods" signifies weakness (classified under *a* in the scheme). In the following quote, the same attribute of "democratic methods" is used to signify immorality connected with strength (this represents a residual meanings according to the scheme).

> For a long time past, the Western democracies have been trying to enlarge the present conflict. This has been their sole political aim. (March 9, 1940)

The next quote shows how the same meaning of immorality connected with strength is signified by the attribute of "undemocratic methods" (this corresponds to c in the scheme). Furthermore, when this same attribute is applied to the Germans rather than the British, it has the meaning of morality connected with strength (this corresponds to f in the scheme).

> There is just one thing which the British understood about National Socialism—its forcefulness. Therefore, they recognized that to oppose it a man of dynamic character was necessary. They settled on Churchill. . . . But there is the German kind of dynamism—progressive, elastic and revolutionary—and there is the brutal type, devoid of any instinct, except social and military prejudices, as typified by Churchill. (June 9, 1940)

The general Nazi practice on the subject of democracy is to refer scornfully to the "so-called Allied democracies." As it is impossible to tell whether the scorn is directed against the "so-called" or against the "democracies," there is the double implication, first, that the Allied governments are not democratic, and, second, that even if they were, democracy is in itself an evil.

It is interesting that the three groups of ambivalent attributes which have the highest elasticity should be, of all groups listed, the ones used with the German side as a subject reference most frequently (28 per cent of total references as compared with 22 and 19 per cent in those groups of attributes with a predominantly moral or immoral meaning) and most intimately related to Nazi ideology with its stress on youth, action and planning. One would perhaps suppose that attributes closely related to the ideology of the propagandist would have more stable meanings than those marginal to it. The fact that this is not so is not merely further proof of the opportunistic character of Nazi ideology. Rather, it sheds light on the status of ideas in Nazi politics in general.

The Nazis do not attach any intrinsic value and any stable

meaning to the ideas which according to their claims are important to them. The elasticity of those ideas which are most intimately connected with Nazi ideology proves that these ideas, too, are used instrumentally. These ideas, too, are subordinate to what really matters to the Nazis: success and power.

Chapter 10. Notes

1. Cyril Falls, *The Nature of Modern Warfare*, New York, 1941, p. 9.

2. Thomas Hobbes, *Leviathan* (Everyman's Library ed.), p. 64.

3. Cf. especially, Rupert von Schumacher and Hans Hummel, *Vom Kriege zwischen den Kriegen*, Stuttgart, 1937.

4. *Red Star* (October, 1942), quoted in the *N. Y. Times* of Oct. 11, 1942.

5. On June 20, Hitler received Petain's note announcing the names of the four French plenipotentiaries.—For the periodization, cf. Hamilton Fish Armstrong, *Chronology of Failure*, New York, 1940.

6. Within the five types, however, we also distinguish between agitation in the form of commands or suggestions, and agitation for actions or attitudes.

7. This, to be sure, is a particular kind of weakness and strength respectively, but may for certain purposes be distinguished from military, economic and all other kinds of weakness and strength.

8. To insure reliability of the coding procedure we have established rules for the way in which the answers to these questions have to be found.

9. Although these attributes and actions have been listed as single words, each category includes any word of approximately the same meaning; nine groups of attributes with related meanings were eventually formed in order to facilitate the technical problem of studying elasticity. See p. 241.

10. From now on the word "attribute" will be used to signify both attribute and action.

11. If during the final coding a new attribute was found which seemed of sufficient importance to be included in our list, we re-examined the coded material to be sure that this attribute had not occurred before.

12. Strictly speaking, statements having France as a subject reference.

13. There were no entries for "unity" (of Germany with France). In the following discussions, tables and graphs, "division" will always be included whenever we speak of "weakness," German domestic unity being included in "strength" in any case.

14. It is quite possible that this pattern is reversed in German propaganda to this country.

15. It may be objected that when Nazi propagandists tell Frenchmen "England is responsible for this war" or "The British Government consists of warmongers," the *effect* on the French audience may not be very different from that of Nazi assertions that England dragged *France* into the war. However, according to our rules, we have coded the former statements as "assertions of guilt," the latter as "exploitation," since the

classification of content must not depend on an appraisal of its presumable effect.

16. With the exception of the difference between Periods IV and V, when *both* curves *rise*.

17. The reader should keep in mind that we are talking about statements in which "the English," or "the French" or "the Allies" are *subjects*. When the German propagandist declares "Germany shall defeat France," he talks about France, but "Germany" would be the subject reference, and the statement would be coded as *German* strength. We have also coded *object references,* but report only on findings pertaining to subject references.

18. This statement really contains two simplifications: (1) Propaganda may lie about, distort or slant military news (instead of merely communicating the knowledge of facts "objectively"). Since Germany was overwhelmingly victorious in her campaign against the West, she had less reason for departing from the truth than, say, in the Russian campaign. Cf. on this problem, Hans Speier, "The Radio Communication of War News in Germany," *Social Research,* Vol. VIII, November 1941 (dealing with German *domestic* broadcasts during the campaign against France), and *German Military Communiqués,* Research Paper No. 2 of the Research Project on Totalitarian Communication (mimeographed). (2) By revealing corruption of, and exploitation by, political individuals and groups, propaganda may communicate the knowledge of *facts* in spite of its moral language.

19. These six meanings are also indicated in the schematic scheme of page 241.

20. A word of explanation is necessary for our classification of attributes as being "positive" or "negative." As can be seen, this distinction does not refer to German or Enemy side as do the directions; neither does it necessarily follow the wording of an attribute. To have a consistent and easily applicable aspect of classification for all attributes, we considered as positive the wording which connotates strength while we considered as negative the wording connotating weakness. Thus "attacking" would be considered positive, "non-attacking" negative; however, "undemocratic methods" would also be positive, because in German propaganda it is associated with strength while "democratic methods," associated with weakness, would be classified as a negative attribute.

Chapter 11

STANDING DIRECTIVE FOR PSYCHOLOGI-
CAL WARFARE AGAINST MEMBERS OF
THE GERMAN ARMED FORCES *

June 1944

By

RICHARD H. S. CROSSMAN

[Mr. Crossman, as Deputy Chief of PWD/SHAEF, was the chief author of this Standing Directive. General R. A. McClure and his other deputies contributed much to its formulations. D.L.]

Scope and Purpose of this Directive

1. This Standing Directive lays down the general lines to be followed in all forms of white propaganda directed to German armed forces in the West. It is intended as a Standing Directive, valid both before and after D-Day. It will be supplemented from time to time by special directives, as well as by the weekly Central Directive prepared by PWE/OWI in collaboration with PWD/SHAEF. Unless expressly stated, however, these directives should be regarded as supplementary to, and not as cancelling, the present Standing Directive, which has the approval of PWE/OWI.

2. The Moscow Declaration laid down the principle that the individual would be held responsible for his war crimes. This applies equally to the soldier and to the civilian; a uniform neither aggravates nor mitigates the guilt of the individual, thus the Declaration ruled out the suggestion of mass reprisals.

3. But it has also been made clear by our Governments that they are determined to destroy not only the Nazi system, but the concept of the Wehrmacht, which has been both the initi-

* Reprinted from *Sykewar: Psychological Warfare Against Germany,* by Daniel Lerner, published by George W. Stewart, Publisher, Inc., New York, 1949.

ator and the willing instrument of recurring German attempts to dominate other peoples. Nothing in the implementation of this directive must compromise that issue.

4. It is recognized that in the execution of Psychological Warfare it is a fundamental principle not to antagonize the audience. Direct denunciation or direct offence against known susceptibilities will therefore be avoided in all Psychological Warfare against the enemy armed forces. On the other hand, nothing will be done to encourage or condone the concept of German militarism and the attitudes of mind behind it, both of which we are pledged to destroy.

5. Psychological Warfare is not a magic substitute for physical battle, but an auxiliary to it. By attacking the fighting morale of the enemy, it aims at: (a) reducing the cost of the physical battle, and (b) rendering the enemy easier to handle after surrender.

6. The conduct of Psychological Warfare therefore forms part of the conduct of military operations, and must be co-ordinated with that of other arms of war. It is the task of Psychological Warfare to assist the Supreme Commander in fulfilling his mission against the enemy with the most economical use of troops and equipment.

7. The use of Psychological Warfare in military operations must however be strictly subordinated to the long-term policy of our Governments, in the sense that nothing must be done with the object of undermining fighting morale during operations which would prejudice Government policy to Germany after the war. To this end, this Standing Directive for Psychological Warfare during operations is preceded by a summary of standing high-policy directives.

8. These high-policy directives define not the strategy of the campaign which Psychological Warfare will conduct against German fighting morale, but the limits within which it must, for policy reasons, be confined.

Standing High-Policy Directives

9. No specific promises will be made concerning the treatment of Germany after the war, other than those expressly made by Government spokesmen. In particular there must be no suggestion that the Atlantic Charter applies to Germany by right.

10. On no account must there be any suggestion or implication:—

  (I)   that we recognize any claim of the German Army to be absolved from its full share of responsibility for German aggression on the grounds that its part is merely professional and nonpolitical and that it does no more than obey orders;

 (II)   that we recognize the possibility of divorcing the "fighting war" from the atrocities which the German soldier has committed or condoned, e.g., the taking and shooting of hostages and the murder of prisoners;

(III)   that we would be prepared to allow German militarism to survive in any form.

11. The following are the points on which our Governments have committed themselves:

(a) Demilitarisation of Germany.

(b) Punishment of war criminals.

(c) Liberation of territories overrun by Nazi Germany, including Austria.

(d) Occupation of Germany.

(e) Destruction of Nazism and German Militarism.

(f) Prevention of such economic distress in Germany as will be detrimental to the rest of the world.

(g) Ultimate restoration of Germany to a place "in the world family of democratic nations."

The key quotations on these points are given in Annex I. Note that (d), (f) and (g) are only general commitments, and may not be elaborated in Psychological Warfare unless and until specific Government statements are forthcoming on these points.

APPRECIATION OF STRENGTH AND WEAKNESS OF GERMAN FIGHTING MORALE WITH SPECIAL REFERENCE TO PSYCHOLOGICAL WARFARE

Note: Except where specifically stated, the following generalizations apply to the German Army, not to the Air Force or Navy.

12. *Strong Points*

  (I) *The Habit of Discipline.* The habit of uncritical obedience to authority, rather than any ruthless enforcement of discipline from above, remains the strongest factor in German morale today. This factor may not decrease sharply until the German Army as a whole is broken on the battlefield, since the retreats and defensive battles to which the Wehrmacht is now committed automatically place greater reliance on higher authority than offensive campaigns of the 1940 type.

(II) *Comradeship*. The ideal of comradeship has been keenly cultivated in the German Army, particularly since 1933. The German NCO forms a transitional stage between soldier status and officer status, a fact which strengthens this sense of comradeship. It has furthermore been immensely deepened by the Russian campaign.

(III) *Professional Pride*. The average German's conviction that the best life is the soldier's life, plus the social fact that the highest calling in Germany is the soldier's calling, constitutes a great source of strength.

Added to this the German soldier, and often the non-German soldier serving in the Wehrmacht, is convinced:—

(a) that he is privileged to be serving in the finest army in the world, permeated with a code of soldierly honour which rules him and his officers alike;

(b) that the Wehrmacht is the embodiment of the highest physical and spiritual attainments of German culture;

(c) that the Wehrmacht is therefore the *nonpolitical* guardian of the future of the German race;

(d) that, as a fighting machine, German "quality" can *probably* succeed in throwing back both Anglo-American and Russian "quantity."

(IV) *Material Interests*. The German Army represents, for the reasons stated in subparagr. (III) above, an honoured career with considerable material benefits. (Pay allowances and especially food are good compared with civilian standards in Germany.) Thousands of officers (especially those of junior and field rank) and tens of thousands of NCOs (particularly in specialist trades) have signed on not simply for the duration, but for periods varying from 7-14 years, or longer, and are fighting not only to preserve the German Army as a war machine, but as a means of livelihood.

(V) *The Bolshevik Bogey*. The guilty fear of Russian vengeance, linked with the Teuton dislike of the Slav and general fear of Bolshevism, has convinced the average German soldier that "anything is better than defeat in the East."

German propaganda has deliberately enlarged and intensified this fear, in the following ways:—

(a) It has largely succeeded in persuading the soldier that the Anglo-Americans are so dominated by the Bolshevik Colossus that they would be powerless to save Germany.

(b) It has filled the gap created by the absence of specific United Nations policy to Germany with atrocity stories of forced labour in Russia, castration, deportation, etc.

(VI) *The Rewards of Victory in the West*. Learning from Mr. Churchill in 1940, the High Command has deliberately capitalized the threat of invasion from the West. It has:—

(a) argued that, if the Anglo-American threat can be frustrated or confined, the German Armies can be switched to the East. This argument has been used to justify the retreats in the East.

(b) argued that a defensive victory in the West will form the basis for the speedy conclusion of a "compromise peace" either with the West or with the East, which would in fact be a German victory.

(c) exploited the bombing of Germany to persuade the soldier that his only hope of regaining what he has lost lies in a German victory in the West.

(d) succeeded in convincing the German soldier that for these reasons one last tremendous effort must and can be made.

(VII) *Summary*

(a) Taken by and large, it must be accepted that the German High Command has rendered the Army largely immune to the two Psychological Warfare campaigns which proved effective in 1918, i.e., Bolshevist propaganda, leading to soldiers' and workers' councils; and democratic propaganda, leading to a revolt of the civilian under arms against the professional soldier.

We should assume that the German Army in the West will, like von Arnim's Army in Tunisia, fight on *as a whole* until it collapses *as a whole*. Indeed defeatism is more widespread at the top than at the bottom.

(b) The High Command has succeeded in actually raising fighting morale during the winter.

(c) For the reason outlined in subparagr. (I) above, no propaganda directed at the frontline German soldier is likely to be effective unless it sounds and looks more positive and authoritative than his own Army Order forbidding him to listen to it.

(d) For the reasons outlined in subparagrs. (II) and (III) above, there is little prospect of dividing the German Army *internally*—i.e., setting men against officers. Furthermore, no propaganda aiming at inducing the surrender of German troops is likely to succeed unless it meets the fundamental objection that by surrender the individual is letting down his comrades.

13. Weak Points

(I) *The Shaken Myth of Invincibility*. The long series of defeats suffered by the Wehrmacht in the Mediterranean and in Russia have shaken—but by no means shattered—the German soldier's faith in the mystic invincibility of German arms which carried his fighting morale up to a high tide of fanaticism in June 1940. Within this general uneasiness are other specific doubts:

(a) *Doubt about the Führer*. Allied propaganda that disasters such as Stalingrad, Tunisia, the Ukraine battle, and the Crimea, were largely due to the prestige policy of hanging on too long to too much, has gone home. Many German soldiers today feel that military operations are being dictated by political and often party considerations. The permeation of the OKW, and of the General Staff, with party generals (notably the C. of S. Zeitzler) is largely blamed for this.

Note: At present, the average soldier, despite an awareness that he has made serious mistakes, is not inclined to blame Hitler, as the generals and other informed persons already do. Hitler is still his lucky tailsman. Göring is also to some extent shielded. Of the German leaders, Himmler, Goebbels, and Ley are the most unpopular. Generally speaking, "The System" or the "Party bosses" are the commonest scapegoat.

(b) *Doubts about Equipment.* German Army Equipment is good, and the German soldier knows it. But his battle experience since 1941 has given him painful proof that, in some respects at least, Allied equipment is not only more plentiful, but better. (Allied MT in Africa, Russian PAK, Russian medium tanks in the East and Allied fighter planes on all fronts are examples.)

The present *"Wunderwaffe"* vogue is in part a wishful thinking reaction to this.

(c) *Doubts about the News.* Despite intense efforts by the High Command, it has not succeeded in making the German soldier accept unquestioningly its interpretation of events. Most German soldiers, when they get the opportunity, read or listen to Anglo-American propaganda and try to find a truth halfway between their own communiques and ours. They assume that "everything is propaganda" and that they, as intelligent people, can read between the lines. Without knowing it, they are of course steeped in Nazi propaganda. They regard as "propaganda lies" such facts as that Germany invaded Poland, or that England has some highly developed social services. They have the useful faculty of forgetting any facts inconvenient to their superiors, and believing they were invented by Anglo-American propaganda. Their outlook is formed, however, not by the direct output of the Propaganda Ministry, but by the educational and propaganda activities of the Wehrmacht. Nevertheless they are open to any propaganda which does not sound or read like "propaganda," and does not offend their sense of "soldierly honour." Unconsciously still, but actively, the German soldier craves for an excuse to stop the useless slaughter which leaves his honour as a German soldier unscathed, and puts the blame on someone or something outside the Wehrmacht. He needs, in brief: (I) facts, which seem to him to be objective, showing that, despite the courage of the Wehrmacht, someone at home has lost the war for Germany; (II) a picture of the future which portrays death and destruction for "the betrayers of Germany" and survival for the German people.

Evidence for the above analysis is provided by the growing success of: (a) Free German Committee broadcasts from Moscow, headed by General Seydlitz, and (b) Radio Calais. Both these transmissions seem to assume an analysis of German fighting morale similar to that above.

(d) *Doubts about the Luftwaffe.* Moreover, the *Air War* brings with it a cause of friction between the Air Force and the Army. German soldiers are beginning to talk like many British soldiers in 1940. This friction, and the resulting blame on "the authorities" is a real if minor chink in German fighting morale.

All these factors are important, in that they provide the soldier with scapegoats for his decline in fortune, and when things go wrong the German's natural reaction is: "I have been betrayed."

(II) *Manpower.* This is perhaps the main *operational* worry of the German soldier. He is disturbed by the enormous losses in men and material which he knows the battles in Russia have cost the Wehrmacht. This uneasiness is heightened by the Allied propaganda barrage on this theme, contrasted with the silence of his own authorities, a silence all the more significant when it persists even under the new OKW policy of simulating complete frankness on operational matters. This general manpower worry breaks down into other specific ones:

(a) The worry that, because of manpower troubles, the ranks of the Wehrmacht are being increasingly filled with foreigners of some twenty nationalities, and that the quality of the army is therefore in danger of "pollution."

(b) The worry that, with almost every one of its field divisions committed already to actual or potential battle-fields, the German Army has no effective central reserve to sustain it.

Both (a) and (b) above apply with particular force to the target of this paper—the German forces in the West. These troops have in their own formations large numbers of foreigners; and most of these divisions have had proof, by their own experience of being switched from West to East and back, that no uncommitted central reserve exists. The great volume of German counterpropaganda on this point is further evidence of its importance.

(III) *A War Gone Wrong.* In building up the picture of the chivalrous Wehrmacht in deadly battle against Bolshevism, the High Command inevitably raises in the German soldier's mind the question why Germany is fighting Britain and America, especially since Hitler denounced in *Mein Kampf* the fatal mistake of the two-front war. The High Command seeks to answer this question by denouncing Anglo-American impotence and arguing that the Jews of Wall Street and the City of London are in conspiracy with the Kremlin. But this argument does not quell a deep uneasiness.

There is also a feeling in the German soldier's mind that the defensive battles which he is now forced to fight are not the battles for which he was trained, nor the battles for which his equipment was designed. There is evidence that the OKW had great trouble, during 1943, in converting officers and men to the technique of the defensive battle which their previous training had largely neglected.

The fear of isolation, a feature of what the Germans used to ridicule as "Maginot-mindedness," is likely to be at its strongest among coastal formations in the West. They are particularly liable to the anxiety lest they be sacrificed as "human land-mines."

(IV) *Loss of Honour.* An increasing number of soldiers are aware of, and uncomfortable about:—

(a) atrocities, especially in Russia. They naturally want to push the blame onto the SS., or simply "those in authority."

(b) the hostility of the occupied territories, including "Nordic" countries like Norway. The German wants to be liked, and the German soldier is puzzled why, despite the correctness of the Wehrmacht, he is so coldly received. He wants to have an explanation which blames someone outside the Army for this failure of the "New Order."

(V) *Respect for Western Powers.* The German has a sense of inferiority to both Britain and America. Many Nazis, for instance, regard National Socialism as the method of making Germany a ruling race "like the British." The German feelings for Britain are a confused mixture of envy, respect and contempt for the old-fashioned. Their feeling for America is different, since they do not feel toward it a racial unity like Britain or Germany, and are suspicious of its "capitalist imperialism." They profoundly respect its riches, production capacity and "smartness," and regard it as the continent of unlimited possibilities.

Intensive propaganda has failed to modify these traditional feelings. *In particular, nearly all German soldiers are confident that they will be treated well as prisoners of war and hope for (if they do not expect) an Anglo-American occupation if the worst comes to the worst.* Furthermore, they are feverishly anxious for Anglo-American appreciation of "the chivalry" of the Wehrmacht.

(VI) *The Shadow of the Two-Front War.* It is improbable that German fighting morale in the West will be seriously undermined before a successful Anglo-American landing, provided there is no great German disaster in the East. But the moment we can announce a decisive breakthrough will be a moment of profound psychological crisis, greater even than the shock of Mussolini's collapse last year.

Meanwhile, the advance of the Russian troops *into Europe* must reduce the persuasiveness of the argument that Hitler is deliberately yielding space in the

East to ensure victory in the West. Gradually the German soldier begins to ask whether Hitler's strategy is not precisely what United Nations strategy desires, and whether the Second Front is not having its effects even before it starts.

The Strategy of Psychological Warfare

14. The foregoing analysis suggests that, provided there is no catastrophe in the East, the weak points in German morale, enumerated above, will begin to counteract the strong points only when the Anglo-American forces have demonstrated that they can use their quantitative superiority.

15. It is impossible to predict at what phase of the operations this change in German morale will come. On this point Psychological Warfare will be guided by G-2. Already, however, it is possible to lay down two phases in the psychological warfare campaign:

    (a) The phase before and after D-day, up to change in German morale (referred to as *Phase* A).

    (b) The phase after the change (referred to as *Phase* B). The present Directive deals with *Phase* A.

16. In Phase A all psychological warfare against German troops must be regarded as *preparatory*. This must be a period *not of direct assault* or of open appeals for surrender, but of steady repetition of the facts, full recognition of which will bear sudden fruit in Phase B.

Even after D-day this unemphatic reiteration of facts should be continued until evidence from G-2 indicates that it is time to move into Phase B.

17. During this phase psychological warfare will concentrate on the following tasks:

    (I) *Long-term tasks*

    (a) Maintenance and increase of belief in the reliability of the Anglo-American word, and of unity between the Russians and ourselves.

    (b) Creation of an atmosphere in which the German soldier gradually comes to feel that, since defeat is certain, he has fulfilled his soldierly duty and can now follow the example of the German Army in Tunisia.

(II) *Short-term tasks, pre D-day*

(a) Stimulation of defeatism through a sense of Anglo-American superiority in men and materials; combating the fear of Bolshevism by a cautious build-up of Anglo-American strength.

(b) Exploitation of German confidence in the good treatment of prisoners of war, so as to decrease German fighting spirit and undermine German fear of defeat. Simultaneously, familiarization of the German soldier with official Allied statements on the place of Germany in Post-War Europe.

(c) Exploitation of the Russian offensive as exemplifying the certainty of a German defeat in a two-front war.

(d) Exploitation of the German fear of sabotage and resistance by occupied peoples, including foreign workers.

(e) Exploitation of a sense of isolation through the Allied threat to German communications.

(f) Exploitation of the air offensive to stimulate distrust between the air force and the army and to undermine confidence in the possibility of successful resistance.

(III) *Short-term tasks, post D-day.* After D-day the following tasks should be added to those in (II) above:

(a) Stimulation of distrust of foreigners in the German Army by open incitement of these foreigners.

(b) Special attacks on the morale of troops on the flanks of the fighting. Since these troops will not be actually engaged, they will probably form the best target for propaganda. In this campaign, emphasize the failure of the Luftwaffe and the German Navy to prevent the landings.

METHODS TO BE EMPLOYED IN CARRYING OUT THE ABOVE CAMPAIGN

18. *Long-term tasks*

(I) *Maintenance and increase of belief in the reliability of the Anglo-American word and in unity between the Russians and ourselves.*

(a) Throughout this phase all psychological warfare in all media, whether tactical or strategic, will remain factual and objective, avoiding terms, phrases, or pictures which the German soldier will dismiss as "propaganda." In particular, all boasting and sneering will be scrupulously avoided; there will be no direct appeals to the soldier's self-interest. There will be no attempts at a chummy or intimate style. All psychological warfare will give the impression of Anglo-American reliability, reticence, soldierly dignity and decency.

(b) Use every opportunity to demonstrate practical collaboration between ourselves and the Russians. This is preferable to ideological dissertations on United Nations Unity.

(II) *Creation of an atmosphere in which the German soldier gradually comes to feel that, since defeat is certain, he has fulfilled his soldierly duty and can now follow the example of the German Army in Tunisia.*

Do not assume that the German soldier is yet convinced that defeat is certain. He is keyed up and may maintain a relatively high morale for some time after D-day.

Concentrate, therefore, on those facts which the German soldier can accept as facts, illustrating the inevitability of ultimate defeat.

Make no open appeals for deserting. Similarly, make no open appeals to fear, e.g., of the air offensive. Treat the German soldier as a man who, if openly incited by the enemy to cowardice, will do the opposite.

Show the increasing isolation of Germany's position in the world and the gradual weakening and disintegration of the satellites, the increasing restrictions being imposed on Germany by the neutrals, and the defeats suffered by her Japanese allies.

19. *Short-term tasks pre-D-day*

(I) *Stimulation of defeatism through a sense of Anglo-American superiority in men and materials; combating the fear of Bolshevism by a cautious build-up of Anglo-American strength.*

Do not try to heighten the tension by a deliberate

war-of-nerves campaign. The German will see through this and dismiss it as propaganda. But provide all material available, especially technical material, on the leadership, organization, equipment and training of the Anglo-American armies.

Continue to provide facts showing the failure of the U-boats.

Show that the Mediterranean fronts are draining away German reserves needed for the two essential fronts.

(II) *Exploitation of German confidence in the good treatment of prisoners of war so as to decrease German fighting spirit and undermine German fear of defeat. Simultaneously, familiarization of the German soldier with official Allied statements on the place of Germany in post-war Europe.*

Continue and increase the campaign illustrating the treatment of German prisoners of war. But avoid, especially in leaflets, a "display" which looks like commercial publicity. In radio propaganda, increase as far as possible broadcasts about, and by, German prisoners of war.

It is probable that many German soldiers are not familiar with even a few statements available on United Nations intentions with regard to post-war Germany. These statements should now be plugged in leaflets and radio. Equally, the fact should be emphasised that the Nazis are deliberately concealing from the German soldier the real intentions of the United Nations.

(III) *Exploitation of the Russian offensive as exemplifying the certainty of a German defeat in a two-front war.*

Destroy the illusion that the German retreat in the East is deliberately planned, by showing the intimate connection between Russian and Anglo-American strategy. Hitler is no longer the master of his own strategy. It is dictated to him by the two-front strategy of the United Nations.

Treat the Mediterranean as a theater in which we have compelled the Germans to fritter away first-class manpower and reserves vitally needed for the decisive battles on the two major fronts.

(IV) *Exploitation of the German fear of sabotage and resistance by occupied peoples, including foreign workers.*

Never appeal directly to German fear of sabotage and resistance. Confine yourself to plain facts. Do not spoil these facts by headlines such as "Martyrs of Gestapo Terror."

Build up the impression that resistance in occupied Europe, and to a lesser extent in Germany, is an organized part of the Anglo-American strategy.

Stress, where possible, facts indicating the decline of effective police control in Germany and German-occupied Europe. Here again, do not interpret these facts to the Germans, but let them speak for themselves. *Make no references before D-Day to foreigners serving in the German Armies in the West.*

(V) *Exploitation of a sense of isolation through the Allied threat to German communications.*

Make the German soldier (especially in the coastal divisions) feel he is a "human land mine," by stressing the significance of attacks on German communications.

Stress that the Atlantic Wall is 1000 miles long, and that the German High Command can meet a threat at only one point by stripping reserves from other points. The German assumes that there will be several landings: so should we.

(VI) *Exploitation of the air offensive to stimulate distrust between the air force and the army and to undermine confidence in the possibility of successful resistance.*

"Fear propaganda" designed to intensify the effect of bombs has been rendered unnecessary by the bombs themselves. In treating the air offensive, concentrate on its strictly military significance as an essential part of our invasion strategy. Avoid giving any impression that we are trying to break German morale. Seek indirectly to arouse resentment against the fact that air power, which the Nazis claimed as their invention, has now been turned against Germany. Give the impression that the efforts of the Luftwaffe cannot make up for Anglo-American production superiority and for the mistakes of the German leadership.

Remember that production figures—unrelated to battle figures—no longer impress the German soldier. Not the number of aircraft produced, but the effects of air superiority, impress him. This applies also to all forms of manpower and material superiority.

20. *Short-term tasks post D-day*

(I) *Stimulation of distrust of foreigners in the German Army by open incitement of these foreigners.*

On and after D-Day a special campaign will be launched of direct incitement to desertion, addressed to foreigners in the German Army of the West. It will have two objects: (I) to influence the foreigners, (II) indirectly to influence the German troops. A special directive will be issued on this subject.

(II) *Special attacks on the morale of troops on the flanks of the fighting.*

During the actual fighting we cannot expect that the German troops engaged will be receptive to anything but combat propaganda.

Strategic radio and leaflets should in this period be directed chiefly to the German troops on the flanks, as well as to foreigners throughout the German Army. The treatment should remain formal and objective and avoid boasting or creating an atmosphere of undue excitement. Every effort should be made to obtain "hot" statements from prisoners of war for use by radio and leaflet.

Every effort should be made to demonstrate to these troops the influence of sea power on the operation. In particular the following themes should be used:

(a) Allied command of the sea, and of the air over it, gives us the power to launch attacks with the maximum of surprise over a very wide range.

(b) Allied command of the sea excludes the free use of sea communications along the Atlantic Wall, communications which would be invaluable if land communications are destroyed or hampered.

(c) The German Navy cannot cope both with the assault and its follow up, and with the trans-Atlantic traffic bringing more and more men, weapons and supplies.

(d) To the troops on the flanks of the breach in the Atlantic Wall, emphasize the power and effectiveness of naval bombardment.

(e) Complete Allied control of the Mediterranean offers freedom of action for further attacks on the Continent.

Part III

THE ORGANIZATION OF PURPOSE
AND PERSONS

EFFICIENT ORGANIZATION of propaganda requires, first of all, a *clear* conception of the purpose to be served by the organization. The purpose also must be *shared* as well as clear. For the function of organization is to provide the channel through which an aggregate of diverse individuals can best apply a *common* purpose to a given situation. The particular form any organization takes is important only as it serves this function. Organization, too, is instrumental.

The chapter by Lasswell specifies several alternative ways of organizing purpose open to those with a "policy conception of propaganda." The next two chapters, by Linebarger and Davis, contain vigorous statements of two such purposes—emphasizing, respectively, a total "warfare psychologically waged" and a "strategy of news."

The "organization of persons" is an extremely complicated problem, particularly when those persons are propagandists. Bruce Lockhart writes of his own British propaganda organization during World War II: "I cannot say that PWE was an easy team. Every good propagandist must possess the qualities of a prima donna or . . . must be born with one eye." His chapter is a vivid recollection of a central problem in any organization of propagandists: "a tendency to try to make foreign policy by means of propaganda instead of being content to support policy by propaganda." The OSS Assessment Staff report on personnel screening and vetting suggests that propagandists also might be assessed on such a factor, among others, as their readiness to serve rather than make policy. The chapter by Doob deals with skill, rather than temperament, components for effective service in a propaganda organization, by analysis of the World War II experience with social scientists in the Overseas Branch of OWI.

The integration of purpose and persons, which is the function of organization, calls for optimum decisions on the matters discussed in preceding chapters: selection and clarification of propaganda goals, selection and allocation of persons best able to formulate strategies and conduct operations to achieve these goals. Certain factors inherent in the structure of national power lie beyond the immediate control of propaganda organization but must be taken into account by it—as, for example, "The Number One Voice" which Reston discusses. Zacharias illustrates, on the other hand, how lesser voices can be handled efficiently through organization of voice status to suit policy purpose. Jackson directs our attention to another set of problems inherent in the national structure: the integration of "Private Media and Public Policy." In a country whose mass media of communication are for the most part privately owned and operated, this is a matter of the first importance.

Two main points are shared by these writers. First, the efficiency of a propaganda organization depends largely on the degree to which its personnel hold a clear and common conception of their purpose. Second, it depends upon the nature of that purpose—i.e., the policy to be instrumented by propaganda. Whereas the first is mainly a matter of internal administration, the second depends upon the total political context of which propaganda is but one subordinate dimension. The policy framework within which any propaganda organization must operate is defined not by propagandists, but by politicians. It is the latter who make the policies—with respect to purse, persons, purposes—by which a propaganda organization falls into place alongside the other instruments of statecraft.

It is for this reason that we have subtitled this volume "Materials For American Policy." The papers here collected report experiences, codify lessons, make recommendations. There they must stop; the decisions will be made elsewhere. Wise policy will consult experience, in propaganda as in other special fields. But the general rule remains: Propagandists propose; statesmen dispose.

Chapter 12

POLITICAL AND PSYCHOLOGICAL WARFARE

By

HAROLD D. LASSWELL

PSYCHOLOGICAL WARFARE is a recent name for an old idea about how to wage successful war. The idea is found in the oldest manuals of military strategy. Sun Tzu's *The Book of War,* written in China in the fifth century B.C., stressed the importance of destroying the enemy's will to fight through such means as surprise and noise. "In night fighting," Sun Tzu wrote, "beacons and drums are largely used; in day fighting, a great number of banners and flags, and the enemy's eyes and ears are confounded." The same aim could be accomplished by spreading tales of the treachery of trusted leaders and of the overwhelming forces at the command of the enemy. *The Book of War* also advised the assassination of enemy leaders in order to create panic. Another suggestion made by Sun Tzu was that a commander should avoid struggle to the bitter end and gain victory at a minimum cost.

Essentially the same guiding principles can be found in the military literature or the prevailing maxims of the ancient empires of India and the Near East. The East Indian political classic, Kautilya's *Arthasastra,* for example, contains advice on how to destroy enemy morale and build up one's own. Secret agents, it suggests, should circulate among the enemy soldiers and spread rumors of their certain defeat. As for one's own forces, "Astrologers and other followers of the king should infuse spirit into the army by pointing out [its] impregnable nature."

The basic idea is that the best success in war is achieved by the destruction of the enemy's will to resist, and with a minimum annihilation of fighting capacity. The political aim is limited destruction. Neither the enemy's armed forces nor the whole population nor the physical facilities should be totally obliterated. On the contrary, the political goals are limited. Usually the purpose is to see that in the enemy country there be installed a leadership that will turn it into an ally, or at least into a non-hostile power.

In the case of our own wars with Germany, at no time was it our serious policy to destroy the whole German people. In World War II, the destruction of German lives and property through bombing was intended to bring the conflict to the quickest possible conclusion. The ultimate object was the substitution for the Nazi regime of leaders and forms of government willing to support the sort of national structure and international order in which we have confidence.

In World War II, strategic air power was clearly not a "psychological" instrument in the same sense that radio broadcasts to the German people were. Yet in war, all strategy and tactics aim at *an economy of means in the accomplishment of its objectives*. How, then, can we distinguish Psychological Warfare from other forms of warfare?

The most distinctive act of Psychological Warfare is this:— *it uses the means of mass communication in order to destroy the enemy's will to fight*. When the old Chinese armies went into battle with an array of musical instruments and a forest of banners to impress the enemy soldiers, they were relying upon the use of means which are ordinarily specialized for the communication of emotion or information. The same was true of the use of tale-bearers to undermine the unity of the enemy by exaggerating the strength of the forces on the other side or by stirring up sedition against the leaders.

Mass communication, it should be stressed, is not exclusively a matter of the word, spoken or printed, or picture. It uses other media also, such as physical acts and material devices. This is notably true of assassination. While the act of killing cannot be considered a conventional method of communication, yet it has been used often to affect political attitudes. *The act of assassination was expected to have an impact upon the intention of the enemy to fight that would be far out of proportion to the physical damage done to his capacity, or to the physical capacity made use of in the killing.* We are looking at the conduct of war in the perspective of psychology when we are seek ing to widen the gap between the physical destruction of capabilities on both sides and the magnitude of the impact upon the enemy's intention to resist.

By this time it should be obvious that Psychological Warfare is a reminder of the fundamental conception of all strategy rather than a specific technique. Why, then, do we speak of it at all?

The fact is that fundamental principles of warfare are continually falling into neglect from which it is necessary to rescue them. Generals and admirals are always caught between two opposing tendencies in using their tools of war. One tendency is to magnify the specific importance of the physical and personnel instruments; the other is to subordinate these instruments to a larger plan in which they may be economized, and hence cut down somewhat in apparent importance. This means that men who specialize on ships become devoted to every detail of how the ship can be built, supplied, and handled in war. Artillery specialists are absorbed in the designing, building and tactical application of guns. Regardless of the physical weapon, or of the personnel devoted to the weapon, there is a vast concentration of understanding and loyalty, the result of which is to magnify the visible role of the weapon in the conduct of war. "Gadget love" is a snare for the unwary in the same way that love of the horse or the camel or the elephant appealed to the cavalryman of the past.

A term like Psychological Warfare comes into vogue when circumstances appear to confer some new importance upon economy in the use of physical weapons as a means of destroying the enemy's will to fight. In World War I the word that performed this task was "propaganda." That, too, was not a conception limited to the printing of newspapers or of leaflets for clandestine circulation among enemy soldiers and civilians. There was "propaganda of the deed," a term borrowed from social revolutionaries, which emphasized the importance of assassinating or the taking of emotionally significant cities or the importance of surprise and the cultivation of revolutionary aims against enemy governments.

World War II saw the term Psychological Warfare performing the function that had been performed by propaganda in the first World War. The word originated and gained significance in Germany as the Germans who were defeated in World

War I began to look into the causes of that "collapse." The experts for the German General Staff believed that they had been bested in the use of the instruments of mass communication (often referred to by the term "propaganda"), and also by the failure to exploit all of their weapons with the maximum impact upon the enemy's will as the chief criterion.

The vogue of the expression "Psychological Warfare" came in part from the rapid expansion of specialized psychologists in Germany, the United States, and in other Western countries. The psychologists wanted "a place in the sun"; that is, they were eager to demonstrate that their skills could be used for the national defense in time of war. Early in the Second World War a group of Americans translated some of the important German literature into English for the purpose of opening the eyes of the military to the usefulness of psychology, not only in testing for specific aptitudes, or in propaganda, but in considering every phase of the conduct of war under modern conditions.

When we say, therefore, that Psychological Warfare is a new name for an old idea, and for an idea that is continually growing dim, we are in no way detracting from the importance of the term. Although the Russians paid little attention to the expression, they were even more completely aware of the essential idea than the Germans. For the leaders of the Soviet Union had seized power largely by combining propaganda with other acts upon tottering governments and upon discontented masses. The vocabulary of the Soviet leaders did not have to be refreshed by another word for conceptions thoroughly understood and applied.

Actually, the idea of Psychological Warfare is somewhat less comprehensive than other terms with which it is closely linked. The more inclusive conception is that of "political warfare," which covers the use of more than the means of mass communication or the handling of weapons in order to maximize impact upon the will to resist. Political warfare adds the important idea that all instruments of policy need to be properly correlated in the conduct of war.

Diplomacy, for example, can be used to keep potential enemies neutral, or to detach allies from the enemy. Diplomacy may also be used to bring the war to an early end by making secret arrangements with disaffected elements in the enemy country. When we speak of diplomacy, we have in mind the making of official commitments. Whereas mass communication aims at large audiences, diplomacy proceeds by means of official negotiation. Representatives of various powers deal directly with one another. Often diplomacy can be made most effective when it is properly correlated with Psychological Warfare (in the sense of both symbol propaganda and "propaganda of the deed").

Political warfare also includes the use of economic means besides the instruments which have been enumerated above. In order to preclude the use of minerals or other resources by an enemy, available stocks may be purchased in neutral countries. It may be important to coordinate propaganda with these operations in order to gain the tacit cooperation of officials in neutral countries who might otherwise interfere.

In considering Psychological Warfare and other instruments of policy connected with it, it should be kept in mind that they can be employed in peace as in war, with the necessary change of emphasis. The difference between war and peace is not always sharply defined, as is seen by the current "cold war." War can be said to exist when active hostilities are going on between two powers, or when the resumption of hostilities is expected at any moment.

The chief instruments of policy in war and peace are:

> Diplomacy
> Propaganda
> Economics
> Arms.

In war the emphasis upon arms is of outstanding importance:

> Armed Warfare
>> Physical Warfare
>> Psychological Warfare
> Political Warfare
>> Diplomatic Warfare
>> Propaganda Warfare
>> Economic Warfare

Peacefare and warfare are the two patterns which are assumed in the instruments of total policy at all times.

Political warfare thus includes operations in relation to allies, neutrals, and the home audience. Psychological Warfare includes propaganda directed against the enemy, together with the use of arms to create the greatest impact upon the enemy's will to fight at the least cost of capability. Enemy intentions are the target.

Chapter 13

WARFARE PSYCHOLOGICALLY WAGED *

By

PAUL M. A. LINEBARGER

PSYCHOLOGICAL WARFARE, in the broad sense, consists of the application of parts of the science called psychology to the conduct of war; in the narrow sense, psychological warfare comprises the use of propaganda against an enemy, together with such military operational measures as may supplement the propaganda. Propaganda may be described, in turn, as organized persuasion by non-violent means. War itself may be considered to be, among other things, a violent form of persuasion. Thus if an American fire-raid burns up a Japanese city, the burning is calculated to dissuade the Japanese from further warfare by denying the Japanese further physical means of war and by simultaneously hurting them enough to cause surrender. If, after the fire-raid, we drop leaflets telling them to surrender, the propaganda can be considered an extension of persuasion —less violent this time, and usually less effective, but nevertheless an integral part of the single process of making the enemy stop fighting.

Neither warfare nor psychology is a new subject. Each is as old as man. Warfare, being the more practical and plain subject, has a far older written history. This is especially the case since much of what is now called psychology was formerly studied under the heading of religion, ethics, literature, politics, or medicine. Modern psychological warfare has become self-conscious in using modern scientific psychology as a tool.

In World War II the enemies of the United States were more fanatical than the people and leaders of the United States. The consequence was that the Americans could use and apply any

* Reprinted from *Psychological Warfare*, published by Combat Forces Press, Washington 1948.

expedient psychological weapon which either science or our version of common sense provided. We did not have to square it with Emperor myths, the Führer principle, or some other rigid, fanatical philosophy. The enemy enjoyed the positive advantage of having an indoctrinated army and people; we enjoyed the countervailing advantage of having skeptical people, with no inward theology that hampered our propaganda operations. It is no negligible matter to be able to use the latest findings of psychological science in a swift, bold manner. The scientific character of our psychology puts us ahead of opponents wrapped up in dogmatism who must check their propaganda against such articles of faith as Aryan racialism or the Hegelian philosophy of history.

Psychological Warfare as a Branch of Psychology. Good propaganda can be conducted by persons with no knowledge of formal psychology. The human touch, the inventive mind, the forceful appeal—things such as these appear in the writings of gifted persons. Thomas Paine never read a word of Freud or Pavlov, yet Paine's arguments during the Revolutionary War played subtly on every appeal which a modern psychologist could catalogue. But war cannot, in modern times, assume a statistical expectation of talent. Psychology makes it possible for the able but ordinary statesman or officer to calculate his persuasion systematically and to obtain by planning those results which greater men might hit upon by genius.

What can psychology do for warfare?

In the first place, the psychologist can bring to the attention of the soldier those elements of the human mind which are usually kept out of sight. He can show how to convert lust into resentment, individual resourcefulness into mass cowardice, friction into distrust, prejudice into fury. He does so by going down to the *unconscious* mind for his source materials. (During World War II, the fact that Chinese babies remain unimpeded while they commit a nuisance, while Japanese babies are either intercepted or punished if they make a mess in the wrong place, was found to be of significant importance in planning psychological warfare.)

In the second place the psychologist can set up techniques for finding out how the enemy really does feel. Some of the worst blunders of history have arisen from miscalculation of he enemy state of mind. By using the familiar statistical and questionnaire procedures, the psychologist can quiz a small cross section of enemy prisoners and from the results estimate the mentality of an entire enemy theater of war at a given period. If he does not have the prisoners handy, he can accomplish much the same end by an analysis of the news and propaganda which the enemy authorities transmit to their own troops and people. By establishing enemy opinion and morale factors we can hazard a reasoned forecast as to how the enemy troops will behave under specific conditions.

In the third place, the psychologist can help the military psychological warfare operator by helping him maintain his sense of mission and of proportion. The deadliest danger of propaganda consists of its being issued by the propagandist for his own edification. This sterile and ineffectual amusement can disguise the complete failure of the propaganda *as* propaganda. There is a genuine pleasure in talking-back, particularly to an enemy. The propagandist, especially in wartime, is apt to tell the enemy what he thinks of him, or to deride enemy weaknesses. But to have told the Nazis, for example, "You Germans are a pack of murderous baboons and your Hitler is a demented oaf. Your women are slobs, your children are halfwits, your literature is gibberish and your cooking is garbage," and so on, would have stiffened the German will to fight. The propagandist must tell the enemy those things which the enemy will need; he must keep his private emotionalism out of the operation. The psychologist can teach the propaganda operator how to be objective, systematic, cold. For combat operations, it does not matter how much a division commander may dislike the enemy; for psychological warfare purposes, he must consider how to persuade them, even though he may privately thirst for their destruction. The indulgence of hatred is not a working part of the soldier's mission; to some it may be helpful; to others, not. The useful mission consists solely of making the enemy stop fighting, by combat or other means. But when the soldier turns to propaganda, he may need the advice of a psychologist in keeping his own feelings out of it.

Finally, the psychologist can prescribe media—radio, leaflets, loudspeakers, whispering agents, returned enemy soldiers, and so forth. He can indicate when and when not to use any given medium. He can, in conjunction with operations and intelli-

gence officers, plan the full use of all available psychologica
resources. He can coordinate the timing of propaganda with
military, economic or political situations.

The psychologist does not have to be present in person t
give this advice. He does not have to be a man with an M.D
or Ph. D. and years of postgraduate training. He can be presen
in the manuals he writes, in the indoctrination courses for psy
chological warfare officers he sets up, in the current propagand
line he dictates by radio. It is useful to have him in the field
particularly at the higher command headquarters, but he is no
indispensable. The psychologist in person can be dispense
with; the methods of scientific psychology cannot.

Propaganda can be conducted by rule of thumb. But only
genius can make it work well by playing his hunches. It ca
become true psychological warfare, scientific in spirit and de
veloped as a teachable skill, only by having its premises clearl
stated, its mission defined, its instruments put in systemati
readiness, and its operations subject to at least partial chec
only by the use of techniques borrowed from science. Of all th
sciences, psychology is the nearest, though anthropology, soc
ology, political science, economics, area studies and other spe
cialties all have something to contribute; but it is psycholog
which indicates the need of the others.

Psychological Warfare as a Part of War. An infantry office
does not need to study the whole nature of war, in order t
find his own job. Tradition, military skill, discipline, soun
doctrine—these have done the job for him. Sun Tzu, Vegetiu
Frederick, Clausewitz and a host of lesser writers on war hav
established the place of combat in war, and have appraised i
general character.

How much the traditional doctrines may be altered in th
terrible light of atomic explosion, no one knows; but thoug
the weapons are novel, the wielders of the weapons will still b
men. The motives and weaknesses within war remain ancier
and human, however novel and dreadful the mechanical e
pedients adopted to express them.

Warfare as a whole is traditionally well defined, and psych
logical warfare can be understood only in relation to the who
process. It is no mere tool, to be used on special occasion.
has become a pervasive element in the military and securi
situation of every power on earth.

Psychological warfare is a part of war. The simplest, plainest thing which can be said of war—any sort of war, anywhere, anytime—is that it is *an official fight between men*. Combat, killing, and even large-scale group struggle are known elsewhere in the animal kingdom, but war is not. All sorts of creatures fight; but only men declare, wage, and terminate war; and they do so only against other men.

Formally, war may be defined as the "reciprocal application of violence by public, armed bodies."

If it is not *reciprocal*, it is not war. The killing of persons who do not defend themselves is not war, but slaughter, massacre, or punishment.

If the bodies involved are not *public*, their violence is not war. Even our enemies in World War II were relatively careful about this distinction, because they did not know how soon or easily a violation of the rules might be scored against them. To be public, the combatants need not be legal—that is, constitutionally set up; it suffices, according to international usage, for the fighters to have a reasonable minimum of numbers, some kind of identification, and a purpose which is political. If you shoot your neighbor, you will be committing mere murder; but if you gather twenty or thirty friends together, tie a red handkerchief around the left arm of each man, announce that you are out to overthrow the government of the United States, and *then* shoot your neighbor as a counterrevolutionary impediment to the new order of things, you can have the satisfaction of having waged war. (In practical terms, this means that you will be put to death for treason and rebellion, not merely for murder.)

Finally, war must be *violent*. According to the law of modern states, all the way from Iceland to the Yemen, economic, political, or moral pressure is not war; war is the legalization, in behalf of the state, of things which no individual may lawfully do in time of peace. As a matter of fact, even in time of war you cannot kill the enemy unless you do so on behalf of the state; if you had shot a Japanese creditor of yours privately, or even shot a Japanese soldier when you yourself were out of uniform, you might properly and lawfully have been put to death for murder—either by our courts or by the enemies'. This is among the charges which recur in the war trials. The

Germans and Japanese killed persons whom even war did not entitle them to kill.)

The governments of the modern world are jealous of their own monopoly of violence. War is the highest exercise of that violence, and modern war is no simple reversion to savagery. The General Staffs would not be needed if war were only an uncomplicated orgy of homicide—a mere getting-mad and throat-cutting season in the life of man. Quite to the contrary, modern war—as a function of modern society—reflects the institutional, political complexity from which it comes. A modern battle is a formal, ceremonialized and technically intricate operation. You must kill just the right people, in just the right way, with the right timing, in the proper place, for avowed purposes. Otherwise you make a mess of the whole show, and —what is worse—you lose.

Why must you fight just so and so, there and not here, now and not then? The answer is simple: you are fighting against *men*. Your purpose in fighting is to make them change their minds. It is figuratively true to say that the war we have just won was a peculiar kind of advertising campaign, designed to make the Germans and Japanese like us and our way of doing things. They did not like us much, but we gave them alternatives far worse than liking us, so that they became peaceful.

Sometimes individuals will be unpersuadable. Then they must be killed or neutralized by other purely physical means— such as isolation or imprisonment. (Some Nazis, perhaps including the Führer himself, found our world repellent or incomprehensible and died because they could not make themselves surrender. In the Pacific many Japanese had to be killed before they became acceptable to us.) But such is man, that most individuals will stop fighting at some point short of extinction; that point is reached when one of two things happens:

Either, the defeated people may lose their sense of organization, fail to decide on leaders and methods, and give up because they can no longer fight as a group. This happened to the American Southerners in April, 1865. The President and Cabinet of the Confederate States of America got on the train at Richmond; the men who got off farther down the line were "refugees." Something happened to them and to the people about them, so that Mr. Davis no longer thought of himself as President Davis, and other people no longer accepted his commands. This almost happened in Germany in 1945 except for Admiral Doenitz.

Or, the defeated people can retain their sense of organization, and can use their political organization for the purpose of getting in touch with the enemy, arranging the end of the war, and preparing, through organized means, to comply with the wishes of the conquerors. That happened when Britain acknowledged American independence; when the Boers recognized British sovereignty; when Finland signed what Russia had dictated; and when Japan gave up.

Sometimes these things are mixed. The people might wish to make peace, but may find that their government is not recognized by the enemy. Or the victors may think that they have smashed the enemy government, when the new organization is simply the old one under a slightly different name, but with the old leaders and the old ideas still prevailing.

It is plain that whatever happens wars are fought to effect a psychological change in the antagonist. They are then fought for a psychological end unless they are wars of extermination. These are rare. The United States could not find a people on the face of the earth whose ideas and language were unknown to all Americans. Where there is a chance of communication, there is always the probability that one of the antagonistic organizations (governments)—which have already cooperated to the extent of meeting one another's wishes to fight—will subsequently cooperate on terms of primary advantage to the victors. Since the organizations comprise human beings with human ways of doing things, the change must take place in the minds of those specific individuals who operate the existing government, or in the minds of enough other people for that government to be overthrown.

The fact that war is waged against the minds, not the bodies, of the enemy is attested by the comments of military writers of all periods. The dictum of Carl von Clausewitz that "war is politics continued by other means" is simply the modern expression of a truth recognized since antiquity. War is a kind of persuasion—uneconomical, dangerous, and unpleasant, but effective when all else fails.

Chapter **14**

WAR INFORMATION *

By

ELMER DAVIS

EXECUTIVE ORDER 9182, which established the Office of War Information on June 13, 1942, defined as its primary purpose the facilitation of the development of an informed and intelligent understanding, at home and abroad, of the status and progress of the war effort, and of the war policies, activities, and aims of the Government. The various duties laid on the O.W.I. by the Order are all contributory toward this end.

That is to say, the O.W.I. is a war agency, which owes its existence solely to the war, and was established to serve as one of the instruments by which the war will be won. We in O.W.I. do not overestimate the contribution we can make to victory, but we do not underestimate it, either. We know that the war is going to be won primarily by fighting, but we can point to plenty of proof in history, both recent and remote, that victory of the fighting forces can be made easier by what is called psychological or political warfare, the prosecution of which has been entrusted primarily to this Office. We are in a sense an auxiliary to the armed forces—an organization whose operations can pave the way for their operations and make their success easier. We may be a minor auxiliary, but if what we do succeeds in shortening the war by one single day it will save the United States Government as much money as this Office is likely to cost in several years.

There is ample proof that if we do the job right, we may succeed in shortening the war. Great generals of all time have recognized the value of psychological warfare and propaganda as adjuncts to the work of their fighting forces. The armies of Genghis Khan, whose conquests are still without parallel, were

* Reprinted by permission of the author and Public Affairs Press.

preceded by secret agents who worked on the populations of the countries he was about to attack, spreading defeatism and division, and softening them up so that they had less heart to put up a really tough fight when the Mongol armies came along. And if there had been radio broadcasting in those days, never doubt that Genghis Khan would have used it. In modern times, everybody knows that the victories of Hitler's armies have been immensely facilitated, particularly in France, by the psychological preparation that softened up not only a good part of the French people, but still more a good part of the Government. Hitler is using that same weapon on us, too; has been using it for years past; and we would be fools not to use it on him and his allies as well.

Hitler and Genghis Khan are discreditable characters; my colleagues and I have no particular desire to emulate them. But fortunately there are more respectable precedents. Two of the best jobs ever done in all history in the field in which this Office is instructed to operate abroad were done by Americans. The first was the achievement of Benjamin Franklin, operating out of Paris in the years from 1777 till the Revolution had come to its triumphant conclusion, to which he had so greatly contributed. Franklin's work, to be sure, was much more extensive than that of the Overseas Branch of the O.W.I.; it included diplomacy and secret-service work, as well as propaganda. But purely on the propaganda side the job he did remains a classic. In France, and the other continental countries, he was constantly encouraging the people who sympathized with us and constantly making new converts, by pointing out not only that we had a good cause—that we were fighting for liberty and self-determination; but that our victory would contribute to the interests of France; and by maintaining that that victory was bound to come. It came faster because he had persuaded people that it was coming anyway. Also, Franklin's propaganda was steadily active in England, not only providing arguments to the considerable elements in that country which sympathized with the revolted colonists, but working on the feelings of the much larger group which was beginning to feel that maybe the war was a bad investment—spreading defeatism, persuading them that they were fighting only in the interest of the King and a few West Indian planters, and not of the nation. There is not a single element in what is now called psychological warfare that Franklin did not employ. None of us in the O.W.I. believes that we are as smart as Franklin, but we are going to do the best we can.

And the second classic job in this field was done by Woodrow Wilson in 1918, working partly direct, by his own speeches, and partly through the agency of George Creel's organization. Most of us are old enough to remember this of our own knowledge; but if you want further proof, I can call to witness the most expert and successful propagandist of our time, who got his first experience of propaganda when he was serving in the German Army—Corp. Adolf Hitler. He writes in *Mein Kampf:*

"To what terrific consequences a rightly directed propaganda may lead could be observed for the first time during the war, though unfortunately it all had to be studied on the other side. What we failed to do the enemy did with unheard-of skill and a calculation that seems truly the work of genius. The war propaganda of the English and Americans was psychologically correct. In the beginning it sounded crazy and impudent; later it was no more than unpleasant; and finally it was believed. After 4½ years a revolution broke out in Germany, whose slogans came from the enemy's war propaganda."

Hitler, you observe, studied carefully the technique of Wilson and the other Allied leaders and learned from it a great deal which he has since employed for deplorable ends. But propaganda is an instrument; it may employ truth instead of falsehood in its operation (as Wilson did, and as the O.W.I. intends to do); and it may be directed to worthy instead of unworthy purposes. To condemn the instrument, because the wrong people use it for the wrong purposes, is like condemning the automobile because criminals use it for a getaway. The job of political warfare that Wilson accomplished in softening up the will to resistance of the German people did not win the war by itself, even though the German militarists do say so, to escape the admission that their armies got licked; but it certainly shortened the war by some months, and in so doing it saved many thousands of American, as well as other, lives. In the work of Franklin and Wilson this Office has not only honorable precedents to follow but high standards to shoot at; the job is in many respects more difficult than it was in Wilson's day, but if we attain even a reasonable degree of success we shall make somewhat easier the task of our armed forces; we shall save time and money and lives.

Yet if the job is in some ways harder than 25 years ago—thanks to the far more severe repression of speech and opinions in enemy countries and countries controlled by the enemy, another factor perhaps works to our advantage, and certainly makes the need of this sort of activity even greater than it was then. Thanks to this very repression, to the endeavor of totalitarian governments to suppress all news and all opinion except what they choose to give out, the truth itself has become a more powerful weapon than ever before. Many millions of people are completely dependent for any truthful account of what is going on, on what we and our Allies tell them; and merely to know the truth is going to inspire them to a more stubborn endurance and resistance to the endeavors of the enemy to make them accept their defeat as final.

Let me say that at home and abroad we are telling the same story, telling the truth. The O.W.I. was established, in the phrasing of Executive Order 9182, "in recognition of the right of the American people and of all other peoples opposing the Axis aggressors to be truthfully informed." We endeavor to see to it that the enemy peoples are truthfully informed because we believe the truth is on our side, not only as to the nature and issues of this war, but as to who is going to win it. Some things must, of course, be held back on the ground of military security. But we are going to tell nothing but the truth, and we intend to see that the American people get just as much of it as genuine considerations of military security will permit.

Chapter 15

THE PROPAGANDIST AND THE
POLICY MAKER *

By

ROBERT BRUCE LOCKHART

ONE OF MY first efforts was to eliminate an undesirable eagerness on the part of our experts to indulge in wordy warfare with the German Propaganda Ministry. However entertaining and occasionally useful it may be to score off the enemy, propaganda is not and should not be a duel of dialectics between the political warriors of the rival propaganda organisations. It should be addressed to the masses. German propaganda may have inspired fear of Germany. I do not believe that it made a single friend for Germany apart from Germans.

For this tendency the new title of political warfare was largely responsible. Certainly the name was not always an advantage, for both the ministers and the government departments on whose goodwill P.W.E. was dependent did not appreciate the difference between propaganda and political warfare and merely assumed that the new name was a misguided attempt by the propagandists to increase their own importance.

In point of fact, many new technical methods of propaganda were introduced during the war, of which perhaps the most valuable was the deduction of enemy intentions from enemy propaganda. Some of the new methods were overdone. For instance, after one or two initial successes the practice of committing the Germans to the capture of a key position (for example, Stalingrad) by a date, which from the best military opinion we knew was highly unlikely, was carried to an excess which defeated its own ends. An essay could be written on the differences between propaganda and political warfare.

* Reprinted from *Comes the Reckoning*, published by Putnam & Co., Ltd., London, 1948.

Perhaps the truest definition of the latter is that political warfare practises every form of overt and covert attack which can be called political as distinct from military. It seeks both to counter and by intelligent anticipation to forestall the political offensives of the enemy. It demands a highly specialised intelligence service of its own and, above all, an accurate estimate of the enemy's intentions. It relies not only on open and truthful propaganda, but also on a whole series of secret or "black" operations which can be suitably classified under the headings of subversion and deception. These operations include so-called "secret" broadcasting from stations supposed to be operated in or close to enemy and enemy-occupied territory by subversive enemy or enemy-occupied elements.

I cannot say that P.W.E. was an easy team. Every good propagandist must possess the qualities of a prima donna or, as Ernst Toller once said, must be born with one eye. The department was composed almost entirely of temporary officials who had plenty of *esprit de corps* but considerably less knowledge of official procedure. There was no lack of brains, especially in the organisation at Woburn where Rex Leeper had assembled and trained a varied array of talent which gave the form and shape to the propaganda policy which was finally adopted. But at all times, and particularly during the first two years of the war, there was a tendency to try to make foreign policy by means of propaganda instead of being content to support policy by propaganda. This tendency was strongly resented by Ministers and by the Foreign Office and the service departments.

Actually political warfare is neither an exact science nor a separate art. As the handmaid of official policy and of military strategy, it is dependent on the calculations and errors of government. At the same time it must be supple with an instinctive feeling for the element of chance in human affairs. Above all, it must on occasions act with great speed in order to kill an enemy lie which otherwise might do great harm. It has therefore to take its directives not only from ministers and Chiefs of Staff who are not always readily available but also from the incidence of time and events.

Inevitably, therefore, the propagandists chafed under the restraints of official policy and were inclined to regard Whitehall as an obstacle which had to be circumvented by intrigue rather than eliminated by persistent persuasion and argument.

Most of these attempts to by-pass the permanent departments were detected, caused an infinity of trouble, and did great harm to P.W.E. Early in February, 1942, the Joint Planners, a section of the Chiefs of Staff organisation composed of members of the three service departments and the Foreign Office, were considering a request from the War Cabinet for a paper on the state of morale in the occupied countries of Europe. One member suggested that P.W.E. should be asked to prepare the memorandum. The suggestion was rejected on the ground that P.W.E. was "wild and irresponsible."

To be fair, there were faults on both sides. The permanent departments, especially the Foreign Office, were slow to realise the importance of broadcasting to a Europe that was cut off from every other means of communication, and without constant pressure by P.W.E., even if at times it was unwisely exerted, it is doubtful if we should ever have progressed beyond the cramping limits of excessive caution. Having been a permanent civil servant in the first world war and a temporary one in the second I think it fair to say that in war-time the temporary departments suffer from lack of experience and excess of enthusiasm and that the reverse applies to the permanent departments. In P.W.E. I made it my principal task to try to hold a fair balance between the enthusiasm of the propagandists and the caution of the permanent officials.

The composition of P.W.E. was extraordinarily varied. It contained a handful of professional soldiers and civil servants. The rest were drawn from almost every walk of life and included journalists, business men, advertising experts, schoolmasters, authors, literary agents, farmers, barristers, stockbrokers, psychologists, university dons, and a landscape gardener. I do not think that any one profession provided any initial advantage of training. A propagandist is born and not made. The journalists were undoubtedly the best exponents of propaganda. They wrote the best leaflets. They had the best understanding of the value of the spoken and written word, and in a department which had always to work at top speed they alone had the requisite sense of urgency. Being used to ephemeral work, they were not so good on policy and sometimes felt frustrated by the hampering necessity of consistency. Our schoolmasters were excellent. The dons included some brilliant men, but were inclined to resent criticism. With one exception the advertising experts were a disappointment. I have an open mind about psychologists. We employed three, and one, at least, did useful work for our German section. Psychological analysis has undoubtedly a place in political warfare, but it was not sufficiently tested in the war to justify any firm conclusion. My personal view is that in propaganda an ounce of first-hand experience of a country is worth a ton of theoretical knowledge, and this theory applies not only to our psychologists but to all the propagandists we employed.

On account of the shortage of men we relied for staff mainly on women who were vastly in the majority. Taken by and large, they were admirable in efficiency and in conduct. Two were expert propagandists who ran their own section with men under them. Several excelled in administrative work. All showed a spirit of cooperation and loyalty which to me at any rate was always a consolation in times of trouble. Brooks's secretary and my own were entrusted with all our Top Secret information, and, as far as security is concerned, I believe firmly, and I think the belief is widely held in Whitehall, that women keep official secrets far better than men including most Ministers. Pessimists, who take a gloomy view of the future of this country, may reap a morbid satisfaction from the German theory that the first sign of decadence in a country is when the women become superior to the men. Personally I shall be satisfied if Britain continues to be served by her women-folk as well as she was during the war.

Our activities, apart from our secret work, were mainly concerned with broadcasting and the dissemination of leaflets. With the exception of a short interval for maintenance purposes, broadcasting went on by day and by night. Every twenty-four hours 160,000 words went out over the air in twenty-three languages. Twenty-two per cent. of this total of over a million words weekly went to Germany. It was perhaps too high a proportion, for in my opinion the best work of the European Service of the B.B.C. was done in the occupied countries. Leaflets were distributed by the Royal Air Force from the first day of the war and also by balloon. They ranged from single sheet leaflets to miniature illustrated newspapers and long before the end of the war they had set a new high standard for this form of production. A special feature of our work was the production of miniature magazines and even books which were distributed, partly, by air and, partly, by secret methods. Reviews like *La France Libre* and a book of Mr. Churchill's speeches were reduced to the size of a folded lady's handkerchief and, nevertheless, were so beautifully printed that the text could be read with ease and comfort by the naked eye. Both in content and in attractiveness they were, I think, the best propaganda productions of any country.

Both broadcasting and leaflets to the occupied countries presented no great difficulties. We were appealing to friends who were eager—sometimes, indeed, too eager—to listen to our broadcasts and to pick up our leaflets and miniature magazines. In our task of maintaining morale in these countries we collaborated closely with the Allied Governments in London. That we achieved excellent results is borne out not only by the evidence of the oppressed peoples themselves but also by the fierce penalties which the Germans imposed with increasing savagery on listeners to the foreign broadcasts of our European Service.

In our propaganda to Germany, however, we were handicapped from the start by a problem which was never solved. This was the vexatious question of what we called a "hope clause" for Germany. For a long time there was no official policy about the future of Germany, and we were left to grope our way as best we could. But we were never allowed to make any promises in our propaganda. When eventually the policy of unconditional surrender was officially announced, it imposed a severe restriction on the opportunities for successful propaganda. Indeed, it was undeniably a propaganda asset to Germany, and Dr. Goebbels employed it constantly in his propaganda to his own countrymen. Put in plain language, the argument he used was: "Some of you Germans may not like us Nazis, but if the Allies win they will wreak on us all a peace of revenge in comparison with which the Treaty of Versailles will seem Utopian." To enforce his point, he plastered the walls of the chief German cities with huge posters containing extracts from Lord Vansittart's *Black Record*.

The problem with which the Government were faced was: "Were there sufficient so-called 'good Germans' to justify a promise of a reasonable peace provided that they turned against Hitler before the end of the war?" On the proper answer to this question the House of Commons and, I imagine, the whole country, were divided. It was a personal and not a Party issue, and even in the Labour Party there were deep cleavages of opinion. After the debate on political warfare in February, 1942, Mr. Eden and sometimes Mr. Bracken used to receive two separate Parliamentary Propaganda Committees. I attended as adviser on the current affairs of our department. One Committee took what I may call the Vansittart line and complained querulously of P.W.E.'s softness towards the Germans. The other Committee, of which Commander King-Hall was the mainspring and which advocated a hope clause, took exactly the opposite line and with equal vigour protested against the harshness of our German propaganda.

We propagandists favoured the hope clause, but the difficulty was to win approval for a formula which would not conflict with the official policy of unconditional surrender. Many attempts were made both by the British and the Americans, but they came to nothing, and with the understandable object of preserving national unity at home the Government did their best—and in war-time it is a powerful best—to avoid public discussion of the problem.

Certainly nearly all members of Parliament regarded themselves as experts on propaganda, held strong views on the subject, and more often than not had their own pet German *émigré*.

For what it is worth, my own opinion is that, so long as a German victory or even an inconclusive peace seemed possible to Germans, the "good Germans" were powerless to cause any serious disruption of the German military machine.

Nevertheless, there is now a considerable amount of evidence, taken mainly from captured German documents, which indicates that anti-Nazi Germans, including high officers of the army, listened-in assiduously to both our "white" and our "black" broadcasts and that until the official announcement of "unconditional surrender" our propaganda was having an increasing effect. Obviously its big chance would have come at the moment when German hopes of winning the war were beginning to wane. This moment coincided with the formula of "unconditional surrender."

The absence of a hope clause was, therefore, a severe handicap to our German propaganda. I do not cavil at the Government's policy or lack of policy. It is difficult to prepare for peace when one is fighting for very existence; doubly difficult when a country is as unprepared for war as ours was. But the fact should be noted that in January, 1941, when Mr. Harry Hopkins came to England to find out how we proposed to win the war, he was informed that the three lines of our attack on Germany were (1) blockade; (2) bombing and (3) propaganda and subversion. There was then no prospect of attacking the Reich itself by land. These lines of the politico-strategic conduct of the war were confirmed by the American Chiefs of Staff during Mr. Churchill's visit to Washington in December, 1941.

Yet at the time no serious impetus was ever given to our propaganda efforts from on top. It was due, I think, partly to the pressure of graver events and partly to ignorance of the subject in Whitehall. The ignorance bred scepticism, and together they were a formidable hurdle. The Chiefs of Staff were always willing to help us to solve our problems but, to begin with at least, they erred on the side of over-simplification. When we explained to them our difficulties about the hope clause for Germany, one of them, assuming that all propaganda was deception, provided an admirable solution. "Why don't you take the King-Hall line in your propaganda and keep the Vansittart line for the peace terms?"

Unfortunately, open propaganda is always a responsibility of the Government's and—to Mr. Eden's credit be it said—we were never allowed to make in our propaganda any commitment which the Government were not prepared to fulfil. If we approached even the borderline, I was certain to be rebuked. But in the first years of the war the Foreign Office were no better educated in the technique of propaganda than the service departments, and even those officials who wished most to help us sometimes tumbled into traps. When Hungary and Roumania were restive about the ultimate fate of Transylvania, I would receive a suggestion: "Why don't you tell the Hungarians in your Hungarian broadcasts that Germany is going to let Roumania keep Transylvania and tell the Roumanians in your Roumanian broadcasts that she is going to give it to Hungary." With patience and good humour I had to explain not only that in Transylvania there were people who spoke both languages but also that Dr. Goebbels employed a large staff of linguists to listen in to all our foreign broadcasts in the hope of discovering inconsistencies in our policy and exposing them to the world, and that of course we did the same.

I do not think for one moment that during the period of German military ascendancy our propaganda, even if given greater support, could have achieved more than it did. And that was very little indeed as far as Germany was concerned. You cannot undermine morale in the hour of military success, and not even Hitler himself could have stopped the German people from shrieking *Sieg Heil* in unison when after twenty-five years the bitterness of defeat seemed to have been wiped away by the most resounding of victories.

Nevertheless, Whitehall's ignorance of the technique and possibilities of propaganda and, more particularly, of broadcasting was unnecessarily prolonged. This was a minor misfortune for which the pre-war planning of our propaganda activities was responsible. Apart from the defects of organisation, an initial mistake was made in establishing the enemy propaganda department at Woburn, and this defect was aggravated by the obstinacy of a department, which had done most valuable pioneer work, in resisting for so long every attempt to bring it back to London. I have always felt that, if it had been established from the beginning in or near Whitehall, its efficiency would have been increased, its merits more quickly recognised, and many vexatious delays and inter-departmental wrangles avoided. I am no lover of the bureaucratic state, but the senior officials of the British civil service bring to the study of most problems the knowledge of a vast experience, nor are they lacking in goodwill. On the other hand the initial attitude of the propagandists was ostrich-like, and surely never in Whitehall has there been a better example of a situation in which great possibilities were sacrificed for petty considerations.

Chapter 16

THE ASSESSMENT OF MEN *

By

OSS ASSESSMENT STAFF

1. The Nature of The Task

THE TASK confronting the OSS assessment staff was that of developing a system of procedures which would reveal the personalities of OSS recruits to the extent of providing ground for sufficiently reliable predictions of their usefulness to the organization during the remaining years of the war. In this sentence everything hangs on the meaning of "sufficiently reliable predictions."

It is easy to predict precisely the outcome of the meeting of one known chemical with another chemical in an immaculate test tube. But where is the chemist who can predict what will happen to a known chemical if it meets an unknown chemical in an unknown vessel? And even if all the properties of all the chemicals resident in a given laboratory are exactly defined, is there a chemist who can predict every chemical engagement that will take place if Chance, the blind technician, is in charge of the proceedings? Can a physician, steeped though he may be in the science of his profession, say for certain whether or not the body he has just examined will contract contagious jaundice next summer in Algiers? How, then, can a psychologist foretell with any degree of accuracy the outcomes of future meetings of one barely known personality with hundreds of other undesignated personalities in distant undesignated cities, villages, fields, and jungles that are seething with one knows not what potential harms and benefits? Fortune—call the old hag or beauty what you will—can never be eliminated from the universe of human

* Reprinted from *Assessment of Men,* published by Rinehart & Co., New York, 1948.

interactions. And this being forever true, prophetic infallibility is beyond the reach of social scientists.

Furthermore, we would guess that no matter how substantial are the advances of scientific psychology, the best series of predictions of *individual* careers—apperception operating as it does —will involve the play of experienced intuitions, the clinical hunch, products of unconsciously perceived and integrated symptomatic signs. The assessment of men—we trust that Samuel Butler would agree—is the scientific art of arriving at sufficient conclusions from insufficient data.

Within reach of those who are trained in assessment, we hope, are "sufficiently reliable predictions," or "sufficient conclusions," that is to say, predictions or conclusions which will serve, by the elimination of some and the better placement of others, to decrease the ultimate failures or unsatisfactory performers, by such a number that (i) the *amount saved* plus (ii) the *amount of harm prevented* plus (iii) the *amount gained* is greater than the cost of the assessment program. The *amount saved* can be roughly computed in terms of the average expenditure of money and time (spent by other members of the organization) in training, transporting, housing, and dealing with an individual who in the end proves to be incapable of discharging his duties properly. The most important item, the *amount of harm prevented*, is scarcely calculable. It consists of the friction, the impairment of efficiency and morale, the injury to the reputation of an organization that results from the actions of a man who is stupid, apathetic, sullen, resentful, arrogant, or insulting in his dealings with members of his own unit or of allied units, or with customers or citizens of foreign countries. To this must be added the irreparable damage that can be done by one who blabs. Diminution in the number of men of this stamp—sloths, irritants, bad actors, and free talkers—was one of the prime objects of the assessment program. The *amount gained* is equally hard to estimate. It consists of the average difference between the positive accomplishments of a failure and of a success. An unsatisfactory man, by filling an assignment, deprives the organization of the services of a man who might be capable of a substantial contribution. Some OSS schemes, in fact, were entirely abandoned because in each case the man who arrived in the theater to undertake the project was found to be unsuitable. Thus every pronounced failure costs the organization a good deal of time and money, lowers the efficiency and reputation of one of its units, and, by taking the place of a competent man, prevents the attainment of certain goals.

Needless to say, no OSS official was urged to weigh these subtleties and come out with an answer in dollars and cents. For even if it had been possible to make such an estimate, no use could have been made of it, since the one figure that was needed for an evaluation of the assessment program was not obtainable: the percentage of failures among the thousands of unassessed men and women who had been recruited prior to December, 1943. The available records were not accurate or complete enough to give the staff at Station S this level against which to measure its results, and so at the outset we had to face the fact that we would never know certainly whether we had been an asset or a liability to the OSS.

The chief over-all purpose of the OSS assessment staff—to eliminate the unfit—was similar to that of the conventional screening board, but in certain other aspects the task of the former was unique: the number and nature of the billets to be filled by "bodies," the adequacy of the information about the different assignments, the types of men who came to be assessed, the conditions under which the work was done, the kinds of reports that were required, and so forth.

2. The Promise of Assessment

There is much evidence to support, and no evidence to contradict, the assumption that the psychologists and psychiatrists of the assessment staff are virtually unanimous in their opinion that the OSS system of examination and diagnosis was better than any with which they had previously been familiar. Certain parts of the program, to be sure, were not considered valuable by all of us, but, taken as a whole, the series of procedures gave the members of the staff a surer sense of "knowing a man," more confidence in their formulations and recommendations than they had ever enjoyed before under similar circumstances, that is, when called upon to size up large numbers of men and women in a relatively short time.

Although the all too human tendency, common to members of a congenial group, to overvalue their own productions must certainly be included among the determinants of the staff members' favorable verdict, and although their conviction that assessees would behave in the field as they did at assessment was probably greater than was justified, nevertheless it seems that, in the absence of conclusive scientific proof of the special merits and defects of the system, the consensus of an experienced and ever-critical staff is a reasonably good index of the worth of the procedures.

In this section, however, we are not concerned with the question of the efficacy of our system of assessment under the conditions imposed by the OSS, but rather with the question of its probable utility in the future; and here the members of the staff are agreed that it could be developed into an extraordinary instrument for accomplishing three important purposes simultaneously: (1) the selection of the most suitable persons for important jobs; (2) the advancement of our understanding of personality; and (3) the adequate training of clinical psychologists and psychiatrists.

Some men are inclined to the opinion that only those sciences which can offer unequivocal quantitative proofs of their accomplishments are worthy of financial or institutional backing. Fortunately for psychology, however, there are a few who judge otherwise, who take the absence of tangible evidences of accomplishment as an indication that the science in question is a young one and, therefore, in need of special support for its development.

The fact that the initial researches, the explorations, and pilot studies of workers in a young science have not led to any definite or startling results is no argument against the encouragement of that science. As Pasteur answered to a questioner who was skeptical of the value of the infant science of bacteriology, "What good is a baby?" Every science must pass through the stages of infancy, childhood, puberty, and adolescence before it reaches the point of maturity at which even the near-blind can see its worth. Since this is inevitably the case, the more encouragement that is given to an immature science the sooner will it arrive at the desired stage of conceptual and practical effectiveness. Let us take an extreme case and assume, for the sake of argument, that it is true, as some have claimed, that not until after 1900 did medicine pass from the stage of doing man more harm than good to that of doing him more good than harm; and then ask ourselves, what would have been the most enlight-

ened attitude to hold toward medicine a hundred years ago?
To abolish it or refuse to support it because it was doing more
harm than good? Or to encourage it so that some day it would
do more good than harm? Let a man with severe diabetes, pernicious anemia, syphilis, or acute appendicitis answer this question. The point is that the scientific method of observation,
tentative interpretation, hypothesis making, and verification is
almost certain to succeed *in the long run* whether the objects
of concern be animal, vegetable, or mineral. Some sciences have
already attained a large measure of success, have proved their
usefulness and can pay their way; but there are others which
have not yet reached the stage of self-sufficiency and so must
turn to public-spirited individuals, to government, to cultural
institutions, or to foundations for assistance.

Faced by a diversity of plans for scientific research, decision
as to institutional or financial support should, in each case, hang
largely on the best obtainable answers to four questions: (1)
How important to man's welfare would be the ordered knowledge that is the special goal of the given science? (2) What are
the chances that the specific objectives of the proposed research
will prove to be strategic in the advance of this science? (3) Are
the methods selected for attaining these objectives likely to be
successful? (4) Is the available staff of scientists equal to the
undertaking?

To us it is self-evident that the science of man stands above
all other sciences in the rank order of importance, especially
today, at this critical point in the evolution of our species. Never
so urgent has been the need for knowledge of the determinants,
components, and consequences of social forces and interactions,
the need for adequate means of surveying, measuring, interpreting, predicting, and controlling the behavior of men. Today's
special urgency is the result of the present perilous gap between
man's power to create and to manipulate physical forces *effectively* and his power to create and to manipulate them *wisely,*
a gap which is correlated with the wide discrepancy which now
exists between the state of perfection of the physical sciences
and the state of imperfection of the social sciences. One of the
chief aims of our time must be to diminish this discrepancy,
because material science has taken on the character of a cancer-
ous growth, and, if not balanced by the development of a usable
social science *operating in the service of humanistic values,* it

will surely pass from the state of doing man more good than harm to that of doing him more harm than good, if not of demolishing his most valued institutions.

It is within the broad framework of a great plan to advance the basic social sciences all along the line that the present scheme for a research assessment agency, or institute, should be envisaged.

The essential characteristics of the system of assessment we are advocating are as follows:

1) *Social setting:* The whole program is conducted within a social matrix composed of staff and candidates, which permits frequent informal contacts and, therefore, many opportunities to observe typical modes of response to other human beings.

2) *Multiform procedures:* Many different kinds of techniques are employed, running all the way from standardized tests to uncontrolled situations, special attention being given to the interview, to projective techniques, and to performance tests.

3) *Lifelike tasks:* Assessees are given lifelike tasks in a lifelike environment: the tasks are complicated, requiring for their solution organization of thought at a high integrative level, and some of them must be performed under stress in collaboration with others.

4) *Formulations of personality:* Sufficient data are collected and sufficient time is available to permit conceptualization of the form of some of the chief components of the personality of each assessee, this formulation being used as a frame of reference in making recommendations and predictions.

5) *Staff conference:* Interpretations of the behavior of each assessee are discussed at a final meeting of staff members, and decisions (ratings and recommendations) are reached by consensus.

6) *Tabulation of assessments:* The formulations of personality, the ratings of variables, and the predictions of effectiveness are systematically recorded in a form which will permit statistical treatment and precise comparisons with later appraisals.

7) *Valid appraisal procedures:* Special attention is devoted to the perfection of appraisal techniques, so that reliable measures can be obtained of the validity of each test in the assessment program and of the ratings of each variable.

This brief summary should be sufficient as a reminder of the chief features of the methodology described in this volume. The three major objectives of an agency or institute committed to these principles in peacetime would be as follows:

Selection of the Most Suitable Men for Important Positions. —Since the OSS system of assessment is more expensive and time-consuming than other systems, it cannot be recommended when the task is that of picking several thousand men a year for jobs of minor significance, particularly if the qualifications for these jobs are chiefly technical. But our system of assessment is preferable, we believe, whenever (1) an institution or a combination of institutions must pass on the suitability of about four hundred to one thousand candidates a year; (2) the quality of the selectees is a matter of considerable importance; and (3) the requirements include the ability to work effectively with others, either as leader or as cooperator.

Although one thousand candidates a year are about the upper limit for an assessment staff of twelve men administering a three-and-a-half-day program, there is no limit to the number of candidates who can be properly examined if the institution to be served is willing to increase the number of assessment units. Also, although a one-day assessment is not advisable at this stage in the development of the methodology, it should be noted that one staff, administering a streamlined program of this length, can handle over two thousand candidates a year.

The quality of the selectees is a matter of considerable importance (1) if a good deal of time, talent, and money must be spent in training them (e.g., selectees for Annapolis or West Point), and/or (2) if they will eventually be in a position either to benefit greatly or to injure greatly the cause of the people or of the institution they are serving (e.g., business executives, government officials, educators), and/or (3) if it will be difficult to discover their deficiencies and replace them promptly once they are appointed (e.g., foreign representatives of a government or of a business concern).

Since the system of assessment described in this book includes, or can be adjusted to include, not only all the pertinent standardized tests which are used today by personnel psychologists but, in addition, numerous other more inclusive procedures not heretofore employed, and since this system also embraces, as an integral part of the whole program, a procedure for evaluation which will reveal the specific errors made and thus lead inevitably to a continuous series of technical improvements, it is bound to become, provided its development is in the hands of properly trained psychologists and psychiatrists, the most effective system of assessment. Therefore, it can be recommended, first of all, on the basis of the practical service it is capable of performing.

In this connection two consequences of the operation of an assessment program of the OSS type are worth mentioning: on the one hand, the science of psychology will be greatly benefited by having to demonstrate the validity of its theories and techniques under the exacting conditions imposed by a purposeful organization; and, on the other hand, the administrators of the organization will be benefited by the gradual acquisition of psychological knowledge pertinent to the treatment of its personnel.

Chapter **17**

THE UTILIZATION OF SOCIAL SCIENTISTS IN THE OVERSEAS BRANCH OF THE OFFICE OF WAR INFORMATION *

By

LEONARD W. DOOB

MANY SOCIAL scientists employed by the government or in the armed services during the war found their research and scientific wisdom not eagerly accepted, wisely interpreted, or sensibly followed by policy-makers. Unlike some of the old-time departments, the war agencies had no established procedure for utilizing social science. Social scientists had a place on the ever-changing organization charts, sometimes merely because it was vaguely felt that all kinds of brains, even academic, were necessary to win a total war. Often they had to carve out for themselves the specific rôles they wished to play. They functioned not in accordance with the charts, but within what Mansfield and Marx [1] call informal organizations of their own making.

In many situations, there was discrepancy between what social scentists thought they could do and what the policy-makers were prepared to let them do. Some sought deliberately to bridge the gap by promoting and marketing their disciplines and themselves. Like their colleagues in the natural sciences, they wished to be consulted when problems involving their own expertness were involved.

The informal techniques that social scientists employed in behalf of social science and themselves are worth recording because certainly similar ones must often be utilized whenever social scientist meets policy-maker. They should be mentioned to any social scientist about to enter government service, so that

* Reprinted from *American Political Science Quarterly,* vol. XLI, No. 4 August 1947.

he can at least be aware of the problem and more easily survive the initial period of disillusionment and misery. They belong, it seems, within the purview of the student of public administration.

What follows in this article is a necessarily abbreviated case history of the writer's experience in one war agency. It is deliberately somewhat autobiographical, so that the raw materials may be presented as concretely as possible. Naturally, the social-science demands of the Overseas Branch of the Office of War Information were not typical, nor does this writer—a psychologist—claim to represent anyone except himself. It can only be hoped that other social scientists will record their own similar and dissimilar experiences and produce a more general guide-book for social science in government.

1. Types of Research

By executive order, the Overseas Branch of the Office of War Information—as distinguished from the better known but smaller Domestic Branch—was the government agency charged during the last war with responsibility for transmitting official American propaganda to enemy countries and for disseminating "information" in the name of the United States to allied and neutral countries outside the Western hemisphere. Within an active theater of operations, this responsibility was shared with military and naval aut orities and sometimes taken over by them. Every conceivable vehicle of communication was employed, extending from a short-, medium-, or long-wave radio program to a lecturer on American literature in one of the British Dominions, or from a slick magazine to a greeting from the American people printed on a soap wrapper. Concealed or "black propaganda" (like rumor-spreading) did not concern the OWI, since all of its "white propaganda" and information were clearly labelled as coming from this country.

In the accepted jargon of government, a sharp distinction was drawn and actually existed between policy-makers and operators. A policy-maker contributed to the formulation of a propaganda directive or criticized propaganda output before or after its dissemination. Propaganda directives of the OWI were written in Washington with or without the help of other government agencies, but they became official government policy only after being approved by the Department of State and the War and Navy Departments. An operator, on the other hand, "implemented" the directives through one of the communication media. At all times his production was "controlled"—or was supposed to be controlled—by policy-makers or their representatives.

Research in the Overseas Branch was divided into three types: policy, operations, and background. Policy research, which was almost always classified as secret or confidential, consisted of facts and generalizations which helped policy-makers write directives for countries that were, or might eventually be, reached by the OWI's propaganda. The "state of morale" in Germany and Japan, for example, was frequently assayed; obviously, it was said, one kind of propaganda is needed for people with a high morale and a different kind for those whose morale is sinking. Operational research, which was never classified, contained facts or pseudo-facts of interest to operators. If a directive commanded that the people of one country be told that Germany's morale was high or low, a research group uncovered items allegedly demonstrating the Reich's mental state. Background research, which was either restricted or not classified at all, fell somewhere in between, but generally strove to increase the insight of operators.

The research resulted in reports that varied in length from a sentence to a volume. The size of an obscure town or the latest propaganda line employed by Radio Tokyo was determined in response to a face-to-face, telephoned, teletyped, telegraphed, cabled, or radioed request. At the other extreme were weekly reports analyzing significant events inside a country, often with the aid of tables and graphs indicating the frequency with which a given propaganda theme was being employed on the radio, in the press, or by both. Then facts were merely assembled in a form convenient for operators; for example, there was a daily publication listing, under convenient rubrics, quotations from foreign journalists and newscasters which could be incorporated into feature stories or radio scripts. Some intricate research also was carried on, such as an anthropologist's attempt to delineate the character structure of a few countries on the basis either of prisoner-of-war interrogations or of interviews conducted with scattered informants residing in the United States.

The OWI's research cannot easily be classified as belonging to one rather than another social science. In fact, it may be seriously questioned whether much of it had anything at all to do with social science, unless social science be defined broadly as simple fact-gathering about people. From a social-science viewpoint, the problem for policy research was real enough, since it was always a variant of one of the following questions: what is happening inside a particular country, what are the people doing and thinking, what are the leaders plotting and planning? The answers to such questions, however, required adequate data before any social science could be systematically employed. Such data were lacking. Often fairly important reports existed, but, because they were of necessity highly classified and/or came from other agencies and governments with which effective liaison was gradually established, they could be distributed only to a few key researchers. The OWI never developed its own intelligence-gathering facilities overseas, even in countries where the people themselves could have been studied. Other agencies asserted that this was their function, although they seldom discharged it satisfactorily. The outposts' budgets, moreover, were usually so limited that their chiefs felt compelled to dispense with the frill of data-collecting and to concentrate their manpower on useful and more pressing tasks, *viz.*, operations or administration. One top social scientist was able to recruit an excellent staff to do research in one of the liberated countries, but soon after he had completed some first-rate reports a quarrel with the commanding officer of the military group under whom he worked in that theater brought the entire project to an end. In a sense, too, the OWI's inability to secure the information it needed resulted from the scattering, both in Washington and abroad, of research related to propaganda and information and of competent personnel.

By and large, therefore, it can be said that the data at hand secured all the analysis they deserved. Sometimes, in fact, the analysis was too refined and represented a deductive leap into the unknown, motivated by the social scientist's desire to use his social science or by his impulse to compete with journalists on their own terms. Far too many risky and dogmatic inferences concerning the state of morale in enemy countries, for example, were made on the basis of radio transcripts and newspapers simply because these data were at hand by the train-load. What was seldom done was to pool the available data and information of all experts in order to determine systematically—in terms of social-science principles—how people might respond to propaganda. Instead, the easier and quicker solution was simply to consult one of the self-styled or recognized experts concerning the desirability of the propaganda innovation. This was a hit-and-miss approach in a situation in which no one except an omniscient deity will ever know in detail what hit and what missed. The social scientist could not protest, inasmuch as his own position was too vulnerable; if he talked in terms of principles or theories, he ran the risk of being called a "professor" and of delaying fast-moving operations.

2. Administrative Organization

Research was permitted within the Overseas Branch because each policy-maker and operator in his own way paid lip-service to "facts" and was convinced that someone ought to collect and perhaps analyze them. Journalists, cooped up in an office or an army establishment, were worried because the conditions of war prevented them from running down the facts; they looked upon research workers as glorified, if not qualified, "leg-men" for a city editor. Men from the fields of advertising and radio had previously grown accustomed to some type of market research to bolster their intuition and they claimed they needed a substitute. There was always the feeling that the OWI, young and lusty though it was, deserved its own research organization equally with its occasional rival, the Office of Strategic Services, or like the big, mature respectable agencies of State, War, and Navy. Some officials, furthermore, were stricken with the desire to build an empire for purposes of ego-gratification or civil-service classification—and a good corps of slaves to do research impressed everyone, except the sleuths from the Bureau of the Budget, as something all good empires should have. The top administrators of the OWI, who feared that a large research appropriation might antagonize those sleuths as well as congressional committees, attempted to curb such expansionist tendencies, frequently with much success.

Almost every kind of organization plan for research was tried. During the existence of the Overseas Branch, there was a research group at each level of the agency, and the various groups

had administrative and functional responsibility to all imaginable policy-makers, operators, and administrators. At one time,
it is fair to say, only the fiscal office and the janitor did not have
to worry directly about the kind of research being conducted or
the promotion of a bilingual clerk. A central Bureau of Overseas Intelligence in Washington contained approximately one
hundred people who concentrated on policy research, and who
also wrote background and operational reports. For administra-
tively obscure but politically evident reasons, the principal
policy-makers in Washington were permitted to have their own
research staffs or did research themselves. The large operating
offices in New York and San Francisco had sections called Operations Intelligence and other research groups which supplied
implementing materials to operators. Yet here again some of the
operators had their own research staffs or trusted no one but
themselves to carry on the work. Similarly, the outposts located
throughout the world and the combat propaganda teams functioning close to enemy lines collected intelligence which might
or might not be sent back to the United States. Some of these
groups, though inadequately staffed, prepared their own policy
and operational reports.

From the viewpoint of the utilization of research and the
elimination of duplication, no one administrative system
seemed better than another. All that reorganization accomplished was to place a group in a different position on the organization chart. The decisive factor was not organizational but
geographical and human. Duplication of effort, for example,
was largely avoided, at least in the United States, through informal agreements and constant contact between people who
liked and trusted each other.

3. Research Personnel

In the Overseas Branch, it was by no means thought that
social scientists alone had the ability to make sense out of heterogeneous data; journalists, with their traditional "nose for
news," were frequently considered better equipped to piece the
facts together. In some instances, less capable journalists and
radio men, who did not quite live up to the Branch's standards
in their profession, were sentimentally retained but farmed out
to research. The conviction existed that a national, almost re-

gardless of what his previous training had been, was *ipso facto* an authority on the nation from which he had come or fled. His expertness might be questioned if he showed bias one way or the other regarding, for example, the issue of communism, but otherwise he tended to be accepted as a one-man panel truly representative of the millions in his homeland with whom he might have had no contact for years. It was amazing to observe that such individuals were sufficiently courageous or foolish to dare foretell in detail precisely how an entire nation would respond to a propaganda appeal. Nationals of a foreign country, of course, had to be employed for purely linguistic reasons, but very quickly many of them—too many of them, in this writer's opinion—were permitted to transcend their rôle as translators, announcers, or clerks. In addition, there were a few individuals —approximately five or ten per cent—who would be recognized as social scientists inside or outside any academic community; and they tended to occupy the most prominent and important research positions.

This policy of mixing social scientists, journalists, and nationals was not necessarily deplorable. The snap judgment of the journalist could not be dismissed or ignored by the social scientist who felt himself intellectually paralyzed by the paucity of reliable or unreliable data. In such a situation, he excelled only as a critic. His training tended to make him less subjective, less ethnocentric, less prone to generalize from biased data, and —all in all—less likely to be dogmatic. A critic is seldom popular, and the research race in the OWI tended to be won by the swift and the glib. In a competition between shrewd or wild guesses and scientific hypotheses or theories, the social scientist has or should have an ace up his sleeve: verification. Verification during the war was generally out of the question, or at least consisted of ambiguous or out-of-date sense-perceptions. The OWI, in large part through no fault of its own, was definitely not a good testing-ground for social science or social scientists.

4. Research Morale

As in any organization, the research worker's morale fluctuated as a function of personal circumstances and the *esprit* he had established with his immediate associates. Three factors, however, seemed to effect almost everyone. In the first place, an individual was happier if convinced that he had access to "inside" information, which almost always was classified intelligence originating in another government agency (especially the Department of State) or an OWI outpost. Then the completion and circulation of a report brought satisfaction just as the spirits of an academic social scientist rise when an article or book he has written is published, even though the OWI reports never bore the names of their authors. But, most important of all in wartime, was evidence that operations or policy, or both, had been affected by a report.

Only by examining actual output could an individual determine whether or not operational material provided by him, or one of his general propaganda suggestions, had been utilized. The enormous production of the OWI, however, never permitted a complete survey. Very frequently, operations expressed gratitude to research and stated that a particular report had been incorporated into a script or story.

The writer of a policy report, on the other hand, could always determine whether or not his contribution had been influential by consulting the weekly directive. Although these directives were classified as confidential, they were made available to most of the research workers, and the principal one—called the Central Directive for the entire organization—was read aloud and discussed at weekly meetings. Many of the directives, moreover, contained not only a list of "do's" and "don'ts," but also a concise background summary of trends and events which gave a partial explanation for the propaganda policy, and which might contain research materials.

Some individuals inside the OWI tortured themselves with another thought, which then affected their morale: was the dissemination of propaganda or information itself an important contribution to the war effort? The doubt might concern the OWI effort regarding a particular country like Albania or Burma; even if a radio program were actually heard, and even if eventually stockpiled materials were distributed after the nation had been liberated, was it worth while to expend the effort? Such soul-searching naturally was not confined to research workers, but often pervaded the Overseas Branch. It was sometimes stimulated by congressional or newspaper attacks upon the OWI. Or it occurred when the individual himself felt guilty because his was an intellectual job and not a task in a

combat area—the way to win a war, the phrasing went, i
through bombs and not words. The OWI and the individual
themselves, therefore, provided a set of justifications, few c
which were rationalizations. If psychological warfare coul
shorten the war only by a few minutes, it was said, thousand
of lives would be saved, and so every propagandist's supereg
could feel at ease. Evidence concerning the effectiveness c
propaganda (such as the number of prisoners carrying surrende
leaflets or the enemy's effort to refute an American propagand
line), moreover, was frequently at hand and widely displayec
Usually the OWI'er managed to stop thinking before he reache
the point of asking the ultimate question; as a research worke
he was happy if he affected policy or operations.

Social scientists, in addition, faced a morale problem of thei
own. Most of them quickly realized that for the reasons alread
outlined, they could not function as specialists. Why, then, di
they remain in the Overseas Branch if they had little or no op
portunity to use their talents? Each man and woman no doub
had his own answer. Some did move into other agencies whos
research fields looked greener, or returned to their colleges an
universities. Others wanted to move, but were persuaded t
continue. Those who remained—and the writer has the impre
sion that many more remained than left—were simply intrigue
by the OWI. They were convinced that propaganda was an im
portant weapon and that—however humbly—they were helpin
to wield it. For the duration, they allowed most of their socia
science skills to hibernate, even as men and women in the arme
forces were compelled frequently to forget their professions
trades, or personal preferences. A few kept hoping that som
day or week or year they would be permitted to collect the dat
they required. Still others felt the challenge of trying to mak
as much of social science as possible work under unfavorabl
circumstances. There was always the thrilling possibility of be
ing sent overseas. *Esprit* inside the organization was sometime
high, and it was considered poor sportmanship to desert one
colleagues. No doubt every academic individual liked his cor
tact with "real life" outside the campus; he could personall
witness how one government agency functioned in wartime, an
he could work with people from the other side of the intellectu
tracks. Anyone interested in propaganda as such was able t
meet propagandists and to observe, perhaps, what made the

tick and fail to tick. Many social scientists in the OWI had a grandstand seat at the propaganda game because they were expected to carry research water to the players.

5. Promotion of Research

As chief of the Bureau of Overseas Intelligence, the writer realized that social-science research, especially projects requiring execution overseas, had to be promoted. He knew that the administrators were sympathetic toward bright and sound ideas within budgetary limits. He never convinced himself, however, that additional policy research was basically either necessary or feasible.

For one thing, he concluded that research could play only a negligible rôle in the formulation of OWI directives which were so dependent on the country's political policies and so constantly affected by military and naval clamor regarding security. By and large, it must be said, the propaganda implications of political and military policies were seldom considered. What the OWI was usually compelled to do was to justify or propagandize in favor of decisions already made. The policy of unconditional surrender for Germany, which may have stiffened German resistance, was perhaps a wise one in the long run, but here it need only be suggested that no research could be carried out in the OWI to estimate its wisdom in advance, and none could be tolerated to ascertain the desirability of publicizing its existence, since the OWI obviously had to conform to the wishes of the President. Similarly, the appeals to be employed by combat teams in calling upon a particular group of enemy soldiers to surrender required no systematic research; instead, only a few elementary facts about the conditions of those troops were required, and these were obtainable from Combat G–2. Policy makers were correctly convinced that propaganda had its best opportunity to be effective during a military or political lull; but the directives written at such a time stemmed almost exclusively from common sense and not from research, and, in addition, they were bound by general American policy and security considerations.

The OWI's propaganda principles, consequently, tended to be unsubtle and elementary, with or without research backing. The usual procedure was not to obtain the psychological facts, but to psychologize concerning the situation at hand. It was quite possible to conceive of genuine research on a social-science level which might or should affect policy, such as the state of public opinion in a country as measured by a refined survey; yet such research, as has been pointed out, was not permitted. Some information—like a stray report from an OWI outpost, the State Department, or the OSS—often seemed worse than no information at all because inadequate information could be misleading. But policy-makers found what they frankly called "hot dope"—such as gossip about a dictator's mistress or an estimate of whether a neutral country would remain neutral—more intriguing and important than an out-of-date appraisal of basic factors affecting a country or its people. Under these circumstances, the writer eventually abandoned research and during the last year of the war became Policy Coördinator of the Overseas Branch.

While in charge of research in Washington, however, the writer did manage to overcome his paralyzing inhibitions and to promote research. He found himself most successful among policy-makers whose respect, or at least affection, he had won through means not at all related to the research itself or social science in general. Specifically, this meant being liked personally by the policy-maker, humbly pointing out that the research would not be an encroachment upon the individual's own empire of assistants, forcefully indicating that the results could improve the directive and thus redound to his credit, etc. Certain background reports were sent to the OWI outposts, and the ensuing letters of thanks and approval were then employed as proof that research was necessary. In addition, responsible and capable section chiefs within the Bureau were encouraged to cultivate working relations and friendships with the policy-makers of their areas. In this way they acquired an awareness of the policy-makers' problems on a day-by-day basis. Lest they succumb completely to the charms of these masters and undertake impossible or useless tasks, they were not permitted to begin work on an assignment until the Bureau chief or his deputy was convinced that the request sprang from a real need and not from whimsey, a distinction not always easy to make

In the field of operations, too, deliberate promotion was carried on, first because it was felt that the writer's Bureau could make a contribution and second, because the Bureau's existence could be only partially justified by its reports to policy-makers. At the outset, it was essential to diminish the hostility of operators in New York toward research in Washington. They distrusted members of the Bureau because the latter were not operators; journalists in general, for example, held sociologists and political scientists in rather low repute because they felt that they themselves secured better "facts" and certainly secured them more rapidly. Then there was always some friction between the Washington and the New York offices, the same type of friction which exists between the editorial and news-gathering staffs in most newspapers, except that in this instance it was intensified by geographical separation and by a series of internecine struggles for power which, though at an end, left bad feelings in their wake. It was important, therefore, quickly to build up trust and confidence. This was achieved on a purely personal basis. Each week the chief or one of his staff journeyed to the New York office and for a period of forty-eight hours breathed only the atmosphere of operations. Careful observation of the OWI machine was made; key individuals were regularly interviewed so that their research needs could be ascertained or anticipated; and food and drink served as catalysts to build up genuine friendships. A chief of one of the operating bureaus, for example, was determined that his empire would never be invaded by anyone from Washington, especially a research worker—and he held this belief throughout the war, drunk or sober. But many of his subordinates were less neurotic and could easily be convinced that even a Washington bureau could help them in specific ways. After a period of time, this man winked at the service which "Washington" was providing because he must have realized that the reports were improving the quality of his own output and hence were in line with his own ambitions.

The courting of operators in this fashion sometimes led to impossible demands. The word "research" seemed to suggest to some that a miracle could be quickly wrought and that the innermost secrets of any enemy or occupied country ought to be immediately discovered and made available for operations. Or sometimes a round-up report for background purposes was requested which would have terrified a team of scholars with ten years, and not ten days, at their disposal to complete the job. Another type of miracle considered useful by operators involved spot news or intelligence which, if it existed, was too highly classified to be disseminated. In this connection the Bureau performed a most useful service which won the gratitude of operators: it learned how to censor and alter certain classified materials in such a way that they could be employed without jeopardizing security and yet without losing too much of their original punch. Gradually a principle of liaison between research and operations emerged: requests were accepted only when operators understood the capabilities and limitations of the Bureau and only when they could demonstrate to a responsible representative of the Bureau that the report would be useful and not just "interesting to know."

An intimate relation between operators and research worker was mutually beneficial. The operator obtained information he could use (after in some instances the utility had been pointed out to him) and the research worker learned in detail not only what information the operator needed, but also in what form that information should be presented. One of the most effective techniques the writer ever employed, in his immodest opinion, to win the respect of some key journalists was to write a few reports in journalistic style. This seemed to convince them that he did not live in the clouds, that he appreciated their problems, and that consequently he might possibly grasp their research needs in the future.

The fact that a good relation between operators in New York and research workers in Washington depended so much on personal contact rather than on formal duties was indicated by another situation which was similar in almost all respects except that of geography. The Washington offices in general were unable to establish or retain effective liaison with the OWI office in San Francisco. The same problems existed, but they were never adequately solved because frequent trips were out of the question. The telephone, the teletype, and the mail were not adequate substitutes. Both the Bureau of Overseas Intelligence and San Francisco's Operations Intelligence made conscientious efforts to prevent duplication, to have research performed by the group most capable of performing it, etc. but—in comparison with the Washington-New York link—relatively little was accomplished.

6. *Marketing of Research*

It is difficult to say in general whether or not research was eagerly accepted by the OWI's policy-makers and operators. So much depended, as has been intimated, on who did the research. Information with the highest prestige originated outside the Overseas Branch, and it produced submission simply because it came from another agency. Hardboiled journalists in the OWI frequently knew perfectly well that a report from State, War, or Navy was essentially worthless, but they could not disregard the logical or illogical conclusions drawn therefrom for fear of offending the agency involved and, as a result, of having the OWI hauled up before the Joint Chiefs or the Secretary of State. Within the Overseas Branch, there was a tendency to give more credence to research carried on within one's own section than to that produced by another group.

Policy-makers were more than eager to be guided by research findings when a report seemed, or could be employed, to justify one of their own propaganda ideas, and especially when the respectable departments were opposed to the idea. At a crucial meeting, for example, the representative of the War Department might say that he considered the directive proposal "bad propaganda," a phrase which naturally meant absolutely anything or nothing. The OWI official could reply by saying that "the boys in research have some dope which shows that this is what is needed." To which the man in uniform might respond, "Oh, well, if that's the case—this is none of our business, since security does not seem to be involved." In the policy sphere there was no respect as such for the kind of report any research group produced, because everyone knew that the facts were limited and the analyses unavoidably tentative and inconclusive.

Whether or not policy recommendations were made by research workers depended on the policy-maker involved. During an early period of the Overseas Branch, the top policy-maker—in this writer's opinion, a most capable but erratic man—believed that only he had the brilliance to formulate policy. His ears and mind, consequently, were opened to no one he did not personally like. Since he felt justifiably hostile and contemptuous toward a cavalry *(sic)* officer who for reasons pertaining to the OWI's public relations had been appointed intelligence chief, he paid little or no attention to the Bureau.

His two successors did not believe that they alone possessed all the propaganda wisdom inside the OWI, and therefore suggestions from the Bureau were acceptable and frequently utilized. As time went on, the chief of the Bureau was invited to attend most of the important policy meetings. There he could determine some of the areas of ignorance among policy-makers and later make an effort to have his Bureau supply a relevant report.

At these meetings, too, he could advance suggestions for the new directive. The suggestions he made might have their origin in research, in some principle of social science which he happened to consider applicable to the problem at hand, or simply in common sense. If he had research to buttress his argument, so much the better. But he successfully affected policy by pitching into the discussion and succeeding or failing on the basis of what he said. Whether or not in this rôle he was functioning as a research worker, a social scientist, or just a more or less intelligent human being, is a purely academic question. Research and social science, in short, were the excuse which enabled him to get into the policy discussions in the first place. This point must be clearly understood. Expressed differently, it suggests that in some situations, where social science data are inadequate or where social science itself can provide only principles or a way of approach to a problem, the social scientist must hurl himself into the debate, participate on an equal or unequal footing with men and women who are not social scientists, toss some of his scientific scruples to the winds, and fight for what seems to him to be valid or even good. A strict adherence to the scientific *credo* in such circumstances leaves the social scientist impotent and sterile as far as policy is concerned. He is faced with these alternatives: to keep quiet, stay within the confines of his research, and leave the decision to others; or to speak up, go beyond his research and social science, and thus share in the decision. Certainly, this writer asserts, the judgment of a social scientist ought to be no worse than the judgment of someone outside the fold when the problem concerns other human beings; and maybe it can be better in some instances.

A question of social or scientific ethics, however, arises in this connection: should the social scientist attempt to add prestige to his argument by always representing himself as a social scientist? The reply each individual gives is obviously a function of his own conscience. The solution of the writer was clear-cut if somewhat self-righteous. When he argued from data, he indicated their nature as well as their limitations. When principles seemed to give rise to his point of view, he named the principles, suggested how valid they were generally thought to be by his colleagues, and never stated that the propaganda universe would collapse if these dicta were disobeyed. When he spoke from what seemed to him to be common sense, he unequivocally and appropriately labelled his thoughts. This procedure did not necessarily make him sound verbose or pompous, for a simple phrase could convey the distinction. "According to reports we have . . . ," "psychologists generally believe that . . . ," or "in my personal opinion . . ." managed, it was hoped, to specify the esteem he merited. Naturally there must have been a positive or negative "halo effect" which caused some of his protagonists to forget the tag, but at least the effort was made not to bluff or to pose as an expert when technical expertness was only partially present or completely absent.

There was no way to force an operational report into a story, script, motion picture, or some other medium. The operator was the technician whose judgment had to be accepted if not respected. One could argue and argue, but the only convincing challenge was, "If you don't use this, then how are you going to implement the current directive?" The operator even then might use different material, or perhaps claim that the directive could not be implemented with the type of information available. If an operator, for whatever reason, once employed research material which he himself had not collected, and if his product won approval within the office, then of course he was more likely to trust the research group in the future.

One of the frequent complaints of operators in the New York and San Francisco offices was that the policy directives would prescribe a propaganda line for which there was no operational material. Representatives of research were able to help alleviate this difficulty. As each new directive was being discussed, they indicated whether or not the propaganda line was feasible in terms of available material. Often they also suggested that a propaganda theme be adopted for the reason that non-classified material was at hand. If the theme became part of the directive, then the operators were more or less dependent upon research for implementation. In fact, during the last few years of the OWI's existence, a list of reports from the Bureau which had been compiled, or which would be ready by an indicated deadline, was attached to the Central Directive; thus the week's research could be planned in terms of the Directive and the operators could depend on the Bureau for implementing material.

Reports had to be tailored to the readers, their interests, and their peculiarities. In general, brevity was almost always desired. Most policy-makers and operators had neither the time nor the training to examine long reports whose conclusions were indecisive, and whose factual information was surrounded by verbal hedging. A concise summary at the beginning sometimes helped. After some experimentation, it was found that few research workers could write a satisfactory report. The style of social scientists, for example, tended to be wordy and too involved. As a result, a small group of editors in the Bureau of Overseas Intelligence assumed the functions of translating first drafts into simple English and, if necessary, into "journalese"; of studying the research and stylistic requirements of the different groups in the Overseas Branch; and of distributing copies of the reports to the most appropriate people. No report could coast along on the prestige of social science, first, because social science had little prestige, and second, because—in the nip-and-tuck of war, empire-building, and the public relations of the OWI—coasting led nowhere.

7. Outside Obstructions to Research

The difficulties and problems facing the research worker in the Overseas Branch so far have been confined to those originating inside the agency. There were, in addition, some nuisances from the outside whose presence would never have been missed; no, indeed, they would never have been missed! First of all, social scientists from academic institutions sometimes breezed into the offices of policy-makers not familiar with social science for the purpose of making a proposal which they considered sensational and important. They had to be treated politely for the sake of the OWI's budget and reputation. Generally this was a waste of time. In a few instances, the visitors were hired or utilized as consultants and began to collect data. Finally—

and usually much too late—they sent in a report and felt that the job was finished. Actually, the job was not finished. The policy-maker would read the first and maybe the second page of their report, say "how interesting," and then pass it to a colleague whose desk was also littered with unread or undigested reports. Eventually the document was filed and only an efficient secretary could locate it, if anyone ever again asked to see it. Generally, nobody did. What these consultants failed to realize was a simple, mundane matter: research could not be superimposed on the working organization from the outside and, if it was, someone inside the agency had to assume the unattractive responsibility of sticking the nose of the relevant officials right into the report. The consultants suffered from the delusion that officials inevitably would beat a path to their mousetraps, when in truth the officials had many other interests in life. One consultant, after he had spent months wiggling himself into the research which he and his financial backer had decided was essential, convinced himself afterwards that he had been called in by the OWI and hence could not be held responsible for his senseless interloping.

There were also a few social scientists not on the payroll of the OWI—and some not on the payroll of any government agency—who acquired enormous prestige for themselves either because they knew and were respected by very important officials in Washington, because they previously had published many books, or because they had trained large numbers of students then under civil service. Some top official of the OWI would hear of one of them, perhaps at a cocktail party or perhaps through a friend in another agency. Then he would wonder why research workers in his own agency were not employing the techniques associated with that social scientist. In some instances the techniques or practical modifications thereof were in actual use, in others they were just not applicable. More time was lost before the top official's thinking on the subject could be set reasonably straight.

8. Personal Adjustment

Service in the Overseas Branch as a research worker was trying for the writer in innumerable ways. Most of all, he found it difficult, as the phrase would have it, to be diplomatic. He had been undiplomatic inside another war agency before he arrived at the OWI. There he had followed a custom of telling people—policy-makers or operators—to visit the nether regions when in his opinion this was the advice they truly deserved. He had learned the valuable lesson, as frankness increased his frustrations, that he would be more useful as a social scientist and happier as a human being if he treated almost every individual like a psychiatric patient who had to be understood in the gentlest possible fashion before he could be expected to swallow the pill of research. In the Overseas Branch, this meant being pleasant to what seemed to be millions of people—which, for this writer, was quite a strain. The adoption of a psychiatric approach, it should be parenthetically added, was fruitful in ways related and unrelated to the performance of duty. In trite but very meaningful fashion, it was possible to like some people when they were better understood, and the subsequent perception that the feeling was reciprocated proved gratifying. By and large, moreover, the members of the OWI were very highly motivated, worked exceedingly long hours, were productive to the extent that their talents and the organizational set-up permitted, and represented as decent if heterogeneous a group of individuals as anyone might ever meet. Under such circumstances, the strain of removing egocentrism, the ethnocentrism of social science, and a heavily reinforced system of personal habits in social relations could be tolerated. A similar problem faced the writer when he worked exclusively on the policy level. Then he learned that you could lead an operator to a directive, but you could not make him implement it—no matter how strict the system of controls—unless he understood it, approved of it, and/or had trust in the policy-maker.

9. Summary

1. In the Overseas Branch of the OWI, social science as such possessed relatively little meaningful prestige among journalists, advertising men, public relations counsels, executives, and others ordinarily concerned with mass communication media in American society. In a vague sort of way, such individuals believed that social science in the abstract was probably pursuing worthwhile objectives, but that those objectives had little or no practical importance, and certainly were of no great interest

to them in their professional work. The writer is convinced that contact with social scientists during the war did not alter this viewpoint.

2. Social scientists in the OWI did not really display their wares, and they did not do so largely because they could not. They were judged on their merits after an initial prejudice had been overcome. They had to prove that they could be useful, and it did not matter whether that utility was derived from research, from social science, or from common sense.

3. Social scientists who deliberately sought to be useful, therefore, were impelled to adapt themselves to the people and problems confronting them. This required a kind of plasticity which had no relationship whatsoever to social science and the organization chart, but which the individual had to possess or acquire as quickly as possible. He learned to function in a situation teeming with problems in social science, but lacking the data of social science. In this light, the Overseas Branch itself became a major research project, and it was a project whose intricacies could not be intuited by self-appointed consultants from the outside.

4. Research had to be constantly promoted and, when the report was completed, the findings had to be marketed. No research worker ever had the guarantee that his research was really needed, although he had all kinds of verbal expressions to the effect that it was wanted. He could never be sure that what he did would be utilized unless his chief, or he, assumed the responsibility of following through.

Chapter 17. Notes

1. Harvey C. Mansfield and Fritz Morstein Marx, in Fritz Morstein Marx (ed.), *Elements of Public Administration* (New York, 1946), Chap. 13.

Chapter **18**

THE NUMBER ONE VOICE *

By

JAMES RESTON

THE PRESIDENT of the United States influences opinion by every public act. The soldiers and the diplomats may or may not command the attention of the people by what they say or do, but the electorate is never indifferent to the slightest activity in the White House. No matter who he is, the President is a symbol of his office and his country. Even the least competent chief executive is the successor of Washington and Lincoln. Consequently, when he speaks, he speaks for America, he influences the lives of Americans, he represents or misrepresents the ideal every man has in his mind of what the President should say or do, and for these reasons, men listen when he speaks.

Moreover, the whole apparatus of the most modern and extensive system of rapid communications ever gathered together in one country is constantly at his disposal. Everything he says or does is news. If he goes to Congress to address the federal legislature, the major radio networks record every word and the television cameras transmit every flicker and expression of his face. If he goes to the country for the week end, he is followed by a battery of reporters and cameramen. If he gets a new dog, or expresses a preference for a picture, or has a daughter who sings, or acquires a new gadget for his desk, the object of his interest is subjected to the same careful scrutiny as a new policy sent to Congress.

The fierce competition of the private agencies gathering and disseminating news provides the President with a ready audience on almost every occasion. He is the "big story." Only a few

* Reprinted from *Public Opinion and Foreign Policy,* edited by Lester Markel, published by Harper & Bros. for the Council on Foreign Relations, New York, 1949.

papers and agencies assign reporters to the State Department and the Defense Departments in Washington, but almost all are represented at the White House. Whenever the President holds a press conference, at least 150 reporters attend.

The competition is so sharp that, when the press conference ends, the scramble of reporters for the telephones is a menace to life and limb, and this competition to report what the President says is not restricted to the representatives of press associations, newspapers and the radio. The magazine writers, the newsreel reporters, and even the book publishers are equally eager to have access to material, critical or merely descriptive, about the President and his administration. The President, consequently, more than any member of his administration or any political competitor, because of the preeminence of his office and the competition of the various news agencies, can be assured of getting his views before the people whenever he likes.

He can, for example, appoint committees to study the question at issue and release their findings to the public. On the basis of the study he can have legislation prepared and send it to Congress with a message stating or re-stating his reasons for wishing action. He can go personally to Congress and address both houses in joint session if he believes the matter at issue warrants such dramatic action. He can arrange to make a public speech on the subject whenever he chooses, or simply ask for radio time in order to carry his argument to the people. He can comment on the question at his meetings with the press and radio reporters. He can take it up with his Cabinet, authorizing them to discuss the question openly on Capitol Hill or in public speeches. He can have a message prepared for the newsreel cameras and either deliver the message himself or arrange to have it delivered by some prominent government official.

The President of the United States, in short, is in a unique position to influence the views of his fellow citizens: he is part symbol, part executive, part actor, part "graven image." No man in history ever had such an opportunity to reach so many people so quickly, and so often, with the assurance of an attentive audience as he. That is why, in any study of public opinion in the United States, it is vital to survey the influences that play upon the President and the uses he makes of his great power.

Chapter 19

DECISIVE BROADCAST *

By

ELLIS M. ZACHARIAS

It was on June 9, 1945, at 8:25 A.M., that I made my fifth broadcast, in which I incorporated the message sent from Switzerland by the prominent Japanese newspaperman Jiro Taguchi to Foreign Minister Togo in Tokyo. A copy of this dispatch had been obtained through the superb efforts and espionage technique of the Swiss branch of the Office of Strategic Services and was a splendid example of their co-operation when they sent it to me as of possible value for inclusion in my campaign. We immediately recognized the great significance of this message but also the paradox of the situation. The addressee was the same Togo who on December 6, 1941, as foreign minister of the Tokyo government, had confronted Ambassador Grew in the latter's abortive attempt to get President Roosevelt's message through to the Emperor at midnight on December 6, while riding high on the waves of impertinence and confidence.

We could not escape the thought that the wheel of history had indeed made a full turn, and the involvement of one of the protagonists of the Pearl Harbor treachery added a piquant touch to the diplomatic spectacle. Mr. Taguchi was another protagonist. He had represented a jingoistic Japanese newspaper in Germany for several years and had prided himself on being in the confidence of the Nazis' inner circle. But now it was his turn to be humiliated, to offer humble advice to the broken foreign minister, counseling him to sue for peace if he wanted to avoid Germany's fate.

Taguchi went far beyond giving advice. He took upon him-

* Reprinted from *Secret Missions*, published by G. P. Putnam & Sons, New York, 1946.

self the responsibility of trying to conduct peace negotiations in Bern, Switzerland, by approaching our minister there, Mr. Leland Harrison. He employed the good offices of several neutral intermediaries to lend added weight to his overtures. But it was by no means an official approach. Taguchi was acting as a free-lance peacemaker, and consequently his suggestions could not be taken seriously. However, his activities were seconded by the efforts of other Japanese in Bern, including representatives of great financial concerns, who added their endorsements to the pleas of Taguchi, hoping thereby to elicit an answer for transmittal to Tokyo.

By then peace feelers were coming in to Washington in amazingly large numbers. The most persistent of these came via the Vatican, although it must be emphasized that the Vatican acted only as a mere transmitting agency and made no recommendations of its own.

It was reported that the Emperor himself was seeking mediation by the Pope through the Archbishop of Tokyo, who happened to be the brother of a former foreign minister, the late Yosuke Matsuoka. This provided still another ironical touch, since Matsuoka had once been the strongest advocate of German-Japanese co-operation and had become the stooge of Hitler and Ribbentrop. Indeed, it was Matsuoka who had taken a leading position among the warmongers during 1941 and upon his return from a trip to Berlin had urged immediate hostile action, having guaranteed to Hitler that Japan would enter the war by seizing Singapore, which act, however, was not supposed to involve the United States. While one member of the Matsuoka family was thus instrumental in unleashing the war, another member was now making strenuous efforts to stop it short of the invasion of Japan proper. The Vatican was informed openly that the Archbishop of Tokyo was acting upon the Emperor's behest and that his role was merely that of an intermediary. But occasionally he added his own to the purported pleas of the Emperor, and some of them were remarkable for the urgency with which they implored the Pope "to do something."

These approaches began to reach the Vatican in April and continued throughout May, blowing hot and cold, playing a primitive form of psychological warfare by today protesting Japan's determination and strength, and tomorrow admitting complete exhaustion and failure. It was easy to recognize the crudeness of the diplomatic show being staged in Tokyo; and while we regarded these pleas as a possible indication of Japan's anxiety to conclude peace at the earliest moment, it was impossible to evaluate the requests because of the ambiguous nature of the campaign.

Without making a direct move, we registered these overtures as possible straws in the wind and adapted our campaign to them. In my opinion the most significant and probably the most enlightened approach was that of Taguchi. The urgency of his advice was well calculated to impress Togo and his circle in Tokyo. He placed special emphasis on a fatal German miscalculation. The Germans had deluded themselves with the thought that the Allies did not have sufficient fighting spirit to carry the war to total victory. As I revealed this passage of the Taguchi radiogram to my listening audience in Tokyo, I commented: "Do not these words have a familiar ring? Have you not heard leaders among you say that the United States does not have the spiritual strength to wage war to its predestined end? Mr. Taguchi described this fatal miscalculation of the Germans as the result of basing strategy upon imaginary ideas which have no foundation in reality. Has not the strategy of Japan been built upon a similar, nay, an identical basis?"

Taguchi reiterated this analysis as he pointed out that the same spirit which had induced Hitler to prolong the war after the collapse of the first Russian campaign had again prevailed after Stalingrad. "Instead of meeting the changed situation with political wisdom," he wrote to Togo, "instead of considering the future interests of the nation, they took, and intensified, oppressive measures."

By then Japan was following Germany's example. She was intensifying police measures to keep the people in line and to bolster their fading enthusiasm for what came to be labeled the "Hundred-Year War." Special sessions of district attorneys were held in Tokyo by the Minister of Justice, Mr. Matsuzaka; and the Procurator General, Nakano, was placed in charge of "morale promotion," which by then had become morale enforcement. My purpose in citing Taguchi's dispatch was far more than just to provide an intelligence scoop to enliven my broadcasts. I was quite explicit in drawing conclusions for my Japanese listeners, who are habitually slow in arriving at decisions unless assisted in their thinking. "The outstanding lesson which clear-sighted men like Mr. Taguchi learned from Germany's defeat was this," I said: "The continuation of a hopeless war not only failed to help Germany but compromised the entire future of that country. Mr. Taguchi said that the cost was immense. German cities were destroyed; the middle class disappeared; securities were turned into wastepaper; and in the very words of Jiro Taguchi: 'Everybody lost everything. The German nation lost its sovereignty.' "

This was a powerful argument, since reliable information now indicated that all Japan hoped to salvage from the war was her sovereignty. This word has a peculiar significance for the Japanese. It has a theocratic undertone in addition to its legalistic meaning. Sovereignty is closely linked to the sovereign in a combination of sacred-secular interpretation reminiscent of the feudal interpretation of the term, when the sovereign was God, the last representative of an unbroken line of divine rulers descended from the Sun Goddess, an irrational dogma elevated to the rank of anachronistic political philosophy.

Admiral Suzuki, the new premier, was particularly concerned over this question of peculiar Japanese sovereignty. He was very close to the Emperor, having been grand chamberlain for many years. The imperial house and the classical interpretation of the imperial institution were deeply imbedded in his mind and heart. What he called the "national structure" of Japan meant the divinity and political prerogatives of the Emperor. This was his guiding principle, and now he was concentrating his efforts toward saving Japan by saving her national structure, i.e., the continuity of the ruling house said to be "unbroken for ages."

On the other hand, he was more than willing to heed the Emperor's desire to bring about peace—but his loyalty to the Emperor made him refrain from doing anything about it until he could ascertain what the Allies had in mind regarding the future fate of the imperial house. In his plight he decided upon what in retrospect appears to have been a desperate move. In June he instructed Mr. Sato, the Japanese ambassador to the Kremlin, to make representations to Marshal Stalin and ask him to intervene with the Western Allies on Japan's behalf in order to obtain a further clarification of the unconditional surrender formula, and, if possible, peace terms. What he really wanted was an assurance that Japan's sovereignty would be respected even if she had to pay for the privilege with her empire.

The fact that such a peace plea had been forwarded to Stalin, and Japan's plight bared to the Soviet leaders, did not receive here the attention it seemed to warrant. The Soviet Union by Suzuki's move was given a clear indication of Japan's inner plight and her willingness to surrender. Thus when on August 8, 1945, the Russians joined in the war against Japan, they acted upon intelligence provided by the Japanese themselves that they were at the end of their rope. Russia joined in the war in the knowledge that Japan had admitted defeat.

It is left to the judgment of history to explain why it was necessary for the Soviet to take its course of action and why the Allies, assuming they knew of Japan's approaches to the Soviet, refused to exploit the opening provided by Japan herself. If the detailed interpretations of the unconditional surrender formula had been forthcoming in June rather than the end of July, the war would have ended without Soviet participation and before the dropping of the atomic bombs on Hiroshima and Nagasaki. Although the historical perspective is insufficient as yet to provide a complete picture as it existed in June 1945, it is an undeniable fact that the diplomatic situation provided an opportunity for peace many weeks before mid-August, at which time it was generally thought that Japan had bowed to the supernatural force of the atom bomb.

There always existed considerable confusion in Washington and, indeed, throughout the country regarding the diplomatic concept of the term unconditional surrender, and it became obvious that a further clarification of the unconditional surrender formula was necessary, not merely for the Japanese but for the people of the United States as well.

We presumed that the policy of the United States was formulated in five documents: one was the Atlantic Charter which distinctly stated that it applied to victor and vanquished alike; another was the 1944 New Year's declaration of Generalissimo Chiang Kai-shek. The third was the series of declarations issued after the Casablanca, Teheran, and Yalta conferences. The fourth was President Truman's proclamation of May 8, 1945, concerning unconditional surrender; the fifth was Justice Jackson's declaration on war criminals. With these documents in mind and their application clearly outlined, I felt that contrary to general belief we did have a concrete policy, and from then on my campaign was based on making this policy known to the Japanese.

By the end of June the plight of the Japanese had become desperate, and as Admiral Suzuki received no answer to his plea from Russia, he called an extraordinary session of the Diet in which he discussed in remarkably frank terms the entire war situation.

We recognized the significance of this move and gathered around the ticker bringing to our office the momentous speech. It was evident from the very outset that while Suzuki was talking of war, he was thinking of peace. Now, it was no longer a material consideration such as the retention of Manchuria or Korea which prevented him from saying in so many words that he would accept our terms. The only doubt which still forestalled a decision was the future status of the Emperor. "I have served His Imperial Majesty over a period of many years," Suzuki said, "and I am deeply impressed with this honor. As bold as it may seem, I firmly believe there is no one in the entire world who is more deeply concerned with world peace and the welfare of mankind than His Imperial Majesty the Emperor. The brutal and inhuman acts of both America and England are aimed to make it impossible for us to follow our national policy as proclaimed by the Emperor Meiji. I hear that the enemy is boasting of his demand of unconditional surrender by Japan. Unconditional surrender will only mean that our national structure and our people will be destroyed. Against such boastful talk there is only one measure we must take—that is to fight to the last."

With our knowledge of the background of this extraordinary session and of Suzuki's speech, I made an important broadcast to the Japanese on July 7 inviting them to ask openly for peace. "Japan must make the next move," I said in clearly accentuated words. "Japan must make her choice without delay, for reasons which Admiral Suzuki knows. I have told you before that the time is running out for Japan. You must move and move quickly. Tomorrow it may be too late."

We analyzed the speech again for future action, and as subsequently proven by events and confirmed by Suzuki himself, our analysis was accurate. Our problem now was the method by which we could reassure Suzuki on this score, and indicate that there was no decision to destroy what he ambiguously described as the national structure of Japan.

This time our answer was not confined to another broadcast. Instead, there was selected a method as devious as those chosen by the Japanese themselves. We decided to answer Premier Suzuki in an anonymous letter written to a reputable American newspaper and to bring this letter to his attention in the quickest manner possible. The *Washington Post* was selected as the vehicle with full cooperation of its editors. The letter contained all the answers to Suzuki's query. Some of its passages may be worth quoting:

> Insofar as Japan is concerned, the clamor for an "explanation" of the unconditional surrender formula is difficult to understand, since it has been both specified and clarified in various official documents. Our policy of unconditional surrender can, therefore, be stated in simple terms:
>
> (1) Unconditional surrender is the manner in which the war is terminated. It means exactly what General Grant had in mind when he stated his terms to General Lee, namely, the acceptance of terms without qualifying counter-arguments.
>
> (2) The conditions which will obtain after surrender have been explicitly stated in the Atlantic Charter, the Cairo Declaration, Generalissimo Chiang Kai-shek's declaration of New Year's Day, 1944, President Truman's declaration of May 8, 1945, and Justice Jackson's statement on war criminals. These documents contain the conditions of which Japan can avail herself by surrendering unconditionally and thereby fulfilling the prerequisite of peace, namely, the cessation of hostilities.
>
> (3) The Atlantic Charter and the Cairo Declaration clearly state that we seek no territorial aggrandizement. The Atlantic Charter, moreover, assures certain definite benefits to victors and vanquished alike.
>
> (4) American military law, based upon historical precedents as well as a decision of the United States Supreme Court, clearly specify that conquest or occupation does not affect the sovereignty of a defeated nation, even though that nation may be under complete military control. . . .
>
> If the Japanese desire to clarify whether or not unconditional surrender goes beyond the conditions contained in the five documents cited above, they have at their disposal the regular diplomatic channels, the secrecy of which precludes any public admission of weakness. They are aware that we know that Japan has lost the war. Such an inquiry could not pos-

sibly be misinterpreted, or display any weakness beyond that which now actually exists in Japan. It is presumed that this was the meaning and purpose of Mr. Grew's statement and in this sense it deserves the fullest endorsement of the American people.

If, as Admiral Suzuki revealed in the Diet, their chief concern is over Japan's future national structure (Kokutai), including the Emperor's status after surrender, the way to find out is to ask. Contrary to a widespread belief, such a question can be answered quickly and satisfactorily to all those who are concerned over the future peace of the Orient and the world.

The letter attracted considerable attention in the United States, and the *Washington Post* was bombarded by callers who wanted to learn the identity of its anonymous author. My telephone also rang. Washington correspondents, accurately gauging the technique, tried to make me confess authorship. Typical of the many efforts to determine the source of the letter was a syndicated article by Duke Shoop, Washington correspondent of the *Kansas City Star*, who wrote:

A provocative open letter inviting the Japanese to open negotiations on unconditional surrender is being widely discussed here since it is believed that Captain E. M. Zacharias, the "official American spokesman" of American radio broadcasts to the Japs, is the author. . . . This provocative letter is like something out of a mystery thriller, but it is not at all out of the question that some such method might be taken to convey further to the Japanese what we mean by unconditional surrender. Through neutral countries they have almost immediate access to comments in American newspapers. Whether this was the purpose or not, the letter is a significant contribution to the psychological phase of the war which has its purpose advising the Japanese of what unconditional surrender does and does not mean.

The letter was reprinted in many American dailies from coast to coast. We felt certain that it would be picked up in Washington by the listening posts of the Japanese government.

Simultaneously another broadside was prepared along more conventional lines. I was now called upon to prepare a radio script on the highest diplomatic level. I fully recognized my tremendous responsibility and devoted special attention to this one talk. We worked on the script day and night for almost a week, drafting and redrafting it, listening to suggestions, submitting it for approval, weighing every single word with the greatest of care. When at last I went to the broadcasting studio, I had its fourteenth draft in my pocket.

For this broadcast we selected a little room specially built for highly classified recording to guarantee security. As unobtrusively as possible, guards were posted around the studio to see that no unauthorized person could obtain advance information of what I was to say. But this secrecy was maintained for only a short period. When my recordings were put on the air a few days later, the text of the broadcast was released to the American press by the OWI, using this publicity as another means of reinforcing and emphasizing the message.

I was introduced as "an official spokesman of the United States government," in line with the stipulation of the operation plan. But the Japanese had indicated doubt as to my true authority. Was I "official spokesman" in fact, as well as in name? Did my statements carry higher endorsement? Or was I merely a cog in the wheel of the American propaganda mill? With the release to the press we hoped to dispel their doubts, and the reception which the American newspapers accorded to this talk surpassed our most optimistic expectations. The news of this broadcast broke on July 21, and the evening papers were the first to feature it. "U.S. Warns Japan to Quit Now, Escape Virtual Destruction," headlined the *Washington Post*, and next morning the *New York Times* gave it front-page display and reprinted the whole broadcast. Other prominent papers similarly featured it.

The broadcast reiterated the themes of my letter to the *Post*. The message it carried was incorporated in four sentences: "The leaders of Japan have been entrusted with the salvation and not the *destruction* of Japan. As I have said before, the Japanese leaders face two alternatives. One is the virtual destruction of Japan followed by a dictated peace. The other is unconditional surrender with its attendant benefits as laid down by the Atlantic Charter." The urgency of the situation was formulated in words which were adapted to Japanese psychology when I said: "Your opportunity to think over these facts is rapidly passing. . . . If the Japanese leaders still prefer to delay and hope for miracles, they should remember that the cemetery of history is crowded with the graves of nations—

nations which were doomed to extinction because they made their decision too late."

In the midst of the domestic clamor which was manifested in editorials printed in virtually every American daily, the Japanese kept a significant silence. As I waited for their answer, I visualized the conclaves going on in Tokyo, in which possible strategy and tactics were being discussed in an endeavor to find the most propitious answer. As it was, we did not have to wait long. The Japanese answer was delivered at 12:15 A.M. (EWT) on July 24, by another Inouye, Dr. Kiyoshi Inouye this time, who was introduced as Japan's outstanding authority on international relations. I remembered him quite well as a former professor at the University of Southern California, at Tokyo University, and as delegate to various international conferences.

The message entrusted to Dr. Kiyoshi Inouye was of momentous importance. In effect, he was to indicate Japan's willingness to *surrender unconditionally,* if and when Japan was assured that the Atlantic Charter would apply to her. He stated: "Should America show any sincerity of putting into practice what she preaches, as for instance in the Atlantic Charter excepting its punitive clause, the Japanese nation, in fact the Japanese military, would automatically, if not willingly follow in the stopping of the conflict. Then and then only will sabers cease to rattle both in the East and the West."

This was not the final word of the campaign. But it was the next to last. In retrospect, the Inouye broadcast of July 24 must be accepted as evidence of the Japanese decision to terminate the war then and there; to terminate it on the basis of the terms outlined in my series of previous broadcasts culminating in my twelfth talk. The Japanese answer was delivered on the eve of the Postdam Declaration in which the meaning of unconditional surrender was clearly outlined and spelled out. It was delivered *thirteen days* before the first atomic bomb was dropped on Hiroshima, and more than two weeks before the Soviet's entry into the war. Japan was ready for surrender. To reap our harvest we had only to shake her like a tree full of ripe apples.

Subsequent investigations on the spot after Japan's surrender revealed that the Emperor was fully aware of our psychological warfare activities and had access to the monitoring service. He felt that we understood clearly the situation inside Japan and that at the end of June 1945 the time had come to seek peace.

Several Japanese in high positions who were in constant touch with the Emperor were thoroughly interrogated. One official of the Foreign Office said: "The Zacharias broadcasts were influential especially in government circles," and added: "The outstanding feature of the Zacharias broadcasts was the difference between unconditional surrender and dictated peace. The Japanese knew how Germany was being administered under such a peace. Zacharias promised that if Japan accepted unconditional surrender they would have the benefit of the Atlantic Charter. The people began to look with favor on such terms, claiming that it was not what the militarists had said. It seemed to the people that Zacharias' explanation of unconditional surrender offered a way out."

Mr. Toshio Shiratori read the copies of my broadcasts at the Foreign Office. At first he was somewhat skeptical, then became a thorough believer. A copy of each broadcast was taken to the Emperor by Mr. Matsuda. He stated that the information in these talks influenced those in the Emperor's circle as well as the Emperor himself.

Another official in the Foreign Office stated: "The broadcasts of Captain Zacharias were the object of unusual attention." He felt that these talks were influential because (a) they claimed to represent the official views of the United States government; and (b) they reiterated the pledge of President Truman that the Japanese would not be enslaved.

The highest and latest official word on this subject was received in a letter from Mr. Dennis McEvoy. It was dated August 29, 1946, and was sent just after McEvoy's return from Tokyo, where he had gone after V-J Day to set up *The Reader's Digest* in Japanese.

It will be recalled that Mr. McEvoy, as a first lieutenant of Marines, was a member of the unbeatable team in the psychological warfare against the Japanese high command. His letter reads:

> Just before leaving Tokyo I had dinner with Prince and Princess Takamatsu, whom you knew and mentioned in your first broadcast. The Prince told me on this occasion that "the Captain Zacharias broadcasts provided the ammunition needed by the 'peace party' to win out against those elements in the Japanese government who wished to continue the war to the

bitter end"—and after looking over personally the fortifications the Japanese had prepared for us, I am convinced it would have been a very bitter end indeed. The Prince's statement was in exact accord with the estimate of the situation which you made before you began to talk to the Japanese on the radio. Other pre-war contacts of mine in Japan, both in and out of the government, who were in a position to observe the crucial political situation which terminated in Japan's surrender, confirmed Takamatsu's assertions. I believe that this is rather convincing evidence of the tremendous value of your work in helping bring the war to an early close, thereby saving countless lives.

There was unanimity among Japanese newspapersmen that our propaganda not only shortened the war but made the bloodless occupation of Japan possible. This was the goal set forth in the "decision" of my Operation Plan 1-45.

Chapter 20

PRIVATE MEDIA AND PUBLIC POLICY *

By

C. D. JACKSON

AMERICAN MOVIES are seen by millions of Europeans. News gathered by American wire services is printed in many hundreds of European newspapers. American newspapers, magazines and books are on sale in most European countries.

All this adds up to a vast amount of American private activity in Europe that affects public opinion, particularly the opinions of many Europeans who are not reached by our official propaganda. Although this activity is privately financed, it is a fundamental part, in some countries the most important part, of the whole complex of activities which can help to make Americans better understood abroad.

In this book it has already been argued—and, it is hoped, demonstrated—that in the cold war of words all our deeds abroad, all our writings, all our publications, all our expressions of thought must be weighed according to their propaganda impact. That is why all private activities affecting public opinion abroad have, in effect, a propaganda aspect, using the word without an invidious sense and in its true meaning. That is why in the Economic Recovery Plan specific provision was made for helping to promote the circulation of American publications and American ideas in Europe.

Because of this propaganda aspect, private activity affecting public opinion abroad places a large responsibility on those who conduct it. They can do much to create an honest and helpful impression of America, or, by misusing their opportunity, they

* Reprinted from *Public Opinion and Foreign Policy*, edited by Lester Markel, published by Harper & Bros. for the Council on Foreign Relations, New York, 1949.

can do great harm to America's world position and to America's foreign policy—and thus to their own enterprises.

The operations abroad of American private industry in the information field can be grouped in four major categories: (1) press services, (2) newspapers and periodicals, (3) motion pictures, and (4) books.

This chapter is an attempt to analyze for each category the extent of the activity, its effectiveness and the possibilities of an increase in effectiveness. The facts given and the conclusions reached are drawn from original research, from the reports of the thirty-four correspondents who contributed to these studies [1] and from the writer's experiences and observations in the field.

1. Press Services

To understand the activities of the American press associations in Europe we must consider the newspapers which they serve, either directly or through sale of their services to the various central news agencies. European newspapers, suffering from severe newsprint restrictions, bear little resemblance to the newspapers of the United States. They rarely exceed ten pages and usually consist of four to six. Compared with our own papers they carry little advertising. With the exception of a few outstanding newspapers published in England and on the Continent, they are mainly party journals, more often devoted to editorializing than to the printing the news. Many of them run the less responsible members of the American press a close race in playing up "yellow news."

There has been an extraordinary post-war increase in the number of European newspapers which get their news from the three major American news services—the Associated Press, the United Press and the International News Service. In 1939 the AP had just begun to break in to the overseas news market; today it serves 1,493 newspapers and radio stations outside the continental United States, of which 469 are in Europe. The UP during the same period increased the number of overseas customers which it serves directly from 485 to 1.058. INS enlarged the number of its overseas clients, from 100 to 495. Competition among the services for these foreign customers is keen.

The American associations send out daily news reports somewhat similar in content to their reports for domestic papers, but generally with special emphasis on news of interest to the foreign market. In their foreign operations the associations are confronted with two special problems: (a) Too often the more serious dispatches about American events and American policies are side-tracked by foreign editors in favor of sensational material—stories about Hollywood divorces, gangland murders and the like. (b) In countries behind the Iron Curtain there is much evidence that the reports are distorted in the interest of Communist propaganda.

With regard to the selection of sensational items by European editors, the associations are in a difficult position. In the domestic field they operate on the principle that the news agency supplies the reports and the rest is up to the newspaper editors. This principle often results in distorted emphasis in the domestic press, but the distortion is mitigated by the variety of news media available to the American public. In the foreign field, however, the facilities for correcting distortions do not exist, and therefore the problem is much more complex. Thus there is indicated a large task of education, the task of convincing foreign editors and foreign readers of the importance of having the kind of news service that will give them a true picture of America. Obviously, this is a long-term assignment.

But time presses and, therefore, such short-term measures as can be adopted must be adopted without delay. The news agencies should examine their overseas operations with extreme care because of their great importance in the psychological struggle. There have been charges that they are not doing the fully effective job that is needed. They might well put to themselves questions such as these: Is our foreign service too sensational? Do we give it the attention it deserves? Do we man it properly at home and watch it carefully abroad?

With regard to the deliberate distortion of news in Communist countries, that is a more delicate problem. The American news services have contracts to supply news reports to countries behind the Iron Curtain. The question is raised as to whether or not these contracts are detrimental to our interests. It is not a new problem, even though it has never before existed in its present intense form. Writing seven years ago of his long campaign against control of news sources and outlets by the old Reuter agency, Kent Cooper, general manager of the Associated Press, said:

> In the . . . postwar era a free press and freedom of international news exchange everywhere must be guaranteed. There can be no permanent peace unless men of all lands can have truthful, unbiased news of each other which shall be freely available at the source to all who seek it there, wherever that may be. The flow of news must not be impeded. Those whose business it is to get the news at the source must be under no restraint or dictation by governments. This can come to pass only when, as to news collection, all the barriers are down.[2]

These words are more meaningful today than ever before; their implementation, however, presents many difficulties. For example, the Associated Press has made a series of short-term experimental agreements with the central news agencies (that is, the official government agencies) of the countries behind the Iron Curtain—Russia, Czechoslovakia, Poland, Hungary, Rumania and Yugoslavia. Under the agreements, the AP report is supplied to these agencies on the condition that they do not change the facts or the meaning of what they receive. AP correspondents stationed in these countries are expected to observe and report on material used under these agreements. But such inspection is difficult; it requires a great deal of time and diligence; often misrepresentation is accomplished by selection and emphasis, rather than distortion of facts.

One thing is certain, that the Communist agencies operate on the theory that theirs is a propaganda job and a service to the state, and their aim is not the objective presentation of the news which is the goal of the true American newspaper. In Communist countries the official propaganda offices are in direct charge of the press, and the distortion is dictated from above. The ethical question is raised: Should the wire services sell news reports when they know those reports are going to be twisted to misrepresent American life?

On the affirmative side there is the argument that if the American news agencies refuse to sell to Communist countries, they will deprive the readers in those areas of any chance of getting anything in the nature of a fair report; by sending the report there is always the chance that some favorable news may trickle through. On the negative side there is the argument that the news agencies, by permitting their reports to be used for Communist propaganda purposes, are lending the prestige of the

American news-gathering organizations to Communist purposes.

2. Newspapers and Periodicals

American newspapers and periodicals distributed abroad are read by a relatively small but influential audience. Some are English-language publications which are circulated chiefly among government officials, civil servants, professors, teachers, jornalists, business men and students. Others are published in various foreign languages and have a greater mass potentiality.

Many of the American newspapers and periodicals read abroad are printed abroad. A number of United States publishers have established branch publishing offices overseas, both to print and to distribute their publications.

The *New York Herald Tribune,* daily European Edition (English language), printed in Paris, has a circulation of 63,000[8] in Western Europe, Germany and Austria, the Middle East and North Africa.

During the United Nations sessions in Paris last fall the *New York Times* began distribution of a special air-mail edition overseas—an edition composed and printed in New York and flown overseas for distribution within twenty-four hours of publication. It also prints an Overseas Weekly (English language) which has a total circulation of 24,000 (in Germany 10,000).[8]

The *Rome American,* an English-language daily published in Rome, is distributed principally in Italy, Greece, Saudi Arabia, with token distribution elsewhere in Europe. Circulation is approximately 25,000.

The *Reader's Digest* has done the most extensive job in overseas publishing. Starting before the war with an English edition printed in Britain, on V-J Day it was putting out editions in Spanish, Portuguese, Arabic (since discontinued), Swedish, Finnish, Danish and Norwegian. Since 1945 it has added Japanese and French, plus two more English editions for Australia and South Africa, a Canadian edition (in English and French) and an edition in German. The combined circulation of all these editions totals 4,275,000.

Newsweek prints two special English-language editions abroad, one in Paris (circulation 44,519[3]) for Europe and Africa, the other in Tokyo (circulation 26,221[3]) for the Pacific area.

Time International English-language editions include Canadian and Latin American publications, an edition printed in Tokyo and Honolulu for Asia and the Pacific, and an edition printed in Paris for Europe, Africa and the Middle East. Combined circulation: 261,546.

Life International (English language), published fortnightly in the United States for distribution abroad, has a circulation of 252,082.

McGraw-Hill translates four of its trade publications into Spanish for Latin American audiences: *El Automovil Americana* (16,000), *El Farmaceutico* (8,000), *Ingenieria Internacional Construccion* (9,000), *Ingenieria Internacional Industria* (11,000). It also puts out three international editions in English: *The American Automobile Overseas* (10,000), *Pharmacy International* (2,700), *McGraw-Hill Digest* (15,000).

Several other Spanish-language magazines are published in the United States for Latin America; among them are *La Hacienda* (circulation 25,884), *Norte Revista Continental* (circulation 126,095) and *Cine-Mundial* (circulation 55,000).

Another group of magazine publishers has engaged in international publishing to the extent of turning over to local publishers in various countries the reprint rights to their magazines, either in the original English or for translation into the language of the country. Such locally reprinted United States magazines include *Omnibook, Magazine Digest,* and some of the Macfadden and Fawcett publications.

A third group of publishers regards the foreign market simply as an extension of its domestic market, exporting copies of its regular United States editions for limited subscription and newsstand sale abroad. The major firms in this group are Curtis Publishing Company, Crowell-Collier, Look and Hearst International.

A fourth group of publishers, mostly comic book and pulp-fiction concerns, looks on the foreign market as a dumping ground for surplus or unsold newsstand copies left over from its domestic distribution. Before the war there was a substantial demand for these surpluses in the English-speaking countries. The demand presumably is still there but those countries, along with many others, have passed, or are about to pass, laws prohibiting the "dumping" on their markets of second-hand or backdate foreign magazines.

The American publishers who print abroad pay their printing costs in local currencies, but their paper is dollar-purchased and shipped, their editorial content is dollar-created, and their American personnel abroad are dollar-paid. Almost all circulation income, and part of advertising income, is received in local currency which foreign governments are generally reluctant or unable to convert into dollars. Because of this economic disadvantage, provision was made by Congress to permit the exchange of a limited amount of Marshall Plan dollars for such blocked currencies.[4] This established one of the links between government and private enterprises in the overseas operation.

It should be recognized that there are certain American publications circulated abroad that do not contribute to a proper understanding of America. Some are guilty of sensationalism and distortion. Some elaborate on phases of American life or politics that tend to diminish our prestige in Europe. Some carry across the seas the personal axes they grind at home; thus they give the European reader a one-sided view of controversies that he cannot understand without a knowledge of American politics or business. Still others—and not only the comic book publishers—look upon Europe as a dumping ground for their surplus material without regard to the impression that material may create. Obviously this kind of journalism benefits neither the nation nor, in the long run, the enterprises themselves.

3. Motion Pictures

More people see American films in Europe and in the rest of the world than at home. Eric Johnston, President of the Motion Picture Association of America and of the Motion Picture Export Association, estimates the foreign audience for American films at 110,000,000 weekly, the domestic audience at 90,000,000. Movie houses all the way across Europe, including Russia, depend on the American product. British theaters, for example, require about 350 new feature pictures a year, but Britain's film industry produces only 50 or 60. In France 60 percent of all films shown are American; in Belgium about 70 percent. Even in Soviet Russia, Pravda recently felt it necessary to castigate the provincial movie theaters for giving more time to old American pictures than to new Soviet films. American films—with foreign-language subtitles—reach large numbers of Europeans who cannot or do not read American newspapers or periodicals. Thus the motion picture has a strong propaganda impact.

The foreign market is an economic necessity to Hollywood. Film costs are so geared that sales overseas provide the entire margin of profit for the industry. In the post-war years this income has been hard hit by the dollar shortage abroad and by restrictions imposed in many countries on the import of American films. Consequently, competition for the foreign market is keener than ever among the major studios.

Most American films distributed abroad are produced by the ten leading film companies which are members of the Motion Picture Export Association.[5] There are a few independents in the field, but their share of new films for the foreign market is less than 9 percent of the total.

The foreign market for American films falls into two categories. First, there are the countries—embracing 90 percent of the overseas market—where there is, in theory at least, an open market, although there may be commercial restrictions limiting the number of film imports. Second, there are the countries—embracing about 10 percent of the market—where either military occupation authorities or Communist governments operate as distribution monopolies for all motion pictures; they are Germany, Austria, Japan, Korea, Indonesia, the Soviet Union, Poland, Czechoslovakia, Yugoslavia, Hungary, Rumania and Bulgaria. In all these countries importers of American films must deal either with military authorities or with Iron Curtain film monopolies.

In countries in the first category film exporters operate on their own. They have their own agents overseas and arrange for their own distribution on a competitive basis. What quotas there are, are set by the importing countries. For example, France recently limited imports of American films to 121 a year; other foreign films to 65. In dividing the American quota, the French Government assigned eleven licenses each to the ten members of MPA. The other ten were assigned to non-member producers.

Although the Motion Picture Association of America has no control over the pictures its members send to these countries, the member companies do more than 90 percent of the export business. They receive guidance from the Association's Selectivity Department, whose job it is to "review all films contemplated for export and to advise the exporting company as to suitability for release in various countries." Films are classified as "Group I—suitable; Group II—not advisable; and Group III—unsuitable." Two members of the Selectivity Department operating in Hollywood study scripts before and during production and suggest changes designed to improve the export suitability rating.

The Selectivity Department has no set code by which it judges pictures or scripts. Its objective is to eliminate objectionable elements from a picture during production or to persuade a member company not to ship overseas a completed picture "which might be detrimental to the prestige of the United States if released abroad." For example, the Selectivity Department of the Association would not approve for export a motion picture which contained a sequence holding up to ridicule or contempt the electoral process in the U.S.A. The department may adjudge a picture "suitable" for some countries but "unsuitable" for others. It might find, for example, that English-speaking nations have the necessary background for a certain film but that the same film would mislead Slavic countries as to American institutions. But, in any event, the department's recommendations are not binding; the final decision is up to the distributor.

To deal with countries in the second categroy MPA in 1946 set up the Motion Picture Export Association (MPEA). In the occupied countries, all films selected by MPEA must have the approval of the occupying authorities. In the Iron Curtain countries MPEA follows this procedure: It selects a predetermined number of titles from its stockpile of several thousand unreleased features and offers them as a block to the film monopoly which contracts to take a given number from the list offered. For example, Poland in 1947-48 contracted for 65 films selected from a list of 100; Czechoslovakia bought 80 selected from a list of 120; last fall Mr. Johnston closed a deal with the Soviet Union under which Russia agreed to buy 20 films from a list of 100; Yugoslavia agreed to take 25 from the same list.

In preparing these lists the Export Association has a relatively free hand since all its member companies divide the receipts of the Export Association on a predetermined basis and therefore are not interested in pressing for selection of their own pictures as against a competitor's. With several thousand films to choose from and 350-450 additional pictures added to its available product annually, the officers of the Export Association first prepare a basic release list containing films of various types —musicals, comedies, action pictures, romances, dramas, etc. The basic schedule is submitted to the MPA Selectivity Department which passes judgment on suitability or unsuitability of the list submitted. Here are some of the standards applied: "Does the picture in any way distort, exaggerate or mislead in its portrayal of Americans or the American way of life?" "Is there too much vice or violence in the picture?" "Would the film give serious offense to the governments or people of one or more MPEA territories?" "Will the film encounter serious cutting at the hands of local censor boards?"

Thus Hollywood does have the machinery for selection of "the best American films" for export. In practice, however, the MPA's Selectivity Department rates very few films as "unsuitable." MPA explains the low figure by the fact that objectionable features are generally eliminated on the Hollywood set. (MPEA of course discards many more because its foreign market is restricted.) Therefore, by Hollywood's standards, practically the entire production of MPA members is rated as "suitable" for foreign consumption.

There are many critics who do not go along with Hollywood on this. They contend that many Hollywood pictures create, and contribute to, distorted impressions of American life abroad; that there is considerable emphasis on the sensational aspects of the domestic scene; that the impression left with the foreign movie-goer—who cannot step out of a movie theater into the realities of American life—is one of an America hell-bent for crime and fun in noisy and gaudy terms. These critics argue that there is no real selectivity practiced in Hollywood; that in effect "marketability" carries as much or more weight than "suitability" in the selection of export films.

Hollywood defends both its motives and the quality of its product. With regard to motives, Eric Johnston says, "Hollywood is acutely aware of its responsibility as the guardian of a great medium of mass communication. Its record in peace . . . will measure up to any other instrument of expression. . . . The average foreign movie-goer regards our pictures with respect because Hollywood has not tried to make it appear that American democracy is Utopia."

With regard to quality, Hollywood argues that the critics are misinformed. Examples such as the following are cited:

"Not long ago, some of our government and private critics were horrified because 'The Grapes of Wrath,' a picture based on the Steinbeck novel, was shown abroad. 'Too seamy!' they cried. 'That's a side of American life better untold outside our borders.'

"Yugoslavia pirated a print of the film and showed it under the title, 'The Paradise That Is America,' gleefully pointing to the plight of our migrant workers in the days of drought and depression as a typical, permanent American condition. The Communists thought they had a damning weapon against democracy in their hands.

"Our critics and the Communists were both wrong. The thing that impressed the Yugoslav audiences was that the migrant workers drove away in their own jalopies when the police chased them out of the tent-and-shanty town."

Again: " 'Ali Baba and the Forty Thieves' has been the most popular American film shown in Czechoslovakia, running for nearly six months in Prague. The Czechs found great satisfaction in this legend where the heavy-handed dictator is eventually overthrown by the common people."

The examples are interesting. There are other films that have been good propaganda. For example, in the Italian elections in the Spring of 1948, American films were extremely effective.[6] There is a widespread feeling, however, that such films are in the minority—in short that Hollywood is not doing the job it could do in explaining America to Europeans.

4. Books

American books, sold abroad either in the original or in translation, are highly influential in intellectual circles. American novels are widely read. American scientific works are in great demand because of America's preeminence in scientific fields.

Before World War II American book publishers, entirely wrapped up in promoting and developing their domestic market, were not at all export-conscious. Not more than 2 percent of their total book output went abroad. Britain and France at that time were exporting between 30 and 40 percent of their production; they regarded the overseas book trade as an instrument of foreign policy.

During the war American book publishers, working with OWI, furnished a vast quantity of books to liberated countries, an activity which stimulated them to give serious thought to post-war possibilities. In October 1945, they combined their efforts in the foreign field by forming as a "chosen instrument" a non-profit corporation, the United States International Book Association.

With a membership that eventually included 124 publishers (among them all the leaders in the industry), with the blessings of the State Department and with $125,00 of government money, USIBA set out to follow in the footsteps of OWI. Its announced purpose was to make United States books "freely and economically available throughout the world, and make the best products of our technology, education, culture and entertainment at least as fully known and easily available abroad as the books of any other nationality."

USIBA set up book centers in foreign capitals, organized book fairs and traveling book exhibitions in several countries, arranged for short-wave broadcasting of reviews of American books, distributed a monthly book list abroad, and compiled a definitive bibliography of scientific, medical and technical books. These activities attracted much attention to American books, and contributed in large measure to the $2,000,000 sales handled by USIBA during its first year of existence.

Originally set up as a two-year experiment, USIBA was hitting its stride after this first year, but then its members came to a parting of the ways and decided to go back to operating abroad on the old every-man-for-himself basis.

In 1947, despite the demise of USIBA and the continuance of foreign exchange restrictions, officially reported exports of American books to all countries showed a substantial gain over 1946, from $18,700,000 to $24,000,000. The 1947 exports were almost five times what the Department of Commerce reported in 1938.[7] If mail shipments had been included, the 1947 total would have been increased to approximately $50,000,000. Comparing this figure with an estimated 1947 book production of $352,000,000, we get an export quota of 15 percent.

The breakdown of 1947 exports by geographic areas, however, shows that only a relatively small proportion of the American books sold abroad go to the areas where the cold war is being fought most bitterly. Of the officially reported exports in 1947 amounting to $24,000,000, sales valued at $7,700,000 were made to Canada. Only 28 percent ($6,889,000) went to Europe. European sales were distributed as follows:

	Dollar volume	Percent of total
Western Europe	$6,033,511	24.8
Germany [8]	56,579	.2
Russian satellite countries	319,840	1.3
Russia	252,450	.1

The exports of American books to overseas markets in 1948 declined about 20 percent from 1947 total. The United States Department of Commerce estimates the dollar volume of sales abroad last year at approximately $19,000,000. The prospect for a reversal of this downward trend in book distribution abroad is not regarded as good so long as the present restrictions on dollar exchange obtain in most of the countries of the world.

The question here, as with the other media of the press, is whether the book industry should not realize the importance of the contribution it could make to the job abroad and, accordingly, again set up an organization, a "chosen instrument," to do that job.

5. The Basic Issue

In all four fields—news agencies, newspapers and magazines, motion pictures, and books—the basic issue is the same. It is the issue of whether those who control these media will recognize and assume their responsibility abroad.

Even though it has been said before in this book, it should be said again: that the American press when it operates abroad is in effect doing a propaganda job, as well as undertaking a commercial venture; that there is too little appreciation of the fact that Europe is an ideological battleground. Private information organizations should not see Paris in terms of Chicago, or Rome in terms of New York. Once they leave our shores, our newspapers, magazines and films are more than newspapers, magazines and films; they are representatives of America.

Private enterprise should develop an increased awareness of

its international responsibility, an awareness that would result in better news, better movies, better books in Europe. And it must jealously guard against distortion.

Finally, the efforts of private enterprise should complement the government's efforts—and *vice versa*. Only this kind of teamwork can wipe out the areas of ignorance abroad about American ways, American motives and American policy—and, unless they are wiped out, our whole program will be injured immeasurably.

Chapter 20 Notes

1. See p. x, *Public Opinion and Foreign Policy*.
2. Kent Cooper, *Barriers Down*, New York, Farrar & Rinehart, 1942, p. 9.
3. Includes circulation among U. S. military personnel as well as among foreign civilians.
4. The first agreements under this provision were announced in December, 1948.
5. Allied Artists, Columbia, Loew's, Paramount, RKO, Twentieth Century-Fox, United Artists, Universal-International, Warner Brothers and Republic Pictures. All these except United Artists are also members of the Motion Picture Association.
6. See Chapter Ten, 199-200, *Public Opinion and Foreign Policy*.
7. Yearly exports as reported by the U. S. Department of Commerce, *not including mail shipments*, were:

	To Canada	To all countries
1938	$2,130,476	$ 5,219,314
1944	5,009,350	8,676,382
1945	5,762,525	11,605,243
1946	7,644,416	19,406,101
1947	9,701,363	24,294,851

8. The German figures do not include American books distributed through such governmental agencies as the Department of the Army, the Department of State and the Library of Congress. For the fiscal year 1948, $785,000 was allotted to the Department of the Army for the purchase of American books.

Part IV

THE EVALUATION OF PROPAGANDA EFFECTS

THE EFFECTIVENESS of propaganda activity, even when directed toward so specific and short-range a goal as surrender among enemy troops, is difficult to evaluate. The problem becomes more complicated as propaganda is integrated with the other instruments of policy in the successful achievement of wider goals. What relative weight shall we assign to psychological warfare—as compared with military operations, industrial production, diplomatic negotiation—in winning a war? Victory is clearly a very complex "effect," the outcome of a large number and variety of activities convoked to a common purpose.

The first step in evaluating effects achieved is clarity about effects desired. Such clarity begins with recognition that the general purpose of all propaganda is redistribution of power in the audience—as, indeed, this is the general purpose of all political activity. The distinctive aspect of propaganda is its mode of operation: propaganda alone, among the tools of policy, alters power-relevant behavior by modifying attitudes through manipulation of symbols. The symbols manipulated are mainly those of identification and expectation, and the behavior elicited consists of revised demands on self and others. The elaboration of these propositions is the subject of Lerner's chapter on a perspective for evaluating effectiveness.

Such a perspective calls for configurative analysis of concrete propaganda situations. The chapter drawn from the Strategic Bombing Survey specifies "some social and psychological factors in morale," with a clear view of the multidimensional context in which behavior actually occurs. The Shils-Janowitz chapter analyzes data on *Wehrmacht* morale with respect to key variables in primary group behavior, thereby providing a valuable case-study of a propaganda campaign whose purpose was "disintegration."

The Padover-Gittler-Sweet report on Aachen was probably the most important single document produced by Psychological Warfare field intelligence during World War II. Its arrival at SHAEF occasioned initial shock and subsequent re-examination of our operations, both in psychological warfare and military government. Although written under the stress of war conditions in a combat zone, it is here reproduced precisely in its original form. It serves as a vivid demonstration of how evaluation on a current basis can redirect propaganda activity—if made within the context that propaganda aims at redistribution of power and with a keen sense of the power-relevant effects desired.

The chapter by Herz applies such a perspective to an appraisal of the gigantic leaflet operation in War II. Warburg gives a rapid survey of effects achieved in all the main theaters of war, bearing in mind the relation of propaganda to other policy instruments. The chapter by Speier concludes the volume by reconsidering the past as a guide to the future of psychological warfare.

Chapter 21

EFFECTIVE PROPAGANDA: CONDITIONS AND EVALUATION

By

DANIEL LERNER

GOEBBELS ONCE said: "Propaganda has no policy, it has a purpose." In this way the ingenious obscurantist emphasized that propaganda is the tool, not the master, of policy. A less cynical, more accurate way to make the point is this: Propaganda always has some policy. The policy probably will not be made by propagandists, and it probably will not remain forever the same. Since policy is the sequence of governing decisions in any body politic, it is likely to fluctuate through time as changing conditions alter issues and modify alternatives. Although its policy may shift, however, the purpose of propaganda remains constant: to serve that policy with maximum effectiveness.

The problem under discussion is how we can evaluate the effectiveness of propaganda activity in world politics. We state the view that reliable evaluation requires clarity on: (1) the nature of policy goals; (2) the function of propaganda, along with the other instruments of policy, in promoting these goals; (3) the conditions essential for effective propaganda; (4) the effects which propaganda can be designed to achieve; (5) the canons of evidence by which the actual achievement of these effects can be estimated. Under these five heads we review briefly some central problems in the evaluation of recent and current propaganda experience.

The Nature of Policy Goals

Policy is a sequence of decisions governing the behavior of a person, group, nation, or world body politic. The policymakers of any community, however large or small, are those whose

344

decisions enunciate the continuing goals, stakes, and rules-of-the-game which are observed by all members in good standing of the community. The scope of such decisions is conditioned by various characteristics of the particular body politic, notably the stability of its long-range goals; and by various characteristics of its environment, notably the threats and dangers to stability.

Long-range goals are affirmations of ultimate and mediate purposes of life in the body politic. As such, they are inevitably formulated in resonant symbols of ambiguous reference: liberty, equality, fraternity, peace, security, salvation, abundance, democracy, enlightenment, A World Commonwealth of Human Dignity. Ambiguity is inevitable because such words are historical in their origin and career. As the particular circumstances which generated them are modified through time, the contents of these symbols change. The task of policy is continually to respecify their operational meaning so that the vision of the future which these symbols embody may survive the changing needs and demands of present events. One policy function, then, is to maintain the stability of long-range goals by overcoming threats and dangers in the current environment.

Such threats and dangers may be internal to the community, e.g., the effort of a special group to seize disproportionate shares of the public power. Or it may be external, e.g., the attempt of a rival community to impose its own decisions by force. Faced with such threats and dangers, policymaking consists of choosing among the available alternatives those present actions most likely to enhance the long-range goals of the community.

The Propaganda Function

The actions among which policymakers must choose involve two different, but interrelated, kinds of activity: saying and doing. A fundamental fact which has been inadequately articulated is that talking *is* acting. Talking, indeed, is the way of acting which probably occupies the greatest part of our lives. Yet, "mere talk" is often deprecated by such phrases as "talk is cheap." In American society, particularly, "action" is equated with *doing* and is over-valued at the expense of talking. This preference, however, is more enlightening as part of the cultural folklore than as a description of typical American behavior. Here as elsewhere, the most effective action is that which integrates words and deeds to a common purpose.

In the arena of world politics, which directly concerns us here, policy uses four instruments to achieve its goals: propaganda, diplomacy, economics, war. These dominate, respectively, in strategies of persuasion, negotiation, bargaining, and coercion. Their respective vehicles are symbols, contracts, commodities, and violence.

Of the four, persuasion is undoubtedly the most pervasive mode of political intercourse. It is essential to the effective function of the others, in war as in peace. If the "party of the second part" is sufficiently persuaded by one's symbols, then the negotiation of diplomatic contracts becomes easier or unnecessary. Also, there is not much use applying economic sanctions unless you make clear why the other community is being deprived of commodities and what it can do to remove such semi-coercive measures. The same is true with even greater urgency when violence is employed, which explains why no war is fought without some declaration of "war aims" to clarify the conditions under which peaceful relations may be restored.

These remarks indicate the distinctive function of propaganda in the service of policy. The policy function, we have said, is to promote by present actions the attainment of goals in the future. War, economics, and even diplomacy serve this purpose by operations upon the material environment. The propaganda function is to advance policy goals by manipulating the symbolic environment. What people *believe about* the future shapes their responses to present events. And it is these beliefs about the future—the *structure of expectations*—which propaganda attempts to modify on behalf of policy goals.

Some Conditions of Effective Propaganda

The manipulation of expectations is an instrument with powerful uses, but also with definite limits. The uses will be better served if the limits are clearly understood. The fundamental limitation is inherent in the instrument: its strategy is *persuasion* and its vehicle is *symbols*. Propaganda does not change *conditions* but only *beliefs about* conditions; it cannot force people to change their beliefs but can only persuade them to do so.

Under what conditions are people most likely to be persuaded by symbols to modify their expectations of the future, and consequently their behavior in the present? This question is in need of systematic investigation. Several main points are clear, however, from recent experience. We may summarize these lessons by stating four essential conditions of effective propaganda:

(1) The *attention* of the audience must be secured.
(2) The *credence* of the audience must be secured.
(3) The *predispositions* of the audience must include the modifications sought by propaganda as plausible alternatives to present expectations.
(4) The *environment* of the audience must permit the courses of action prescribed by the modified structure of expectations.

These conditions seem obvious upon statement. To persuade a man to do what you tell him, you must first get him to listen to you. Once you have his attention, you must get him to believe what you say if he is to take your message seriously. His credence gained, what you tell him to believe must be within the realm of his existing predispositional structure of expectations and aspirations. It is a waste of words to try to persuade a loyal citizen that he would rather see his nation lose a war than win it; no such alternative preference is possible within his predispositional set. But it may be quite possible to persuade the same man, once you have his attention and credence, to believe that the nation is going to lose a war.

Such a modification of expectations by propaganda may be facilitated by focussing attention on other existing aspirations in the audience, e.g., by pointing out that such long-range goals as world peace or national dignity will be better served by ending the war now in defeat than by prolonging it in vain efforts to achieve victory. On the other hand, policy may require propaganda to make no concessions to audience aspirations— e.g., unconditional surrender. Whether or not audience aspirations are invoked to help modify audience expectations constitutes a policy decision of great importance for the propagandist. What we wish to emphasize here, however, is that, whether audience aspirations are explicitly respected or implicitly rejected, predispositions define the limits within which audiences can be effectively persuaded to modify their expectations.

A fourth condition of effective propaganda is that the actions required of the audience by their modified expectations should be feasible in the environing circumstances which define for them the limits of meaningful behavior. It would make no sense, for example, to call on Soviet citizens in Vladivostok (even if we had persuaded them to believe that their present regime was headed for disaster and that their future happiness depended on its removal) to assassinate Stalin or imprison the Politburo. In the environment which limits their feasible alternatives of behavior, propaganda which called for such action would not be meaningful. Indeed, the impracticability of such action might lead to the utter rejection of our statements, otherwise plausible, because they impose obligations impossible to fulfill. (See chapter 24, page 416.)

What types of action, then, *can* propaganda require of audiences whom it has persuaded?

Typical Aims of Propaganda

The aims of propaganda always include audience actions which alter the distribution of power in ways advantageous to the policy of the propagandist. Propaganda does aim, as most current writers claim, to "change attitudes" (modify expectations, in our terminology). But this is only the means by which propaganda gets to its ultimate aim of influencing behavior. It would be of small consequence, for example, that the Voice of America persuaded some Russians that Americans are peace-loving democracies rather than imperialistic warmongers, if this changed attitude (expectation about our future behavior) made no difference in the behavior of these Russians now or in the future.

It is important to recognize that the behavioral consequences of modified expectations need not appear immediately. Indeed some of the most important consequences of any attitude-alterations appear only in the longer-range future. Propaganda adjusts the timing of the behavioral consequences it seeks to the short-range or long-range aims of its policy goals.

What are some of these aims toward which propaganda is typically directed? Dr. Hans Speier has distinguished five "natural aims" of propaganda: (1) submission (2) subversion (3) cooperation (4) privatization (5) panic. His elaboration of these categories demonstrates their utility for clarifying the final aims of propaganda activity. They are valuable, too, for evaluating the effectiveness of a particular propaganda campaign when it is concluded.

For current evaluation of ongoing propaganda activity, other schema may be used. Take a simple example:

	Self	Rival
Power		
Purpose		

This fourfold table illustrates a usable framework for the evaluation of current propaganda, before sufficient time has elapsed for the types of overt action categorized by Dr. Speier to have occurred. Suppose the final aim is to secure the *submission* of certain groups within a rival power. Research has shown that there is no doubt of our power among this audience; what keeps them rivalrous is doubt of our purpose. The propaganda task is to persuade these groups that our purpose is virtuous *by their standards*. Evaluation of our propaganda must gauge the value of each item in terms of its effectiveness in strengthening this image of our moral purpose among the audience. This would call for continuous content analysis of both our propaganda output and of audience responses to that output, to indicate whether we are achieving the effects we desire. This is no substitute for the final payoff in action, but a way of continuously reminding ourselves of our goal and of checking whether our current activity is advancing us in the desired direction.

Conversely, suppose our final aim is to activate *subversion* against the rival regime among these groups within its population. The intelligence estimate is that expectations among the audience about *our* power and purpose are irrelevant to this aim. The relevant points are: that these groups are already persuaded that our rival's purpose is immoral, that their action is delayed only by their fears that the power of the rival regime is too great against their own means. (In such a situation, our policy may use other instruments besides propaganda, e.g., sanctions which deprive the rival regime of essential power-com-

modities while we increase the means of the subversive group.)
The main propaganda aim in such a situation, however, would
be to position the subversive group and the rival regime as
Self: Other (removing the irrelevant propagandist power from
the scene); and then to increase the confidence of the subversive
group in its own power, relative to the regime, to the point
where subversive action takes place. Such action, as Dr. Speier
properly emphasizes, is the payoff in terms of which effectiveness must finally be evaluated. A campaign of this sort may take
years, however, and some running measure of current effectiveness is needed during the long period before the payoff point
is reached.

This simple schema can be refined and complicated as required to provide categories relevant to the content of our
propaganda output and of audience affects. It is one among
several that can be used to evaluate propaganda activity on a
current basis. The point we wish to emphasize here is that eval-
ution of propaganda effects achieved requires, first, a framework
which embodies a correct perspective on the effects desired.
Next it requires rather strict canons of evidence by which to
test the effects achieved. To illustrate the needs, we review
briefly the methods used to evaluate on a current basis the effectiveness of Allied psychological warfare against the Germans
in World War II (Sykewar).

Types of Evidence on Effects *

Four general types of evidence are usually adduced to show
that propaganda has, or has not, been effective: (1) responsive
action; (2) participant reports; (3) observer commentaries; (4)
indirect indicators. All of these postulate, logically, that propaganda output and effects constitute a stimulus-response situation from which conclusions must be *inferred*. The four types
of evidence named above are arranged, methodologically, in increasing remoteness from the concrete stimulus-response situation, i.e., in increasing length of the inference from propaganda
stimulus to propaganda effect. Unfortunately, evidence usually
grows more abundant as remoteness increases. This becomes
clear as we briefly characterize each in turn.

* This section is adapted from the author's book entitled *Sykewar: Psychological Warfare Against Germany, D-Day to VE-Day* (1949), pp. 289-301.

(1) *Responsive action* is behavior which can more plausibly be attributed to propaganda stimuli than to any other stimuli in the environment. In the ideal case, a 1:1 ratio can be established: e.g., immediate surrender of German troops precisely as directed by a combat loudspeaker broadcast. More often, the inference from propaganda stimulus to audience response must cross a wider gap, but the crossing still can be made with confidence: e.g., Sykewar output directed Frankfurt citizens to hang white flags from their windows and thereafter American troops arrived to find many white flags hanging. Since these flags corresponded in detail with Sykewar instructions, and since no other source gave similar instructions, it could safely be inferred that this was direct responsive action.

Such evidence, though desirable, is rare. It requires, also, analysts trained to avoid two logical fallacies. We must avoid, first, the pitfall of assuming (*post hoc propter hoc*) that any action which conforms to the directive stimulus is a response, i.e., that an action is an effect simply because it happens after a stimulus. Second, the fallacy of displaced inference must be avoided: e.g., that Frankfurt residents hung out white flags as directed properly leads to an inference that *this particular response* was stimulated by a particular propaganda stimulus; it does not lead to any conclusion (except as one item in a distribution) that this or any other propaganda acts did or did not *change Frankfurt attitudes toward surrender*. There may have been *no* change in such attitudes—i.e., those who hung white flags in 1945 may have been ready to do so in 1940. Or, whatever change did occur may have been stimulated by other acts —i.e., bombing, rationing, news of a son's death on the eastern front. This second caution in evaluating the evidence of responsive action is particularly important because so much propaganda activity, especially of the sort called "strategic" (rather than "tactical"), aims at long-range behavioral effects attained by repetition, attrition, and the gradual modification of predispositions.

(2) *Participant reports* on propaganda effects by the persons stimulated constitute a less reliable kind of evidence than responsive action. No verbal report on one's own private responses can be quite as conclusive as observable action in the public domain. For, it is clear, a person's report on his internal behavior frequently—whether by mechanisms beyond his con-

trol or by design—misrepresents what actually went on inside. When such participant reports are treated as indexes they may be quite useful, as is shown by the study of trends in *Wehrmacht* morale (chapter 9).

The caution to be observed in handling such data, after their reliability has been established within reasonable limits of confidence, is that *indexes to* morale are *not identical with* morale. An inference is required, and the inference must account for relevant variables which determine whether a given "attitude" will in fact lead to a given "action." To illustrate with one index that was used by evaluators of both German and Japanese morale in the recent war: Diminished loyalty to the leader will be sufficient motivation for some soldiers to surrender; it will be necessary but not sufficient for others; for still others it will have little or no bearing on the readiness to surrender. The analyst must have the relevant variables isolated, and accounted for, when he undertakes to *infer* future actions (such as surrender) from present indexes (such as loyalty to the leader) in particular cases.

(3) *Observer commentaries,* though made by witnesses to the presumed stimulus-response situation, are notoriously treacherous. The stock illustration of danger inherent in such testimony is the case of the six witnesses to an automobile accident who, when asked to report what they had seen, gave six candid and circumstantial and confident—*and contrary*—versions of the event.

The tests applicable to data from observer commentaries are the reliability and heterogeneity of sources. Each source is tested separately for *reliability*—and approved when past information it supplied has regularly been accurate, disapproved when it has not. (Ideally in large intelligence operations, sources should be ranked on a calibrated scale of reliability, to enable all analysts to assign identical weightings and thus objectify "confidence.") All sources together are tested for *heterogeneity*—which is a function of their number, variety and independence. This test postulates that the probability of accuracy for any specific item reported increases with the *number* of *different* sources which *independently* report it as accurate.

(4) *Indirect indicators* are measures of effectiveness which are not at all involved in the particular stimulus-response situation being evaluated. Such a measure, for example, might be

a high correlation between increasing size of audience to a propaganda source and increasing frequency of reference to this source among other audience channels of information. The analysis of audience communications is generally a fertile source of data on effectiveness, and particularly when such refined and precise techniques as Content Analysis are employed. Both the uses to be made of such data, and the cautions to be observed in gathering and analyzing them, are stated clearly in our study of German propaganda to France (chapter 10).

In Conclusion

Propaganda is effective when it modifies audience behavior in ways advantageous to the policy it serves. Policy goals thus define one set of limits for propaganda activity—by postulating what is *desirable*. Another set of limits is defined by audience predispositions—which determine what is *possible*. Propaganda strategy manipulates the terrain bounded by these policy and audience considerations. The propagandist's maxim must be: Know thy goals: know thy conditions.

For the main conditions given the propagandist—i.e., that aspect of the current political situation with which he is most directly concerned—are the predispositions of his audience. What we here call predispositions, psychologists at other times have called attitudes, instincts, motivations. The term used is less important than clarity about its operational meaning. Our point is that the propagandist works upon the identifications and expectations of the audience in order to modify their demands and deeds in desired directions. Whatever names one chooses, we must be clear that the propagandist is concerned with that part of man's psyche which controls his behavior.

The reason: to make a man *do* what he says, the propagandist must persuade that man to *believe* what he says. Belief is always, in some degree, a function of desire. Hence the propagandist is concerned with the desires of his audience and their possible modification. Effective propaganda consists in persuading the audience to *want to do* that which the propagandist wants them to do. For this, more than skilful chicanery is needed. Lincoln's aphorism is still relevant: You can't fool all of the people all of the time. Any long-run view of propaganda effectiveness postulates that audience desires must be understood and respected; often indeed, when they cannot be altered, these desires must be granted.

It is in such cases that the intelligence function serves policy. Properly conceived, intelligence is the continuous evaluation of the effectiveness with which our propaganda modifies conditions (including audience predispositions) in behalf of goals. Intelligence in this sense is indispensable to both policy and propaganda. Its findings should form the basis on which our formulation of goals and our propaganda strategy are continuously revised in the light of our knowledge of changing conditions. Not only audience predispositions, but also our own predispositions, are variables in the continuing process of world politics. Democratic wisdom begins with the recognition that policy can not do more—and should not do less—than the *most* of what is possible with the *least* sacrifice of what is desirable. Nothing less than this provides an adequate perspective for talking about propaganda effectiveness.

Chapter 22

SOCIAL AND PSYCHOLOGICAL FACTORS
AFFECTING MORALE *

By
USSBS MORALE DIVISION

NOT ALL GERMANS subjected to bombing were willing to give
up. A thorough-going analysis of the effectiveness of bombing
must explore the reasons why this is so. Who were these people
who were willing to keep going to the very end? What sort of
opinions and ideas did they have? Were they altogether immune
to the effects of bombing?

Among the factors which made the morale of some individuals higher than that of others, personal identification with the
Nazi cause was by all odds the most important. Other psychological characteristics which were related to high morale were
continuing belief in the adequacy of defense measures, a sense
of vested interest in German victory, belief in V-weapons, and a
tendency not to be apprehensive of the future. These results do
not mean that the morale of persons with such characteristics
was invulnerable to bombing. Nazis, for example, actually
showed depressed morale as a result of bombing more frequently than others; but their initial morale was so much
higher that bombing was insufficient to bring it down to the
level of the non-Nazis. It was found, however, that fear and
terror in the presence of bombing bore no relation to the practically more important aspects of morale, such as willingness
to surrender. The persons who became extremely frightened
were no more willing to give up than were those who remained
calm.

* Reprinted from United States Strategic Bombing Survey, *The Effects of
Strategic Bombing on German Morale* I, 33-37 (Government Printing Office,
1947).

Nazi Identification

Level of Morale. Belief in Nazi ideas and the Nazi cause had more influence than any other factor on the morale of the German civilian. It was, in fact, more important than direct bombing experience, for ardent Nazis subjected to heavy bombing retained better morale, as a group, than did non-Nazis who were not bombed at all. This was true for all aspects of morale with the possible exception of the purely emotional reactions of fear and terror brought on by the raids; Nazis seem to have been frightened almost as much as other Germans.

Two indices of Nazi identification were used. The first was simply an admission of membership in the Nazi Party organization, which was subject to possible error on two counts. Some members had joined for bread-and-butter reasons rather than because of belief in Nazi doctrines and, on the other hand, some doubtless failed to admit their membership. Hence a second index was obtained. The interviewers rated each respondent for degree of Nazi identification on the basis of all the information gained during the interview, particularly on the types of Nazi beliefs expressed. For example, a respondent might disclaim adherence to Nazi ideas but would go on to remark that it was nice to have a good Aryan people like the Americans as an occupying force.

Twenty percent of the sample admitted that they were members of some Nazi organization, exclusive of the Hitler Youth

TABLE 1

MEDIAN MORALE INDEX B

	Heavy bombing	Medium bombing	Light bombing	Un-bombed
Nazi party members......	32.5	29.5	31.5	31.5
Nonmembers	29.0	27.8	28.7	30.7
Difference	3.5	1.7	2.8	0.8
Ideological Nazis	36.5	35.0	36.2	38.8
Non-Nazis	26.5	26.8	28.4	29.0
Difference	10.0	8.2	7.8	9.8

High scores mean high morale on morale index B.

groups. Ten percent were identified as ideological Nazis, 57 percent as non-Nazis, and 33 percent as falling between.

Tables 1–4 furnish examples of the consistently higher Nazi morale on a few of the morale measures. All other measures tell essentially the same story, with the minor qualification already noted that the differences in the percentage of Nazis and non-Nazis expressing fear under bombing are on the whole unreliable, even though these differences show the same trend as those on other measures of morale.

TABLE 2

PERCENT WILLING TO SURRENDER

	Heavy bombing	Medium bombing	Light bombing	Un-bombed
Nazi party members.......	43	49	38	37
Nonmembers	60	57	50	53
Difference	17	8	12	16
Ideological Nazis	20	30	12	14
Non-Nazis	65	53	57	65
Difference	45	33	45	51

In the tables of this chapter the base of the percentages is the number of people falling in each cell. For example, in table 2, 43 percent of *Nazi Party members who were heavily bombed* said they were willing to surrender. Sixty percent of *nonmembers heavily bombed* were willing to surrender, etc.

TABLE 3

PERCENT REPORTING WAR WEARINESS

	Heavy bombing	Medium bombing	Light bombing
Nazi party members	73	76	53
Nonmembers	73	73	63
Difference *	0	(3)-	10
Ideological Nazis	42	42	37
Non-Nazis	76	79	65
Difference	34	37	28

* Difference in parentheses is in direction opposite from expectation.

TABLE 4

PERCENT EXPRESSING INTENSE FEAR OF BOMBING

	Heavy bombing	Medium bombing	Light bombing
Ideological Nazis	32	38	29
Non-Nazis	42	40	35
Difference	10	2	6

It is evident from these tables that the classification of Nazis on the basis of ideology brings out greater morale differences than classification by party membership. This is consistently true.

The Effects of Bombing on Nazis

As already indicated, the consistently higher morale of Nazis should not be interpreted as meaning that they were invulnerable to the effects of bombing. Tables 1–4 bear out the statement that bombing had its effects on Nazi morale. Each of these measures shows a falling off, with the possible exception of the party member category in Table 1, when unbombed are compared with heavily bombed. There are 27 morale measures on which it is possible to compare the drop in morale for Nazis and non-Nazis. In 16 of the 27 measures the differences between bombed and unbombed Nazis were greater than similar differences for non-Nazis.

The morale measures on which Nazis showed a greater morale drop than non-Nazis include, among others, willingness to surrender (schedule B), time lost from work, fear and depression, apathy and fatigue, a feeling that the respondent suffered more personally than others, interference with work routine because of loss of sleep.

Belief in Adequacy of Defensive Measures

On the whole, people who felt that the air-raid shelters, anti-aircraft, and post-raid measures were inadequate had lower morale than the civilians who thought these measures adequate. Again, bombing served to bring the satisfied and dissatisfied groups closer together by lowering the morale of those who considered defensive measures adequate. Increased bombing lowered morale more among individuals who felt everything possible was being done than among those dissatisfied with defensive measures. Perhaps people satisfied with the steps taken to protect them found the situation all the more hopeless under heavy air attack. Since, in their eyes, everything possible was being done, the psychological impact of the raids was all the greater.

TABLE 5

BELIEF IN ADEQUACY OF DEFENSIVE MEASURES AND MORALE

	Median morale index (A)		
	Heavy bombing	Medium bombing	Light bombing
ARP unsatisfactory	31.1	32.7	30.6
Everything possible was done	29.0	28.7	22.5
Difference	2.1	4.0	8.1
Dissatisfied with shelters	30.3	31.6	29.5
Satisfied with shelters	30.0	29.5	27.8
Difference	0.3	2.1	1.7
Ack-ack inadequate	31.1	31.5	29.5
Ack-ack adequate	29.0	28.4	27.0
Difference	2.1	3.1	2.5
Post-raid services unsatisfactory	30.6	30.9	31.0
Post-raid services good	29.7	30.0	27.8
Difference	0.9	0.9	3.2

High scores indicate low morale on index A.

The question inevitably arises whether this apparent relation of morale to belief in adequacy of defense is real or whether it occurs because Nazis, who have the highest morale, are disposed to avoid criticism of defensive measures provided by the government. The relation turns out to have meaning, for the differences demonstrated persist when the results are analyzed separately for those with Nazi ideology and those with other views.

Vested Interest in German Victory

German morale was influenced not only by Nazi conviction and by belief in the adequacy of counter-measures, but also by a sense of vested interest in German victory. The Nazi Propaganda Ministry did its best to exaggerate the community of interest and the common fate of the German people. Some Germans, however, realized they had much more to gain from victory than others, and there were those who felt they would be benefited by an Allied victory. This feeling of vested interest was ascertained by asking people how they would have fared if the Germans had won the war, and how they expected to get along under Allied occupation.

Those who felt they would have fared better under a German victory than under Allied occupation were classified as having a vested interest in German victory. Those who felt they would have fared worse under German victory than under Allied occupation were classified as having a vested interest in Allied victory. Civilians showing the greatest vested interest in German victory maintained their morale in many cases until the end of the war (tables 6 and 7). Bombing, however, did produce some war weariness and defeatism, even in this highly motivated group. The effect of bombing upon the opposite group (those who thought they would be better off if the Allies won) was less clear-cut. It led to war weariness earlier in the war, but it did not increase the proportion of people wanting unconditional surrender.

TABLE 6

PERCENT WILLING TO SURRENDER UNCONDITIONALLY

	Heavy bombing	Medium bombing	Light bombing	Un-bombed
Vested interest in German victory	31	31	25	13
Vested interest in Allied victory	62	65	65	68
Difference	31	34	40	55

Again, it has been found that the fact of having a vested interest in German victory is not the same as Nazi identification, for its relation to morale persists when Nazis are excluded.

TABLE 7

MEDIAN TIME AT WHICH INDIVIDUALS NO LONGER WANTED
TO GO ON WITH THE WAR

	Heavy bombing	Medium bombing	Light bombing	Un-bombed
Vested interest in German victory	Oct. 1944	May 1945	Sept. 1944	May 1945
Vested interest in Allied victory	Mar. 1943	June 1943	Feb. 1943	Jan. 1945
Difference (in months)	19	23	19	4

Belief in V-weapons

Great hopes were pinned on the development of V-weapons by certain parts of the German population. This was commented on by various official reports such as that from the security police in Braunschweig in 1944:

> The hopes of further secret weapons are after all the only factor having a positive effect on morale. Everything which propaganda sets forth concerning the new weapon is received and discussed with burning interest.

The analysis of interview material reveals that persons who accepted the propaganda on this subject were on the whole a high morale group.

TABLE 8

MEDIAN SCORE ON MORALE INDEX B

	Heavy bombing	Medium bombing	Light bombing	Un-bombed
Great belief in V-weapons	32.2	33.1	33.8	36.0
Complete rejection	26.3	26.2	27.2	27.6
Difference	5.9	6.9	6.6	8.4

High scores indicate high morale.

TABLE 9

PERCENT WILLING TO SURRENDER

	Heavy bombing	Medium bombing	Light bombing	Un-bombed
Great belief in V-weapons	46	36	32	30
Complete rejection	79	64	54	70
Difference	33	28	22	40

It is doubtless true that belief in V-weapons depended to some extent on acceptance of Nazi claims in general or on some more general factor of morale. It was not, therefore, altogether a cause of high morale but was in part a result of it. There is evidence, however, that the acceptance of this belief did operate to affect morale attitudes as long as the belief persisted, for 5 percent of the sample mentioned spontaneously that failure of the V-weapons to materialize made them believe Germany would lose, and of those respondents who never reached the point of wanting to give up, 4 percent gave as their reasons the hope for the new weapons.

Fear and Sensitivity

Some of the individual differences in morale which relate to beliefs, attitudes, and motives are in part a reflection of deeply-lying personality characteristics. No completely adequate measures of personality were possible in the cross-sectional study but there were inquiries yielding information on objectively produced fear and sensitivity on the one hand, and about subjective fear on the other.

Objectively produced fear can be distinguished from sensitivity, or subjective fear, in that it grows directly out of terrifying situations and is common to most people, whereas sensitivity relates to subjective processes, to apprehensions and expectations which differ markedly between individuals. The latter is, therefore, more truly a personality trait.

In general, when people were questioned about their emotional experiences during raids, they reported more in terms of objectively produced fear than in terms of subjectively induced fright. The fear experienced during air attacks was not correlated with willingness to surrender or with most of the other aspects of morale. Thirty-six statistical comparisons were made between measures of emotional reaction to bombing and morale attitudes. Only 3 of the 36 indicated any relationship between fear and the various dimensions of morale. Thus, for example, the frightened in this sense are no more willing to give up than are those reporting no fear. As already suggested, this was also true of Nazis. No matter how strong the identification with Nazi ideas, the sheer objective terror of an air raid produced fear in the individual experiencing it. The immediate effect of the experience was very much the same for all, regardless of other aspects of morale. Table 10 illustrates the absence of a relationship between degree of fear and willingness to surrender.

TABLE 10

PERCENT WILLING TO SURRENDER

	Heavy bombing	Medium bombing	Light bombing
Intense fear	21	82	58
Little or no fear	55	58	46

The same phenomenon has been observed in battle, where men with good behavioral morale will experience fear under terrifying circumstances almost as much as men who run away. It is not so much whether people become frightened as what they do about it that affects the outcome.

When, however, subjective fear or sensitivity was studied indirectly through queries about people's apprehensions, a relation was found between morale and timidity. German civilians were asked about the expectation that their lives would be upset by the war. The apprehensive people, who felt the war would seriously affect their lives, had poorer morale than their stolid countrymen who had not anticipated the trials of war and air attacks. Anticipation, instead of helping to cushion the shock, proved to be a symptom, like worry, related to poor morale.

On the other hand, the apprehensive are not consistently more susceptible to the effects of bombing than are more stolid persons. On some measures, as in the first portion of table 12, they show even less consistent decline in morale as a result of bombing than do the less apprehensive.

TABLE 11

PERCENT WILLING TO SURRENDER

	Heavy bombing	Medium bombing	Light bombing	Un- bombed
Expected life to be upset	62	56	47	50
Did not so expect	51	52	45	44
Difference	11	4	2	6

TABLE 12

PERCENT BELIEVING LEADERS DID NOT HAVE PEOPLE'S INTERESTS AT HEART

	Heavy bombing	Medium bombing	Light bombing	Un- bombed
Expected life to be upset	46	48	39	39
Did not so expect	33	37	32	22
Difference	13	11	7	17
Thought a great deal about war	43	47	34	31
Did not think much about war	31	36	45	25
Difference	12	11	(11)	6

Table 12 also shows that the passive or stolid individuals who thought little about the war had higher morale than their more imaginative colleagues. Bombing lowered the morale of both groups, but in this case those who thought a great deal about the war were slightly more affected, when the unbombed are compared to the heavily bombed.

Socioeconomic Status

Socioeconomic status was determined from the information regarding education and occupation of the respondent.

The most striking result of the analysis of morale by socioeconomic status is the consistently lower morale revealed by the people with low status. This is true of all morale measures analyzed and at all levels of bombing. Since this group starts with such low morale even when unbombed, the drop with increased bombing is relatively slight. In the other higher status groups there is a marked drop in morale with increased bombing.

TABLE 13

PERCENT WILLING TO SURRENDER

	Heavy bombing	Medium bombing	Light bombing	Un- bombed
High status	55	59	38	33
Middle status	58	53	51	48
Low status	63	62	61	61

However, these differences do not persist when degree of Nazi identification is controlled. Nazi identification and high socioeconomic status tended to be identified to such an extent that the apparent effects of the latter were wholly due to the higher morale of the Nazis.

Religious Affiliation [1]

On all but one measure of morale analyzed, Protestants showed slightly higher morale than Catholics. On this one measure (morale index B) there was no difference.

TABLE 14

PERCENT WILLING TO SURRENDER

	Heavy bombing	Medium bombing	Light bombing	Un- bombed
Catholic	66	63	73	57
Protestant	54	51	48	52

Other Individual Differences

A number of other variables were examined and found without effect on morale. Notable among those which showed no consistent effects were age, sex,[2] and marital status. Region is shown to be an important factor in morale in chapter 1 of volume II.

Chapter 22. Notes

1. See further reference to the role of the church in ch. 7, pt. II, vol. I, and to religious activity in ch. 1, vol. II.

2. In ch. 2, vol. II it is reported that women showed greater loss in morale than men. The index used there is based chiefly on emotional components of morale. In the civilian interview material women showed about the same loss as men on measures of willingness to surrender. The markedly greater loss in the study of captured mail is probably due to the fact that the morale measure there is based on emotional components; that, in other words, women's emotional reactions were more affected by bombing than those of men, but not their attitudes toward surrender.

Chapter **23**

COHESION AND DISINTEGRATION
IN THE WEHRMACHT *

By

EDWARD A. SHILS AND MORRIS JANOWITZ

I. The Army as a Social Group

THIS STUDY is an attempt to analyze the relative influence of
primary and secondary group situations on the high degree of
stability of the German Army in World War II. It also seeks to
evaluate the impact of the Western Allies' propaganda on the
German Army's fighting effectiveness.[1]

Although distinctly outnumbered and in a strategic sense
quantitatively inferior in equipment, the German Army, on all
fronts, maintained a high degree of organizational integrity
and fighting effectiveness through a series of almost unbroken
retreats over a period of several years. In the final phase, the
German armies were broken into unconnected segments, and
the remnants were overrun as the major lines of communication and command were broken. Nevertheless, resistance
which was more than token resistance on the part of most
divisions continued until they were overpowered or overrun in a way which, by breaking communication lines, prevented individual battalions and companies from operating
in a coherent fashion. Disintegration through desertion was
insignificant, while active surrender, individually or in groups,
remained extremely limited throughout the entire Western
campaign.

In one sense the German High Command effected as complete a defense of the "European Fortress" as its own leadership
qualities and the technical means at its disposal permitted.
Official military analyses, including General Eisenhower's re-

* Reprinted from *Public Opinion Quarterly* (Summer 1948).

port, have shown that lack of manpower, equipment, and transportation, as well as certain strategical errors, were the limiting factors.[2] There was neither complete collapse nor internally organized effort to terminate hostilities, such as signalized the end of the first world war.

This extraordinary tenacity of the German Army has frequently been attributed to the strong National Socialist political convictions of the German soldiers. It is the main hypothesis of this paper, however, that the unity of the German Army was in fact sustained only to a very slight extent by the National Socialist political convictions of its members, and that more important in the motivation of the determined resistance of the German soldier was the steady satisfaction of certain *primary* personality demands afforded by the social organization of the army.

This basic hypothesis may be elaborated in the following terms.

1. It appears that a soldier's ability to resist is a function of the capacity of his immediate primary group (his squad or section) to avoid social disintegration. When the individual's immediate group, and its supporting formations, met his basic organic needs, offered him affection and esteem from both officers and comrades, supplied him with a sense of power and adequately regulated his relations with authority, the element of self-concern in battle, which would lead to disruption of the effective functioning of his primary group, was minimized.

2. The capacity of the primary group to resist disintegration was dependent on the acceptance of political, ideological, and cultural symbols (all secondary symbols) only to the extent that these secondary symbols became directly associated with primary gratifications.

3. Once disruption of primary group life resulted through separation, breaks in communications, loss of leadership, depletion of personnel, or major and prolonged breaks in the supply of food and medical care, such an ascendancy of preoccupation with physical survival developed that there was very little "last-ditch" resistance.

4. Finally, as long as the primary group structure of the component units of the Wehrmacht persisted, attempts by the Allies to cause disaffection by the invocation of secondary and political symbols (e.g., about the ethical wrongfulness of the

National Socialist system) were mainly unsuccessful. By contrast, where Allied propaganda dealt with primary and personal values, particularly physical survival, it was more likely to be effective.

Long before D-Day in Western France, research was undertaken in the United Kingdom and North Africa on these social psychological aspects of the enemy's forces. These studies were continued after D-Day by the Intelligence Section of the Psychological Warfare Division of SHAEF. Although of course they are subject to many scientific strictures, they provide a groundwork for the evaluation of the experiences of the German soldier and for the analysis of the social organization of the German Army. Methods of collecting data included front line interrogation of prisoners of war (Ps/W) and intensive psychological interviews in rear areas. Captured enemy documents, statements of recaptured Allied military personnel, and the reports of combat observers were also studied. A monthly opinion poll of random samples of large numbers of Ps/W was also undertaken. This paper is based on a review of all these data.

Modes of Disintegration

Preliminary to the analysis of the function of the primary group in the maintenance of cohesion in the German Army, it is necessary to classify the modes of social disintegration found in any modern army:

1. Desertion (deliberately going over to the enemy lines)
   a) by individual action
      (1) after discussion with comrades
      (2) without prior discussion with others
   b) by groups acting in concert
2. Active surrender (deliberate decision to give up to the enemy as he approaches and taking steps to facilitate capture, e.g., by sending emissaries, by calling out, by signalling, etc.)
   a) by single individuals
   b) by group as a unit
      (1) by mutual agreement
      (2) by order of or with approval of NCO or officer
   c) by plurality of uncoordinated individuals
3. Passive surrender
   a) by individuals acting alone

(1) non-resistance (allowing oneself to be taken prisoner without taking effective steps to facilitate or obstruct capture; passivity may be a means of facilitating surrender)

(2) token resistance (allowing oneself to be taken prisoner with nominal face-saving gestures of obstruction to capture)

b) by plurality of uncoordinated individuals

4. Routine resistance: rote or mechanical, but effective execution of orders as given from above with discontinuance when the enemy becomes overwhelmingly powerful and aggressive

5. "Last-ditch" resistance which ends only with the exhaustion of fighting equipment and subsequent surrender or death. (This type of soldier is greatly underrepresented in studies of samples of Ps/W. Therefore the study of Ps/W alone does not give an adequate picture of the resistive qualities of the German soldier.)

A more detailed description of each of the above classes will be useful in the following analysis:

Desertion involved positive and deliberate action by the German soldier to deliver himself to Allied soldiers for capture by crossing the lines, e.g., by planfully "losing himself" while on patrol and "blundering" into the enemy's area of control or by deliberately remaining behind during a withdrawal from a given position so that when the Allied troops came up they could take him.

In *active surrender* by the group as a unit, the positive act of moving across to enemy lines was absent but there was an element common with desertion in the deliberate attempt to withdraw from further combat. Like many cases of desertion, the decision to surrender as a group was arrived at as a result of group discussion and mutual agreement. The dividing line between active surrender and desertion brought about by lagging behind was shadowy. There were other forms of group surrender which were clearly different from desertion, e.g., the sending of an emissary to arrange terms with the enemy, the refusal to carry out aggressive orders, or to fight a way out of encirclement.

In *passive surrender,* the intention of a soldier to remove himself from the battle was often not clear even to himself.

The soldier who was taken prisoner by passive surrender might have been immobilized or apathetic due to anxiety; he might have been in a state of bewildered isolation and not have thought of passive surrender until the perception of an opportunity brought it to his mind. Non-resistant passive surrender frequently occurred in the case of soldiers who lay in their foxholes or hid in the cellars or barns, sometimes self-narcotized by fear, or sometimes deliberately waiting to be overrun. In both cases, they made only the most limited external gestures of resistance when the enemy approached. In the second type of passive surrender—token resistance—the surrendering soldier desired to avoid all the stigma of desertion or surrender but nevertheless showed reluctance to undertake aggressive or defensive actions which might have interfered with his survival.

An examination of the basic social organization of the German Army, in terms of its primary group structure and the factors which strengthened and weakened its component primary groups, is first required in order to account for the stability and cohesion of resistance, and in order to evaluate the impact of Allied propaganda.

II. The Function of the Primary Group [3]

"The company is the only truly existent community. This community allows neither time nor rest for a personal life. It forces us into its circle, for life is at stake. Obviously compromises must be made and claims be surrended. . . . Therefore the idea of fighting, living, and dying for the fatherland, for the cultural possessions of the fatherland, is but a relatively distant thought. At least it does not play a great role in the practical motivations of the individual." [4]

Thus wrote an idealistic German student in the first world war. A German sergeant, captured toward the end of the second world war, was asked by his interrogators about the political opinions of his men. In reply, he laughed and said, "When you ask such a question, I realize well that you have no idea of what makes a soldier fight. The soldiers lie in their holes and are happy if they live through the next day. If we think at all, it's about the end of the war and then home."

The fighting effectiveness of the vast majority of soldiers in combat depends only to a small extent on their preoccupation with the major political values which might be affected by the outcome of the war and which are the object of concern to statesmen and publicists. There are of course soldiers in whom such motivations are important. Volunteer armies recruited on the basis of ethical or political loyalties, such as the International Brigade in the Spanish Civil War, are affected by their degree of orientation toward major political goals. In the German Army, the "hard core" of National Socialists were similarly motivated.

But in a conscript army, the criterion of recruitment is much less specialized and the army is more representative of the total population liable to conscription. Therefore the values involved in political and social systems or ethical schemes do not have much impact on the determination of a soldier to fight to the best of his ability and to hold out as long as possible. For the ordinary German soldier the decisive fact was that he was a member of a squad or section which maintained its structural integrity and which coincided roughly with the *social* unit which satisfied some of his major primary needs.[5] He was likely to go on fighting, provided he had the necessary weapons, as long as the group possessed leadership with which he could identify himself, and as long as he gave affection to and received affection from the other members of his squad and platoon. In other words, as long as he felt himself to be a member of his primary group and therefore bound by the expectations and demands of its other members, his soldierly achievement was likely to be good.

Modern social research has shown that the primary group is not merely the chief source of affection and accordingly the major factor in personality formation in infancy and childhood. The primary group continues to be the major source of social and psychological sustenance through adulthood.[6] In the army, when isolated from civilian primary groups, the individual soldier comes to depend more and more on his military primary group. His spontaneous loyalties are to its immediate members whom he sees daily and with whom he develops a high degree of intimacy. For the German soldier in particular, the demands of his group, reinforced by officially prescribed rules, had the effect of an external authority. It held his aggressiveness in check; it provided discipline, protection, and freedom from autonomous decision.[7]

Army units with a high degree of primary group integrity suffered little from desertions or from individually contrived surrenders. In the Wehrmacht, desertions and surrenders were most frequent in groups of heterogeneous ethnic composition in which Austrians, Czechs, and Poles were randomly inter-mixed with each other. In such groups the difficulties of linguistic communication, the large amount of individual resentment and aggressiveness about coercion into German service, the weakened support of leadership due to their inability to identify with German officers—all these factors hampered the formation of cohesive groups.

Sample interviews with Wehrmacht deserters made in North Africa in 1943 and in France and Germany in 1944 and 1945 showed an overwhelmingly disproportionate representation of elements which could not be assimilated into primary groups. A total of 443 Wehrmacht Ps/W captured toward the end of the North African campaign, consisting of 180 Germans, 200 Austrians and 63 others (Czechs, Poles, Yugoslavs, etc.), had very markedly different tendencies towards desertion: 29 per cent of the Germans were deserters or potential deserters; 55 per cent of the Austrians fell into these two classes, as did 78 per cent of the Czechs, Poles, and Yugoslavs. Of the 53 German deserters, only one declared that he had "political" motives for desertion. In the Western European campaign, the bulk of the deserters came from among the "Volksdeutsche," [8] Austrians, Poles, and Russians who had been coerced into German military service. It was clear that in view of the apolitical character of most of the deserters, the grounds for their desertion were to be sought among those variables which prevented the formation of close primary group bonds, the chief of which were insuperable language differences, bitter resentment against their coerced condition, and the unfriendliness of the Germans in their units.

Among German deserters, who remained few until the close of the war, the failure to assimilate into the primary group life of the Wehrmacht was the most important factor, more important indeed than political dissidence. Deserters were on the whole men who had difficulty in personal adjustment, e.g., in the acceptance of affection or in the giving of affection. They were men who had shown these same difficulties in civilian life, having had difficulties with friends, work associates, and their own families, or having had criminal records. Political dissidents on the other hand, when captured, justified their failure to desert by invoking their sense of solidarity with their comrades and expressed the feeling that had they deserted when given a post of responsibility their comrades would have interpreted it as a breach of solidarity. For the political dissident, the verbal expression of political dissent was as much anti-authoritarianism as he could afford, and submission to his group was the price which he had to pay for it.

The persistent strength of primary group controls was manifested even in the last month of the war, when many deserters felt that they would not have been able to have taken the initial step in their desertion unless they had discussed the matter with their comrades and received some kind of legitimation for the action, such as a statement of approval.[9] And, on the other hand, the same ongoing efficacy of primary group sentiment was evident in the statements of would-be deserters who declared they had never been able to cross the threshold because they had been told by their officers that the comrades who remained behind (i.e., the comrades of the men who had deserted) would be shot. Hence, one of the chief forms of disintegration which occurred in the last stages of the war took the form of group surrender in which, after ample discussion within the unit, the authorization of the leading personalities and often of the NCO's had been granted for the offering of token resistance to facilitate capture, or even for outright group surrender.

Factors Strengthening Primary Group Solidarity

The Nazi nucleus of the primary group: the "hard core." The stability and military effectiveness of the military primary group were in large measure a function of the "hard core," who approximated about ten to fifteen per cent of the total of enlisted men; the percentage was higher for non-commissioned officers and was very much higher among the junior officers.[10] These were, on the whole, young men between 24 and 28 years of age who had had a gratifying adolescence in the most rewarding period of National Socialism. They were imbued with the ideology of *Gemeinschaft* (community solidarity),[11] were enthusiasts for the military life, had definite homo-erotic tendencies and accordingly placed a very high value on "toughness," manly comradeliness, and group solidarity.[12] The presence of a few such men in the group, zealous, energetic, and unsparing of themselves, provided models for weaker men, and facilitated the process of identification. For those for whom their charisma did not suffice and who were accordingly difficult to incorporate fully into the intimate primary group, frowns, harsh words, and threats served as a check on divisive tendencies. The fact that the elite SS divisions and paratroop divisions had a larger "hard core" than other divisions of the army—so large as to embrace almost the entire group membership during most of the war—accounted for their greater fighting effectiveness. And the fact that such a "hard core" was almost entirely lacking from certain *Volksgrenadier* divisions helped to a considerable extent to account for the military inferiority of these units.

One of the functions of the "hard core" was to minimize the probability of divisive political discussions. There was, of course, little inclination to discuss political matters or even strategic aspects of the war among German soldiers. For this reason widespread defeatism concerning the outcome of the war had little consequence in affecting behavior (until the spring of 1945) because of the near impossibility—objective as well as subjective—of discussing or carrying out alternative plans of action.

In contrast with the "hard core," which was a disproportionately large strengthening factor in the integrity of the military primary group, the "soft core" was a source of infection which was by no means comparable in effectiveness. Unlike the first world war experience in which anti-war attitudes were often vigorously expressed and eagerly listened to by men who were "good comrades," in the second world war the political anti-militarist or anti-Nazi who expressed his views with frequency and vigor was also in the main not a "good comrade." There was a complete absence of soldiers' committees and organized opposition, even in March and April 1945 (except for the Bavarian Freiheitsaktion which was constituted by rear-echelon troops). On isolated occasions, the Western Allies were able to exploit a man who had been a "good comrade" and who, after having been captured, expressed his defeatism and willingness to help end the war; he was thereupon sent back into the German line to talk his comrades into going over with him to the Allied lines. Here the "soft core" man exploited his comradely solidarity and it was only on that basis that he was able to remove some of the members of his group from the influence of the "hard core."

Community of experience as a cohesive force. The factors which affect group solidarity in general were on the whole carefully manipulated by the German general staff. Although during the war Germany was more permeated by foreigners than it had ever been before in its history, the army was to a great extent carefully protected from disintegrating influences of heterogeneity of ethnic and national origin, at least in crucial military situations. German officers saw that solidarity is fostered by the recollection of jointly experienced gratifications and that accordingly the groups who had gone through a victory together should not be dissolved but should be maintained as units to the greatest degree possible.

The replacement system of the Wehrmacht operated to the same end.[13] The entire personnel of a division would be withdrawn from the front simultaneously and refitted as a unit with replacements. Since new members were added to the division while it was out of line they were thereby given the opportunity to assimilate themselves into the group; then the group as a whole was sent forward. This system continued until close to the end of the war and helped to explain the durability of the German Army in the face of the overwhelming numerical and material superiority of the Allied forces.

Deterioration of group solidarity in the Wehrmacht which began to appear toward the very end of the war was most frequently found in hastily fabricated units. These were made up of new recruits, dragooned stragglers, air force men who had been forced into the infantry (and who felt a loss of status in the change), men transferred from the navy into the infantry to meet the emergency of manpower shortage, older factory workers, concentration camp inmates, and older married men who had been kept in reserve throughout the war and who had remained with the familial primary group until the last moment. The latter, who were the "catch" of the last "total mobilization" carried with them the resentment and bitterness which the "total mobilization" produced and which prevented the flow of affection necessary for group formation. It was clear that groups so diverse in age composition and background, and especially so mixed in their reactions to becoming infantrymen, could not very quickly become effective fighting units. They had no time to become used to one another and to develop the type of friendliness which is possible only when loyalties to outside groups have been renounced—or at least put into the background. A preview of what was to occur when units became mixed was provided by the 275th Fusilier Battalion which broke up before the First U.S. Army drive in November. Thirty-five Ps/W interrogated from this unit turned out to have been recently scraped together from fifteen different army units.

The most ineffective of all the military formations employed by the Wehrmacht during the war were the Volksturm units. They ranged in age from boys to old men, and were not even given basic training in the weapons which they were supposed to use. Their officers were Nazi local functionaries who were already objects of hostility and who were therefore unable to release a flow of affection among equals. They had moreover not broken their family ties to the slightest extent. They still remained members of a primary group which did not fuse into the military primary group. Finally, they had no uniforms. They had only brassards to identify them and through which to identify themselves with one another. The mutual identification function of the uniform which plays so great a role in military units was thereby lost. As soon as they were left to their own devices, they disintegrated from within, deserting in large numbers to their homes, hiding, permitting themselves to be captured, etc.

Factors Weakening Primary Group Solidarity

Isolation. The disintegration of a primary group depends in part on the physical and spatial variables which isolate it from the continuous pressure of face-to-face contact. The factor of spatial proximity in the maintenance of group solidarity in military situations must not be underestimated. In February and March of 1945, isolated remnants of platoons and companies were surrendering in groups with increasing frequency. The tactical situation of defensive fighting under heavy American artillery bombardment and the deployment of rear outposts forced soldiers to take refuge in cellars, trenches, and other underground shelters in small groups of three and four. This prolonged isolation from the nucleus of the primary group for several days worked to reinforce the fear of destruction of the self, and thus had a disintegrative influence on primary group relations.[14] A soldier who was isolated in a cellar or in a concrete bunker for several days and whose anxieties about physical survival were aggravated by the tactical hopelessness of his situation, was a much more easily separable member of his group than one who, though fearing physical destruction, was still bound by the continuous and vital ties of working, eating, sleeping, and being at leisure together with his fellow soldiers.

This proposition regarding the high significance of the spatial variable for primary group solidarity and the maintenance of the fighting effectiveness of an army is supported by the behavior of the retreating German Army in North Africa in 1943, and in France and Germany in September-October 1944 and March 1945. As long as a retreat is orderly and the structure of the component units of an army is maintained, strategic difficulties do not break up the army. An army in retreat breaks up only when the retreat is poorly organized, when command is lost over the men, so that they become separated from their units and become stragglers, or when enemy penetrations isolate larger or smaller formations from the main group.[15]

Stragglers first became a moderately serious problem in the German Army in October 1944. On October 22, 1944, General Keitel ordered that a maximum of one to three days be allowed for stragglers to reattach themselves to their units. The previous limit had been five days. The aggravation of the straggler problem was further documented by General Blaskowitz's order of March 5, 1945, according to which the category of stragglers was declared to have ceased to exist. Soldiers who lost contact with their own units were directed to attach themselves immediately to the "first troops in the line which he can contact. . . ."

Familial ties and primary group disintegration. Prisoners of war remarked with considerable frequency that discussions about alternative paths of action by groups of soldiers who were entirely defeatist arose not from discussions about the war in its political or strategic aspects, but rather from discussions about the soldiers' families.[16] The recollection of concrete family experiences reactivated sentiments of dependence on the family for psychological support and correspondingly weakened the hold of the military primary group. It was in such contexts that German soldiers toward the end of the war were willing to discuss group surrender.

To prevent preoccupation with family concerns, the families of German soldiers were given strict instructions to avoid references to family deprivations in letters to the front. In the winter and spring of 1945, when Allied air raids became so destructive of communal life, all telegrams to soldiers at the front had to be passed by party officials in order to insure that no distracting news reached the soldiers. On the other hand, care was taken by party and army authorities that soldiers should not be left in a state of anxiety about their families and to this end vigorous propaganda was carried on to stimulate correspondence with soldiers at the front. For those who had no families and who needed the supplementary affection which the army unit could not provide, provisions were made to obtain mail from individuals (including party officials) who would befriend unmarried or family-less soldiers, with the result that the psychic economy of the soldier was kept in equilibrium.

There was, however, a special type of situation in which the very strength of familial ties served to keep the army from further disintegration. This arose towards the end of the war, when soldiers were warned that desertion would result in severe sanctions being inflicted on the deserter's family.[17]

Toward the end of the war, soldiers tended to break away from the army more often while they were on leave and with their families, and therefore isolated from personal contact with their primary group fellows. When soldiers returned to visit their families, then the conflict between contradictory primary group loyalties became acute. The hold of the military primary group became debilitated in the absence of face-to-face contacts. The prospect of facing, on return to the front, physical destruction or a prolonged loss of affection from the civilian primary group, especially the family, prompted an increasing number of desertions while on furlough.

All of these factors contributed to loosen the solidarity of the German Army, especially when the prospect of physical destruction began to weigh more heavily. Severe threats to the safety of the civilian primary group created anxiety which often weakened the hold of the military primary group. When the area of the soldier's home was occupied by the enemy or when the soldier himself was fighting in the area, there was strong disposition to desert homeward. One such soldier said: "Now I have nothing more for which to fight, because my home is occupied."

The strong pull of the civilian primary group became stronger as the coherence of the army group weakened. But sometimes, the former worked to keep the men fighting in their units, i.e., when they reasoned that the shortest way home was keep the group intact and to avoid capture or desertion. Otherwise there would ensue a long period in an enemy P/W camp. On the other hand, in event of the defeat of a still intact army, there would be only a short period of waiting before demobilization.

Demand for physical survival. The individual soldier's fear of destruction ultimately pressed to weaken primary group cohesion; nevertheless it is striking to note the degree to which demands for physical survival could be exploited by Wehrmacht authority to the end of prolonging resistance. Where the social conditions were otherwise favorable, the primary bonds of group solidarity were dissolved only under the most extreme circumstances of threat to the individual organism—in situations where the tactical prospects were utterly hopeless, under devastating artillery and air bombardment, or where the basic food and medical requirements were not being met. Although aware for a long time of the high probability of German defeat in the war and of the hopelessness of the numerous individual battles, very many German soldiers continued to resist without any serious deterioration in the quality of their fighting skill. But where the most basic physiological demands of the German soldier were threatened with complete frustration, the bonds of group solidarity were broken.

Concern about food and about health always reduces the solidarity of a group. Throughout the war, and until the period just before the end, German army medical services were maintained at a high level of efficiency; the decline in their efficiency coincides with the deterioration in the morale of the men. Special care was also observed in the management of the food supply and accordingly few German soldiers felt that the food supplies were inadequate. Indeed, as late as October 1944, only 15 per cent of a sample of 92 Ps/W declared that they were at all dissatisfied with army food. By January, however, the situation changed and Ps/W reported increased preoccupation with physical survival, with food, and the shortage of clothing. Soldiers in certain units were beginning to "scrounge." The extreme cold of the winter of '44-'45 also began to tell on the men whose military self-esteem was being reduced by the raggedness of their uniforms and the failure to obtain replacements for unsatisfactory equipment.

Thus, to keep groups integral, it was necessary not only to provide positive gratifications but also to reduce to a minimum the alternative possibilities of increasing the chances for survival by leaving the unit. For this reason the Nazis sought to counteract the fear of personal physical destruction in battle by telling the men that accurate records were kept on deserters and that not only would their families and property be made to suffer in the event of their desertion, but that after the war, upon their return to Germany, they, too, would be very severely punished. They were also told by their officers that German agents were operating in American and British P/W cages in order to report on violations of security and on deserters. A Wehrmacht leaflet to German soldiers mentioned the names of two deserters of the 980th Volksgrenadiere who were alleged to have divulged information and stated that not only would their families be sent to prison and suffer the loss of their property and ration cards, but that the men themselves would also be punished after the war. In actuality, they were often punished in the P/W camps by the extreme Nazis who exercised some control in certain camps.

For the same reason, as long as the front was relatively stable, the Wehrmacht officers increased the natural hazards of war by ordering mine fields to be laid, barbed wire to be set up, and special guards to be posted to limit the freedom of movement of isolated and psychologically unattached individuals who, in situations which offered the chance of safely withdrawing from the war, would have moved over to the enemy's lines. Although the number of avowedly would-be deserters remained very small until near the end of the war, even they were frequently immobilized for fear of being killed by the devices set up to prevent their separation from the group. The danger of destruction by the Allies in event of desertion also played a part in keeping men attached to their military units. As one

P/W who had thought of desertion but who never took action said, "by day our own people shoot at us, by night yours do."

Another physical narcissistic element which contributed somewhat to resistance on the Western front was fear of castration in event of the loss of the war. (This was effective only among a minority of the German soldiers.) The guilt feelings of the Nazi soldiers who had slaughtered and marauded on the Eastern front, and elsewhere in Europe, and their projection onto the enemy of their own sadistic impulses, heightened their narcissistic apprehensiveness about damage to their vital organs and to their physical organism as a whole. Rumors of castration at the hands of the Russians circulated in the German Army throughout the last three years of the war and it is likely that they were largely the result of ruthless methods on both sides.

The Nazis perceived the function of fear of personal destruction in the event of capture as a factor in keeping a group intact after the internal bonds had been loosened. There were accordingly situations in which SS detachments deliberately committed atrocities on enemy civilians and soldiers in order to increase the anxieties of German soldiers as to what would befall them in the event of their defeat and capture. This latter policy was particularly drastically applied by the Waffen-SS in the von Rundstedt counter-offensive. It appears to have been an effort to convince German soldiers that there were no alternatives but victory or resistance to the very end and that surrender or desertion would end with slaughter of the German soldiers, as it had in the cases of the Allied soldiers. This was not effective for the mass of the German soldiers, however, who were becoming convinced that the law-abiding British and Americans would not in most situations harm them upon capture.

The dread of destruction of the self, and the demand for physical survival, while breaking up the spontaneous solidarity of the military primary group in most cases, thus served under certain conditions to coerce the soldier into adherence to his group and to the execution of the orders of his superiors.

III. The Role of "Soldierly Honor"

American and British soldiers tend to consider their wartime service as a disagreeable necessity, as a task which had to be performed because there were no alternatives. For the German, being a soldier was a more than acceptable status. It was indeed honorable. The King's Regulations which govern the British Army (1940) begin with the statement that the army consists of officers and men serving for various lengths of time. The German equivalent in the Defense Laws of 1935 opens with a declaration that "military service is a service of honor for the German people, the Wehrmacht is the armed barrier and the soldierly school of the German people."

Emphasis on the element of honor in the military profession has led in Germany to the promulgation of elaborate rules of conduct regulating the behavior of both officers and men in a great variety of specific military and extra-military situations.[18] The explicit and implicit code of soldierly honor, regulating the responsibilities of officers for their men, determined behavior in battle and established conditions under which surrender was honorable. It also provided a very comprehensive body of etiquette. This elaborate ritualization of the military profession had a significantly positive influence on group solidarity and efficiency during periods of stress. "Honor" rooted in a rigid conscience (superego) served in the German Army to keep men at their tasks better than individual reflection and evaluation could have done. When the individual was left to make decisions for himself, the whole host of contradictory impulses toward authority of officers and of the group as an entity was stimulated.

Domination by higher authority was eagerly accepted by most ordinary soldiers, who feared that if they were allowed to exercise their initiative their *innere Schweinhunde,* i.e., their own narcissistic and rebellious impulses, would come to the fore. On the other hand, rigorous suppression of these impulses constituted an appeasement of the superego which allowed the group machinery to function in an orderly manner.

The belief in the efficacy and moral worth of discipline and in the inferiority of the spontaneous, primary reactions of the personality was expressed in the jettisoning of the German Army Psychiatric Selection Services in 1942. When the manpower shortage became stringent and superfluities had to be scrapped, the personnel selection system based on personality analysis was one of those activities which was thought to be dispensable. Apparently taking individual personality differences into account was thought to be too much of a concession to moral weakness which could and in any case *should be* overcome by hard, soldierly discipline.

Strength as an element in honor. For persons who have deeply-lying uncertainties over their own weaknesses, who fear situations which will reveal their weakness in controlling themselves and their lack of manliness, membership in an army will tend to reduce anxieties. Subjugation to discipline gives such persons support; it means that they do not have to depend on themselves, that someone stronger than themselves is guiding and protecting them. Among young males in middle and late adolescence, the challenges of love and vocation aggravate anxieties about weakness. At this stage fears about potency are considerable. When men who have passed through this stage are placed in the entirely male society of a military unit, freed from the control of adult civilian society and missing its gratifications, they tend to regress to the adolescent condition. The show of "toughness" and hardness which is regarded as a virtue among soldiers is a response to these reactivated adolescent anxieties about weakness.

In the German Army, all these tendencies were intensified by the military code, and they accounted for a considerable share of the cohesion and resistance up to the very last stages of the war. Among those at the extreme end of the scale—the "hard core" of Nazi last-ditch resisters—in whom the preoccupation with strength and weakness is to be found in most pronounced form—this attitude was manifested in unwillingness of some to acknowledge defeat even after capture.

The honor of the officer. To control the behavior of officers and to protect soldierly honor, the Court of Honor procedure of the Imperial Army was reestablished when the Nazis came into power. Its function was to adjudicate disagreements and quarrels between officers in an authoritative way, and it did succeed in minimizing disagreements and unpleasant tensions among officers in both professional and private affairs which might otherwise have endangered solidarity of the group by division among those in immediate authority. The settlement, which was arrived at in secret by officers of the same rank as those involved in the dispute, was almost always accepted without a murmur by both parties. Its minutely detailed procedural and substantive rules reduced to a minimum the possibility that an officer might feel that the collective authority which ruled over him was weak, negligible, or impotent in any sphere. The code went so far as to empower the court to recommend suspension from duty simply on the grounds of *unehrliche Gesinnung* (dishonorable attitude) derogatory to the status of the officer class. External discipline penetrated thus into even the most private sphere to give assurance that soldierly honor would be operative even in the recesses of the individual mind.[19] The officers' court of honor not only served as an "external superego," but by its continuous emphasis on "honor" and "dishonor," it heightened the sensibilities of the officers to the demands of their own superego.

One of the most elaborated aspects of soldierly honor as related to combat behavior dealt with the conditions under which surrender could be honorably performed. In this respect, great stress was laid on the oath which bound soldiers not to desert or surrender, and much casuistical effort was expended to make surrender compatible with soldierly honor. In some cases soldiers arranged circumstances in such a way as would appear to others, as well as to themselves, that they had been captured against their will. In other cases, surrender was excused as legitimate according to accepted military standards. In a few cases, fortification commanders required that a token round of phosphorous shells be fired against their position in order to satisfy the requirements of their honor. Deserters often attempted to appease their conscience by ingenious arguments to the effect that the oaths which they took were signed with pencil, or that the sergeant who administered the oath turned his back on them, or that they had been forced into signing the oath which was incompatible with the "requirements of a free conscience."

The stout defense of the Channel ports, which denied vital communication centers to the Allies, was in large part the result of the determination of the commanding officers whose sense of military honor required them to carry out to the letter orders for resistance, regardless of the cost in men or of the apparent strategic futility of their operation.

Even after the extreme reverses in February and March of 1945, German colonels and generals sought to have their units captured and overrun in an approved manner. Captured German senior officers often declared that they had been aware of certain defeat in their sector but, despite this, they took little or no action to terminate hostilities. The most positive action some of them were able to take was to follow their instructions to hold fast in such a manner as to facilitate the capture of their own command posts when they were not able to retreat. But the various subterfuges to make their surrender or capture acceptable to their superego were apparently insufficient, and after capture their sense of guilt for having infringed on the moral requirements of officership usually produced regressive manifestations in the form of elaborate self-justifications for their inadequacy. In some cases it went to the extreme form of imagining how they would justify themselves in the event that Hitler were to confront them at the very moment and were to ask them why they had allowed themselves to be captured.

The reluctance of senior and general officers to enter into negotiations to surrender on their own initiative was of course not due exclusively to motivations of conscience; it was buttressed by the efficient functioning of the security system. The failure of the July 20 *Putsch* resulted in the carefully contrived isolation of senior commanding officers and their domination by Nazi secret police. The establishment of an independent chain of command for National Socialist *Führungs-offiziere* (Guidance Officers) was an additional technique established for spying on generals. Aside from their morale duties, which are described elsewhere, these fanatical Nazi Guidance Officers at higher headquarters busied themselves in reporting on German generals who appeared to be unlikely to carry out orders for final resistance.

Company grade and battalion officers on the whole behaved similarly to their superiors. The deterioration of their effectiveness which occurred was due in greater measure to the great reduction in their numbers rather than to any loss of skill or determination. At the end, the German Army suffered severely from being underofficered, rather than poorly officered. As early as January 1945, the ratio of officers to enlisted men fell to about 50 per cent of what it had been under normal conditions.

Tension between officer's honor and solicitude of men. There was, however, a difference between the behavior of junior and senior officers, which can in part be explained by the former's closer physical proximity and more extensive contact with their men. The sense of obligation which the junior officer felt for the welfare of his men often tempered his conception of the proper relations between soldierly honor and surrender, especially when he was in a position to recognize that there was no military value in further resistance. Nonetheless, desertion by German officers was extremely rare, and only occasionally did they bring about the group surrender of their men; more typically they protected their soldierly honor by allowing themselves to be overrun.

Senior non-commisisoned officers displayed a sense of military honor very similar to that of junior officers, but even closer identification with their comrades precipitated a crisis in loyalties which weighed still more heavily on their consciences. Ordinarly, soldierly honor and primary group solidarity are not only congruous with one another but actually mutually supporting. In crisis situations, however, the divergence between them begins to appear and loyalty to the larger army group (the strategically relevant unit), which is an essential component of soldierly honor, enters into contradiction to loyalty to the primary group.

Until the failure of von Rundstedt's counter-offensive, soldierly honor on the part of senior NCO's tended to outweigh primary group solidarity wherever they came into conflict with each other. As the final Allied drive against the homeland developed, they became less disposed to carry out "last-ditch" resistance, but when captured they showed signs of having experienced guilt feelings for not having done so. The recognition of the overwhelming Allied strength in their particular sectors, together with physical absence from the immediate environment of their superior officers (which was a function of the decreasing ratio of officers to men) made it possible for them to offer only token resistance or to allow themselves to be overrun. They relieved their consciences by declaring that further bloodshed would have served no further *military purpose.*

The infantry soldier's honor. The code of soldierly honor and its ramifications took a deep root in the personality of the German soldiers of the line—even those who were totally apolitical. Identification with the stern authority associated with the symbols of State power gave the ordinary German soldier a feeling that he became strong and morally elevated by submitting to discipline. For these people a military career was a good and noble one, enjoying high intrinsic ethical value. Even apathetic

and inarticulate soldiers sometimes grew eloquent on the values
of the military life.

The most defeatist soldier, who insisted that he longed to be
captured and that he offered little or no resistance, was careful
to point out that he was not a deserter, and showed anxiety lest
the conditions under which he was captured might be interpreted as desertion. This was of course to some extent the result
of the fear that German police would retaliate against his family if his company commander reported that he had deserted
and that the Nazis would seek revenge against him, either in
the P/W camp, or after the war in Germany. But at least of
equal significance was his desire to maintain his pride in having
been a good soldier who had done his duty.[20] Anti-Nazi German soldiers who went to some length to inform the interrogators of their anti-Nazi political attitudes felt no inconsistency
in insisting that despite everything they were "100 per cent
soldiers." Only a very small minority admitted freely that they
deserted.

IV. Relations with Authority: Officer-Man Relations

The basis of the officers' status. The primary group relations
in modern armies, especially in the German Army, depend as
much on the acceptance of the various authorities to which the
soldier is subjected as on mutual respect and love between individuals of equal rank. The non-commissioned and the junior
officers are the agents on whom the individual soldier depends
in his relationships with the rest of the army outside his immediate group, and in his relations with the outer world (the
home front and the enemy). They have charge of his safety, and
they are the channels through which flow food, equipment, and
other types of supplies as well as chance symbolic gratifications
such as decorations, promotions, leave, etc. For the German
soldier, with his authoritarian background, the officer-man relation is one of submission to an overriding authority.

An exceptionally talented regular German Army officer, bred
in the German military tradition, once tried to summarize to
his interrogator what made the German Army "work": political indoctrination and "pep talks" were "all rot"; whether the
men would follow him depended upon the personality of the
officer. The leader must be a man who possesses military skill:

then his men will know that he is protecting them. He must be a model to his men; he must be an all-powerful, and still benevolent, authority.

He must look after his men's needs, and be able to do all the men's duties better than they themselves in training and under combat conditions. The men must also be sure that their officer is duly considerate of their lives: they must know that he does not squander his human resources, that the losses of life which occur under his command will be minimal and justified. In the training of NCO's for officers, the German Army acted on the basis of such maxims, despite the Nazi Party's propagandistic preoccupation with such secondary aspects of morale as political ideology.

The positions of the officer and of the NCO were dependent on discipline and on the sanctions by which discipline is maintained and enforced. During training the Wehrmacht laid down the most severe disciplinary rules. In combat, even before Germany's military fortunes began to contract, life and death powers over the troops were vested in lower commanders. At the same time elaborate precautions were taken to control and even to counteract their severity in certain spheres of behavior. Officers were warned against senseless and unnecessary insults directed against their men. Special orders were issued and particular attention was paid in the training of officers to fatherly and considerate behavior in relations with their men; the combination of sternness and benevolence was strongly counseled. Numerous small indications of affection such as congratulations on birthdays and on anniversaries, and fatherly modes of address, e.g., "Kinder" (children), were recommended as helping to build the proper relations between officers and men.

The results of this approach to status relationships appear to have been good. Differences in privileges between officers and enlisted men in combat units almost never emerged as an object of complaint on the part of enlisted Ps/W. On the contrary, complaints of "softness" were more frequently directed against officers and enlisted men in the rear. The infantry soldier seldom attempted to attribute deficiencies in military operations to his immediate superiors. Spontaneous praise, in fact, was frequent.

German soldiers—both officers and men—greatly appreciated the ceremonial acknowledgment of hierarchical differences as expressed, for example, in the military salute. Captured Germans who saw the American Army in Great Britain before D-Day were often contemptuous of an enemy who was obviously so lax in dress and salute. Many of them said that the American Army could not be expected to fight well since the relations between officers and enlisted men were so informal. "This is no army." Such views of the value of the ceremonial aspects of discipline persisted in defeat. Ps/W taken late in the war, when they commented on American officer-man relations, often remarked with incredulous wonderment: "I don't see how it works!"

Not only was the position of German officers strengthened by their mixture of severe dominion and benevolence, but additional support for their authority came from the provision for the blameless gratification of primitive impulses and from the sanctioning of all types of aggressive social behavior outside the army group. Private personal transgressions of "civil" ethics were regarded as of slight importance, since they were outside the limits of the "manly comradeship" of the military primary group. Drunkenness and having women in the barracks were crimes which the officers overlooked; in occupied and enemy countries the latitude in personal and private transgressions was even greater. Provision was made for official houses of prostitution in which soldiers could reassure themselves about their manliness without disrupting the disciplinary structure of the Wehrmacht. This combination of practices lowered the probability of tensions in officer-man relationships.

NCO's and junior officers. In battle, leadership responsibility devolved in actuality on senior NCO's (the opposite numbers of American platoon sergeants) and on the company grade officers. Only seldom did a line soldier see his battalion commander and even less frequently was he spoken to by him. Thus battalion commanders and other higher officers played a less central role in the personality system of the German soldier. They were therefore less directly related to the solidarity of the military primary group.

Nearly all non-commissioned and commissioned officers of the company grade level were regarded by the German soldier throughout the Western campaign as brave, efficient, and considerate. It was only in the very final phases of the war that Ps/W occasionally complained that they had been abandoned by their officers, and there was reason to believe that such complaints were justified not by facts but by the resurgence of uninhibited hostility against officers who, having been defeated, could now be looked upon as having shown weakness.

In addition, the slight increase in anti-officer sentiment which occurred during the last two months of the war, may be related not to the decline in competence, courage, or devotion on the part of the officers, but rather to the fact that the heavy losses of the Wehrmacht's trained junior officers had led to a large reduction in the ratio of the junior officers to men. In consequence, in order to use the available officers most economically, it was necessary to "thin" them out.[21] This resulted in a reduction in the amount of face-to-face contact between officers and men and in reduced feeling of the officers' protective function. And this, in turn, sometimes tipped the balance of the submissiveness-rebelliousness scale, in the successful manipulation of which lay the secret of the effective control of the German Army.

The junior officers of the Wehrmacht were, in general, very well selected. They were better educated than the average German, and had received extensive preliminary training. Although Nazi Party politics played a role in the general selection of officers (despite the façade of a non-political Wehrmacht) the junior officer ranks never became a field of patronage. High technical and personality requirements were made of all candidates for officership, Nazi and non-Nazi.

These facts were appreciated by many of the more intelligent enlisted Ps/W who testified that the influence of highly placed friends or of Party connections had practically no effect on an officer candidate's chances for selection, if he lacked the necessary qualifications for making a good officer.

Equally important in the provision of firm, "hard," and protective leadership, were the senior non-commissioned officers, who were everywhere appreciated as the most solid asset of the Wehrmacht. Until 1943, more than half of the NCO's who became Ps/W had belonged to the pre-1935 German Army. These men were neither very interested in politics nor very aggressive, but were thoroughly trained, solid men who were doing their job out of a deeply-rooted sense of duty to the soldierly profession.

As the war progressed, their numbers declined and less well-trained men took their place. In the last stages of the war, when the speed in reforming units was increased, the top non-commissioned officers often did not have sufficient time to promote the growth of strong identifications between themselves and their men. In February 1945, for the first time, Ps/W began to complain that "they didn't even have time to learn our names." The disintegration which set in in the Wehrmacht at this time was in part due to the declining value of the NCO as a cohesive factor in the military primary group.

Senior officers. The High Command and the senior officers, although generally esteemed, were not directly relevant in the psychological structure of the military primary group. They were in the main less admired than the junior officers because their physical remoteness made it easier to express hostile sentiments against them; they stood between the Führer and the junior officers and NCO's. And while the latter three obtained a positive affect from the ambivalent attitude toward authority of so many of the soldiers, the general officers themselves were made to some extent into the recipients of the hostile component of the soldier's authority-attitude. The failure of the *Putsch* of July 20 served to lower the esteem in which the High Command was held, although in general there was not a very lively reaction to that incident. Stalwart Nazis viewed it as a case of treason, and for the time being the concentration of their hostility on generals whose names were announced in public increased their confidence in those generals whom the Führer left in charge. Other soldiers, less passionately political, were inclined to turn their backs on the unsuccessful plotters because of the weakness manifested in their failures. But the situation was only temporary, and in any case the officers on whom the men in the field felt they depended were but little affected. The loss of prestige of the immediate officers was too small to make any difference in battle behavior, while senior officers in whom confidence had declined to a greater extent were too remote in the soldier's mind to make much difference in his combat efficiency.

V. Secondary Symbols

From the preceding section it is apparent that the immediately present agents and symbols of political authority—junior officers, NCO's, and conceptions of soldierly honor—were effective because of their consistency with the personality system of the individual soldier. In this section, we shall examine the effectiveness of the remoter—or secondary—agents and symbols of state authority.

Strategic aspects of the war. For the mass of the German Army, the strategic phases of the war were viewed apathetically. The ignorance of the German troops about important military events, even on their own front, was partly a result of the poverty of information about the actual course of the war—itself a part of Nazi policy.[22] But the deliberate management of ignorance need not always result in such far-reaching indifference as the German soldiers showed. Deliberately maintained ignorance would have resulted in a flood of rumors, had the German soldiers been more eager to know about the strategic phases of the war. As it was, there were very few rumors on the subject—merely apathy. Three weeks after the fall of the city of Aachen, there were still many prisoners being taken in the adjoining area who did not know that the city had fallen. For at least a week after the beginning of von Rundstedt's counter-offensive, most of the troops on the northern hinge of the bulge did not know that the offensive was taking place and were not much interested when they were told after capture. Of 140 Ps/W taken between December 23-24, 1944, only 35 per cent had heard of the counter-offensive and only 7 per cent said that they thought it significant.[23]

Some exception to this extensive strategic indifference existed with respect to the Eastern front. Although the German soldiers were extremely ignorant of the state of affairs on that front and made little attempt to reduce their ignorance, still the question of Russians was so emotionally charged, so much the source of anxiety, that it is quite likely that fear of the Russians did play a role in strengthening resistance. National Socialist propaganda had long worked on the traditional repugnance and fear of the German towards the Russian. The experience of the German soldiers in Russia in 1941 and 1942 increased this repugnance by direct perception of the primitive life of the Russian villager. But probably more important was the projection onto the Russians of the guilt feelings generated by the ruthless brutality of the Germans in Russia during the occupation period. The shudder of horror which frequently accompanied a German soldier's remarks about Russia was a result of all of these factors. These attitudes influenced German resistance and the consequent diffusion of their attitudes among their comrades. They also took effect by making soldiers worry about what would happen to their families if the Russians entered Germany. Of course, it should also be mentioned that this fear of the Russians also made some German soldiers welcome a speedier collapse on the Western front in the hope that a larger part of Germany would fall under Anglo-American control.

Before the actual occupation, only a small minority expressed fear of the consequences of an Anglo-American occupation. The continuing monthly opinion poll conducted by the Psychological Warfare Branch, mentioned elsewhere, never showed more than 20 per cent of the prisoners answering "yes" to the question, "Do you believe that revenge will be taken against the population after the war?" Those who feared retribution were confirmed Nazis. Yet the general absence of fear of revenge did not cause a diminution of German resistance.

Neither did expectations about the outcome of the war play a great role in the integration or disintegration of the German Army. The statistics regarding German soldier opinion cited below show that pessimism as to final triumph was quite compatible with excellence in fighting behavior. The far greater effectiveness of considerations of self-preservation, and their vast preponderance over interest in the outcome of the war and the strategic situation, is shown by German prisoner recall of the contents of Allied propaganda leaflets (see Table 1). In the last two months of 1944 and the first two months of 1945, not less than 59 per cent of the sample of prisoners taken each month recalled references to the preservation of the individual, and the figure rose to 76 per cent in February of 1945. On the other hand, the proportion of prisoners recalling references to the total strategic situation of the war and the prospect of the outcome of the war seldom amounted to more than 20 per cent, while references to political subjects seldom amounted to more than 10 per cent. The general tendency was not to think about the outcome of the war unless forced to do so by direct interrogation. Even pessimism was counterbalanced by the reassurances provided by identification with a strong and benevolent Führer, by identification

TABLE 1

TABULATION OF ALLIED LEAFLET PROPAGANDA THEMES
REMEMBERED BY GERMAN Ps/W

	Dec. 15-31 1944	Jan. 1-15 1945	Jan. 15-31 1945	Feb. 1-15 1945
Number of Ps/W	60	83	99	135
Themes and appeals remembered:				
a. Promise of good treatment as Ps/W and self-preservation through surrender	63%	65%	59%	76%
b. Military news	15	17	19	30
c. Strategical hopelessness of Germany's position	13	12	25	26
d. Hopelessness of a local tactical situation	3	1	7	7
e. Political attacks on German leaders	7	5	4	8
f. Bombing of German cities	2	8	6	—
g. Allied Military Government	7	3	—	—
h. Appeals to civilians	5	4	2	—

(The percentages add up to more than 100% since some Ps/W remembered more than one topic. Only Ps/W remembering at least one theme were included in this tabulation.)

with good officers, and by the psychological support of a closely integrated primary group.

The ethics of war and patriotism. Quite consistently, ethical aspects of the war did not trouble the German soldier much. When pressed by Allied interrogators, Ps/W said that Germany had been forced to fight for its life. There were very few German soldiers who said that Germany had been morally wrong to attack Poland, or Russia. Most of them thought that if anything had been wrong about the war, it was largely in the realm of technical decisions. The decision to extirpate the Jews had been too drastic not because of its immorality but because it united the world against Germany. The declaration of war against the Soviet Union was wrong only because it created a two-front war. But these were all arguments which had to be forced from the Ps/W. Left to themselves, they seldom mentioned them.

The assumption underlying these arguments was that the strong national state is a good in itself. But it was not, in fact, the highest good for any but the "hard core." In September

1944, for example, only 5 per cent of a sample of 634 Ps/W said that they were worried about anything other than personal or familial problems, while in the very same survey, more than half of the Ps/W said they believed that Germany was losing the war or that they were at best uncertain of the war's outcome. In brief, fear for Germany's future as a nation does not seem to have been very important in the ordinary soldier's outlook and in motivating his combat behavior. As a matter of fact, as the war became more and more patently a threat to the persistence of the German national state, the narcissism of the German soldier increased correspondingly, so that the idea of national survival did not become an object of widespread preoccupation even when it might have been expected to become so.[24]

Ethical-religious scruples seem to have played an equally small role. Although there were a few interesting cases of Roman Catholic deserters, Roman Catholics (except Austrians, Czechs and Polish nationals) do not seem to have deserted disproportionately. Prisoners seldom expressed remorse for Nazi atrocities, and practically no case was noted of a desertion because of moral repugnance against Nazi atrocities.

Political ideals. The significance of political ideals, of symbols of political systems, was rather pronounced in the case of the "hard core" minority of fervent Nazis in the German Army. Their desire for discipline under a strong leader made them enthusiasts for the totalitarian political system. Their passionate aggressiveness also promoted projective tendencies which facilitated their acceptance of the Nazi picture of an innocent and harmless Germany encircled by the dark, threatening cloud of Bolsheviks, Jews, Negroes, etc., and perpetually in danger from inner enemies as well. But for most of the German soldiers, the political system of National Socialism was of little interest.

The *system* was indeed of very slight concern to German civilians also, even though dissatisfaction increased to a high pitch towards the end of the war. Soldiers on the whole were out of touch with the operation of the Party on the home front. Hence the political system impinged little on their consciousness. Thus, for example, of 53 potential and actual deserters in the Mediterranean theater, only one alleged political grounds for his action. The irrelevance of party politics to effective soldiering has already been treated above: here we need only repeat the statement of a German soldier, "Nazism begins ten miles behind the front line."

Nor did the soldiers react in any noticeable way to the various attempts to Nazify the army. When the Nazi Party salute was introduced in 1944, it was accepted as just one more army order, about equal in significance to an order requiring the carrying of gas masks. The introduction of the *National Socialistische Führungsoffiziere* (Guidance, or Indoctrination Officer), usually known as the NSFO, was regarded apathetically or as a joke. The contempt for the NSFO was derived not from his Nazi connection but from his status as an "outsider" who was not a real soldier. The especially Nazified Waffen SS divisions were never the object of hostility on the part of the ordinary soldier, even when the responsibility for atrocities was attributed to them. On the contrary, the Waffen SS was highly esteemed, not as a Nazi formation, but for its excellent fighting capacity. Wehrmacht soldiers always felt safer when there was a Waffen SS unit on their flank.

Devotion to Hitler. In contrast to the utterly apolitical attitude of the German infantry soldier towards almost all secondary symbols, an intense and personal devotion to Adolf Hitler was maintained in the German Army throughout the war. There could be little doubt that a high degree of identification with the Führer was an important factor in prolonging German resistance. Despite fluctuations in expectations as to the outcome of the war the trust in Hitler remained at a very high level even after the beginning of the serious reverses in France and Germany. In monthly opinion polls of German Ps/W opinion from D-Day until January 1945, in all but two samples over 60 per cent expressed confidence in Hitler,[25] and confidence in January was nearly as high as it was in the preceding June. During this same period considerably more than half of the German soldiers in seven out of eight polls said they believed that it was impossible for the German Army to defeat the Allies in France. Only when the German Army began to break up in the face of overwhelming Allied fire power and deep, communications-cutting penetrations, did confidence in Hitler fall to the unprecedentedly low level of 30 per cent. Even when defeatism was rising to the point at which only one-tenth of the prisoners taken as of March 1945 believed that the Germans had any chance of success, still a third retained confidence in Hitler.[26]

Belief in the good intentions of the Führer, in his eminent moral qualities, in his devotion and contributions to the well-being of the German people, continued on an even higher level. This strong attachment grew in large part from the feeling of strength and protection which the German soldier got from his conception of the Führer personality.

For older men, who had lived through the unemployment of the closing years of the Weimar Republic and who experienced the joy of being reinstated in gainful employment by Nazi full-employment policies, Hitler was above all the man who had provided economic security. This attitude extended even to left wing soldiers of this generation, who denounced the National Socialist political system, but found occasion to say a good word for Hitler as a man who had restored order and work in Germany. For men of the generation between 22-35, who had first experienced Hitler's charisma in the struggles to establish their manliness during late adolescence, Hitler was the prototype of strength and masculinity. For the younger Nazi fanatics, he was a father substitute, providing the vigilant discipline and the repression of dangerous impulses both in the individual and in the social environment; for them he had the additional merit of legitimating revolt against the family and traditional restraints.

Prisoners spoke of Hitler with enthusiasm, and even those who expressed regret over the difficulties which his policies had brought on Germany by engendering a two-front war and by allowing the Jews to be persecuted so fiercely as to arouse world hatred—even these men retained their warm esteem for his good intentions. They found it necessary to exculpate him in some way by attributing his errors to dishonest advisors who kept the truth from him, or to certain technical difficulties in his strategic doctrines which did not in any way reflect on his fundamental moral greatness or nobility.

It was difficult for German soldiers, as long as they had this attitude toward Hitler, to rebel mentally against the war. Time after time, prisoners who were asked why Hitler continued the war when they themselves admitted it was so obviously lost, said he wouldn't continue the war and waste lives if he did not have a good, even though undisclosed, strategic reason for doing so, or if he didn't have the resources to realize his ends. Nazis as well as non-Nazis answered in this way. Or else they would say, "the Führer has never deceived us," or, "he must have a good reason for doing what he does."

There was obviously a fear of rendering an independent judgment of events among the German soldiers and a desire for some strong leader to assume the responsibility for determining their fate. American and British soldiers often complained that the complexity of the army organization and strategy was so great and their own particular part was so small that they could not see the role of their personal missions. Their failure to see the connection made them miserable because it reduced their sense of personal autonomy. In the German Army, on the other hand, there was no difficulty for soldiers who were used throughout their lives to having other persons determine their objectives for them.

It is also possible that the very high devotion to Hitler under conditions of great stress was in part a reaction formation growing from a hostility against lesser authorities, which emerged as the weakness of these authorities became more manifest. In the last year of the war, hostility and contempt on the part of the German soldiers toward Nazi Party function-aries and toward Nazi Party leaders below Hitler (particularly Goebbels and Goering) was increasing. After the *Putsch* of July 20, hostility toward senior Wehrmacht officers also in-creased somewhat, although it never reached the levels of hostility displayed by civilians against local civilian Party offi-cials and leaders. It is possible, therefore, that guilt created in ambivalent personalities by giving expression, even though verbally, to hostility against subordinate agents of authority, had to be alleviated by reaffirmed belief in the central and highest authority.

Weakening of the Hitler symbol. As the integral pattern of defense was broken down, however, and as danger to physical survival increased, devotion to Hitler deteriorated. The tend-ency to attribute virtue to the strong and immorality to the weak took hold increasingly, and while it did not lead to a com-plete rejection of Hitler, it reached a higher point than at any other stage in the history of National Socialism. The announce-ment of Hitler's death met an incapacity to respond on the part of many soldiers. There seemed to be no willingness to question the truth of the report, but the great upsurge of preoccupation with physical survival as a result of disintegration of the military primary group, the loss of contact with junior officers and the greatly intensified threat of destruction, caused a deadening of the power to respond to this event. For the vast horde of dishevelled, dirty, bewildered prisoners, who were being taken in the last weeks of the war, Hitler was of slight importance alongside the problem of their own biological survival and the welfare of their families. For the small minority who still had sufficient energy to occupy themselves with "larger problems," the news of Hitler's death released a sort of amorphous resentment against the fallen leader whose weakness and immorality had been proven by the failure of his strategy. But even here, the resentment was not expressed in explicit denunciations of Hitler's character or personality. The emphasis was all on technical deficiencies and weaknesses.

The explanation of the deterioration and final—though probably only temporary—hostility toward Hitler may in part be sought in the average German soldier's ambivalence toward the symbols of authority. This psychological mechanism, which also helps to explain the lack of a significant resistance movement inside Germany, enables us to understand the curve of Hitler's fame among the German people. Hitler, the father symbol, was loved for his power and his great accomplishments and hated for his oppressiveness, but the latter sentiment was repressed. While he remained strong it was psychologically expedient—as well as politically expedient—to identify with Hitler and to displace hostility on to weaker minority groups and foreigners. But once Hitler's authority had been undermined, the German soldiers rejected it and tended to express their hostility by projecting their own weakness on to him.

Thus the only important secondary symbol in motivating the behavior of the German soldiers during the recent war also lost its efficacy when the primary group relations of comradeliness, solidarity and subordination to junior officers broke down, and with it the superego of the individual, on which the effective functioning of the primary group depends.[27]

VI. Nazi Machinery for Maintaining Army Solidarity and Fighting Effectiveness

Administrative machinery and personnel. Even before the outbreak of the war, the Nazi Party took an active hand in the internal high policy of the Wehrmacht and in the selection of the Chief of Staff and his entourage. From September 1939 to the signing of the capitulation in May 1945 this process of Nazification continued steadily until the Wehrmacht was finally rendered powerless to make its own decisions. Nazi Party control over the Wehrmacht was designed to insure (1) that Nazi strategic intentions would be carried out (2) that capitulation would be made impossible and (3) that internal solidarity down to the lowest private would be maintained.

Most ambitious and successful of the early efforts at Nazification were the recruitment and training of the special Waffen SS (Elite) Divisions. These units initially contained only fanatically devoted Nazi volunteers and had officer staffs which were thoroughly permeated with Nazi stalwarts. They became the Nazi Party army within the Wehrmacht, and their military prowess greatly enhanced the prestige of the Nazi Party and weakened the position of the General Staff.

At the outbreak of the war, the domestic security and police services inside the Reich were completely unified under the command of Himmler. Although the Wehrmacht had its own elaborate system of security, elements of the *Sicherheitsdienst* operated in occupied areas, in conjunction with the Wehrmacht. As the fortunes of war declined, the Nazi Party accelerated the extension of its security and indoctrination services over the Wehrmacht. The security net around the German High Command was drawn most tightly in response to the 20th of July *Putsch*. In addition to those officers who were executed, a large number of doubtful loyalty were removed or put into commands where they could be closely supervised.

As the German troops retreated into Germany, SS and state police units, instead of the Wehrmacht military police, were given the normal military function of maintaining the line of demarcation between the front lines and the rear areas. A captured order, issued by the CO of the SS forces in the West on September 21, 1944, indicated that these units would have the task of preventing contact between the civilian population and the troops, as well as the arrest and execution of deserters from the army.[28] In addition to these security procedures, the Nazis made effective use of exploiting the individual German soldier's fear of physical destruction as was described above in the section, *Demand for physical survival.*

But these measures were of a negative nature. In order to strengthen the traditional Wehrmacht indoctrination efforts, the Nazi Party appointed in the winter of 1943 political indoctrination officers called *National Sozialistische Führungsoffiziere* (NSFO), to all military formations. Later in September 1944, when the Nazis felt the need for intensifying their indoctrination efforts, the position of these officers was strengthened by the establishment of an independent chain of command which enabled them to communicate with higher headquarters without Wehrmacht interference.[29] The NSFO's were given the power, in cases of "particular political significance or where delay implies danger" to report immediately and directly to NSF officers of higher commands and upward to the highest command, irrespective of routine communication channels. To interfere with the NSFO chain of command was made a military crime. The NSFO "organization" came to publish or directly supervise most of the publications and radio stations for the troops, and to prepare the leaflets which were distributed to or dropped on the German troops. Their job also included periodic indoctrination meetings. The official publication for the indoctrination of the officers' corps, *Mitteilung für die Truppe,* which had been published throughout the war by the Wehrmacht, was also taken over by Nazi Party functionaries *(NS Führungsstab der Wehrmacht)* in November 1944.

The NSF officers, with their independent chain of command, also became security officers of the Nazi Party. They spent a great deal of time prying into the morale and political convictions of higher officers in order to warn headquarters of the need to replace men of faltering faith.[30] Captured German generals, perhaps motivated by a desire to exculpate themselves, told how during the closing months of the war, they came to feel completely subjugated by the indoctrination officers. They reported that these Nazi junior officers maintained an independent reporting system on senior officers and often said, "You're done if he gives a bad account of you."

The final step in the Nazi Party encroachment on the admin

istration of the Wehrmacht came when the *levee en masse,* the *Volkssturm,* was raised. Here, the Nazi Party assumed complete control of training and indoctrination and units were to be turned over to the Wehrmacht only for actual deployment. No doubt the Wehrmacht was glad to be relieved of this unpopular task, as well as the even more unpopular task of organizing the Werewolf resistance, which the Nazi Party assumed for itself completely.

Propaganda themes. The most striking aspect of Nazi indoctrination of their own men during combat was the employment of negative appeals and counter-propaganda, which attempted less to reply directly to the substance of our claims than to explain the reasons why the Allies were using propaganda.

The Nazis frankly believed that they could employ our propaganda efforts as a point of departure for strengthening the unpolitical resolve of their men. They had the legend of the effectiveness of Allied propaganda in World War I as a warning from which to "conclude" that if the Germans failed to be tricked by propaganda this time, success was assured. A typical instance of this attitude was contained in a captured order issued by the Officer in Command of the garrison of Boulogne on September 11, 1944, in which he appealed to his men not to be misled by Allied propaganda. The German order claimed that the propaganda attack in the form of leaflets was in itself an expression of the weakness of the Allied offensive, which was in desperate need of the port for communications. During the same period, an NSF officer issued an elaborate statement in which he reminded the garrison at Le Havre that the "enemy resorts to propaganda as a weapon which he used in the last stages of the first world war," in order to point out that German victory depended on the determination of the German soldier to resist Allied propaganda.

In the fall and winter of 1944, the campaign to counteract Allied propaganda by "exposing" it was intensified and elaborated. (This method had the obvious advantage that direct refutations of Allied claims could largely be avoided.) *Mitteilung für die Truppe* (October 1944), a newspaper for officer indoctrination, reviewed the major weapons in the "poison offensive." They included: attacks against the Party and its predominant leaders ("this is not surprising as the enemy will, of course, attack those institutions which give us our greatest strength"); appeals to the Austrians to separate themselves from the Germans ("the time when we were split up in small states was the time of our greatest weakness"); sympathy with the poor German women who work in hellish factories ("the institution must be a good one, otherwise the enemy would not attack it").

Other themes "exposed" in leaflets were: the enemy attempts to separate the leaders from the people ("Just as the Kaiser was blamed in 1918, it now is Hitler who is supposed to be responsible"); the enemy admits his own losses in an exaggerated way in order to obtain the reputation of veracity and to lie all the more at the opportune moment.

Even earlier in the Western campaign, the Germans followed the policy of stamping Allied leaflets with the imprint, "Hostile Propaganda," and then allowing them to circulate in limited numbers. This was being carried out at the same time that mutually contradictory orders for the complete destruction of all enemy propaganda were being issued. The explanation, in part, is that the Nazis realized that it would be impossible to suppress the flood of Allied leaflets, and therefore sought to clearly label them as such and to employ them as a point of departure for counter-propaganda.

The procedure of overstamping Allied leaflets was linked with follow-up indoctrination talks. Such indoctrination lectures, which were conducted by the Nazi NSFO's, became towards the end of the war one of the main vehicles of Nazi indoctrination of their own troops. Ps/W claimed, although it was probably not entirely correct, that they usually slept through such sessions, or at least paid little attention, until the closing *Sieg Heil* was sounded. At this late date in the war, emphasis on oral propaganda was made necessary by the marked disruption of communications. Radio listening at the front was almost non-existent due to the lack of equipment; when in reserve, troops listened more frequently. Newspapers were distributed only with great difficulty. More important were the leaflets which were either dropped by air on their own troops or distributed through command channels.

"Strength through fear." Major lines of the negative approach employed by these leaflets in indoctrination talks, in the rumors circulated by NSF officers, stressed "strength through fear," particularly fear of Russia and the general consequences of complete destruction that would follow defeat.

Because of the German soldier's concern about the welfare of his family living inside Germany, Nazi agencies were constantly issuing statements about the successful evacuation of German civilians to the east bank of the Rhine.

Equally stressed in the strength through fear theme were retaliation threats against the families of deserters, mistreatment of prisoners of war in Anglo-American prison camps, and the ultimate fate of prisoners. The phrase *Sieg oder Sibirien* (Victory or Siberia) was emphasized and much material was released to prove that the Anglo-Americans planned to turn over their prisoners to the Russians. When the U.S. Army stopped shipping German Ps/W to the United States, Nazi propaganda officers spread the rumor among German soldiers "that the way to Siberia is shorter from France than from the United States."

Statements by Ps/W revealed that shortly before the Rundstedt counterattack, speeches by NSFO's were increased. One of the main subjects seems to have been weapons. In retrospect, the intent of the directives under which they were working was obvious. Attempts were made to explain the absence of the Luftwaffe, while the arrival in the near future of new and better weapons was guaranteed.

Psychological preparation for the December counter-offensive was built around the Rundstedt order of the day that "everything is at stake." Exhortations were backed up with exaggerated statements by unit commanders that large amounts of men and material were to be employed. Immediately thereafter, official statements were issued that significant penetrations had been achieved; special editions of troop papers were prepared announcing that 40,000 Americans had been killed.

Such announcements received little attention among the troops actually engaged in the counter-offensive because of the obvious difficulties in disseminating propaganda to fighting troops.

Nevertheless, after the failure of the counter-attack, the Nazis felt called upon to formulate a plausible line to explain the sum total result of that military effort, especially for those who felt that better military judgment would have resulted in a purely defensive strategy against Russia. On January 25, *Front und Heimat* announced that the December offensive had smashed the plan for a simultaneous onslaught: "The East can hold only if the West does too. . . . Every fighting man in the

West knows that the Anglo-Americans are doing all they can, although belatedly, to start the assault on the Fortress Germany. Our task in the West now is to postpone that time as long as possible and to guard the back of our Armies in the East."

Despite the obvious limitations on the efficacy of propaganda during March and April 1945, the Nazis continued to the very end to keep up their propaganda efforts. Due to the confusion within the ranks of the Wehrmacht and the resulting difficulties of dissemination, the task devolved almost wholly on the NSFO's who spent much of their time reading to the troops the most recent orders governing desertion. Leaflets called largely on the Landser's military spirit to carry on. One even demanded that he remain silent (zu schweigen). The Nazis taxed their fancy to create rumors as the last means of bolstering morale. Here a favorite technique for stimulating favorable rumors was for CO's to read to their men "classified" documents from official sources which contained promises of secret weapons or discussed the great losses being inflicted upon the Allies.

VII. The Impact of Allied Propaganda on Wehrmacht Solidarity

The system of controls which the social structure of the Wehrmacht exercised over its individual members greatly reduced those areas in which symbolic appeals of the Allies could work. But the millions of leaflets which were dropped weekly and the "round-the-clock" broadcasts to the German troops certainly did not fail to produce some reactions.

The very first German Ps/W who were interrogated directly on their reactions to Allied propaganda soon revealed a stereotyped range of answers which could be predicted from their degree of Nazification. The fanatical Nazi claimed, "No German would believe anything the enemy has to say," while an extreme attitude of acceptance was typified by a confirmed anti-Nazi who pleaded with his captors: "Now is the moment to flood the troops with leaflets. You have no idea of the effect sober and effective leaflets have on retreating troops." But these extreme reactions of soldiers were of low frequency; Nazi soldiers might admit the truth of our leaflets but usually would not accept their conclusions and implications.

The fundamentally indifferent reaction to Allied propaganda was most interestingly shown in an intensive study of 150 Ps/W captured in October 1944 of whom 65 per cent had seen our leaflets and for the most part professed that they believed their contents. This was a group which had fought very obstinately, and the number of active deserters, if any, was extremely small. Some forty of these Ps/W offered extended comments as to what they meant when they said they believed the contents of Allied leaflets.

> Five stated outright that they believed the messages and that the leaflets assisted them and their comrades to surrender.
>
> Seven declared they believed the leaflets, but were powerless to do anything about appeals to surrender.
>
> Eight stated that they believed the contents, but nevertheless as soldiers and decent individuals would never think of deserting.
>
> Twenty-two declared that events justified belief in the leaflets, but they clearly implied that this had been of little importance in their battle experiences.

In Normandy, where the relatively small front was blanketed with printed material, up to 90 per cent of the Ps/W reported that they had read Allied leaflets, yet this period was characterized by very high German morale and stiff resistance.

Throughout the Western campaign, with the exception of periods of extremely bad weather or when the front was fluid, the cumulative percentage of exposure ranged between 60 and 80 per cent. (This cumulative percentage of exposure was based on statements by Ps/W that they had seen leaflets sometime while fighting on the Western front after D-Day. A few samples indicated that penetration during any single month covered about 20 per cent of the prisoners.) Radio listening among combat troops was confined to a minute fraction due to the lack of equipment; rear troops listened more frequently. In the case of both leaflets and radio it was found that there was widespread but desultory comment on the propaganda, much of which comment distorted the actual contents.

Not only was there wide penetration by Allied leaflets and newssheets, but German soldiers frequently circulated them extensively among their comrades. A readership study of *Nachrichten für die Truppen,* a daily newssheet published by the

Allied Psychological Warfare Division, showed that each copy which was picked up had an average readership of between four and five soldiers—a figure which is extremely large in view of the conditions of combat life. Not only were leaflets widely circulated, but it became a widespread practice for soldiers to carry Allied leaflets on their person, especially the "safe conduct pass" leaflets which bore a statement by General Eisenhower guaranteeing the bearer swift and safe conduct through Allied lines and the protection of the Geneva convention. There is evidence that in certain sectors of the front, German soldiers even organized black-market trading in Allied propaganda materials.

It is relevant to discuss here the differences in effectiveness between tactical and strategic propaganda. By tactical propaganda, we refer to propaganda which seeks to promise immediate results in the tactical situation. The clearest example of this type of propaganda is afforded by "across the lines" loudspeaker broadcasts, which sometimes facilitated immediate capture of the prisoners of war—not by propaganda in the ordinary sense, but by giving instructions on how to surrender safely, once the wish to surrender was present.

No sufficiently accurate estimate is available of the total number of prisoners captured by the use of such techniques, but signal successes involving hundreds of isolated troops in the Normandy campaign have been credited to psychological warfare combat teams. Even more successful were the loudspeaker-carrying tanks employed in the Rhine River offensive, when the first signs of weakening resistance were encountered. For example, the Fourth Armored Division reported that its psychological warfare unit captured over 500 prisoners in a four-day dash from the Kyll River to the Rhine. Firsthand investigation of these loudspeaker missions, and interrogation of prisoners captured under such circumstances, establish that Allied propaganda was effective in describing the tactical situation to totally isolated and helpless soldiers and in arranging an Allied cease fire and thereby presenting an assurance to the German soldier of a safe surrender. The successful targets for such broadcasts were groups where solidarity and ability to function as a unit were largely destroyed. Leaflets especially written for specific sectors and dropped on pin point targets by fighter bombers were used instead of loudspeakers where larger units were cut off. This method proved less successful, since the units to which they were addressed were usually better integrated and the necessary cease fire conditions could not be arranged.

Less spectacular, but more extensive, was strategic propaganda. Allied directives called for emphasis on four themes in this type of propaganda: (1) Ideological attacks on the Nazi Party and Germany's war aims, (2) the strategical hopelessness of Germany's military and economic position, (3) the justness of the United Nations war aims and their unity and determination to carry them out (unconditional surrender, although made known to the troops, was never stressed), (4) promises of good treatment to prisoners of war, with appeals to self-preservation through surrender.

Although it is extremely difficult, especially in view of the lack of essential data, to assess the efficacy of these various themes, some tentative clues might be seen in the answers given to the key attitude questions in the monthly Psychological Warfare opinion poll of captured German soldiers.[31] Thus, there was no significant decline in attachment to Nazi ideology until February and March 1945. In other words, propaganda attacks on Nazi ideology seem to have been of little avail, and attachment to secondary symbols, e.g., Hitler, declined only when the smaller military units began to break up under very heavy pressure.

Since the German soldier was quite ignorant of military news on other fronts, it was believed that a great deal of printed material should contain factual reports of the military situation, stressing the strategical hopelessness of the German position. As a result, the third most frequently recalled items of our propaganda were the military news reports. It seems reasonable to believe that the emphasis on these subjects did contribute to the development of defeatist sentiment.

Despite the vast amount of space devoted to ideological attacks on German leaders, only about five per cent of the Ps/W mentioned this topic—a fact which supported the contention as to the general failure of ideological or secondary appeals. Finally, the presentation of the justness of our war aims was carried out in such a way as to avoid stressing the unconditional surrender aspects of our intentions, while emphasizing postwar peace intentions and organizational efforts; much was made of

United Nations unity. All this fell on deaf ears, for of this material only a small minority of Ps/W (about 5 per cent) recalled specific statements about military government plans for the German occupation.

As has been pointed out previously, the themes which were most successful, at least in attracting attention and remaining fixed in the memory, were those promising good treatment as prisoners of war. In other words, propaganda referring to immediate concrete situations and problems seems to have been most effective in some respects.

The single leaflet most effective in communicating the promise of good treatment was the "safe conduct pass." Significantly, it was usually printed on the back of leaflets which contained no elaborate propaganda appeals except those of self-preservation. The rank and file tended to be favorably disposed to its official language and legal, document-like character. In one sector where General Eisenhower's signature was left off the leaflet, doubt was cast on its authenticity.

Belief in the veracity of this appeal was no doubt based on the attitude that the British and the Americans were respectable law-abiding soldiers who would treat their captives according to international law. As a result of this predisposition and the wide use of the safe conduct leaflets, as well as our actual practices in treating prisoners well, the German soldier came to have no fear of capture by British or American troops. The most that can be claimed for this lack of fear was that it may have decreased or undercut any tendency to fight to the death; it produced no active opposition to continued hostilities.

As an extension of the safe-conduct approach, leaflets were prepared instructing non-commissioned officers in detailed procedures by which their men could safely be removed from battle so as to avoid our fire and at the same time avoid evacuation by the German field police. If the Germans could not be induced to withdraw from combat actively, Allied propaganda appealed to them to hide in cellars. This in fact became a favorite technique of surrender, since it avoided the need of facing the conscience-twinging desertion problem.

As a result of psychological warfare research, a series of leaflets was prepared whose attack was aimed at primary group organization in the German Army, without recourse to ideological symbols. Group organization depended on the acceptance of immediate leadership and mutual trust. Therefore this series of leaflets sought to stimulate group discussion among the men and to bring into their focus of attention concerns which would loosen solidarity. One leaflet declared, "Do not take our (the Allies) word for it; ask your comrade; find out how he feels." Thereupon followed a series of questions on personal concerns, family problems, tactical consideration and supply problems. Discussion of these problems was expected to increase anxiety. It was assumed that to the degree that the soldier found that he was not isolated in his opinion, to that degree he would be strengthened in his resolve to end hostilities, for himself at least.

Conclusion

At the beginning of the second world war, many publicists and specialists in propaganda attributed almost supreme importance to psychological warfare operations. The legendary successes of Allied propaganda against the German Army at the end of the first world war and the tremendous expansion of the advertising and mass communications industries in the ensuing two decades had convinced many people that human behavior could be extensively manipulated by mass communications. They tended furthermore to stress that military morale was to a great extent a function of the belief in the rightness of the "larger" cause which was at issue in the war; good soldiers were therefore those who clearly understood the political and moral implications of what was at stake. They explained the striking successes of the German Army in the early phases of the war by the "ideological possession" of the German soldiers, and they accordingly thought that propaganda attacking doctrinal conceptions would be defeating this army.

Studies of the German Army's morale and fighting effectiveness made during the last three years of the war throw considerable doubt on these hypotheses. The solidarity of the German Army was discovered by these studies—which left much to be desired from the standpoint of scientific rigor—to be based only very indirectly and very partially on political convictions or broader ethical beliefs. Where conditions were such as to allow primary group life to function smoothly, and where the primary group developed a high degree of cohesion, morale was high and resistance effective or at least very determined, regardless in the main of the political attitudes of the soldiers. The conditions of primary group life were related to spatial proximity, the capacity for intimate communication, the provision of paternal protectiveness by NCO's and junior officers, and the gratification of certain personality needs, e.g., manliness, by the military organization and its activities. The larger structure of the army served to maintain morale through the provision of the framework in which potentially individuating physical threats were kept at a minimum—through the organization of supplies and through adequate strategic dispositions.

The behavior of the German Army demonstrated that the focus of attention and concern beyond one's immediate face-to-face social circles might be slight indeed and still not interfere with the achievement of a high degree of military effectiveness. It also showed that attempts to modify behavior by means of symbols referring to events or values outside the focus of attention and concern would be given an indifferent response by the vast majority of the German soldiers. This was almost equally true under conditions of primary group integrity and under conditions of extreme primary group disintegration. In the former, primary needs were met adequately through the gratifications provided by the other members of the group; in the latter, the individual had regressed to a narcissistic state in which symbols referring to the outer world were irrelevant to his first concern—"saving his own skin."

At moments of primary group disintegration, a particular kind of propaganda less hortatory or analytical, but addressing the intensified desire to survive, and describing the precise procedures by which physical survival could be achieved, was likely to facilitate further disintegration. Furthermore, in some cases aspects of the environment towards which the soldier might hitherto have been emotionally indifferent were defined for him by prolonged exposure to propaganda under conditions of disintegration. Some of these wider aspects, e.g., particular strategic considerations, then tended to be taken into account in his motivation and he was more likely to implement his defeatist mood by surrender than he would have been without exposure to propaganda.

It seems necessary, therefore, to reconsider the potentialities of propaganda in the context of all the other variables which influence behavior. The erroneous views concerning the omnipotence of propaganda must be given up and their place must be taken by much more differentiated views as to the possibilities of certain kinds of propaganda under different sets of conditions.

It must be recognized that on the moral plane most men are members of the larger society by virtue of identifications which are mediated through the human beings with whom they are in personal relationships. Many are bound into the larger society only by primary group identifications. Only a small proportion possessing special training or rather particular kinds of personalities are capable of giving a preponderant share of their attention and concern to the symbols of the larger world. The conditions under which these different groups will respond to propaganda will differ, as will also the type of propaganda to which they will respond.

Chapter 23. Notes

1. For a further treatment of these problems see Dicks, Henry V., *Love, Money and War,* London: Kegan Paul Rutledge (forthcoming).

2. Report by the Supreme Commander on operations in Europe by the Allied Expeditionary Force, June 6, 1944 to May 8, 1945.

3. "By primary groups I mean those characterized by intimate face-to-face association and cooperation . . . it is a 'we'; it involves the sort of sympathy and mutual identification for which 'we' is the natural expression. One lives in the feeling of the whole and finds the chief aims of his will in that feeling" (p. 23). . . . "The most important spheres of this intimate association and cooperation—though by no means the only ones—are the family, the play group of children, and the neighborhood or community group of elders" (p. 24). . . . "the only essential thing being a certain intimacy and fusion of personalities." (p. 26)

Cooley, Charles Horton, *Social Organization,* New York, 1909.

4. *Kriegsbriefe gefallener Studenten,* 1928, pp. 167-172. Quoted by William K. Pfeiler, *War and the German Mind,* New York, 1941, p. 77.

5. On the relations between the *technical* group and *social* group cf. Whitehead, T. N., *Leadership in a Free Society,* Cambridge, Mass., 1936, Ch. IV.

6. Cooley, *op. cit.,* Part I, pp. 3-57; Freud, S., *Group Psychology and the Analysis of the Ego,* Ch. IV; Mayo, Elton, *The Human Problems of an Industrial Civilization,* New York, 1933; Wilson, A. T. M., "The Service Man Comes Home," *Pilot Papers: Social Essays and Documents,* Vol. 1, No. 2 (Apr., 1946), pp. 9-28; Grinker, R. R. and Spiegel, J. P., *Men Under Stress,* Philadelphia, 1945, Ch. 3; Whitehead, T. N., *op. cit.,* Ch. I, X, VII; also

Lindsay, A. D., *The Essentials of Democracy*, Oxford, 1935, 2nd ed., pp. 78-81.

7. German combat soldiers almost always stressed the high level of comradeliness in their units. They frequently referred to their units as "one big family."

8. Individuals of German extraction residing outside the boundaries of Germany.

9. Approval of desertion by a married man with a large family or with heavy familial obligations was often noted near the war's end. For such men, the stronger ties to the family prevented the growth of insuperably strong ties to the army unit.

10. The "hard core" corresponds to opinion leaders, as the term is currently used in opinion research.

11. Schmalenbach, Hermann, "Die soziologische Kategorien des Bundes," *Die Dioskuren*, Vol. I, München,1922, pp. 35-105; and Plessner, Hellmuth, *Grenzen der Gemeinschaft*, Bonn, 1924.

12. Bluher, Hans, *Die Rolle der Erotik in der männlichen Gesellschaft*. Jena. 1921, Vol. II, Part II especially, pp. 91-109; pp. 154-177.

13. This policy sometimes created a serious dilemma for the Wehrmacht. Increasingly, to preserve the sense of group identity and the benefits of solidarity which arose from it, regiments were allowed to become depleted in manpower by as much as 50 to 75 per cent. This, however, generated such feelings of weakness that the solidarity gains were cancelled.

14. This proposition is in opposition to the frequently asserted view that social solidarity of an intense sort is positively and linearly related to fear of threat from the outside.

15. The Germans in the Channel ports were able to resist so long partly because the men remained together where they were constantly in each other's presence. Thus the authority of the group over the individual was constantly in play.

16. A 36-year-old soldier—a Berlin radio-worker—who surrendered prematurely, said: "During one month in a bunker without light and without much to do, the men often discussed capture. Conversation usually started about families: who was married and what was to become of his family? The subject became more acute as the Americans approached."

17. This threat was never actually carried out. Furthermore, the *Sicherheitsdienst* (Security Service) admitted the impossibility of taking sanctions against the deserter's family because of the difficulty of locating them in the disorder of German civilian life. As the German soldiers became aware of the impotence of the SD in this respect, this barrier against desertion weakened.

18. Demeter, Karl, *Das deutsche Heer und seine Offiziere*, Berlin, n.d., Ch. 3 and 5; Broch, Hermann, *The Sleepwalkers*, London, n.d.

19. Indeed, a well known German general during the period of captivity felt so strongly the pressure of soldierly honor that he always went to sleep wearing his monocle.

20. Frequently German soldiers who were reluctant to desert separated themselves from battle by hiding in cellars or dugouts, waiting to be overrun. Such soldiers often thought it morally necessary to volunteer the ex-

planation for their capture that they had been found by the enemy because they had fallen asleep from exhaustion and had been taken against their will.

21. The absence of officers relaxed disciplinary controls. Thus soldiers who lay in bunkers and who "didn't see any officers for weeks" were more likely to desert or to allow themselves to be captured. The presence of the officer had the same function as other primary group members—he strengthened the superego by granting affection for duties performed and by threatening to withdraw it for duties disregarded.

22. Nazi propagandists, with their hyperpolitical orientation, tended to overestimate the German soldier's responsiveness to politics.

23. The fact that the High Command made no attempt to explain away the defeat of the counter-offensive may have been due, among other things, to its conviction of the irrelevance of strategic consideration in the morale of the ordinary soldier.

24. The proposition often asserted during the war that the Allies' refusal to promise a "soft peace" to the Germans was prolonging the war, i.e., that German military resistance was motivated by fear of what the Allies would do to Germany in event of its defeat, scarcely finds support in the fact that in October 1944, when the German front was stiffening, 74 per cent of a sample of 345 Ps/W said they did not expect revenge to be taken against the German population after the war.

25. See Gurfein, M. I., and Janowitz, Morris, "Trends in Wehrmacht Morale," *The Public Opinion Quarterly*, Vol. 10, No. 1 (1946), p. 78.

26. Much of the reduction of trust in Hitler which occurred in this final period was simply a diminution in esteem for Hitler's technical skill as a strategist and as a diplomat.

27. The mixture of apathy and resentment against Hitler persisted through the first part of the demobilization period following the end of the war, but as life began to reorganize and to take on new meaning and the attitudes toward authority, which sustain and are sustained by the routines of daily life, revived, esteem for Hitler also began to revive. It is likely to revive still further and to assume a prominent place in German life once more, if the new elite which is being created under the Allied occupation shows weakness and lack of decisiveness and self-confidence.

28. Order of Commanding Officer of SS Forces in the West, September 21, 1944.

29. This step was regarded as sufficiently important to be promulgated in an Order appearing over Hitler's signature.

30. Numerous orders menaced officers who might become political dissidents. One such document circulated in Army Group B, dated January 21, 1945, stated that Himmler had drawn up a set of instructions concerning officer offenders which were to be reviewed at least once a month. Political divergences were to be harshly dealt with, regardless of the previous military or political service of the officer in question.

31. Cf. Gurfein, M. I., and Janowitz, Morris, *op. cit.*

Chapter **24**

SOME PSYCHOLOGICAL LESSONS FROM LEAFLET PROPAGANDA *

By

MARTIN F. HERZ

THE EFFECTIVENESS of leaflets which were used in combat propaganda during the past war could be gauged to a much larger extent than was possible in the case of most other forms of propaganda. Continuous prisoner interrogation about the impact of combat leaflets, for instance, permitted the elaboration of certain principles, and their confirmation and subsequent refinement, whereas with respect to the effectiveness of strategic propaganda it has been possible to make only broad and very general observations. Our mistakes in combat propaganda were often readily apparent, while correct psychological judgments could be confirmed by observing the behavior of enemy troops. It is the purpose of this article to set forth some conclusions about leaflet writing and propaganda in general which resulted from this experience.

The Insufficiency of Truth

During the early days of combat leafleting, the psychological warfare field team with the Fifth Army in Italy was partially dependent on shipments of propaganda material from governmental agencies in Britain and the United States. One leaflet sent to Italy seemed a first-rate job. It described, with many pictures and a brief text, the life in "British, American and Canadian Prisoner-of-War Camps." It showed, for instance, a Canadian base camp that had formerly been a hotel, a camp orchestra, a well-groomed prisoner (an officer) sitting in an overstuffed chair, and other prisoners playing billiards or sitting on

* Reprinted from *Public Opinion Quarterly* (Fall 1949).

a porch listening to the radio. Everything this leaflet said or depicted was true. It was thought best, however, to test it first on some of the prisoners in the Aversa P/W enclosure.

As a result of those tests, the entire shipment had to be discarded. The prisoners were by no means uncooperative—in fact, many of them stated that if only they had known that treatment would be as good as it was in Aversa, they would have surrendered earlier. Nevertheless, they simply refused to believe that conditions in P/W camps in America could be as shown on the leaflet.

Although it was true that prisoners in American P/W camps received eggs for breakfast, further testing showed us that this notion was so preposterous to the Germans on the other side of the firing line that they simply laughed at the idea. Since this discredited the balance of our message, it became another favorable truth which we learned to suppress. The same, incidentally, applied to an important strategic propaganda theme, that of war production. We had to refrain from telling the Germans that Henry Kaiser put ships together in five days. Although this spectacular fact was true, we had to stress the less spectacular and more general fact that we were building several times the tonnage sunk by the U-boats. Intelligence on what the Germans believed, and what they could be expected to believe, forced us to do this.

Eventually, as the result of extensive prisoner interrogations, a basic theme on P/W treatment was worked out, which found its widest application on the Western Front. Instead of picturing captivity in the U.S. as the outrageous idyll which it really was, we used the slogan: *"It's no fun being a prisoner-of-war!"* and went on to show that it was a grim but tolerable fate for anyone who had fought hard but who nevertheless had been unable to evade capture. We did point out, however, that being a prisoner had certain redeeming features. The punch line to this type of appeal was: *"Better Free Than a Prisoner-of-War, Better a Prisoner-of-War Than Dead."* That line proved highly effective. Understatement, in this instance, was probably the only viable means of communicating with the enemy.

How Can Effectiveness Be Judged?

At this point, the question may legitimately be asked just how it was known, during the last war, whether a combat leaflet was more, or less, successful. After all, the psychological warfare intelligence officer could only in the rarest instances observe the behavior in battle of those enemy units which had been subjected to a specific leaflet message. Since this question is important to consideration of the following case material, we will dwell on it briefly.

Evidence of effectiveness, or of lack of effectiveness, was obtained chiefly from the following sources: (a) quantity of leaflets found on the persons of prisoners; (b) recollection of leaflets by prisoners, and comments about them; (c) favorable mention, and detailed discussion by soldiers behind the German lines, as reported by cooperative prisoners; (d) detailed description of their surrender by prisoners; (e) preoccupation of German counter-propaganda with specific Allied leaflets, including plagiarism by German combat propagandists; (f) comments by the enemy command, as learned from captured documents on troop morale.

In some cases, where continued dissemination of one special leaflet was deemed desirable, prisoner reactions could even be used to sharpen its effectiveness, as in the case of the well-known SHAEF Safe-Conduct leaflet. The first edition of that leaflet, produced in the early days of the Normandy invasion, showed merely the seal of the U.S. and the British royal crest, together with a standard text in English and German which called upon the Allied front-line soldier to accord his prisoner good treatment. By the time the Safe-Conduct leaflet went into its sixth printing, the following changes had been made as a result of P/W interviews: (a) the German text had been placed above the English; (b) a note had been inserted, stating specifically that the English text was a translation of the German; (c) General Eisenhower's signature had been added; (d) his name had been spelled out, because it was learned that Germans did not recognize the written signature as Eisenhower's; (e) the leaflet was printed in red rather than in green, which made it more conspicuous on the ground; and (f) a note had been added under the word "Safe Conduct," pointing out that the document was valid for "one or several bearers." These improvements resulted from continuous testing of the leaflet's effectiveness.

In planning for propaganda exploitation of our landing at Anzio and Nettuno in January 1944, we provided for dissemination of a leaflet on the main (Cassino) front as soon as we knew that our troops were ashore. In this leaflet we committed the mistake of making specific predictions, speaking of the German retreat being blocked and of a "battle of encirclement" that would commence with the landing operation. When the beachhead was subsequently contained, the Germans were so elated about the falsity of our prediction that they disseminated replicas of our (German-language) leaflet to the American soldiers at the front, jeering at us and delighting in proving us wrong. It need hardly be pointed out that this was rather foolish on their part: our soldiers had never seen our German-language leaflet and did not care what it said. What the Germans might have done, but failed to do, was to disseminate the leaflet *to their own troops,* thus demonstrating the falsity of our propaganda.

The Handling of Propaganda Defeats

The lesson to be learned from this experience would seem to be that it is highly risky to make predictions about a forthcoming operation, and also quite unnecessary. The argument was advanced during the planning stage before Anzio that we "owed it to our boys to assume that they would be successful," since "if they fail, the incidental propaganda defeat won't matter." In other words, it was contended that the propaganda risk was part of the major military risk. Experience proved this attitude to be wrong. While it is necessary to take military (and political) risks, it does not appear to be necessary to take propaganda risks. If facts go against us, we can still salvage some propaganda honor from them by admitting that the facts are against us. If we make false predictions, however, subsequent admissions have much less value because our whole credit has been undermined. Victories, after defeats in battle, may restore the enemy's fear of our weapons; but truth, after falsity, does not necessarily restore the belief in our truthfulness.

The second instance of an Allied propaganda defeat also contains food for thought. We had achieved considerable success with a leaflet which factually and in pictures described the first day in the life of German P/W's captured on the Cotentin peninsula. The leaflet was widely disseminated all over the Western front. When we broke out of the beachhead and captured Paris, the last picture on the leaflet (which showed P/W's being embarked on an LST) was overprinted in red to show that henceforth prisoners would no longer be shipped to America but would remain in enclosures in Western France. This was a correct decision based on interrogations which showed that many Germans, feeling that the war was about to end, were fearful of being shipped to America, from where it would presumably take longer to get home after the armistice.

German counter-propaganda selected this widely disseminated leaflet to "prove" that since "prisoners are no longer sent to America"—they were being shipped to Siberia instead. The accusation was substantiated in no other way. It was very widely made, however, and eventually expanded into the general slogan *Sieg oder Sibirien!* (victory or Siberia) which tied in with Goebbels' brilliant "strength through fear" propaganda on the home front. This confronted us with the problem of how to meet a preposterous falsehood that apparently was having some success in bolstering German troop morale.

After careful discussion, it was decided not to respond directly, because (a) any reply could be picked up by the Germans as similarly spurious "proof" of the correctness of their contention; and (b) we did not wish to give additional currency to the idea of Siberia. It was assumed that every denial of a flagrant lie lends it a certain dignity that it did not possess before. The word "Siberia" was consequently never mentioned in our output, and the German campaign eventually died a natural death. During the entire period, we continued our regular output on P/W treatment, ignoring the question of shipment but playing up somewhat more heavily the guarantee, under the Geneva Convention, that prisoners would be returned home "as soon as possible after the war."

In general, to deny a lie disseminated by the enemy is in most cases merely to give it additional circulation. (The Soviets are experts at picking up a denial and using it to revitalize the original falsehood.) Disputing a specific point with an opponent usually means descending to his level. When the enemy has scored, it is usually best to chalk up the score in his column and then to hit him somewhere else.[1] If we dispute a point with him, we meet him on ground which he has chosen and engage in defensive propaganda. Later it will be demonstrated that defensive propaganda is—at least in combat propaganda— a virtual impossibility. Propaganda is essentially an offensive weapon.

Target: the Marginal Man

The marginal man in propaganda is the man who does not believe everything we say, but who is interested in our message because he does not believe everything our opponents say either. In war, he is the man who distrusts us and has reasons for fighting, but who also has good reasons for not fighting. He is the *potential waverer*. (Real waverers are presumably already convinced, and thus are not strictly marginal targets.) In our combat propaganda we always tried to address ourselves to potential waverers, to the men who despaired of victory but were reluctant to draw the consequences, the men who were still willing to fight but who fought without determination, who would "never surrender" but who might submit to capture "if the situation were hopeless." To address the out-and-out fanatics would have been a waste of time, and would have harmed us with our other listeners and friends. On the other hand, to address directly the defeatists and those waiting to desert harmed us with the potential waverers.

The concept of the marginal propaganda man may be a useful one for peacetime propaganda also. Too much output may be addressed to persons who already agree with us. With battle lines fairly clearly drawn, communications which meet the approval of completely pro-American elements are less important than those which appeal to potential waverers on both sides of the ideological front (i.e., we must not forget potential waverers in our own democratic ranks). That is why public opinion polling on the effectiveness of our peacetime propaganda, if it does not weight its sample in favor of the critical strata of the population, may be misleading. If, for instance, a theme of ours elicits exceptional enthusiasm on the part of extreme rightist elements abroad, while intensifying doubts about us on the part of potential waverers among the democratic left, then such a theme has done us more harm than good.

The reasoning behind this conclusion is similar to that which

made us forego outright appeals to the German soldier to
desert, on the assumption that the desertion-minded would in
any event receive our message warmly, whereas a blunt appeal
for desertion would have harmed us with the potential waverers. For the potential waverer needs more than "just one little
push" to make him topple. To address him with overly partisan, overly direct, overly anti-enemy propaganda might sour
him on us completely. Similarly, if propaganda favoring American "rugged individualism" is directed to potential waverers
abroad who are convinced that they want economic security
most, but who are not yet convinced that it is worthwhile to
surrender freedom for it, equally adverse results might be expected.

Necessity of Concentrating Propaganda Fire

During the war, demands were continuously made upon our
propagandists to "tell the enemy" a large number of things, to
attack him on a variety of fronts and to undermine his credit in
numerous ways. These demands tended to lead to output which
devoted a small amount of attention to a large number of
subjects.

The dispersion of themes in some of our combat propaganda
may also have been caused in part by the advertising and journalism background of many of our propagandists. Yet combat
propaganda and other propaganda addressed to enemy populations in wartime posed quite different problems than domestic
advertising. The advertising man need only imagine that he is
charged with publicizing *Fleetfoot* automobiles in publications
which contain anti-*Fleetfoot* material, both editorial and advertising, in about twenty-five times the lineage that he has at his
disposal. Let him imagine that the publications on which he
must rely to communicate with his public will contain material
such as the following:

> A news item describing how a certain individual sat down at
> the wheel of his *Fleetfoot,* switched on the ignition, stepped on
> the starter, and was blown to smithereens by gasoline fumes
> which had accumulated under the hood, due to imperfections
> of the carburetor. . . . Pictures of the man's funeral. . . . Res-
> olutions of the bereaved of other families similarly stricken to
> boycott *Fleetfoots.* . . . A news item about another *Fleetfoot*

driver who dizzily careened down a steep incline when his brakes failed to function, and a picture of the resulting smashup and carnage. . . . Reports of protest meetings against the slipshod manufacturing methods and repressive labor policies of *Fleetfoot.* . . . Pictures of disorders at the *Fleetfoot* plant, and articles describing the disorganization of the production line, which resulted in rejected parts being inadvertently built into cars on the assembly line. . . . Stories about the cost-cutting policies of the *Fleetfoot* management which brought the elimination of many safety features ordinarily present in other cars. . . . Statistics proving the falling-off of *Fleetfoot* sales and production, and the increase in complaints and fatalities. . . .

To appreciate the situation of the wartime propagandist one need only imagine such items appearing in all newspapers and other media of a country, in a volume many times that of any message that the *Fleetfoot* advertiser can bring to bear. For in a totalitarian country, the mass and insistence of domestic propaganda is altogether out of proportion to what the enemy can offer. Only an occasional leaflet and snatches of radio programs, and often only messages passed on at second hand, can be brought to the attention of the average enemy target. Under such circumstances, it would be idle to speak of the beauty, low price, popularity, engineering advances, etc. of the latest model —as one would do in domestic advertising. There is only one thing, under such circumstances, that can and should be pounded home: namely, that *Fleetfoots* work.

In peacetime, preparatory to possible hostilities, the basic desideratum of propaganda addressed to potential enemy populations is that it should contain proof of our veracity. Praising the excellence of our product is not only secondary but rather beside the point. As we have seen, it would be difficult to sell the beauty and stylishness and engineering advances of *Fleetfoots* to potential customers who are day in, day out, told that *Fleetfoots* are a danger and a menace.

During the last war, many well-meaning critics of our propaganda effort thought that we should have re-educated the Germans while trying to make them surrender. To this day there are some who do not understand why our propaganda to German soldiers did not characterize Hitler as the villain he indubitably was. To convince German soldiers of the iniquity of the Nazi system, however, would have been a task infinitely more difficult and time-consuming than merely to convince them *that they were being defeated and that it was sensible to give up*. Re-education is not a task of psychological warfare, but of postwar reconstruction. Many men surrendered during the last war who had been convinced by our combat propaganda that to fight on was hopeless and that they would be well treated if they gave up. To convince them of the falsity of Nazism and of Hitler's iniquity might have taken many months and perhaps years longer.

The correctness of this finding is well demonstrated by the failures of Soviet Russia's initial combat propaganda effort against Germany during the last war.

Making Excessive Demands Upon the Enemy

All through the bitter winter of 1941 in front of Moscow, when the Soviets might have had an excellent opportunity to appeal to the frustrated attacking troops, German morale was perceptibly stiffened by injudicious, doctrinaire Soviet propaganda. Conversations with Austrian Communists who participated in that propaganda effort reveal that a bitter fight raged between Soviet propagandists and political officers, with the latter insisting that Soviet combat propaganda be "revolutionary." Soviet leaflets thus initially called upon German soldiers in the front-line to "overthrow Hitler in order to save Germany."

It is a well-established principle of psychology that if pressure is put on a person to perform an act of which he is incapable, serious internal strains and disturbances are set up which may even culminate in hostility toward the person who is making the demands. To call on people who are completely incapable of "overthrowing Hitler" to do so in order to attain their salvation, only means that such people will either despair of their salvation or will turn their backs altogether on the message and its source.

The Soviets eventually learned their lesson and strictly divorced their ideological propaganda from their combat propaganda, but only after caricatures of Hitler, messages exalting the bravery of the Soviet Army and denouncing fascism, etc., had done them immeasurable harm. Even after the break had been made, however, the spilling-over of Communist concepts and nomenclature (including occasional domestic propaganda caricatures and words such as "bankruptcy," "lackeys," "cliques") continued to give their propaganda an outlandish flavor, in spite of their brilliant use of captured German generals for combat psychological warfare purposes. It is an axiom of all propaganda of the written word, of course, that the language must be truly that of the recipient—and that any queerness of idiom severely detracts from the effectiveness of the message. This is so obvious that we may forego the pleasure of offering Japanese exhibits which convincingly demonstrate the point.

"Exporting" Domestic Propaganda

Generally speaking, it can be said that domestic propaganda and propaganda addressed to the enemy simply do not mix. It follows that exceptional loathing and hatred of the enemy, perhaps derived from personal humiliation, persecution, and other on-the-spot experiences, do not by any means constitute good qualifications for combat propagandists. Thus persons who returned from Germany and Japan shortly before the war, and considered their primary mission to be spreading knowledge in America about the iniquity and menace of the systems there, found it extremely difficult to achieve the necessary adjustments that would make them useful for propaganda directed toward the enemy civilian populations. Similarly, in combat propaganda, the propagandist's exultation over the enemy's discomfitures should not be too apparent in his output. Leaflets gleefully pointing at weaknesses and absurdities of the enemy, jibing and jeering at his travails, (the "We hear you have a one-legged man in your company" type) generally proved unsuccessful during the last war.[2] It was difficult to prevent the production and dissemination of such material, however, since intelligence officers, for whom propaganda inevitably means capitalizing on all weaknesses and mistakes of the enemy, frequently pressed very strongly for leaflets of this type.

The above point is by no means as obvious as it seems, for while in theory many might agree, in practice it seemed unreasonable to some that we did not fight "ideologically" in our combat propaganda. To clinch this point, therefore, it is well to observe the effect on ourselves of enemy propaganda which incorporated domestic propaganda elements.

One example may be found in German anti-Semitic propaganda. The Nazis, to whom it seemed obvious that the Jews were behind America's entry into the war, found it impossible to contain themselves on that score. As a result, leaflets and radio programs which otherwise might have had a measure of success became even queerer and stranger to the American soldiers—for instance, the Axis-Sally programs with their reference to the "Jewnited States," or leaflets about wartime profiteers which pictured a character named Sam Levy who had been helped up the ladder to fame and fortune by Mr. Mordecai Ezekiel. To the Nazis, the name of a real-life figure such as Mr. Ezekiel seemed a God-given propaganda asset which the propagandist simply could not pass up. After all, did not that name clearly convey the idea of an untrustworthy, scheming and grasping individual? To Germans who had been steeped in Nazi anti-Semitic propaganda it undoubtedly had such a connotation. To American GI's, however, such leaflets looked more like "propaganda" than they would have otherwise, and the entire venture acquired a fatally alien and unreasonable quality.

A second example is afforded by German and Japanese anti-Roosevelt propaganda. Let it not be said that the average American was more loyal to his President or more convinced of Roosevelt's essential honesty than the average German was of Hitler's. Many a German who considered the war a mistake, and perhaps even a crime, nevertheless resented slurs on Hitler, especially when made by the enemy. The same, *mutatis mutandis,* was true of many American soldiers. One anti-Roosevelt leaflet, depicting F.D.R. as The Grim Reaper, had a decidedly adverse (i.e., anti-enemy and morale-strengthening) effect on our troops.

The third, and most recent, example may be taken from the propaganda now being directed to Europe. In this the Soviets, whose propagandists appear to have their hands tied by directives, have without question sinned and failed the most: in Austria, for instance, the Soviet newspaper *Oesterreichische Zeitung,* with its alien make-up, its queer wording ("over-fulfilled the norm," "miasmas of capitalism," etc.) and its preponderance of outlandish news items, has lost nearly all reader interest—although the Austrian Communist paper, which is written by Austrians, is quite another story. War films of all nations, in which enemy soldiers are shown, have met with unfavorable receptions in ex-enemy territory. Plays, such as the eminently successful "Watch on the Rhine," which packed them in on Broadway, elicited general astonishment and dismay over what German and Austrian theatergoers (including violent anti-Nazis) considered to be inaccuracies and "patent propaganda."

Doctrine of Limited Agreement

Thus it can be said that in combat propaganda it would be fatal to expect the enemy to identify himself with our side. Totalitarian enemies do not revolt because they cannot, and they do not change sides because they rarely understand the truth until it is too late. Consequently, we cannot expect an individual enemy to agree with us on more than one point at a time.

In order to find any common ground at all, to find a point of departure for the psychological manipulation of the enemy, it may even be necessary to select a point of his own creed on which to register agreement. During the last war, the elements of the German propaganda position which we used as such "points of departure" were (a) the belief in the excellence of the soldierly qualities of the German infantryman; and (b) the belief that he was being crushed by Allied superiority of materiel, rather than out-fought man for man. No propaganda to enemy targets can be successful unless some such common ground which can be used as a point of departure for the message is found.

As an example of the validity of this doctrine, we may cite *Eine Minute* (One Minute), probably the most successful combat leaflet of the last war. This leaflet is usually passed over by chroniclers of our combat propaganda record because of its seeming lack of originality or insidiousness. Yet it was again and again adjudged the most successful venture of this type (next to the SHAEF Safe-Conduct leaflet). It was found in large numbers on the persons of prisoners, was republished in many variants at various stages of the campaign in the West, and was also reprinted and used with good success by combat propagandists in the Mediterranean Theater. It salved the feelings of the enemy by crediting him, by implication, with great soldierly virtue; it accommodated his alibi of material inferiority; it described him in soldierly (non-political) terms, avoiding any political arguments; it did not overly praise captivity; and it "left the decision to the reader," seemingly not urging him to desert. Also, on its reverse side, along with a dry, curt summary of the essential facts about captivity, it spelled out the behavior necessary to effect surrender.

Propaganda to non-enemy targets is governed by the opposite considerations. In addressing ourselves to an enemy-occupied country, for instance, the audience's identification with our side must obviously be *taken for granted*—even if it does not completely obtain. It must always be assumed that citizens of occupied countries will greet us as liberators when we redeem them. (This assumption also immeasurably lightens the task of consolidation and post-war reorientation propaganda in occupied territories.) To make concessions to the Quisling point-of-view in any particular would be quite out of place.

Wedge-Driving and Appeals to the Unconscious

To "widen the gulf" between two enemy nations, to "drive a wedge" between officers and enlisted men, or to "exploit the cleavage" between elite troops and combat infantry, or "between the party and the people," are ever-cherished objectives of the propaganda directive writer. As objectives they are of course entirely sound. Implementation may, however, involve so many psychological difficulties that more harm than good is done. For sometimes it will suffice for a latent dissatisfaction to be brought out into the open by the enemy, for it to disappear.

Witness the German propaganda at the Anzio beachhead in February 1944, which reasoned quite correctly, that British troops, who had borne the heaviest brunt of the German offensive at Aprilia (Carroceto), were apt to grumble about the seemingly less dangerous role played by the Americans. Several wedge-driving leaflets along such lines were disseminated, including some titillating ones showing British girls being undressed and fondled by Americans. The German approach, however, was so lacking in subtlety that according to British officers on the beachhead the comradeship-in-arms between

British and Americans there was enhanced rather than diminished by the Nazi propaganda effort. Also—possibly through the projection of a theme that was vexing and frustrating to the reader without his being able to do anything about it—anti-German sentiment among British troops may even have increased.

The Japanese combat leaflet writers also attempted to capitalize on the known sex-frustration of American soldiers in the jungles of the South Pacific, but again the result was so crass and clumsy that if it lowered the morale of any American soldier reading such a leaflet, at the same time it quite likely made him want to vent his pent-up feelings upon the enemy. Although there were some abler attempts in the same direction, all suffered from the directness of the appeal: it simply is not for the enemy to remind us of our desire for women, or, for that matter, of our desire to get out of the battle alive. What goes for sex goes even more for cowardice. Enemy media can hardly appeal plainly and directly to the individual's unsoldierly, un-heroic desire for self-preservation. Perhaps it could if he were alone, but since powerful group pressures work upon him, and feelings of duty, comradeship, fear and patriotism intervene, the overt appeal cannot run directly counter to them. German appeals to our GI's, slogans such as "Take it easy, you'll last longer," fall into this category.

Dangers of Black Propaganda

It may be said, in view of the above—and there are many other examples—that to bring out and nourish any subconscious feelings of resentment on the part of the enemy soldier may be beyond the capabilities of "white" propaganda (the source of which is admitted) and instead is a fitting subject for "black" or "gray" propaganda (ostensibly produced by dissident elements within the enemy population, or mentioning no source at all). The difficulty there, however, is that detection of the origin of such propaganda will not only result in heightened hatred against the actual originator for having thus invaded the most private recesses of the enemy's mind, but it will also redound emphatically to the detriment of all "white" propaganda from the same source.

As a good example of this danger, mention might be made

of an Allied "black" or "gray" leaflet of the last war that was designed to fan the sex-starved German soldier's resentment against the alleged increased latitude given foreign laborers in Germany. The leaflet in question showed a swarthy foreign worker shamelessly disporting himself with a naked Teutonic maiden, and was decidedly apt to arouse the passions of a front-line soldier. Had it been possible to conceal the source completely, beyond the shadow of a doubt, this leaflet might well have been a smashing success in undermining German troop morale. As it was, however—and this is a criticism of most of our naive "black" and "gray" activity of the last war—the enemy could easily see from the elaborateness of the leaflet (which in this case was printed in four colors) that this was Allied propaganda. Even though he might agree with the message, he would resent it since it was painful to him. Moreover, since at the same time all our "white" media were laboring hard and patiently to establish the essential honesty and forthrightness of our propaganda, some harm was probably done to the credit of our white media.

No nation can talk out of two sides of its mouth at the same time: we cannot on the one hand speak nothing but the truth and then, with a changed voice and pretending to be someone else—but quite obviously still ourselves—say things which we don't dare to say straight out. Black propaganda must be like the voice of a master ventriloquist which really appears to come out of the mouth of an entirely different individual. In the case of the "gray" leaflet under discussion, the general make-up of the message and especially the elaborateness of its presentation, made it quite obvious that it was not the product of a clandestine printing press in Germany. Had it been possible to create such an impression, however, or had it been possible to make it seem an inadvertent German disclosure, it might have been the important adjunct to our overt program which it was originally intended to be.[3]

On Threats and "Toughness" in Propaganda

There does not appear to be a single case on record in the last war when an ultimatum resulted in surrender of a surrounded enemy unit. On the other hand, we know of many cases when, in the face of a hopeless situation, commanders sent or received emissaries to discuss surrender. Because, in a sense, a totalitarian country at bay resembles a beleaguered fortress, the question of collective surrenders in the face of collective threats is all-important. First of all, it must be said that the threat of force is only effective if immediately followed by force—nothing is more damning than an empty propaganda threat. Second, a message written from the strength of one's position cannot be hedged or qualified, or couched in a defensive tone, and should not attempt to answer imaginary counter-arguments. The German appeal to the American forces in Bastogne, in fact, might have been written by an American fifth columnist in the ranks of a German combat propaganda company, or by American black operators attempting to raise the morale of the defenders. Instead of emphasizing all factors of German strength, the writer attempted to answer all imaginable counter-arguments and thus practically created the impression that the Germans at Bastogne were the beleaguered ones and that the Americans "really had no reason to be as self-confident" as he imagined them to be. This is an excellent example of the general proposition that defensiveness has no place in combat propaganda and little place in any propaganda.

Threats, however, do occasionally have a place in propaganda. In order to describe the conditions under which they may have a salutary effect, it is necessary to differentiate among four basic situations: (a) the situation of the enemy soldier—if he can do something about getting out of the fight, and (b) if he can do nothing about getting out of the fight; similarly (c) the situation of the civilian who is in a position to act, and (d) that of the civilian who can do nothing about the war. If these differentiations are not borne in mind, the effects of propaganda may be diametrically opposed to those which have been intended.

As to the enemy soldier, if he is in any position to surrender, a threat followed up with a display of strength (e.g., overwhelming artillery superiority) may make him ripe at least for capture. If he is in no position to surrender, however—and most members of beleaguered garrisons belong in this category—he is quite likely to be galvanized into especially fanatical resistance by the threat, because of the psychological mechanism of frustration which has been mentioned above.

As to civilians, those who are in no position to do anything about the war—and these constitute the overwhelming majority of the population of all totalitarian countries—will quite likely be embittered by threatening propaganda. Occasionally, however, such bitterness can be exploited for tactical purposes. The Germans are said to have used terror propaganda during their Blitzkrieg in 1940 specifically in order to create panic and encourage civilians to take flight and thus clog the roads. They also attempted to use scare tactics during their Ardennes offensive, when they cynically advised unfortunate French civilians in the Strasbourg-Mulhouse area (where they had temporarily recrossed the Rhine) to "save yourselves—for we will treat you just as well as we have treated your comrades during the last four years!" The Western Allies also used such tactics when, at the behest of Prime Minister Churchill, they unfolded a propaganda effort early in 1945 which was designed to start large numbers of Germans trekking from certain specified "danger areas." These are the only known instances in the last war when threatening propaganda to civilians had the intended effect.

The "Helpless Civilian" Target

By far the most important category of targets, however—in point of numbers, at least—is the civilian population (category "d") that can do nothing to end the war, consisting as it does of persons who cannot even remove themselves from the impact of bombing attacks. To threaten them—however gratifying it may be to the enemy-hating propagandist—is psychologically unsound. Rather, the propagandist must seek, by continuous analysis of the patterns of life in the enemy country, to discover those actions which the enemy civilian can reasonably take in his own interest, and where his own interest coincides with ours. To find such actions may afford the key to propaganda to enemy civilians. In the absence of that key, most propaganda directed to enemy civilians will have little concrete effect on the course of a war. In fact, when it is considered that military defeats in any event constitute psychological blows of the first magnitude against the enemy civilian, it would seem that, prior to the time when mutual-interest situations begin to obtain, little can be gained from propaganda directed toward enemy civilians in wartime, except by way of building up credibility. Thus our enormous leaflet output which was dropped on Germany during the war, on which so little evidence of effectiveness has been obtained, can really be judged only in terms of whether it built up belief in our essential honesty. This confidence was needed in the final months of the war when we were in a position to exploit mutual-interest situations.

This—the seeking of mutual-interest situations—constituted by far the most difficult and delicate psychological warfare research project of the last war. Whereas at the beginning of the war, "tough" propaganda from the West was received with derisiveness; whereas during the invasion period it produced sullenness and frustration; at the end of the war our propaganda was all too often greeted by German civilians with the remark: *"I agree with everything you say, but what am I to do?"* Several leaflets attempted to develop concrete mutual-interest instructions to enemy civilians. In a war against a different country, entirely different mutual-interest situations may obtain. The important lesson is that the earlier such instructions can be formulated and the better they can be presented as being of mutual interest and as being *feasible,* the more successful will propaganda against enemy civilians be.

Chapter 24. Notes

1. In certain cases, of course, denial of an enemy falsehood cannot be avoided. In such instances, the denial will be best made by implication, and without reference to the original lie.

2. There are some exceptions, however, especially in the case of unusually low-morale enemy formations.

3. There are a few cases on record where black propaganda did succeed in "driving wedges"—notably the case of a counterfeit instruction to German officers to "save themselves (run away) in hopeless situations," an order which in any event succeeded in fooling a number of American intelligence officers.

Chapter 25

THE POLITICAL SITUATION
IN AACHEN *

By

S. K. PADOVER, L. F. GITTLER, P. R. SWEET

WE SPENT most of January in Aachen, making a survey of the political situation, particularly the civil administration. We had prolonged conversations with the Oberbuergermeister, the eight Buergermeisters, the Bishop, prominent lesser officials in the civil government, and with average people in the city. We consulted frequently with CIC, with the Special Branch of MG, and with the higher MG officers. Major Hugh M. Jones, MGO, and Major Jack Bradford, Deputy MGO, gave us all the co-operation we desired. We wish to express our appreciation for their helpfulness, as well as to the members of the CIC and Special Branch for their friendly and stimulating assistance.

I. *The Civil Administration*

A. *The Men.* In the last 3 months a new elite has emerged in Aachen, an elite made up of technicians, lawyers, engineers, businessmen, manufacturers, and churchmen. This elite is shrewd, strongwilled, and aggressive. It occupies every important job in the administration. Its leader is Oberbuergermeister Oppenhoff. Almost all the Buergermeisters and key functionaries were chosen by him and most of them think his way. Behind Oppenhoff is the Bishop of Aachen, a powerful figure with a subtlety of his own and a program of the Church. Nearly all of these men have known each other for a long time. Three of the Buergermeisters live together in one house; two in another house. Oppenhoff had been, among other war

---

* This chapter is reprinted from a photostatic copy of the original typescript report to PWD/SHAEF.

duties, the lawyer for the bishop and the diocese. His collaborators are Faust and Op De Hipt, both of them executives in the
Veltrup works. Buergermeister Hirtz and Schefer are old
school-mates. All of these men managed to stay out of the Nazi
party; most of them were directly connected with the town's
leading war industries, Veltrup and Talbot.

Their strong point, especially in dealing with Americans, is
that they are "anti-Nazi" or "non-Nazi." Their proof is that
they never joined the party. How and why did they escape
party membership? Oppenhoff says his circle did not depend
on party membership for their livelihood because they were in
the *freie Berufe*—free professions—or were closely connected
with the Church and thus "could not join." Schefer, now Chief
of Police, was protected from party membership by working as
an assessor for the Wehrmacht High Command in Berlin.
Buergermeister Mies was manager of a big war industry whose
contribution to the Nazi war effort was important enough to
earn him the *Kriegsverdienstkreuz*—War Service Cross—in 1943.
Buergermeister Hirtz was not eligible for Nazi party membership because he says he had a Jewish mother.

These leading officials kept out of the Wehrmacht because
they volunteered their services to the war industry. Some of
them, notably Oppenhoff, Faust and Op de Hipt, sought "refuge," as the Mayor terms it, in Aachen's leading war plant—
the Veltrup works. Veltrup was under the jurisdiction of the
German High Command's Wehrkreiskommando and since
the Wehrmacht was primarily interested in war production,
Veltrup was not ordered to force his group of experts to join
the party.

Although the present civil government's principal leaders
worked hard for the Nazi war effort, Chief Mayor Oppenhoff
and his aides do not feel any "moral guilt" for having contributed to the success and prolongation of a system they profess to dislike and a war they now claim is "unjust." The Chief
Mayor, who "has an answer for everything" (in the words of a
CIC officer), rationalizes that "everyone in Germany contributed to the war in some measure." He claims credit as an anti-
Hitlerite on the ground that he did not serve in the Wehrmacht
or join the party, as if his industrial contribution to Hitler's
war were not far greater than it would have been if he had
been a mere soldier or just a party number. Oppenhoff's mili-

tary status, however, is not clear. We have been told by a friend of his that he was inducted into the Wehrmacht in August, 1944, but removed his uniform on Sept. 12, and hid in Eupen. This would mean that he has never been released from the Wehrmacht.

B. *Their Weltanschauung and Ideas.* A striking fact about this new Aachen elite is its comparative youth. Their ages run from 33 to 50. They all represent the upper middle-class; their earnings in the last 10 years under Hitler have been high—ranging from 7,000 to 200,000 marks yearly, with the average about 30,000 marks. They come from "good" families. None of them suffered under the Nazi regime—or ever, by word or deed, opposed it. The record shows they prospered under Hitler.

The men around Oppenhoff are not democratically-minded. They profess a marked distaste for the Weimar Republic, an abhorrence of multiple-party government, a dread of the working man, and a fearful suspicion of liberal movements. Their clannishness excludes all "outsiders." In varying degrees or tones, one or the other repeats the slogans and cliches of the Nazis or the "eternal German"—that Germany was "dishonored" by the Versailles Treaty, that the latter was too harsh, that France is the permanent hereditary enemy, that Germany was betrayed when the 14 points were not kept, that the Reich is "poor," a "land without space" and must expand. They attribute the outbreak of the war to these "evils" and charge the working-class with being the main support of Hitler.

C. *What Does This Group Have in Mind?* It must be remembered that these men have been operating willingly under a Nazi system for most of their working life and that they grew prosperous under it. They are comparatively young men who have had all their practical business experience under Nazism. Thus they have an anti-democratic "managerial" conception of government as well as of business. It is revealing to hear Buergermeister Faust tell how he was confronted recently at a semi-public conference by an articulate former Social Democrat who spoke out against him with hard critical words. Faust said he was so "shocked and embarrassed" that he could think of nothing to do but "look at his shoes"; in all his experience (he is in the middle thirties), this kind of thing "simply had not been done." Workers in the Nazi Labor Front were never like that.

The most important fact about the Mayor and his group is their "basic plan" for the city of Aachen and the whole *Regierungsbezirk*. Only through an analysis and understanding of this plan can one begin to comprehend all the complications and intrigue which have developed in the civil administration and the MG. The "plan" is also a significant index to what one may expect from similar class-groups in post-war Germany.

The "plan" and its machinery and present development place the Oppenhoff administration outside the sphere of an "emergency" or "temporary" government. The key figure is Chief Mayor Oppenhoff; most of his Buergermeisters, prominent officials, and private contractors follow his lead politically and intellectually.

They are planning the future in terms of an authoritarian, highly bureaucratic state, with a paternalistic small-scale industry based on a hierarchical labor system of skill and handicrafts. Politically it is conceived as small-state Clericalism, and socially it is based on owners and managers of small and medium-sized enterprises, with the support of the skilled "Labor Aristocracy" —foremen, *Meister, Obermeister,* artisans. They do not believe in and intend to resist the organization of popular elections, mass political parties and trade unions. They see "work" and "pride in one's work" and a benevolent employer as the solution to the conflict of parties and class interests. They have a contempt for, and fear of, politically-minded workers. "Give the worker a glass of beer and a loaf of bread" one Buergermeister said sarcastically, "and he is satisfied." He said that German workers "think comically." Another Buergermeister believes Social-Democrats are "un-German."

These views are within the framework of the "Christian Staendestaat," German version of the corporative state-idea, which enjoyed a certain vogue in the depression years and which contributed to the repudiation of the democratic idea in Germany. It was exploited but finally discarded by the Nazis.

Chief Mayor Oppenhoff says his present job of reconstruction is aimed at this goal of a "non-political" (i.e., non-democratic), authoritarian, paternalistic, hierarchical, bureaucratic society. He would not—"*selbstverstaendlich,* of course I would not"— appoint any man to a leading position in his government, "no matter what his ability," if the appointee does not share his basic ideas. Hence, he resists the dismissal of any of his associates, regardless of their past record, if these appointees are "vital" and "indispensable" to the execution of his social-industrial plan. Hence, he makes every effort, despite public criticism and MG pressure, to retain personal control of the Labor Bureau. He wishes to protect the skilled "labor aristocracy" as a socially-privileged cadre that would follow him politically.

The power of this new ruling elite is based on a complicated but cohesive personnel structure within and without the civil government. (1) A core of strong *zielbewusst* men in the administration exercise complete domination and influence on policies and personnel. These men comprise Oppenhoff's most intimate co-workers—Op de Hipt, Faust, Schwippert—recruited from the leadership of Aachen's heavy industry mostly. (Dr. Heusch, also an intimate co-worker, has been arrested by Army as a war-criminal closely connected with the Nazi war machine.) (2) A group of weaker men are the tools of the inner circle, rather than the co-workers—Hirtz, Pontesegger, Mies, Pfeiffer, Schefer, and Faust's and Veltrup's brothers-in-law, Hannapel and Delhaes. (3) Strong men who support the mayor because of his Catholic views and labor policy, but who are German nationalists rather than Rhineland separatists, include the Bishop of Aachen and Buergermeister for School, Breuer. (4) A group of careerists, opportunists and potential profiteers, share the mayor's social views and see material benefits for themselves if the present group consolidates its power. Some of these men have been forced out of the Government by the Special Branch of MG and CIC, but they have been given important private jobs as contractors and business agents.

Since the big immediate job in Aachen is a construction job, contractors hold key positions. The two largest contractors are Bolognini and Huengens. Both were large employers of foreign forced labor and have extremely bad reputations in the town Both built the massive Aachen air-raid shelters and pill-box fortifications. Both now receive their contracts, materials and labor from Hannapel and Delhaes who take their orders from Oberbuergermeister Oppenhoff and Buergermeister Faust. These *Herren* have told us they are planning to invite Herr Veltrup—the former boss of all of them—to turn his talents to the construction field and convert his war-factory to the production of machinery for the building industry. Thus the circle will be complete.

The Mayor has also built up a vast bureaucracy overloading the civil Government. He has 9 main Departments with 67 different Bureaus and 750 employees—about 1 in every 15 Aacheners is on the city payroll. This should be compared to Essen, which, in 1938, had 1 city employee out of 160 inhabitants. In nearby Kohlscheid today, (more than half the population of Aachen), hardly more than two dozen city employees run the town. The same is true of Wuerselen, which has a population of 4,000.

It can be pointed out that most of the men in the Aachen ruling elite are able people, experienced in fairly large enterprises, and can be made useful. They are, however, quite inexperienced in either government or politics, particularly in a policy-making sense. As individuals, they might be fairly inocuous, but as a group, they are tyrannical and naturally are exploiting their position for their own gain and to put the screws on an independent labor organization—a direct challenge to General Eisenhower's Proclamation about German Labor's right to organize into free trade unions.

Since Oppenhoff plans to consolidate a powerful cohesive group and prevent popular representation, he uses purely political criteria, and not efficiency, in picking his men. Witness his statement that he would not hire anyone who does not share his ideas, and his fight against Herr Carl, Labor Buergermeister, the most sincere, able and "efficient" man we found in the city administration. After choosing his men on political criteria, Oppenhoff and his aides then proclaim these men "unpolitical" and "indispensable."

Since "indispensability" is the main rationalization of both the Mayor and the MG for maintaining the local "armaments group" and their satellites in power, let us examine this question. First of all, none of the group has had much experience in government. The Chief of Police was a small-time official in the Wehrmacht Real Estate Division. Buergermeister Hirtz (33 years old) inherited a factory and drew an enormous income from its war contracts, but had almost nothing to do with the factory management. The City Treasurer is a men's clothing-store proprietor. Breuer (Buergermeister for Schools) is a church politician who has not seen the inside of a school since he was a grammar-school teacher 24 years ago. Faust (Industry) is an engineer whose skills are wasted on an administrative job filled with petty bureaucratic details. Op de Hipt, who acts as the Mayor's "executive officer," is principally known as a munitions-factory *Abwehrbeauftragte,* a job of pure Nazi origin amounting to stool-pigeon and Gestapo informer of sabotage and anti-Nazi activity among the workers in the Veltrup arms plant.

The Chief Mayor has threatened repeatedly that he and his aides would resign if Op de Hipt were removed. This former Gestapo informer is supposedly "indispensable." Oppenhoff made the same threat to retain Dr. Heusch as Labor Buergermeister 4 weeks ago. When, despite the local MG's vigorous protest, Heusch was removed from Aachen by Army and held as a "war criminal" for his activities in Russia, Oppenhoff did nothing and the Labor Office manages to operate smoothly without Herr Heusch. Other Germans named "indispensable" have been dropped quickly and without visible ill effects when pressure became too great to ignore. In at least one instance, an "indispensable" German turned out to have been so unimportant that he was not even replaced. The whole bluff of "indispensability" is made ridiculous when one realizes that Aachen is hardly bigger than a village with 11,000 inhabitants —and yet requires the services of 56 American officers and men, 9 mayors and assistant mayors, and 750 employees. On top of it, not only has an anti-democratic group of Nazi-armament makers been put into power, but many actual Nazi Party members hold key positions. (Uneasiness over this situation has been aggravated by our arrival and investigations, and has hastened the efforts to oust some of them.)

C. *Why Nazi Party Members Are Still in the Administration.* Of the 72 "key positions"—defined as such by the Mayor—in the Aachen administration, 22 were held by Party members as of January 20. In some departments the percentage was as high as 50%; in the Finance Bureau it was 71% and its chief, the City Treasurer, has been a party member since 1933. (These figures are from CIC). This does not include 35 additional Party members in lesser positions, nor the high proportion of party members (or those with other party affiliations) who have received licenses to open businesses.

The Mayor, after many weeks of needling from the Special

Branch of MG and CIC, has said he is now ready to dismiss the small fry if he can keep at least "10 or 11" of his "key" people. Evidently he considers them "indispensable" for the carrying out of his "basic plan" to monopolize all political activity—and construction contracts.

The functional importance of a "key position" can be gauged by the example of a man named Anton Filser in the Economics Division. A party member of long standing, Filser is neither a Buergermeister nor head of a section. He is an employee in a secondary post. But his job is vital to the life of the community and subject to quick reaction from the local population. He is in charge of issuing permits for food stores. Of 63 permits issued by Filser, 30 went to Nazi Party members (or wives of members or women who belonged to the Nazi Women's organizations). Filser, incidentally, is a former Aachen wholesale merchant who prospered under the Nazis. (It is possible he may be out of the government in the near future. If so, he may well take up his former trade and thus be in on the ground floor in a business which will prove to be one of the most lucrative in post-war Aachen.)

Oppenhoff takes the following stand: He has the right to hire and fire. MG has given him the prerogative to hire party members or anyone else, and CIC can investigate them later. Oppenhoff says he can "personally vouch for the character" of all party members hired by his aides. He says that if MG does not trust his judgment in appointments, "then, please, *meine Herren,* remove me from office."

Somehow, he does not seem to fear that this threat would be executed. He refers to the CIC in tones of hardly-concealed disrespect, having shrewdly observed that CIC and MG's Special Branch have no decisive power in MG. It is a fact that the recommendations of CIC are not binding upon the MGO unless "security" is involved. Oppenhoff knows that the ultimate decisions rest with the MGO, and with other high MG officers, and so far he has been successful in keeping most of his appointees (friends and war collaborators) in office, despite their party or war-work records.

Oppenhoff says that he will continue to employ in his government two categories of Nazi members: (1) those who were convinced of Nazism in 1933 and "changed their minds later," and (2) those who joined for careerist or other reasons of "necessity, but without inner conviction." He told us this was one of the conditions he gave Lt. Col. S of MG when he accepted the office on 30 Oct. 1944.*

D. *Complications of Getting Rid of Nazi Members and Others.* To oust any party member or any other German undesirable, you run into an administrative maze. It is clear that Oppenhoff has the power, by original agreement, of appointing anyone he desires, with the understanding that CIC will make a "security check" later. But, in practice, once a man is in office, "it takes blasting to get him out," to quote an officer of the Special Branch. The procedure is complicated. Special Branch (appointed by the present MGO to oversee "political security" within the administration; CIC is limited to "military security") may recommend dismissal after examining a German's record. The MGO sends this "Action Sheet" to the American officer in charge of the department employing the man involved. The officer may or may not agree with the recommendation for dismissal. If he does (and this is not always the case), he sends it to the German department chief. The latter then takes it up with Chief Mayor Oppenhoff. They have 10 days in which to take action. In the meantime, Oppenhoff brings pressure to bear to save his appointee. If he does not succeed in doing so, he may give him another job—and the Special Branch, CIC, and the MG have to go through the whole procedure to have the individual dismissed again. Often, because of the complicated bureaucratic structure of the various offices, CIC is unaware for some time of the individual's new job.

Here is the case of a Nazi Party member—Dr. Brehm, a lawyer who took over Oppenhoff's practice when the latter joined the Veltrup armaments works. When Oppenhoff became Chief Mayor, he gave his old friend Brehm a key job in the police department. CIC forced his dismissal. Brehm then got a license as first lawyer to practice in Aachen. He was forced out. Oppenhoff then appointed him head of the *Wohnungsamt* (Housing Bureau). Special Branch and CIC managed to force him out of that post, too. Neither we nor CIC know as yet what the ubiquitous Brehm is doing at this moment.

Bolognini is another case. This former member of the Italian Fascist Party was one of Aachen's big war contractors who built

* [The last names of American officers given in the original text have been deleted here. D. L.]

many of the largest air-raid shelters and fortifications. He is known to have mistreated foreign workers imported for him by the Nazis, and local labor circles speak of him with hatred. Forced out of a post in the Industrial Bureau given him by Oppenhoff, he has now been made the city's building contractor, which, anyone should know, is a post with magnificent potentialities for money-making and future political power.

MG itself has not been blameless in shifting an undesirable from a government job to a "private" one. Dr. Goerres, once Manager of Trade Affairs in the City Economic Division, had been an active party member and had earned from his Fuehrer Hitler a commendation as *Wehrwirtschaftsfuehrer,* Leader of Army Industry. He was finally dismissed, whereupon an MG Officer in the Legal Affairs division gave him a "private appointment" as technical consultant to investigate the affairs of an American corporation in Aachen.

Even more striking is the case of Dr. Gerhard Heusch, an Aachen lawyer and friend of Oppenhoff. Heusch belonged to 5 Nazi Party organizations. In 1941, he became a Major in the Wehrmacht and War Economy Administrator for Ostrov and Pskov in Russia. In January, 1944, after the Russians recaptured his towns and investigated his work, Heusch fled to Aachen, got himself released from the Wehrmacht and took over the Talbot war plant as Managing Director at a salary of 18,000 marks. In November, he turned up in Oppenhoff's "cabinet" as Buergermeister for Labor.

When CIC saw his record, it recommended dismissal. But there was powerful opposition. Oppenhoff declared his friend an "Anti-Nazi" and "indispensable." Major (now Lt. Col.) S, who was mainly responsible for bringing Oppenhoff and his group, "went to bat" for Heusch up to the highest channels in Seventh Corps. S told us he admires Heusch as a "fine" man. While this was going on, Heusch was arrested by still higher echelons as a war criminal, presumably for his "work" in Russia. Oppenhoff, although forced to appoint a new Buergermeister for Labor, is still under the impression that the job is open for Heusch. (Special Branch says the MGO has given his word, however, that Heusch will not be put back into the government. But there is nothing to prevent Oppenhoff from giving his old friend a semi-public job.)

E. *Political Implications of Present Situation.* A review of how Oppenhoff came into power is given below in the section on MG. The fact remains, however, that he is "in," and that he has managed to consolidate the power of his group to a great extent.

There is a tendency, and a danger, at present of stressing the presence of Party members in the Aachen administration. This serves to divert attention from the nonparty people. The basic political problem, which has far-reaching implications, is that Oppenhoff and his aides represent a political authoritarianism that aims to deprive the German people of opportunities promised them by General Eisenhower, President Roosevelt, and Prime Minister Churchill. Oppenhoff, always the clever lawyer, will undoubtedly use his power to circumvent the policies of the Allied High Command wherever they are at variance with his own ideas.

Morally speaking, it is hardly a fitting reward to Allied soldiers to place in power men who did their best to serve Nazi war production in key positions. It is, moreover, hardly just to saddle anti-Nazi Germans, particularly the working people, with a regime that brings back unscrupulous war profiteers and bosses. Anyone who is not of Oppenhoff's persuasion is indiscriminately termed "communistic" by him and many of his co-workers. (See "public opinion," Section III)

The political leadership of Aachen's administration can never be based on a coalition of the democratic and most consistently anti-Nazi elements in Aachen or in the whole Aachen region, so long as Oppenhoff stays in office. Although Aachen's strongest party before 1933 was the Centrist—it had a plurality, not a majority (the second and third strongest parties were those of labor)—the network of mining and industrial towns nearby to the east and north were and still are strongly proletarian in their outlook and politics. These elements, barred from influence in the government of the region, may one day come into bitter conflict with the Oppenhoff "plan."

We will thus be directly responsible for this conflict, which may impair Allied prestige, and alienate precisely those groups on whom we must rely for an anti-militarist and democratic Germany. Most important of all, we are setting the example for an "eternally authoritarian" German regime—where no balance of democratic forces will be tolerated—an authoritarian type of regime which is an historic and traditional threat to European peace and security.

All this would look pretty black if it were ever aired in the American press and, in Congress, MG cannot forever hope to keep the press from discovering the true Aachen story. The popular mood of America toward the "hard" policy of cracking down on all Germans who furthered a brutal Nazi war, is not one against which MG could even hope to defend itself. An angry public opinion at home would undoubtedly force a shakeup in a discredited G-5.

II. *The Position of the Military Government*

A. *The Problem.* Since Aachen has been occupied by the Americans, there have been 3 different MGO's. The present MGO, Major J, has inherited the accumulated errors and civil job-holders; and today the MGO finds himself in the difficult position of trying to discover the former and sifting the latter.

That this situation was allowed to develop may be explained on the ground that MG, at its highest levels, seems to have no sharply-defined policy, and that MG team officers tend to approach their problems from a personal viewpoint. Unless they are given clear unequivocal guidance based on a clear policy of what we want to achieve politically in occupied Germany, MG will continue to flounder in a mess of contraditions, and MG officers will improvise policies according to their own temperament, convictions and personal prejudices. They will continue the dubious policy of attempting to present higher MG echelons with a patently favorable efficiency performance, regardless of its political implications at home and consequences in Germany.

B. *MG's "Performance" Mission.* An MG team is judged on its efficiency and "performance record"—that is, how soon it can get an occupied town functioning, especially in the fields of public health, welfare, utilities, and labor supply. Thus, when an MG team enters a city, its first consideration is functional, not political. (No political intelligence officer accompanies the MG team going into Aachen; in fact, no officer in the team, outside of the medical officer, could speak German or had any firsthand German experience. This situation still exists today.)

An MG team, therefore, will employ almost anybody it believes capable of putting a town on a functioning basis. (How long this "functional phase" lasts is anybody's guess; Aachen presumably is still in this phase.) Thus Nazi sympathizers, Party members, or German nationalists, are appointed by the MG team as the "only available specialists." These specialists, who look extremely presentable and have professional backgrounds similar to those of many MG officers, then place their like-minded friends in secondary positions. As a consequence, MG's initial indifference to the politics of the situation leads in the end to a political mess. Then come the involved attempts to weed out this mess by CIC, and MG officers, concerned with seeing their departments functioning smoothly, find themselves in the unpleasant position either of having to defend Nazis and other undesirables or of starting all over again.

Although no officer concerned with political intelligence as such came into Aachen in the early stages with the first MG team, a certain amount of political intelligence was being gathered by us, the present investigators, during October, 1944. We interviewed many in Oppenhoff's group while they were still in Malmedy, Eupen and in the Homburg Evacuation Center. At that time we wrote extensive reports on the group around Veltrup, their background, ideas and connection with Nazi armament concerns. We pointed out the danger inherent in these men acting as a group and we documented their war records. These reports were distributed, in late October, to First Army, 12th Army Group, and SHAEF. The MG in Aachen, to whom such reports are of immediate value, did not receive them until we personally gave them to the Deputy MGO in early December. Despite the fact that all channels concerned with the political situation in occupied Germany, particularly in Aachen, were fully apprised of the nature of Oppenhoff's group, months have gone by and this information has had no effect.

C. *The MGO's Attitude.* Major J, MGO, realizes there is much local criticism of the Oppenhoff administration, and that the latter is not representative of the city's population. "I am beginning to see," Major J told us in the middle of January, "that the Catholic group here claims too much as being anti-Nazi." He has set up a Special Branch, under two highly capable officers, to investigate and review the record of all city employees and recommend those who should be dismissed. The Special Branch is now working closely with CIC.

Its criteria are based on an employee's "character, efficiency and Nazi Party membership."

Clearly, this leaves loopholes. It does not raise the basic question of whether or not the Oppenhoff group is detrimental to Allied interests. The MGO is apparently not thinking along these lines, and, because his directives do not forbid him to do so, he has no strong objection to employing certain categories of Nazi party members. Future appointments, he said, will be guided by 3 principles: (1) A German must not be an "ardent and active" Nazi; (2) he must be respected in the community; and (3) he must be a man of character—"if the man has character, he will be respected in the community."

The MGO hopes to get rid of some 45 out of 55 Nazi members in key positions. This, however, will take time. "If I can get it done by March," he said, "I'll be satisfied." He believes that one must go slowly in getting rid of Nazi incumbents, because "Where would you find competent people who are not Nazi?"

D. *Why Social-Democrats are not Represented.* It has been emphasized by the MGO that he is not deliberately and consciously choosing appointees who are political conservatives or reactionaries (as most of the present German officials are). MG claims to have no objections to the employment of Social Democrats (What about Communists who used to be numerically strong in this area?) although Oppenhoff's "plan" and policy, in effect, do exclude democratic elements.

The MG has attempted to place one Social-democrat, a former trade union official, in a key position in the Labor Office. This Social-Democrat told us that he refused the job because (1) he felt he would be "used" to force the workers to work while the "better" people could remain idle or begin rebuilding their businesses, and because (2) the Labor Buergermeister (see report on him), whose hands are tied by Oppenhoff, could not guarantee that every man in Aachen who is physically fit would be made to work on communal projects.

Thus, the basic difficulty of the political and material reconstruction of Aachen is rooted in Oppenhoff's "plan" and his aim to safeguard post-war economic opportunities for the group around him.

E. *How The Oppenhoff Group Came Into The Administration.* How did the Oppenhoff group and MG find each other?

Why, will it be asked, did MG select this particular upper-class circle out of the thousands of Aacheners left behind by the Germans? It is now clear that what happened was no accident. The Oppenhoff people were ready to offer their services to the Americans, and the then-responsible MG officers found these men to be "reliable" and to their liking.

Early in September, 1944, after the attempt on Hitler's life had led to the total mobilization of Germany, Veltrup told Oppenhoff and other "leading citizens" to flee to Eupen. They had plans to "work with the Americans," as Oppenhoff says. When Eupen was occupied by U.S. forces, Oppenhoff went to the Civil Affairs officer and offered his services. It was in Eupen, and also in Malmedy, that Major S, Legal Officer of the MG team that was to take over Aachen, found Oppenhoff and the nucleus of the present civil government.

We asked both Lt. Col. S and Oberbuergermeister Oppenhoff each to give us his version of what happened.

What S Told Us

In the latter part of October, Col. C, the CO of the Aachen MG team, finding Aachen a dead and depopulated city, asked Maj. S to find a Mayor. S went to the refugee camp at Brand and to Eupen; he also talked to the Bishop of Aachen. In Eupen the Major got in touch with Oppenhoff and asked him to suggest a suitable Buergermeister and other personnel. "I found out he was a prominent lawyer, an anti-Nazi, and that he worked for Veltrup." S took Oppenhoff along with him and they spent a week travelling and interviewing personnel in various camps. Finally S decided that Oppenhoff was the "best man" to be Mayor of Aachen and he proposed his name to Col. C. The latter agreed. After some hesitation, Oppenhoff accepted the job on one condition, and that was that his name should not be made public. He was inaugurated Mayor on 30 Oct. It should be pointed out that S speaks no German and Oppenhoff no English; the two carried on their negotiations through an interpreter. (Most MG officers speak to their German counterparts through German nationals, whose English we found faulty in many cases.)

Oppenhoff submitted to S a list of 9 Buergermeister, all of them known to him personally. Seven of the 9 were accepted by MG and later approved by the CIC then in town. S himself interrogated each of them, through an interpreter, and among the German people," he told us. S casually admitted that the Bishop of Aachen was helpful ("very much so") and that it was the Bishop who had given him a letter of introduction to Oppenhoff in Eupen.

What Oppenhoff Told Us

Oppenhoff's story differs from that of Major S in some fundamentals. Oppenhoff told us that one day, when he was in Eupen, Major S came to see him; he was accompanied by the Bishop of Aachen (a point which S did not mention and which Oppenhoff asked us not to quote publicly). He was taken in an automobile to Aachen to see Lt. Col. C, with whom he spent 2 and 1/2 hours in conference. They discussed certain individuals whose names the Colonel had on a list. Oppenhoff rejected them and developed his own ideas. He offered to cooperate, he said but only on condition that Germany should NOT be rebuilt along pre-1933 lines—in other words, he refused to work for a republican, democratic Germany.

His idea was to find specialists, not administrators, to head each of the city's departments; he wanted to call these specialists *Verwaltungsraete,* but C and S insisted that they be called *Buergermeister.* He also informed the two MG officers that he would employ Nazi party members if they had had a change of heart; neither C nor S objected. Then Oppenhoff and S toured the camps in search of Buergermeister. In selecting the latter, Oppenhoff did not consult the Bishop, he told us. "I don't believe in bringing in the Church in such matters." He chose only men who fundamentally agreed with his ideas. On October 30 C and S offered him the job of Oberbuergermeister, and after a half hour's reflection, he accepted.

The Bishop's Role

In initiating Aachen's civil government, the role of the Bishop was of primary importance, a fact which neither he nor Major S want publicized now. The Bishop had remained in Aachen during the bombing and shelling; he was found, on 18 Oct., in the Cathedral by an American patrol and was evacuated to an evacuation camp. Thence he was taken to various high American officers for interrogation. How S found him is not clear, but the two were soon in frequent consultation (through a German interpreter).

Officers who were in Aachen in those days told us that Major S and the Bishop saw each other daily, and that despite military difficulties, the Major managed to find transportation and other special privileges for the Bishop, who was, after all, a German citizen. The Bishop was placed under S's protection and he could not be reached except with the latter's permission. Even as late as January, S was seeing the Bishop 2 or 3 times weekly. "S," one officer told us, "guards the bishop like a mother hen."

It may or may not be true that S took no step without consulting the Bishop, but it is a fact that the latter has given his strongest support to Oppenhoff's administration. "All the Buergermeister," the Bishop told us, "are splendid fellows (praechtige Leute). You must trust Oppenhoff; you must leave things to him. If he recommends somebody, believe me he knows what he is talking about."

S, in his capacity of Legal Officer and liaison between MG and the civil administration, continued to protect the Bishop and defend the Oppenhoff group against all comers, including American officers whose business it was to investigate. He was particularly concerned lest PWD or the press find out what the situation was. When we made a survey of Aachen 2 months ago, we were specifically asked by MG not to interview the Buergermeister at the present time. When S heard that we had talked to some of the Buergermeister, he "raised hell" about it, but Major J, the MGO, gave us permission to go ahead. He requested S to give us letters of introduction to the Bishop, as well as to Oppenhoff.

S is no longer in Aachen. He has been promoted to Lt. Colonel, and will join an MG "province" team as chief legal officer.

Even after his departure, the Bishop remains a potent figure with MG. Although he has wisely refrained from overt interference in the city administration, MG displays a certain timidity toward him when it comes to appointments. MG is sensitively conscious that Aachen is a Catholic city, and it assumes, therefore, that the Bishop's voice is vox populi.

This attitude may be traced to S who, apparently, also

accepted the Bishop as the voice, the conscience, and the Parliament of the people of Aachen. The Bishop, incidentally, has no high opinion of the people who make up Aachen's population today. He referred to them, perhaps ironically, as "Friedhofgemuese" (cemetery vegetables). Germans to whom we have spoken either did not know anything about the Bishop, or expressed opposition to the Church's interference in politics, or were plainly hostile to the whole group (insofar as they were aware that the Bishop stood behind Oppenhoff). Apart from that, it is surprising how much an American Military Government—in a combat zone—displays solicitude about the opinions of a German citizen who happens to be an ecclesiastic (and in justice to the Bishop it should be said that he neither tries to interfere openly nor wants it to be known that he is in any way connected with the civil administration).

III. *Public Opinion*

A. *General Ignorance of Situation.* The bulk of the population of some 11,000, concerned with repairing their homes and scrounging for food and furniture, seems to be waiting to see if the civil government will produce any material benefits. There is no definitely crystallized opinion toward the government because public opinion presupposes channels of information, and these are nonexistent. Meetings are not allowed; organizations do not exist; radios do not function because of the lack of electricity. The local population, moreover, knows little about the personalities of the civil government. Even the Bishop is not well known.

Even the articulate watchdogs among the liberals, Social Democrats, and Communists who remained behind do not have any clear knowledge of the persons or policies of the government. These politically alert people do, however, have a "feeling" that something unsavory is going on among the "clique"—as it is widely known—and that Left groups are as unwanted as they are unrepresented in the administration. They have, as yet, no positive knowledge of what they merely suspect—that the Oppenhoff group is determined to prevent party representation on the part of organized labor and to prevent, in fact, labor from ever organizing.

Discontent, however, is frequently vocal. At least one typewritten pamphlet has already made its appearance; it was entitled "What Is Spoken Of in Aachen" and was critical of the Oppenhoff regime. It is worth noting that Lt. Col. S thought the author of the pamphlet should be interned as a "dangerous agitator." Fortunately, MG took no such step. On the contrary, Major B, Deputy MGO, thought it a healthy democratic symptom that Germans showed sufficient interest in government to express honest opinions about it.

B. *Points of Discontent.* Public Dissatisfaction has its roots in (1) the labor policy, (2) Nazi party members in leading positions, (3) the formation of the civil government as a "club" or a "clique" of *Herren,* backed by the Bishop, and (4) the existence of too many employees in the government, too many Buergermeister, and too many privileges that they enjoy. Two young women, whose father was in a concentration camp, summarized their opinion as follows:

"It is the same old *Schieber* (racketeers). But nothing can be done about such things. Germans have always been like that, and will always be. We ask ourselves why a city of 11,000 people needs 8 Buergermeister. Before the Americans came, we had only 1 Buergermeister and 1 assistant. Now these gentlemen have official cars and drive around town while there is no gas for the transportation for the necessities of the people. It's the same old racket."

The most eloquent recognition of the existence of a hostile public opinion is to be found on the door of Labor Buergermeister Carl's office. Carl, a moderate businessman who believes in a three-party system (Right, Center, and Left), is keenly aware of the criticism to which he is exposed on account of his thankless job, and he has posted the following sign:

"Wer der Meinung ist, ihm sei Unrecht geschehen und glaubt, eine berechtigte Beschwerde vortragen zu muessen, wende sich bitte an Herrn Carl, Zimmer 7, 1 Stg. Wir haben fuer jeden Buerger ein offenes Ohr und ein freundliches Wort."

(Whosoever is of the opinion that an injustice has been done to him and believes that he has a just complaint, please see Herr Carl, Room 7, 1st floor. We have an open ear and a friendly word for every citizen.)

D. *The Mayor's Reaction.* The Buergermeister and the other high officials are conscious of the existence of discontent and criticism in the city. But they attempt to brush it off as the expression of cranks and of "dangerous Left elements." Oppen-hoff even gave CIC the names of a few "dangerous" Reds—they happened to be mild (and incorruptible) Social Democrats. Evidently Oppenhoff characterizes all Leftists as "Commu-nists." Before 1933 the Communists were the second largest party in Aachen. Today their strength is still considerable, al-though their leadership is gone. The leadership of the Catholic trade unions ("left wing of the Centrist Party") which were also a strong factor in Aachen and are opposed to the Oppenhoff types, has also disappeared temporarily.

Buergermeister Faust, an engineer who spent the last 10 years working for Germany's war industry, told us that the grumbling comes as a consequence of Allied promises to labor through radio propaganda; he urged earnestly that the Allies should make no promises to German workers, because they might take their new freedom seriously and "do anything." Faust was vague as to the nature of the "promises," but it turned out he was referring to Allied statements that Nazis would be banned from the government and the German people would be given the chance of constructing a democratic policy. This, in the eyes of the Buergermeister, was dangerous incitement.

The source of greatest popular discontent is centered in the labor policy. The refusal to do ordinary work for the good of the community as a whole is widespread—a refusal, incidentally, that was noticeably absent in the Hitler days. Workers will not go on labor projects for the reason that middle class individuals refuse to do the same. The middle class will not work because it has enough food reserves and cash money to get along for some time, and it is also able to find soft positions in the gov-ernment.

Those who do not work for the government manage to obtain permits to open their businesses, and this leaves them out from public work on the excuse that they must do their own rebuild-ing. The workers, therefore, ask angrily why they should be the only ones to do public labor; they ask why the government does not force middle class people to work also. Buergermeister Carl told us candidly that the workers are quite right and that he finds it virtually impossible to make middle class people, espe-cially businessmen, do any public work. When the business people are threatened that force would be employed against them, they denounce the regime as "undemocratic," as "freedom robbers," and as the "same system as the Nazis."

Since the administration, personified by the Oberbuergermeister, who is unfriendly to Buergermeister Carl, is committed to a system of voluntary work—a direct consequence of Oppenhoff's plan of favoring skills and small enterprises as a basis of political power—the workers accuse the government of acting only in the interests of the higher-income groups.

E. *Attitude Toward Party Members.* The presence of known party members in the administration is one of the favorite topics of gossip around the town. As is to be expected, their number is exaggerated, since correct information is lacking. People know that a number of licenses to open stores have been issued by a party member in the government to shopkeepers who are themselves (or their husbands) Nazi Party members. Thus comes the widespread accusation that one must be a Nazi to get a job in the government or to receive a license to do business. This charge, it must be stressed, contains at least 50% truth.

Aacheners, including the politically-seasoned Socialist-Democrats, form their opinion of an official on the basis of whether or not he is a Party member. The Social-Democrats respect conservatives who did not join the party. They are, however, suspicious because not a single Social-Democrat nor a trade union man has an important position in the city government. They know that the administration is formed of a group that once held influential jobs in the two biggest war plants in town —Veltrup and Talbot. They doubt that it was possible for them to stay out of the party. One former Social-Democratic official told us, "Veltrup and Talbot were Nazi factories through and through. They carried out all the labor principles and punishment of the Nazi system. It is incomprehensible to me that the officials of these works are said not to be party members. I doubt it very much. They browbeat the workers into the *Arbeitsfront* and the party, approved of espionage in the plant and denounced so-called 'troublemakers' to the Gestapo. I can't imagine that they were not in the party. If they were not, then there must be something behind it. . . ."

Other workers, some of whom suffered imprisonment for long terms, keep their own records of who is who in the government. They say that they have full trust in the MG selecting officials so long as they are not former party members. They would like to see all party members forced to wear an arm-band —such as the Nazis made foreign workers and Jews wear—and be put into labor battalions for the good of the community. One worker, who is doing labor on the waterworks and whose tubercular 15-year old son was assigned to the collecting and burying of bodies, said: "We imagined it was going to be different. The BBC said all the Nazis would be wiped out. Now you see them everywhere in fine jobs and opening up stores, while the workers are made to do the same work and the business people have the connections to get out of it. Even under the Nazis, the 'better people' had to work alongside the laborer."

E. *"Group" Power*. The most serious objection to the administration is that it represents only one body of opinion. We heard this objection from a businessman, a small manufacturer, a property owner, a former publisher, and an office secretary. Here is a typical comment: "The town officials may be respectable, but there are too many around the Bishop. One hears grumbling. Of course, the Bishop is not objectionable, but there should be people in there from other political camps, men who know the plain people better and have had contact with them for years. The *Herren* in charge now are all *Direktoren* . . ."

F. *Bureaucracy And Self-gain*. Non-political discontent concerns itself with the burden on the people of hundreds of government employes who thereby escape hard work and are ensuring their future. The 8 Buergermeister are accused of using their jobs to lay the groundwork for their own business or professional activity in the future. Otherwise, people say, why are there so many Buergermeister for such a small population? The Buergermeister all live rather well, in villas, and use autos to go back and forth to their jobs. We have heard some Aacheners bitterly complain that these autos are not used to bring in milk for children. "Why cannot the Buergermeister walk a few miles to their homes like the rest of us, or ride bicycles?" Thus all sorts of rumors crop up about the *"Herrenklub"* because they live together and look prosperous.

G. *Conclusion*. It must be pointed out as a warning that the discontent will become more serious when the true face of the civil regime is made known. The Mayor's political plans, for which he is deliberately laying the foundation now, will precipitate a strong counter-movement as soon as these plans leak out to the working class elements. For these plans do not hold even a grain of democracy, as we understand the term. And the working population, which in Germany has always wielded immense political power, is already suspicious, and will be quick to fight for its rights.

Chapter 26

APPRAISAL *

By

JAMES P. WARBURG

FOR REASONS stated in the preceding chapter, Anglo-American strategic propaganda, from the Italian surrender to the invasion of France on June 6, 1944, was badly hampered by the absence of a clear pro-democratic foreign policy. This was especially unfortunate because the Allied propaganda message became unconvincing just when the facilities for transmitting it, particularly by radio, had for the first time become adequate. In other words, just when Britain and America really had a chance to say something, they found that they had nothing much to say.

In the occupied countries, notably in France, Allied propaganda served to maintain the conviction that the Nazis would soon be defeated, but to a large extent this conviction would probably have existed in any case. As for the Germans, the unconditional surrender formula adopted by the Allies at Casablanca in January, 1943, tended if anything to harden their resistance; and Allied propaganda was never able so to interpret the formula as to persuade the German people that they had less to fear from surrender than from a useless continuation of the war.

This is not to belittle in any way the achievements of secret psychological warfare operations conducted by the Allies on the Continent prior to invasion; these were largely responsible for the discipline and subsequent effectiveness of the French Forces of the Interior. Similarly, Allied front-line psychological warfare operations, conducted by PWD against the *Wehrmacht* prior to and in connection with the Normandy landings, did no doubt help considerably to shorten the fighting and to reduce its cost. The same thing is true of similar operations conducted all through the summer and winter campaigns of 1944 and dur-

* Reprinted from *Unwritten Treaty*, published by Harcourt Brace (1946).

ing the spring of 1945, up until the moment of the final German surrender.

Analyzing and summing up the contribution of Allied psychological warfare to the frustration of the Nazi plan of world conquest and to the final destruction of the German armed forces, the writer feels justified in drawing these conclusions:

1. In the period leading up to the outbreak of armed conflict, and even up to the fall of France, Allied psychological warfare was practically non-existent. This was the period when the Nazi nerve war was achieving its greatest triumphs.

2. In the period beginning with Dunkirk and ending with the assumption of the strategic offensive by the Allies in October-November, 1942, first British and then British-American psychological warfare became extremely effective. It succeeded in maintaining the spirit of resistance in the Free World, while at the same time casting the first doubt of his own invincibility into the mind of the Fascist enemy. It opposed to the New Order of Nazi slavery the ideal of a free society based not upon might but upon the rights of man and the dignity of the human race.

3. During the year beginning in November, 1942, Allied strategic propaganda contributed greatly toward driving Italy out of the war; Allied front-line propaganda brought about the surrender of large numbers of German and Italian troops, prevented the French fleet from falling into the hands of the Germans, and delivered the Italian fleet into Allied hands.

4. From the Italian surrender in September, 1943, until the end of the European war in May, 1945, Allied strategic propaganda accomplished but little, due to the absence of a clear pro-democratic foreign policy; but during the same period secret psychological warfare operations and front-line propaganda continued to be effective.

5. Considered by target areas, the results might be tabulated as follows:

Enemy Countries

Germany: Allied psychological warfare never succeeded in breaking down the German will to continue the war. The final surrender of the German armies came, not as a result of an internal revolution, not as the result of a break-down of home morale, but as the result of utter and complete defeat on the field of battle. Front-line propaganda cut down the cost of victory, but did not accelerate it.

Italy: The Italian people were knocked out of the war at least as much by psychological factors as by military defeat. Allied psychological warfare skillfully exploited the sense of guilt already existing in the Italian people and brought them to a state of utter defeatism. Both strategic and front-line propaganda were highly effective.

Satellites: Most of these countries were difficult to reach. It is doubtful whether the people of *Hungary, Rumania* or *Bulgaria* were very much affected by Anglo-American propaganda. Anglo-American reporting of events undoubtedly brought home to them a sense of the hopelessness of their position, but this was secondary to the impact of the defeats inflicted by the Red Army and to Soviet psychological warfare. *Finland,* on the other hand, may have been considerably influenced by Anglo-American efforts to get her out of the war.

Enemy-Occupied Countries

France: There can be no doubt that British and later Anglo-American propaganda were largely responsible for the sustenance of the resistance movement. Instructions for obstructive action and sabotage were faithfully followed throughout the years of occupation, thus rendering great help to the Allied military effort. Much the same thing was true of *Holland, Belgium* and *Norway.* To a smaller degree it was true in *Denmark.*

Greece and *Yugoslavia:* Until Anglo-American policy took its restorationist turn, Anglo-American propaganda and secret activity were effective in helping to keep alive the spirit of resistance. After 1943 they were less effective, yielding first place to Russian influence.

Neutral Countries

Sweden: Anglo-American informational activities, plus economic pressures, succeeded in gaining the sympathy of the Swedish people for the United Nations cause, in spite of the fact that the Swedish people were distrustful and fearful of the Soviet Union. It is doubtful, however, whether these efforts would have been successful had the Germans not invaded Norway. What the Allied information services did accomplish was to get their side of the war story to the Swedish public, which otherwise would have depended entirely upon German sources.

Switzerland: Allied informational activities were less effective than in Sweden, largely because of the difficulties in communication. On the other hand, the Swiss radio could be heard in southern Germany. Both Sweden and Switzerland were valuable listening posts for inside-Germany intelligence. Both countries, especially Switzerland, provided a means of getting certain types of information and propaganda into Germany.

Spain and *Portugal:* Due to the official policy of appeasement, OWI was not permitted by the State Department to make any effort towards winning the sympathy of the Spanish and Portuguese peoples for the anti-Fascist cause. The efforts of both the British and American information services in the Iberian Peninsula were perfunctory and of no real significance to the war. As an example of their utter failure, Spain, until the actual surrender of Germany, was openly trying to bring about a split between the Western Allies and the Soviet Union.

Turkey: OWI succeeded in getting American news in large quantity into the Turkish press. Anglo-American propaganda and diplomacy succeeded in keeping the Turks from joining the Axis in the early stages of the war. They failed to bring the Turks into the war on the side of the Allies while their help would have been of any significance. By the time Turkey did finally declare war, her action was meaningless.

Middle East: In the early part of the war, when Allied military power in the Middle East was mostly a brave bluff, British and even more so American propaganda was largely responsible for keeping the Arab countries from joining the Axis. The British did most of the work, but the most powerful propaganda weapon was the exploitation of the American industrial and military potential.

It is too early to make a similar detailed appraisal of the contribution of our psychological warfare to the winning of the war against Japan.

We do know that Filipino resistance all through the years of Japanese occupation will in all probability become a classical illustration of what psychological factors can do. The Philippine resistance movement was sturdy primarily because, before the war, the United States had for years pursued a policy of true friendship and of helping the Filipinos to attain their independence. This policy stood out in sharp contrast to the traditional colonial policies of the Western European powers. In addition, however, the resistance was greatly aided by constant radio contact with General MacArthur's headquarters, by printed propaganda taken in along with essential supplies by United States submarines, and by other means. When General MacArthur told the Filipinos that he was coming back, they believed him. Eventually the help of Filipino guerrillas saved thousands of American lives.

What effect American propaganda has had upon the Chinese or the peoples of Southeast Asia it is too soon to say. Likewise it will take some time before we have the evidence upon which to base an appraisal of the effect of our propaganda upon Japan. In all probability time will show that, except in the last stages of the war, the effect was negligible. Front line propaganda first began to produce surrenders in sizable quantities during the Okinawa campaign. It also seems that the loss of this island and of Iwo Jima, along with the concentrated air attacks of the B-29's and the destruction of the Japanese Navy, broke the will of the Japanese High Command to continue the struggle. We know that Japan asked the Soviet Union to negotiate peace at about the time Okinawa fell, in June, 1945. We know that the Soviet Union's refusal to be seduced from its agreements with Britain and the United States, plus the Potsdam ultimatum and finally the atomic bomb and the Soviet declaration of war, added the last touches to the collapse of the Japanese fighting spirit.

Both Germany and Japan confounded the prognostications of the experts in the timing and manner of their surrender.

Germany had been expected to yield at the moment when the German General Staff considered further fighting to be useless. This moment, the experts thought, would arrive whenever the Allies succeded in establishing a firm foothold in the West, and before Germany herself had been invaded. Instead, the Germans fought on until the Allies and the Red Army had met in the heart of Germany, and until long after even the youngest private in the Wehrmacht must have known that further resistance was useless.

Conversely, the Japanese war also ran counter to all expectation. The Japanese had been expected to fight fanatically to the last man and the last inch of Japanese soil. Instead, they surrendered with most of their Army intact and their homeland not yet invaded.

In other words, German fighting morale outlasted Germany's physical ability to continue the struggle; Japanese fighting morale collapsed before the limit of physical endurance had been reached.

To what extent the collapse of Japanese morale was due to our psychological warfare operations proper, or to what extent it came simply as the result of the staggering physical and psychological blows inflicted by our armed forces, we shall not know for some time. There is little evidence so far that propaganda played more than a minor part.

One action in the field of political warfare undoubtedly played a considerable part in accelerating the Japanese surrender. This was the decision to allow the Emperor to retain his prerogatives, provided that he agreed to obey the instructions of the Supreme Allied Commander. Whether, in the long run, this will prove to have been a wise decision remains to be seen. Without doubt it saved lives. Also without doubt it will tend, unless there is a revolution, to preserve the social and economic status quo in Japan, under which the Japanese people live in feudal dependence upon the Emperor, the nobility, and the industrial monopolists. In other words, unless there is a revolution, it will tend to preserve in power the ruling clique which has for decades driven Japan into aggression against her neighbors.

We have as yet no means of measuring the revolutionary potential of the Japanese people. Quite possibly it is high. In that case, the Anglo-American policy-makers, in their fear of revolution and their desire to "preserve law and order," may, by preventing an orderly democratic evolution, turn out to have produced the very thing of which they have been most afraid.

Chapter 27

PSYCHOLOGICAL WARFARE RECONSIDERED *

By

HANS SPEIER

Inadequacies of the Term "Psychological Warfare"

THE TERM psychological warfare has gained wide currency in popular and scientific discussions, but its meaning is not clear. For three reasons the term is debated among those who use it freely.

First, warfare cannot readily be expected to be waged in times of peace or, for that matter, against the populations of neutral and allied countries in wartime, unless it is felt that by virtue of being "psychological" this kind of warfare is not "real" warfare. During the Second World War, psychological warfare was indeed regarded primarily as a responsibility of the military who fought the enemy, whereas the civilian Office of War Information never officially professed before the Congress and the public its concern with it. Soon after the end of the war the relationship between the Soviet Union and the Western powers began to be characterized as a state of cold war— incidentally no less ambiguous a term than "psychological warfare"—but while according to many observers of the international scene the traditional distinction between war and peace cannot be applied in the postwar period, no government involved in the cold war has as yet stated that it is engaged in psychological warfare against other nations. Rather, there is

* This paper was prepared for a volume entitled *The Policy Sciences: Recent Developments in Scope and Method,* which is soon to be published by Stanford University Press for The Hoover Institute and Library. This volume will appear in The Hoover Institute's "Studies in World Revolution" (RADIR Project). We are grateful to the officers of The Hoover Institute for generous permission to "reprint" this chapter in advance of its publication there.

talk of "international information" and, reluctantly, of propaganda.

Second, the terms "psychological warfare" and "political warfare" (as the British prefer to call their activities in this field) are misleading if they designate exclusively propaganda to enemy countries in times of war. Wars are waged against enemies in order to defeat them; yet during a war, psychological warfare comprises not only ancillary activities to the same end by certain non-lethal means but also actions which attempt to reach and make friends in the enemy camp.

For yet a third reason, the term psychological warfare is easily misunderstood. When it is used as a synonym for combat propaganda and related activities in wartime, it seems to be implied that other forms of warfare have no psychological effects, but only physical consequences, and are conducted without regard for the mind of the enemy and the moral forces at his command. In this context, then, psychological warfare emerges as a specialized activity which injects into the "unpsychological" wars of the machine age the recollection and rediscovery of man as the agent of aggression, the object of suffering, the human element in bureaucratized strategy and industrialized battles.[1]

The ambiguities of meaning from which the term psychological warfare suffers stems from the lack of a more basic agreement on the nature of war. It is inadvisable as well as tedious to begin this reconsideration of psychological warfare with a proposal of new definitions. The following discussion will cover activities which the reader should feel free to include or exclude from the field of psychological warfare as he delimits it. Fortunately it will be possible to engage in this inquiry without using the word "psychological" at all.

The Ability and the Will to Fight

Military writers are in the habit of distinguishing between the ability and the will to fight. An enemy can be defeated by destroying his capability of resistance, but failing this he will also succumb when his will to fight is broken. These two elements of war are not independent of one another. The will to fight is likely to be stronger if the ability to fight, compared with that of the enemy, promises a chance of success. Capability counts for nothing, however, if resolution to use it is wanting, and within certain limits strong will can offset the disadvantage of inferior capability, particularly when the opponent's resolution and perseverance do not match his superiority of force.

Incapacitation of the enemy by destruction, conquest of territory, capture or denial of men and material, blockade, etc., and incapacitation by demoralizing the enemy are two roads to victory. To assume that only destruction wins wars is tantamount to denying the intellectual and moral elements in war. It is obvious that demoralization, i.e. breaking the will to resist, may in turn be achieved by physical destruction, but statesmen and generals throughout the ages have also used less crude and more ingenious means to win wars. The amount and kind of destruction necessary for victory varies not only with the state of technology but also with the political conduct of the war.

The distinction between capability and will can be profitably applied to the analysis of international relations in times of peace, since in peace as well as in war the status of nations depends upon their ability and their will to change or maintain the prevailing distribution of power. Organized violence by means of military power is not brought to bear upon other nations in times of peace. For the citizen life is safer and more comfortable than it is in wartime. His risk of suffering violent death is low and so are, relatively speaking, his deprivations. The potential use of organized violence, however, bears on the policies which are pursued in peacetime. The same holds true of scientific and technological developments which affect the protective and striking power of arms; of threats, warnings, denunciations of their possible use; of demonstrations that they exist and are efficient; of re-organizations and re-dispositions of the available forces; and of partial mobilizations. Nor are the other instruments of international policy invariably and exclusively reserved for either wartime or peacetime use: diplomacy, espionage, counter-intelligence, economic measures, organizational activities ("fifth columns"), propaganda—all these means are used in the pursuit of international policy in peace as well as in war. The erroneous opinion that the employment of any of these instruments is confined to wartime breeds illusions about the nature of peace, impairs the pursuit of foreign policy goals in peacetime and may render wars, when they come, more ferocious. It is quite possible that the recent popularity of the term "cold war" indicates not only the precarious nature of the postwar relations among the great powers allied during part of World War II but also the unjustified demand that peacetime relations ought not to reflect a struggle for power.

There are, of course, secular trends in the use and function of the instruments of policy. Military force has been applied with fewer political and moral restrictions in the wars of the twentieth century than in the conflicts of the two preceding centuries. Correspondingly, the function of diplomacy in eighteenth century international affairs was more continuous, i.e. less subject to modification and disruption by war, than has been true in the twentieth century. The effort of all great nations during the last four decades in using propaganda as an instrument of foreign policy in peace as well as in wartime has been more formidable that the effort these nations made in this field during the preceding four decades.

Regardless of secular trends in the use of foreign policy instruments and regardless of the different modes of their employment in war and peace, war is not a state of affairs in which military force replaces all other means of policy. Nor is the state of international affairs in periods of peace independent of the balance of national war potentials. The national ability to attain or defend positions of international power, which is put to a test in war, influences the state of peace. So does the will to resist or commit aggression. But it now is necessary to determine more closely what "will" means in this context.

The Will to Fight Reconsidered

Unless we ascertain *whose will* we have in mind when speaking of "the will to fight" we are in danger of committing an anthropomorphic fallacy: clearly, not everybody in a nation at war is really fighting. Unless we ascertain further what is being done and "willed" by those who are not fighting as the nation pursues a given course of action, we miss the various *aims* of "the will" that matter: evidently, not only "the will to *fight*" is necessary for victory. Finally, if we are satisfied with the simple juxtaposition of "capability" and "will," we neglect the intellectual functions in warfare and peacetime foreign affairs: there must be knowledge and thought if a will is to use means for a purpose. The following discussion will attempt to clarify these three issues.

If wars were still waged by armed forces alone and if their leaders could count on blind obedience to command, the only will to fight that would count would be that of the officers—a situation which was approximated in the European wars of the eighteenth century prior to the French Revolution. Soldiers then were disciplined, unhappy and more afraid of their own superiors than of the enemy. Nor did they depend at that time on a continuous flow of freshly-produced supplies to replenish and improve their arms and ammunitions while the war lasted.

Today, war efforts can no longer be sustained from arsenals or loans with which to buy foreign manpower and available weapons. The physical resources of the country must be exploited and the human resources of the whole nation be mobilized in order to insure survival in large-scale war. A large part of the non-combatant population must be put to work in order to equip and re-equip, arm and re-arm the fighting forces of the nation. The industrialization of the economy has changed both the standard of living and the standard of dying. The functional role of the non-combatants in the war effort is buttressed by widespread emotional participation and intellectual interest in the war, which rarely existed prior to the modern nationalistic, literate, age. Finally, civilians as well as the armed forces are exposed to the danger of violent death, since the modern means of destruction permit attacks on the enemy's sources of armament, the urban centers of his industrial war production.

The will to fight is essentially a *will to work* on the part of the civilians in a nation at war. Moreover, while both combatants and non-combatants must be ready to die and suffer deprivation (regardless of any attractions and profits war may offer to some of them), the latter do not need to have a will to kill; the former do. They are victims rather than executioners of violent death. These differences have an important bearing on any intelligent enemy effort to break the national will to resist, and require differentiated warfare.

The large non-combatant part of the population comprises at least four general classes of persons, which are of importance to this analysis.

There are, first, those who hold political power—the political elite. Assuming that they, rather than the rulers of the military hierarchy, determine the policy of the nation as a whole, their "will to fight" is of supreme importance at the outbreak of war, for the conduct of the war and for its conclusion. Similarly, they are responsible in times of peace for the international policy which the nation "as a whole" pursues. But this elite cannot be said to have a will to fight (or not to fight) in the same sense in which such will is asserted in combat. It is more appropriate to speak of the elite's function to decide what is to be done by the nation. Here we are primarily concerned with elite decisions in the field of foreign policy; but the relative stability of the domestic regime bears upon the process in which these decisions are made and its outcome. The conduct of foreign affairs requires, of course, elite decisions which affect the domestic conditions of life, so that the stability of the regime necessarily narrows or widens the scope of choices which confronts the decision-making elite. Instead of ascribing to the political elite a will to fight (or not to fight) we shall therefore speak of its *ability to govern* (at home)—taking it for granted that they have a will to do so if they can—and its *deciding* of *foreign policy*.

Those who hold power govern by means of staffs and control personnel; this personnel will be considered here as part of the elite. The function of this auxiliary personnel is to render it possible for the elite to avoid foolish decisions [2] and to see to it that decisions, whether foolish or not, are acted upon, once they are made. Among other things, the elite relies on foreign intelligence about capabilities and intentions of other powers, domestic intelligence on the stability of the regime and the capabilities of the country, advice in estimating the consequences of alternative foreign and domestic policies, control and suppression of domestic opposition (however defined), and communication with other groups holding less power. Note that the disruption of any of these functions impairs the elite's ability to govern and to make sound decisions, possibly with repercussions on the political elite itself, and particularly in times of war, on the nation as a whole.

The second and largest group of the non-combatants will be considered here as a unit and be called the working population. Its function in modern war has been mentioned. It must have "the will to work." In addition, the working population is required to obey the laws of the country. To the extent that the political elite has authority, instead of merely exercising its rule by means of sanctions, the working population may, therefore, be said to have also a *will to obey* (or not to obey) the law of the elite.

The will to obey meets the minimum requirements of efficiency and authority, but in a well functioning society the working population does in fact always perform "above and beyond the call of duty." If the performance is reduced to mere obedience to orders the control functions of the auxiliary elite personnel are inevitably overloaded.

The relation between the political elite and the working population varies, of course, with the formal and informal political structure of the state. The bearing which this fact has on attempts to break the will to work and the will to obey will be discussed in due course.

The working population comprises people of different skills. Persons of high skill are scarcer than persons of low skill. The loss of experts to the community through death, abduction, desertion or disloyalty, therefore, has grave consequences since they cannot be replaced easily. The top group of such "irreplaceable" skilled specialists within the working population, including selected scientists, administrators, business men, inventors, intelligence experts, engineers, etc., form the civilian key personnel. Like the working population to which they belong, the civilian key personnel must be willing to work and obey. Any successful enemy effort to weaken their will to work and obey, which is especially directed at this part of the community, is likely to have especially high returns not only because substitutes for key personnel are difficult to find but also because malfunctioning members in this group affect the operations of many others. Inefficiency of a charwoman is a nuisance, that of a top administrator a calamity. Moreover, many persons in key positions possess knowledge of high intelligence value. If they become talkative or disloyal, their value to the enemy as a source of information may exceed the value of their elimination.[3]

The non-combatants include a number of dependents, whose age or state of health makes them worthless to the war effort. Their will does not matter. The graphic military term for describing such dependents under conditions of siege warfare will here be used: these non-combatants are useless mouths *(bouches inutiles)*.[4] While useless, such mouths may cry or sing and thus affect the feelings and actions of those who care for them.

Corresponding to the distinction between political elite and working population, we shall speak of military elite and fighting population in the combatant sector of the nation. (There are no military useless mouths, unless one were to regard non-fatal casualties as such.)

It will be assumed that the military elite determines military strategy and tactics in accordance with foreign policy decided by the political elite.[5] Under this assumption, the military elite has a *will to obey* the political elite or must expect sanctions in case of disobedience. In this respect the military elite does not differ in principle from the working and fighting populations. As the military elite holds power over the latter, however, it must have *ability to command* (corresponding to the ability to govern of the political elite). Furthermore, since the military elite and its staffs plan and execute military operations, we shall speak of its *determination of military missions* to attain policy goals. Finally, it shares with the fighting population the *will to fight* (or not to fight), although it should be observed that a large part of this elite holds planning, administrative and other posts which in some ways resemble top positions in civilian life.

Strictly speaking, the *will to obey* military superiors and to act "above and beyond the call of duty" is of greater importance than the will to fight even in the fighting population, inasmuch as under modern conditions of warfare the majority of those "under arms" does not fight the enemy but supports combat troops which do.[6] This division of labor, or rather, of the broad combatant function is reflected in the differential casualty rates of various services and branches in the armed forces. Thus, the Infantry in the U.S. Army, "while constituting about 10 percent of the strength of the Army, accounted for 70 percent of all the battle casualties in World War II.[7] In planning combat propaganda this stratified distribution of risks, which is associated to a significant extent with differences in social recruitment and civilian background, merits close study but for present purposes the whole combatant part of the population will be held to possess a will to fight (or not to fight).[8]

There are of course rare and common skills in the fighting

population as well as among non-combatants, and the existence of key military personnel, distinguished by high skill and highly specialized training, needs special attention. Tribute has often been paid to these experts, because their contributions to war efforts are great. The function of key combatant personnel in war seems to have increased with increasing industrialization of warfare. Illustrations abound: the German shock troops introduced at the end of the First World War after the collapse of linear infantry tactics, the fighter pilots who defended the British Isles in the battle of Britain in 1940, commandos, airborne contingents, etc. An extreme case has been related in Churchill's account of the Second World War. In March 1941 the British succeeded in sinking the German submarine U-47 commanded by "the redoubtable Prien" as well as U-99 and U-100 commanded by two other "tiptop" officers. "The elimination of these three able men," Churchill comments, "had a marked effect on the progress of the struggle." [9]

In summary, a glance at the broadest outline of the functional and political structure of the nation at war has led to a considerable refinement of the notion with which we started and which plays so important a role in psychological warfare. The general notion of "the will to fight" has been replaced by six factors. Consequently, there are six ways of weakening "the will to resist," namely interference with:

1. the deciding of foreign policy (by the political elite),
2. the determination of military missions (by the military elite),
3. the ability to govern (of the political elite),
4. the ability to command (of the military elite),
5. the will to obey (of the military elite, the working population and the fighting population),
6. the will to fight (of the military elite and the fighting population).

If the indispensable functions of the auxiliary personnel attached to the elites are borne in mind, it appears that hostile action against foreign political and military elites can be taken especially by interfering with:

a. intelligence on foreign capability and intention,
b. intelligence on domestic capabilities and obedience,
c. estimates of the consequences of alternative policies,

    d. control of the working and fighting populations and of the military elite by the political elite,

    e. communication with these groups.

Finally, we have found that combatant and non-combatant key personnel are crucial for the functioning of society in peace and war and thus a rewarding target in the international struggle for power. This is due to the fact that key personnel are difficult to replace and often possess information of high intelligence value.

The Democratic Fallacy in Mass Propaganda

The political influence which the mass of the population is constitutionally able to exert upon the elite, i.e., their recruitment and their decisions, determines in large part the structure of the political community. Account must be taken of this structure in the international struggle for power. When the political regime is despotic, the mass of the population has no chance to affect the recruitment of the elite, to fill vacant elite positions, and to pass public judgment on elite decisions. In modern despotism, i.e., in totalitarian regimes, the political elite disseminates its exoteric opinions to the masses of the population. Moreover, the population is tightly organized and thus controlled. All deviant political opinions are either esoteric or are in any case kept secret, because of terroristic measures against those who are alleged to lean toward heresy.

An understanding, however false, of domestic and international events of the past and the future is offered through an official "ideology"—a phenomenon absent in older tyrannies. These ideologies also contain the political definitions of friend and foe, law and moral standards. The ideology invests reality with meaning, however simplified, and provides the masses of the population with permitted language. Ideologies are therefore a comfort in a world which appears incomprehensible and menacing without them. As the political elite blankets the area it controls with approved opinions fitting into the official ideology,[10] it offers security, however costly, to the minds of all as it stabilizes the regime.

In view of these considerations it is folly to expect that the dissemination of another ideology by foreign propagandists can convert the masses of a population living under despotic rule to become adherents to a new ideology or to shake off the shackles of ideology altogether.

The political elite is on guard against the emergence of counter-elites, i.e., those aspirants to power who attempt to reach their goals against the will of the ruling elite. In despotic regimes counter-elites, like less consequential opposition, can operate only under-ground or abroad.

The subordinate military elite is regarded as a potential counter-elite by those who hold supreme power. It is, therefore, distrusted, infiltrated, controlled, and purged from time to time. In the Soviet Union so large a proportion of senior officers were liquidated before the outbreak of the Second World War that the efficiency of Soviet military power was considered in the West to be seriously impaired.[11] Similarly, the National Socialist leaders fought more relentlessly against the German military elite than the resistance of its members to Hitler's regime seemed to warrant.[12]

Since in modern societies the mass of the population cannot overthrow, or actively influence the policies of, despotic regimes without armed domestic or foreign support and without organized leadership, the population at large is no rewarding target of conversion propaganda from abroad. Any notion to the contrary may be called the democratic fallacy of democratic propagandists who disregard the differences in political structure between the regimes under which they and their audiences live.

The will to obey and work or at least the inclination to perform "above and beyond the call of duty" will be weakened as satisfaction with the regime is lessened; but such demoralization is not likely to be furthered by conversion propaganda and may in fact be hindered by it. Dissatisfaction with the regime may result from experiencing deprivations which are unexpected and regarded as unnecessary, futile or unjust. Such experience is not likely to be sharpened by the promotion of strange beliefs, i.e., by ideological propaganda.

Ideological propaganda to the mass of the population living in despotic regimes is sometimes advocated because of the cumulative effect it is alleged to have. As its effect increases over a period of time, it is presumed to lead to explosive action. Evidence for this proposition is lacking.[13] Politically relevant mass action presupposes the destruction or disorganization of controls by means other than propaganda, especially military force or subversion. It also requires leadership by a counter-elite. The control apparatus at the disposal of the elite may crumble in consequence of disruption from without and within, but hardly on account of attempts at converting those who are controlled.

Similar considerations apply to combat propaganda directed at the fighting population. Without prejudice to the need for propaganda directed at the combatant population in time of peace and during a war in stalemate and defeat situations, there can be little doubt that the wartime conditions favoring success of such propaganda are military superiority, victory, pursuit, and stalemate. A propagandist speaking for the side that retreats, has lost a battle, or is militarily weak, must fight uphill. Propaganda in war is an auxiliary weapon. Auxiliary weapons cannot turn the wheel of fortune if the main weapons are blunt, scarce, or lost.

Deviant Political Behavior and Its Inducement

In the conduct of psychological warfare sight must never be lost of the fact that a change in attitudes and private opinions amounts to little if it fails to result in deviant, politically relevant behavior.[14]

Generally speaking deviant, politically relevant behavior comprises all action which weakens the ability of the elites to govern and command. In war, those who fight may cease fighting, fight their own authorities and resist the enemy inefficiently. Those who work or fight may give information to the enemy, cooperate with him by fighting on his side once they are taken prisoner or have deserted. Members of the working population may slow down in their work, commit sabotage, spread rumors, organize those who are disaffected, or engage in illegal activities.

Like mutiny in the armed forces, revolution at home or secession under the leadership of a counter-elite are the most dramatic instances of disorder, weakening the regime or incapacitating it to pursue its foreign policy.

The conditions of politically relevant actions taken by the working population and by those who fight differ significantly in one respect. The latter have, in favorable military circumstances, a chance, however small, to desert or surrender to the enemy if their will to fight is broken. By contrast, the working population has no such opportunities. There is no line its members can cross in order to get out of the war. Once an enemy soldier deserts or surrenders, he increases his chance of survival. If an enemy worker wants to disobey his authorities, he cannot avail himself of the protection of foreign powers; as a rule, not doing what his authorities expect and want him to do considerably decreases the margin of his safety and adds to his chance of violent death by enemy action the risk of losing his life through sanctions by the domestic police.

It is not certain that military personnel can desert more easily in times of peace than in wartime: its moves can be supervised and controlled more closely in garrisons. For example, while the defections of Soviet soldiers during World War II surpassed in magnitude those of any other belligerent nation, the Soviet armed forces stationed in occupied countries after the war live in so strictly enforced isolation from their foreign environment that desertions are rare.

Civilians can leave their country more easily in peace time, despite emigration and immigration laws which restrict such movements particularly from and to countries with despotic regimes. The only groups with ample opportunities to defect are diplomatic and other personnel, including individuals belonging to the civilian key personnel, whose business takes them abroad.

Some of the deviant, politically relevant actions do not require joint efforts but can be taken individually, others cannot possibly succeed without organization. The power interested in breaking or weakening the will to obey must give thought to the *organizational requirements* of the deviant behavior it tries to induce, and to the magnitude of the *risks* incurred by such behavior.

Finally, intelligence estimates must be made of the *self-interests* of enemy non-combatants and combatants in deviant behavior, since these interests may be compatible with the interests pursued by the rival foreign power itself. Such compatability signifies what may be called the chance of alliance in non-combat warfare, and it is a matter of elementary statesmanship to assess the political worth of its exploitation.

Not much need be said here about the measures the rival power can take to help meet the *organizational requirements* of deviant behavior in an enemy regime. These measures range from the formation of counter-elites abroad (governments-in-exile) to their clandestine or overt support if they operate in the enemy country; from giving material aid and organizational assistance to the opposition in the enemy camp (such as arms and communications facilities) to assigning liaison personnel [15] or leadership to them; [16] from advice to bide time to strategic coordination of joint, foreign and domestic, moves against the regime.

Intelligent non-combat warfare attempting to induce deviant actions in the enemy camp must try to reduce the *risks* of such actions and show awareness of the irreducible risks even in its propaganda. Since in war some of these risks can be curtailed by foreign military action, coordination of the use to which the various instruments of policy are put is of great importance if good will, i.e. the will to disobey, in the enemy camp is not to be lost. Apart from military damage to the control apparatus, there are three principal ways of reducing the risks of deviant behavior.

(1) Psychological warfare can be careful to encourage only such actions which in view of the prevailing conditions are feasible without decimating the "resistance" in the enemy camp. If this care is not taken, the directors of the psychological warfare effort will appear either stupid or callous and lose whatever influence they are able to wield abroad.

(2) By the same token, psychological warfare can warn "allies" in the enemy camp of perils which threaten them. For example, RIAS (Radio in the American Sector of Berlin) broadcasts to the Soviet zone of Germany the names of informers so that anti-communists can be on guard against them. Moreover, specific advice can be given on how to minimize or avoid the hazards of deviant behavior. To cite a case of dubious value, during the last war soldiers were occasionally informed by the enemy how to produce undetectable symptoms of diseases which would put them on the sick roll.

(3) Instead of attempting to induce deviant behavior in the enemy population at large—a practice predicated on the absurd assumption that whole populations are imbued with the spirit of heroism and self sacrifice—psychological warfare can concentrate on selected groups whose self-interest, predispositions and organization are conducive to deviation. Work with and through existing cells of resistance and disaffected parts of the

population is likely to be more effective and will boomerang less easily than indiscriminate agitation. Correspondingly, in foreign propaganda, attention must be paid to the fact that talking the way one talks to friends, even though their existence in the enemy camp may be unknown or doubtful, is preferable to a verbal combat with the enemy at large, since such talk is bound to reinforce the opinion of hostile foreign intentions which the enemy elite spreads assiduously in the area it controls. Foreign propaganda of this sort may strengthen rather than weaken the will to obey among the large mass of those who, in situations of stress, derive comfort and security from the support they give to their leaders.

The *self-interests* of groups and individuals in the enemy population which can be exploited for "alliances" through non-combat warfare comprise a wide range of possibilities. Broadly speaking, there may be political interests of ethnic minorities in secession or liberation, a case skillfully utilized by the British against the Austro-Hungarian Empire in the First World War; there may be interests in the removal of controls which are felt to frustrate the aspirations of counter-elites and organized support of the will to disobey, as was the case among the European resistance movements in World War II during the period of German occupation; there may be dissatisfaction with social injustice, etc. Important opportunities for political warfare have arisen throughout history in wars of coalition, since combined national self-interests always are a somewhat brittle foundation for the pursuit of a common policy, particularly in successful offense. In World War II, Goebbels exploited adroitly the mass murder at Katyn to intensify discord between Poland and the Soviet Union, and until the very end of the war, Hitler and his lieutenants hoped for a split between the Western powers and the Soviet Union. Similarly, the Japanese astutely exploited political differences among the Filipinos when at the beginning of 1942 Tojo promised that independence of the Philippines be established at an early date.

Apart from these and other kinds of deviant political self-interest, which are of great value to judicious political warfare, there is elementary self-interest in survival which non-combat warfare can utilize. This is especially true when the employment or the threat of physical weapons intensifies the fear of violent death among the subjects of attack. As has been pointed out, civilians cannot surrender when their courage wanes or their will to obey is broken. They exhibit panic, become apathetic or die. Yet impelled by the need for self-preservation they may also take to flight. Flight in response to propaganda is obviously confined to war time operations when the subjects of attack are warned that they may be killed unless they take precautionary action in order to survive. Since non-combatants are not expected to have a will to fight and are in some measures less reconciled than are combatants to the prospects of death through enemy action, they are perhaps more susceptible to warning than soldiers.

Warnings of impending attack differ from ultimata. An ultimatum tries to force one course of action upon the enemy by threatening severe reprisals if another course of action is followed. By contrast, warnings to non-combatants of attacks to come, which were often delivered during World War II, offer escape from the horrors of action which the warning power has resolved to take. Those who are thus warned are again treated as "allies" rather than as enemies. The political interest of the foreign propagandist in disabling the enemy elite to govern a well organized population is reconciled with the interest of the warned population in its own self-preservation. Instruction or advice to the target population as to what it should do in view of the warning is a more powerful non-combat warfare measure than mere warning which leaves to the resourcefulness of the target population and its government what kind of evasive action to take.

The latter type of pure warning may be illustrated from Admiral Halsey's memoirs. In January, 1943, at Bougainville, the following type of message was dropped in pidgin English on native villages.

> "A serious warning from the big white chief
> to all natives of Puka Passage, Buin, and Kieta:
> This is straight talk. You must listen.
> The village of Sorum has been disloyal, has
> taken orders from the Japs, and has helped the Japs.
> We have now bombed them.
> We have also bombed Pidia, Pok Pok, Toberoi, and
> Sadi when they helped the Japs.
> If any villages help the Japs, we will bomb
> them and destroy them altogether.

We have many planes, many bombs, and many soldiers.
We will not hesitate to carry out this work.
Before long we will come with all the American
Soldiers to dislodge the Japs and kill them all and punish
all natives who helped them.

>That is all.
>You have been warned." [17]

It will have been noted that by having regard for organizational requirements, risk and self interest, those engaged in non-combat warfare play a role quite different from that which the conversion propagandist assumes. The latter is like a missionary, possessed of a faith which he deems superior to that of the heathen, but unlike the missionary he talks from a safe distance. The former identify themselves with the persons whose hazardous political conduct they try to guide; they talk or at least appear to talk to allies and friends. To the extent that their careful consideration of what is expedient from case to case is governed by a sense of responsibility, they are less likely to be tempted by the ruinous gratifications which all tasks of human manipulation offer. Political warfare requires many skills, but also certain moral qualities. Its directors must be able to move against the currents of popular passion and to forego adventurous showmanship. In addition, they must know the foreign policy objectives of their country.

The Range of Planning and the Shaping of Expectations

Decisions reflect varying degrees of foresight. Foreign policy decisions are reactive, when they are taken in response to *faits accomplis;* in this case other powers move according to *their* plans, and the reactive elite "muddles through." Decisions taken according to a plan are not strictly speaking predetermined by that plan but issue rather from a re-examination of a given plan in view of a new situation. In other words, all plans of action embody estimates of future countermoves, and each new decision to respond to a countermove enables the planners to re-examine the adequacy of their foresight as well as to bring their plan up to date. Since the pursuit of a foreign policy is affected not only by the ability to carry out intentions, but also by the execution of the opponent's policy, the foresight becomes dimmer the farther it penetrates the future. It would be irrational to predetermine in a political plan the exact decisions to be taken in the more distant future, because the intervening counter moves are matters of probability rather than fact, and unforeseeable events are matters of chance. Good plans of action are therefore based on the determination of attainable objectives, but since the estimates of what is feasible change with time, they allow for flexibility through a change of moves to reach these objectives. Good plans of action also reflect a preference for initial moves which do not irrevocably commit the decision maker to subsequent moves nor restrict his freedom to revise subsequent moves in view of unforeseen events. If planning ahead frees the political elite from the pressure of unconsidered countermoves, rational (i.e., flexible) planning may be paradoxically said to free it from the pressure of irrational (i.e., rigid) plans. This rationality of planning is well illustrated by a phrase which Churchill repeatedly used in setting forth possible courses of action to be taken against the Axis during World War II: after determining feasible objectives and certain suitable moves to attain them, he pointed out that the moves might have to be modified "as events serve us."

Military elites engage in planning as a matter of course, and in modern wars, at least, are able to state exactly how many days ahead or behind schedule a campaign has progressed. The dependence of modern warfare on the time consuming processes of mobilization, training, the development and production of new weapons as older models become obsolete, and on logistical requirements, renders such planning imperative and constitutes, in fact, a powerful stimulus toward planning the economy of the nation as a whole. Planning in the field of foreign policy is more difficult, chiefly because the control of the future embraced by the plan is shared with opposing elites. The time over which the considerations of political planners range, moreover, is longer than the time range of military plans. Broadly speaking, it is a military short range objective in war to complete successfully a phase in a battle; winning a battle means reaching a medium range objective; and victory in a campaign attains a military long range objective. For the political elite in war, the victorious end of a military campaign is, as it were, tantamount to attaining a political short range objective; the winning of the war is a matter of medium range considerations, and the best utilization of the international distribution of power at the conclusion of hostilities is a long range matter. Any consideration to establish peace forever, i.e., to abolish foreign policy, may be said to be politically out of range or utopian.

There are probably historical and national differences in the extent of foresight which various political elites incorporate into their foreign policy plans and decisions. Given the lack of research on this intriguing subject all propositions concerning it must be hypothetical in nature.

1. Utopianism, including the belief that the international struggle for power can be replaced by a harmony of interests, is associated with a lack of articulateness in defining political objectives of any range.

2. Relative military weakness is associated with attempts to extend the time range of planning or with "reactive" moves.

3. Political elites that have risen to power from a state of persecution (when they were counter-elites) are more likely to plan far ahead than elites without such history.

4. Unless the staff of democratically constituted elites is powerful and has a slower replacement rate than the top elite itself, decisions are "reactive," short range or utopian; by contrast decisions by elites recruited from a political class (e.g., an aristocracy) are governed by considerations of medium and long range objectives.

5. Preoccupation of the political top elite with administrative staff functions is indicative of "reactive" decisions in foreign policy; with domestic intelligence: of short range aims; with foreign intelligence: of medium range objectives; with history: of long range goals.

Propaganda reflects in any case the time range prevalent in the decisions of the political elite. If the policy is reactive, propaganda is likely to be an uninspired news service, because it lacks any relation to policy objectives. In that case news has no political focus and the propagandist cannot establish the "meaning" of the events, although facts often do not speak for themselves and if they do, not the same way to all people.

If the political thinking of the elite is utopian, the propaganda effort will be missionary; against recalcitrant opponents who refuse to become converted it will turn fanatical. Only when the foreign policy objectives of the political elite are both articulate and "within range" can foreign propaganda perform a useful function. It does so, broadly speaking, by deriving the political meaning of events from policy objectives in order to influence the expectations of future events.

For it is the *expectations* of the enemy population on which psychological warfare can exert its most profound influence by disseminating "news." What has happened or what has been done, especially by another power, heightens or lowers expectations and changes their content.

In an intelligent psychological warfare program propaganda does not attempt to convert the foreign population to another ideology by claiming its superiority. Rather, the propagandist tries to *shape expectations* by interpreting events as tokens of the future. In doing so he creates an image of intentions. Moving from ideology to the concrete and specific concerns of the people he talks to, he descends, to use a phrase of Karl Marx, from language to life.

The propagandist can sometimes predict what the enemy elite will do in its domestic policy and what the masses he addresses will have to suffer in consequence. Such propaganda presupposes not only good intelligence about the prospective moves of the enemy elite (e.g., curtailment of food rations), but also reliable estimates that increased deprivations will be resented rather than accepted with patience or austere fervor.

More important, however, are the expectations of the population concerning the plans of the power for whom the propagandist speaks. Theoretically, the propagandist gains access more easily to his own elite than to the secrets of the enemy elite. In practice, however, the effort of the propagandist in influencing expectations depends on the extent to which his own elite permits him to share some of its secrets.

The members of the political elite and its staff concerned with decisions on what is to be done rather than on what is to be said have a natural desire for secrecy, because premature disclosures may enable the enemy to parry prospective moves. Even in Nazi Germany, ruled by an elite that attached great importance to international propaganda, the coordination of propaganda and policy was far from perfect. The propagandist is a professional talker. Who likes to confide secrets to professional talkers? The fallacy hidden in this question lies in the implication that the propagandist will divulge the secrets he learns. As every diplomat knows, it is possible to hide and betray secrets by both silence and talk. By the same token, the propagandist may conceal by talking or reveal by silence [18] what he is supposed not to disclose, but he cannot do either, unless he is informed about the secret. It should be noted, however, that the usual differences in social background and career of "policy makers" and propagandists increase the secretiveness of the former.

The propagandist does of course not need to know all secrets of his political elite. Yet, in order to influence expectations abroad and to be effective in the timing and direction of this effort, he must be able to derive propaganda policy from the foreign policy decisions of the elite. Otherwise he is thrown back to get his inspirations from news or ideology. More generally speaking, the *existence* of policy objectives—short, medium and long range—is a prerequisite of political warfare. The *communication* of these objectives to the directors of propaganda merely insures coordination in the use of policy instruments.

Who, precisely, in the opposing nation is the enemy? Is it the military elite as much as the political elite? Who, in the enemy camp, are potential or actual allies? Which groups should have more power, which less? Is it the foreign policy of the other nation that is to be modified or also its social institutions? Precisely which, if any, of the latter; and in what way? Are revolution and secession permissible, required, or not permissible (since they cannot possibly be a matter of indifference)? If required, precisely what means are to be applied to produce the desired state of affairs: incitement, infiltration, support? If support, what kind? What is the time scale of operations, i.e. the relation of short term to medium term objectives? In war, what are the political long range objectives, if victory is a medium range aim? In peacetime, what are the elements of a desirable relationship between the powers concerned? It is answers to questions of this kind which furnish the basis of political warfare, as distinguished from the gossip of news, the preaching of ideology, the performance of tricks and the projection of the self.

Political Warfare Against Elites

According to the assumption made throughout this essay, the elites are hostile or at least have designs to maintain defensively or attain offensively positions of international power at the expense of other nations. Elite decisions to surrender, to disarm, to form an alliance, to yield or to compromise are goals of political warfare in the same sense in which mutiny in the fighting population, sabotage among the workers, the rise of strong counter-elites or the defection of key personnel may be such goals. Maintaining the assumption of "warfare" as the specific state of international affairs with which we are here concerned, the decisions of other elites, if taken *without interference,* are not only in the interest of the nations they govern but also disadvantageous to the power engaged in political warfare against them. Hence the special task of political warfare to influence enemy decisions in order to reduce the power gain which they are intended to bring about and to turn it possibly into a loss.

Decisions by the political elite concerning foreign policy and the determination of military missions by the subordinate military elite require cooperation among the elite members. It is also necessary that certain staff functions be performed and coordinated. Political warfare can therefore attack the cooperation among elite members or the performance of their staff functions.

Cooperation is dependent upon a modicum of mutual trust. In this respect despotic elites are more vulnerable than democratic elites. It has already been mentioned that the subordinate elite is easily suspected of treason and easily regarded as a potential counter-elite. A study of relations between the political and military leaders in Germany during the Hitler period is especially revealing in this respect.[19] During World War II it was not fully appreciated how easily distrust can be created.[20] A systematic exploitation of these predispositions of a despotic political elite requires reliable intelligence on frictions within the enemy elite and need not be confined to the use of propaganda. It appears that subtler, less public means, such as studied diplomatic indiscretions in neutral countries or the sacrifice of intelligence for the purpose of compromising certain elite members in the eyes of others are more suitable means.

Desertions of elite members are rare and difficult to induce. If they occur, however, they provide great opportunities to political warfare. The sensational defection of Rudolf Hess, Hitler's deputy, was not exploited by the British, which characteristically aroused rather than allayed suspicion of the British on Stalin's part.

There is also evidence from the last war, particularly in the Goebbels Diaries, that propaganda directed at the masses may directly or indirectly through the monitoring services reach the political elite, which is subject to less censorship than the population at large, and thus have an unintended effect. It would therefore appear possible to use this channel of communication with the elite for specified purposes rather than by default. The same holds true of using mass communications for contacts with members of the military elite. Virtually all memoirs of military leaders in the last war frequently cite enemy propaganda statements, and there are a few instances in which action was influenced by them.[21]

More important, however, than these relatively minor weapons in the arsenal of non-combat warfare against enemy elites are the measures that can be taken to interfere with the performance of staff functions. The following remarks are confined to the subject of interference with foreign intelligence and with advice on the consequences of alternative decisions by means of deception.[22]

According to the saying which Plutarch ascribed to Lysander, "Where the lion's skin will not reach, you must patch it out with the fox's," deception has been used throughout history in order to confuse the enemy. All deception is aimed at creating erroneous estimates of enemy capabilities or intentions and thus at inducing counter-moves which are wrong but appear to be right to the enemy.

Like successful secrecy, successful deception produces surprise and helps put the opponent off guard. Secrecy attempts to keep intelligence from the enemy whereas deception provides him with misinformation. If secrecy about the next planned move were complete, the enemy elite would still make the best possible estimate of this move and act in accordance with this estimate. Deception is superior to secrecy in that it attempts to *influence* the estimate; at the same time it aids in obscuring real intent by disclosing a fake intent. Since deception is a form of communication with the enemy elite which it expects to be withheld, the disclosures instrumental to deception must appear either unavoidable or as mishaps: in either case the disclosure may be mistaken by the enemy as the result of its own reconnaissance or intelligence activities. Seemingly unintentional disclosures are studied indiscretions, planted misinformation, etc. Seemingly unavoidable disclosures result from staging a dummy reality in the hope that enemy reconnaissance will spot and mistake it for an indication of genuine capability or intent.

Many paradigmatic forms of deception occur in the animal world. Friedrich Alverdes distinguishes between the following forms of animal deception.[23]

1. *"Sympathese,"* i.e. sympathetic coloration and behavior in relation to the environment in order to deceive for aggressive or protective purposes the sense of sight. Since *"Sympathese"* covers behavior as well as coloration, "playing possum" *("Thatanose")* is included under this heading. So are forms of protective coloration which give the impression that the body of the animal "dissolves" into the environment, e.g., the stripes of the zebra, (called by Alverdes *"Somatolyse"*). Finally there are forms of deception which create the impression that the persecuted, fast moving and vividly colored animal suddenly appears to change into one that is not moving and is protectively colored. Such *"Heteropsie"* may also be directed at the sense of hearing, as in the case of locusts whose whirring stops when they settle down.

2. *Mimesis* consisting in protective similarity with indifferent elements in the environment. Alverdes distinguishes between *"Allomimesis,"* i.e., imitation of inanimate things, *"Phytomimesis,"* i.e., imitation of plants or parts of plants and *"Zoomimesis,"* i.e., imitation of another species.

3. *Mimicry.* Alverdes uses "zoomimesis" to denote cases of deception producing failure to detect, whereas mimicry is deception producing avoidance by adaption of unprotected animals to the appearance of others which are protected by poison, smells, etc.

4. *"Phobese,"* i.e. means which defenseless animals use to ward off their enemies by terrifying colors or behavior.

5. *"Allektation,"* i.e. coloration or behavior which lures other animals into the vicinity of those which prey upon them.

It may be added that animals (especially birds) may simulate being wounded in their flight in order to divert the attention of the aggressor from their young. There are also cases in which animals actively use parts of their environment in order to mask themselves.

The obvious similarity between deception "techniques" in the animal world and those used in human warfare is evident, but should not be over-emphasized inasmuch as man can add to the deception of the senses the deception of the mind. There is then a premium on inventiveness in the field of human deception.

Military history abounds with attempts to mislead the enemy by deceiving his intelligence service through ruses.[24] Military deception is used to mislead enemy intelligence concerning place and time, strength and objectives of offensive or defensive operations in order to induce the enemy either to overlook the imperative need for making a decision or to reach faulty decisions which increase his vulnerability. Major deception schemes to mask operations that involve a large number of combatants are often accompanied by self-deception, i.e., cover-schemes which conceal the purpose of preparing the real operation from those who are supposed to execute it.

It is doubtful that propaganda can effectively contribute to military deception, although some major efforts to that effect were made in World War II. U.S. propaganda after the invasion of Normandy kept calling attention to the possibility of additional landings elsewhere in France in order to tie down German reserves. These verbal efforts would probably have been of little avail, had it not been for the deception measures taken in Great Britain which strengthened German expectations of further landings. As has been pointed out, the effectiveness of communications with the intent to deceive is altogether dependent on the credible appearance of a mishap and on supporting evidence provided by "dummy reality." It is not sufficient to claim that a move is afoot if observable, deceiving preparations of this move are not actually made or if the preparations that are observed clearly deny the claim.

This simple principle of military deception was disregarded by Goebbels who thereby testified to both his ignorance of military matters and his ludicrous over-estimation of the power of cunning. Twice he attempted to deceive enemy intelligence about imminent German offensives. The first effort was directed in June 1941 at creating the impression that England rather than the Soviet Union was about to be invaded by German forces. The scheme involved self-deception at a confidential conference when the department heads of the Propaganda Ministry were told that operations planned in the East had been called off. Then Goebbels himself described in an article published in the *Völkischer Beobachter* the invasion of Crete as a rehearsal for a great airborne operation and implied that an invasion of the British Isles was imminent. On secret orders from Goebbels the article was immediately withdrawn, but not until foreign correspondents had cabled the contents of the article out of the country. As soon as it was known through tapping telephone wires that the order for confiscation had also been telephoned abroad, all foreign lines were closed.[25] It is not known what happened to British and Soviet Russian intelligence estimates in consequence of this ruse, but it is safe to assume that the massing of more than 100 divisions on the German-Russian border spoke louder than Goebbels' propaganda and censorship measures.[26]

A similar ruse was tried by Goebbels in the spring of 1942 in order to divert attention from the impending German summer offensive on the Southern front in the U.S.S.R.[27] It again involved an article by Goebbels and the dispatch of a German journalist first on a trip to the Eastern front, which was much publicized, and then to Lisbon where he was instructed to let it be known in a state of feigned drunkenness that the Germans would attack on the *central* front.

These cases illustrate the wasteful histrionics of zealous propagandists. They do not prove the futility of efforts to mislead enemy intelligence by appropriate means.

It is likely that deception of political elites is more easily accomplished than that of military elites, because in efforts directed at political intelligence relatively less attention need be paid to producing "dummy *capabilities*" or to camouflaging them and more reliance can be placed on the effectiveness of producing false notions of *intent*. A given capability can be used for various purposes and the intent to use it in any definite way cannot be safely derived from it, but the margin of error in deriving intent from capability grows in proportion to the scope of the enterprise under review. Whether or not a field commander is preparing for attack in times of war may be safely derived from the observation of certain unmistakable preparations for battle. Evidence of preparations for war itself may be less conclusive, simply because the political elite may decide to confine the "use" of national capabilities to rendering threats of war more effective. Deception in this case would be successful if the intent of war were conveyed in order to heighten the impact of the threat.

Furthermore, there are many political actions, e.g., the conclusion of treaties, which do not require observable physical capabilities. In these cases, again, induced mistakes in assessing the intent of foreign political elites suffice for deception.

Finally, to the extent that political elites are concerned with longer range objectives, deception bearing on these objectives may succeed without arranging elaborate "dummy capabilities." An illustration may be taken from Hitler's military conferences. On January 27, 1945, Hitler said to General Jodl,[28]

> "I have ordered that a report be played into their hands to the effect that the Russians are organizing 200,000 of our men, led by German officers and completely infected with Communism, who will then be marched into Germany. I have demanded that this report be played into English hands. I told the Foreign Minister to do that. That will make them feel as if someone had stuck a needle into them."

In conclusion, it should be stressed, however, that the use of deception in attempting to influence the expectations and intelligence of opposing political elites is not confined to actions perpetrated by ingenious specialists in trickery. The highest form of political deception consists rather in major political *actions* which lead the opposing elite to misjudge the political strategy it attempts to fathom. Like political warfare in general this kind of deception is no substitute for policy planning: it presupposes the determination of the objectives which deception can help attain, particularly by actions which mislead the opposing elite in assessing the nature of these objectives and their interrelation in time and space.

Chapter 27. Notes

1. I once was asked by an officer, "Does psychological warfare include warfare psychologically waged?"

2. Cf. Harold D. Lasswell's and Abraham Kaplan's proposition, "Upper

elites tend to be skilled in the practices of inter-personal relations rather than of the area in which decisions are to be made." *(Power and Society,* Yale University Press, New Haven 1950, p. 203.)

3. On the importance of secrecy among key scientific personnel *in peacetime,* see H. D. Smyth's *General Account of the Development of Methods of Using Atomic Energy for Military Purposes* (1945), chapt. III. The hypothesis of fission was announced and its experimental confirmation took place in January 1939. "At that time," reports Smyth, "American born nuclear physicists were so unaccustomed to the idea of using their science for military purposes that they hardly realized what needed to be done. Consequently the early efforts at restricting publication . . . were stimulated largely by a small group of foreign born physicists . . ."

4. For an early recognition of this social stratum see Byzantine Anonymous, *Strategikos,* I, 4 ("The useless people who cannot do anything for the common good . . ."), II, 9 (". . . neglected by nature and fate . . ."), and III, 13.

5. In practice, the functions of determining political and military strategies are neither easily distinguished nor always clearly separated. During the Second World War the supreme authority in both spheres of power was in fact held by the same person in the United States, the United Kingdom, China, the Soviet Union and Germany. (The situation differed during the First World War notably in the United Kingdom and Germany.) Concerning the place occupied by "psychological warfare" in the decisions of the political and military elites in World War II, see for the United States: Wallace Carroll, *Persuade Or Perish,* Boston 1948; Ellis Zacharias, *Secret Missions,* New York 1946; Charles A. H. Thomson, *Overseas Information Service of the United States Government,* Washington, D. C., 1948, Part I; Daniel Lerner, *Sykewar,* New York 1949; for Great Britain: Bruce Lockhart, *Comes the Reckoning,* London 1947; for Germany: Derrick Sington and Arthur Weidenfeld, *The Goebbels Experiment,* London 1942 (American edition: New Haven 1943); Rudolf Semmler, *Goebbels—The Man Next To Hitler,* London 1947; *The Goebbels Diaries,* 1942-1943, ed. by Louis P. Lochner, New York 1948.—For the first World War, see Harold D. Lasswell, *Propaganda Technique in the World War,* New York 1927, and Hans Thimme, *Weltkrieg ohne Waffen,* Stuttgart 1932.

6. On January 5, 1951, Senator Taft asked in the Senate, "Is it necessary for this country to provide from sixty to seventy thousand men in uniform and half as many more civilians in order to put a division of 18,000 men in the field?" *(Congressional Record,* Vol. 97, p. 64).

7. Samuel A. Stouffer, et al, *The American Soldier,* Vol. I, Princeton 1949 (Princeton University Press), p. 330.

8. In times of peace, the will to fight should not be taken as a desire to break the peace.

9. Winston Churchill, *The Grand Alliance,* Boston, 1950 (Houghton Mifflin Company), p. 127.

10. Alexander Inkeles, *Public Opinion in the Soviet Union,* Cambridge, 1950.

11. Erich Wollenberg, *The Red Army,* London, 1938.

12. During World War II of 36 Lt. Generals 21 were dismissed by Hitler, 2 were expelled from the Army, and 3 were executed after July 20, 1944. Of 800 officers of the General Staff, 150 are said to have lost their lives as opponents to the regime. See Walter Görlitz, *Der Deutsche Generalstab*, Frankfurt, 1950.

13. But there is evidence for cumulative effects of propaganda on opinions and attitudes, particularly when propaganda is monopolistic. Cf. Joseph T. Klapper, *The Effects of Mass Media*, New York, 1949 (mimeographed by the Bureau of Applied Social Research of Columbia University). Cf. also the review article by Wilbur Schramm, "The Effects of Mass Communications," in *Journalism Quarterly*, December 1949.

14. Goebbels distinguished between *"Stimmung"* and *"Haltung,"* the former being politically irrelevant internalized responses (attitudes), the latter representing externalized responses (behavior) which matter. As long as the authorities can prevent the transition from *"Stimmung"* to *"Haltung,"* Goebbels was entirely right in deprecating concern about depressed *"Stimmung."*

15. E.g. Fitzroy MacLean's airdrop in wartime Yugoslavia to work for the British with Tito.

16. E.g. Lenin's famous journey in a sealed German train to Russia in 1917.

17. Halsey, W. F., and Bryan J., *"Admiral Halsey's Story,"* Whittlesey House, New York, 1947, pp. 150-151.

18. For example, National Socialist propaganda directives (so-called *Sprachregelungen*) prohibited at a certain date during the last war any mention of heavy water in magazines. If *previous* references to heavy water had been noted from time to time, the abrupt silence about the matter would have been a disclosure.

19. Similarly rewarding is a study of military failures and misfortunes of German and Italian commanders during World War II compared with those of British and American generals.

20. Liddell Hart quotes General Blumentritt, "Hitler knew that Field Marshal von Rundstedt was much respected by the army and by the enemy. Allied propaganda broadcasts often suggested that the views of the Field Marshal and his staff differed from those of Hitler. It was notable, too, our headquarters are never subjected to air attacks. Nor was the Field Marshal ever threatened by the French resistance movement—presumably, because it was known that he had always been in favor of good treatment for the French. All these things were brought to Hitler's notice, of course, in reports from his own agents. While he treated the Field Marshal with respect—more respect than he showed other soldiers—he kept him under careful watch." See *The German Generals Talk*, New York 1948, pp. 260-261.

21. See for example the entry under 20 June 1944 in Lt. Gen. Lewis H. Brereton, *The Brereton Diaries* (William Morrow & Co.) New York 1946, p. 289, "Owing to the enormous enemy propaganda on damage done by V-Is, it was decided at commanders' meeting to stage a strong air attack on Berlin tomorrow to counteract it."

22. Interference with the control and communication functions of the auxiliary elite personnel have been touched upon when measures to reduce the ability to govern and command were discussed.

23. Friedrich Alverdes, "Täuschung und 'Lüge' im Tierreich," in *Die Lüge*, ed. by Otto Lippmann and Paul Plaut, Leipzig, 1927, pp. 332-350.

24. See General Waldemar Erfurth, *Surprise* and the introduction to this book by Stefan T. Possony, Harrisburg, 1943 (Military Service Publishing Company), from which the following illustration is taken. During the first World War the British misled the Turks at Gaza to believe that the main blow of Gen. Allenby's forces would fall at the left flank.

"A whole month was spent in sending 'misleading messages by wireless telegraphy in a code which the Turks, by various ruses, had been taught how to solve, without realizing the situation.' In addition, a British staff officer on patrol ride let himself be surprised by a Turkish guard. He feigned to be wounded and ostensibly lost his haversack with an especially prepared notebook, including money, love-letters and several purported orders and military documents. The haversack was picked up by the Turks. The next morning, a notice appeared in the paper that was issued to the Desert Mounted Corps, stating that a notebook had been lost by a staff officer on patrol and that the finder should return it at once to Allenby's headquarters. 'A small party was sent out to search the country for the pocketbook . . . An officer was stupid enough to wrap his luncheon in a copy of these orders, and to drop it near the enemy.' These ruses were successful." (p. 10).

For a few illustrations from World War II, cf. Field Marshal The Viscount Montgomery of Alamein, *El Alamein to the River Sangro*, New York 1949, p. 31 ff., 57, 78-80; Desmond Young, *Rommel*, London 1950, pp. 173-4; Sir Giffard Martel, *An Outspoken Soldier*, London 1949, p. 206; Brereton, *op. cit.*, pp. 273-4; Anthony B. Martienssen, *Hitler and His Admirals*, New York 1949, p. 79, 101; George C. Kenney, *General Kenney Reports*, New York 1949, pp. 268, 281-2, 330, 374, 384, 501; Admiral Halsey, *op. cit.*, p. 197, 207-8; Field Marshal Lord Wilson of Libya, *Eight Years Overseas*, London 1948, p. 40; Sir Frederick Morgan, *Overture to Overlord*, New York 1950; Sir Francis de Guingand, *Operation Victory*, New York 1947, pp. 108, 155-6.

See also Jasper Maskelyne, *Magic-Top Secret*, London (no date).

25. Rudolf Semmler, *op. cit.*, p. 39-42.

26. I am indebted to Miss Jean Hungerford for an examination of the *New York Times*, the *London Times*, the *Daily Mail* and the *News Chronicle* from June 9 to June 22, 1941, for possible public effects of Goebbels' article. The incident was duly reported but was completely overshadowed by reports of the massing of troops on the Russian frontier, the possibility of war between Germany and the U.S.S.R., etc.

27. See the *Goebbels Diaries*, *op. cit.*, pp. 162-227.

28. *Hitler Directs His War*. The Secret Records of his Daily Military Conferences, selected and annotated by Felix Gilbert (Oxford University Press) New York, 1950, p. 118.

INDEX

171

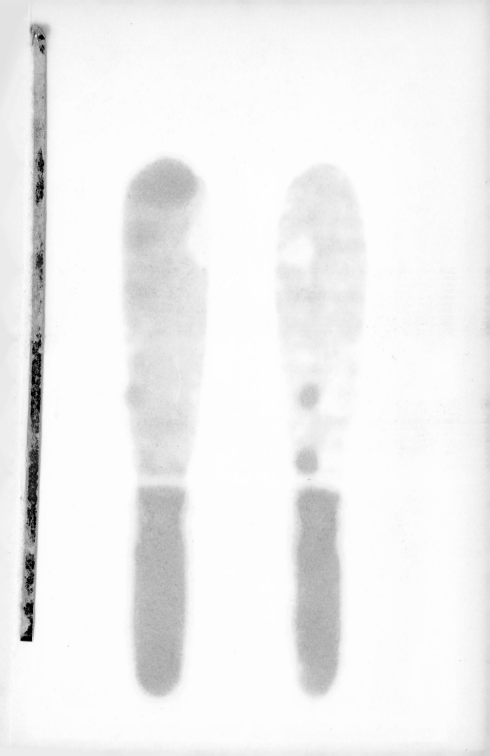